FREEDOM *FROM* RELIGION

RETHINKING ARTICLE 18

A Study in the Light of John Rawls

MEG WALLACE

B.Soc.Sc., LL.B (Hons), PhD

© Meg Wallace 2015

Meg Wallace asserts the moral right to be identified as the author of 'Freedom From Religion'.

Cover design and typeset by Green Avenue Design. Cover photograph by Meg Wallace.

Published by Cilento Publishing, Sydney Australia.

ISBN: 978-0-9925602-4-9

DEDICATION

The timely arrival on the earth of two little boys, grandsons Reuben and Rafael, while I was writing my thesis, provided much pleasure and inspiration to work towards making for them a more tolerant and harmonious world. They are yet unaware of the value of their contribution, and I dedicate this work to them.

ACKNOWLEDGEMENTS

This book is an adaptation and update of my PhD thesis *Freedom of Belief: the Unfulfilled Promise*. The idea behind it was generated by my teaching of human rights and anti-discrimination law as well as working on the ACT Human Rights Act of 2004. In studying the international case-law and mechanics of implementing human rights, I was struck by the contradiction between the rhetoric and reality surrounding the lofty promises of equality and autonomy (not to mention humanitarianism) to which nations piously declare they ascribe.

A central feature of the recognition of human rights is that every individual has an equal opportunity to exercise them. My particular interest has been what is universally known as the 'freedom of religion or belief', the foundational statement of which is Article 18 of the *Universal Declaration of Human Rights* ('UDHR'). But all too often, interpreting and implementing Article 18 has led to individuals or organisations claiming privileged treatment in the guise of the right to 'free exercise', with disregard for the obligation to grant the same right to others. Thus began my quest to better understand the unfulfilled promise of Article 18.

I would like to acknowledge the many friends and colleagues whose support advice and opinions eased the way which sometimes became rocky. Working with a great team on Australia's first Bill of Rights, led by the then Chief Minister of the ACT Jon Stanhope and Professor Hilary Charlesworth, was a tremendous boost to my journey of discovery. Brendan Bailey, Len Sorbello, Elizabeth Kelly and others too many to name who were great mentors and colleagues in promoting human rights policies – take a bow.

I acknowledge also Macquarie staff who contributed to my endeavours, such as Professors Denise Meyerson, who shared ideas with me, Professor Geoffrey Hawker and Dr. Ian Tregenza. Also from Macquarie University is Dr Stephen Mutch, erstwhile state and federal MP, and Honorary Fellow at Macquarie University, with whom I spent many pleasant meals and (at times robust) discussions, and who generated important breakthroughs in my thinking. Ron Williams, who has championed belief rights by challenging religious chaplains in schools in two successful High Court challenges, has been a wealth of personal anecdotes about the unwanted effects of government funded religious chaplains in public schools. His humour and drive have been inspiring.

In Paris, I enjoyed the friendship and generosity in my research of such wonderful people as Phillipe and Christine Bessant, Sam Asayah, Catherine Le Fur and Babu Gogineni from *Libre Pensée*. Nora Binder at the European Court of Human Rights spent time pointing me in useful directions in seeking out decisions and articles. In Geneva I was helped enormously by the staff at the UN Library. Also in London, I found the facilities and staff of the British Library invaluable.

There are others, friends and those I have met, who have kindly shared their views, whatever they are, which have contributed to my understanding of the issues. Special thanks are due to Evan Shapiro, of Cilento Publishing, for getting the book together. He generously responded to requests for last-minute fine-tuning, with impressive results. It was a pleasure to work with him.

As always, I have enjoyed the love and support of my family. My greatest gratitude, though, is to my husband, Dr Max Wallace, who encouraged me to undertake my doctorate, which lead to this book. We have shared much together over many years, and as with my other projects, his support (from cooking to commentary to care) has helped make it all possible.

TABLE OF CONTENTS

DEDICATION 2

ACKNOWLEDGEMENTS 3

TABLE OF CONTENTS 5

LIST OF TABLES... 12

LIST OF LEGISLATION AND TREATIES 13

LIST OF CASES 15

GLOSSARY AND ABBREVIATIONS 23

INTRODUCTION 27

The theories of John Rawls 29

CHAPTER 1 INTERNATIONAL HUMAN RIGHTS: A REVOLUTION............ 33

Human Rights as a revolutionary idea... 33

Human rights and civil liberties 33

Rights and obligations 37

Everyone enjoys the right equally. 39

The idea of belief rights.. 39

Special treatment for Religion?... 40

How do we deal with 'religion or belief' in a pluralist society? 42

Cultural relativism and human rights.. 42

The 'perfectionist' paradigm 44

The 'neutralist' paradigm 44

Conclusion.. 45

CHAPTER 2:BELIEF RIGHTS 47

Introduction 47

The belief provisions... 47

Binding nations further: the ICCPR and ECHR 48

Belief rights as part of the overall aim of Human Rights.................................... 48

Other international declarations on belief rights... 49

The UN International Covenant on Civil and Political Rights (ICCPR) 49

    The United Nations Human Rights Council *51*

The Limited Recognition of Human Rights Treaties... 51

Alternative human rights Declaration... 52

The European Convention on Human Rights and Freedoms (ECHR) 54

The human rights monitoring bodies and their role 55

    The UN Human Rights Council ('HR Council') *55*

    The United Nations Human Rights Committee ('UNHRC') *56*

The European Human Rights tribunals... 58

Non-Discrimination principle 60

Belief rights requires democracy... 61

    Are the international human rights treaties moral or legal pronouncements? *62*

    Human rights at the state level *63*

Conclusion: the globalisation of human rights 66

CHAPTER 3 RAWLS AND BELIEF: LIBERTY **69**

Rawls and non-liberal 'decent' societies: essential human rights........................ 69

Rawls and liberal democratic society: 'basic liberties'...................................... 69

Equal basic liberties in a pluralist society.. 71

Justice: the basic Principles 72

    'Justice as fairness' *73*

    Determining a 'political conception of justice' *75*

    Justice and reason *76*

    Fairness = procedural justice, or one law for all *78*

Liberty and the 'worth of liberty'.. 80

Conclusion 81

CHAPTER 4 THE IMPORTANCE OF EQUALITY **83**

Equality essential to human rights 83

    Political equality versus social and economic equality 84

    Equality in the 'private sphere' 86

    Reconciling liberty and equality 90

Public political culture recognised 91

State, belief and equality 91

Conflicting rights and 'reason' 92

Rawls: Perfectionist, Neutralist or neither? 94

Conclusion 95

CHAPTER 5 SECULARISM AND BELIEF **97**

What is secularism? 97

Weller's four forms of secularism 99

    'Separation of Religion and State (with religiosity)' 99

    'Pillarisation' 99

    'Communalism' 100

    'Secularist Secular Tradition' 100

    Secularism as Political Structure 101

Secularism and Rawls 103

    Rawls fails to recognise his endorsement of political secularism 103

The belief tribunals and secularism 104

    Secularism and Religious Apparel 105

Public Service 108

Conclusion 110

CHAPTER 6 BELIEF PROVISIONS AND STATE-BELIEF ALLIANCE **113**

State-belief relationships Compared 115

State and belief: Approach of the UN 118

State and belief: European organisations 121

Conclusion 124

CHAPTER 7 BELIEF PROVISIONS AND INDETERMINACY 125

Introduction 125

   Terminology.. 125

Muddying the waters: drafting of the belief provisions 127

Approach of the United Nations Human Rights Committee (UNHRC).....128

   The UN and the Belief Declaration.. 130

   The UN and ICCPR General Comment 22 130

Approach of relevant European bodies 132

   The European Council and the ECHR.. 140

Conclusion 141

CHAPTER 8 WHY 'RELIGION'? 143

Religion as belief in the supernatural 144

Special treatment of religious belief..148

Why 'religion'? 152

Conclusion 153

CHAPTER 9 CONSCIENTIOUS OBJECTION: THE 'FORUM INTERNUM' 155

Objection to limitation on manifestation of belief 155

   What is the 'forum internum'? 156

   The belief tribunals and the forum internum 159

Conscientious objection to military service 160

Conscientious objection to other state directives 161

   The basic principle.. 161

   Errors of judgment? The European Commission and Court............ 163

   Other cases of compulsion 166

   Objection to state enforcement of Church taxes 167

The 'public/private sphere' dichotomy 169

Conclusion..169

CHAPTER 10 WHAT'S IS 'MANIFESTING' BELIEF?................................ **171**

Introduction 171

What constitutes manifestation of belief? 172

    UNHRC 172

    European tribunals 173

'Manifestation': it's complicated..173

    UN: Meaning of 'manifestation of belief' 174

    European tribunals: Meaning of 'manifestation' 176

Case Study: Different approaches to limiting belief-based action 178

Conclusion 180

CHAPTER 11 RECOGNITION OF INDIVIDUAL CIRCUMSTANCES **183**

Cultural and religious background 183

The UN: 'specifics of the context' of particular cases 184

The European tribunals: 'margin of appreciation'..............................185

Examples: recognition of circumstances 187

    Relationships counselling 187

    Religious symbols in the classroom.. 189

    Religious symbols at work 193

    Religious 'vilification' and freedom of speech 194

    Education 198

Different tribunal approaches 200

Conclusion 202

CHAPTER 12: THE RESULT: MISSION UNACCOMPLISHED **203**

Special treatment of belief as human rights.......................................203

Non-Western nations...205

'Liberal Democracy' and accommodation of religion 207

    Government alignment with religion 208

    Exemptions from laws of general application 210

Government funding and grants..212

Church exemption from tax 214

Faith-based welfare and financial benefits..216

Negotiating privilege 216

Conclusion 224

CHAPTER 13 THE ANSWER: ACCOMMODATION OR SEPARATION? 227

Why 'no' to state-belief accommodation 227

Proselytising 227

Accommodation tolerates inequality..228

Accommodation and culture..230

Accommodationism tends towards theocracy 231

Neutrality under accommodationism is not feasible..................................233

Why 'yes' to State-belief Separation? 234

State-belief separation = protection rather than privilege 234

State-belief separation = no state interference in personal convictions..........237

Other benefits of state-belief separation..237

Conclusion 238

CHAPTER 14: REALISING THE PROMISE 239

Introduction 239

How do we achieve true belief rights?..239

1. Change of perspective 240

2. Removal of political inequality 241

3. Removal of special consideration of religion..241

4. Due recognition of political secularism..242

5. Requirement of state-belief separation 242

6. Consideration of Rawls's model of 'political liberalism' 243

Article 18 as stated is problematic...244

How would we re-write belief rights?...245

    Constitution or ordinary legislation?.. 245

    Non-establishment of belief? 245

    Example: Fiji Constitution 246

The worth of belief rights..248

BIBLIOGRAPHY 249

INDEX.. 267

LIST OF TABLES

Table 1: Belief rights as set out in the Belief Provisions of International Treaties 22

Table 2: Membership of the United Nations 26

Table 3: The UN Human Right Council and the UN Human Rights Committee 58

Table 4: Rawls's difference between Essential Human Rights and 'Basic Liberties'............. 70

Table 5: State-belief Regimes 115

Table 6: Permitted Limitation of Belief, Expression and Association 136

Table 7: Manifestation of belief: UDHR & Belief Declaration 172

Table 8: Countries with Blasphemy, Apostasy and Defamation of Religion Laws (2011)...224

LIST OF LEGISLATION AND TREATIES

Bill of Rights Act 1990 (NZ), <http://www.legislation.govt.nz/act/public/1990/0109/latest/ DLM224792> 148

Charter of Human Rights and Responsibilities Act (Vic.) 65n62

Cairo Declaration on Human Rights in Islam, Aug. 5, 1990, U.N. GAOR, World Conf. on Hum. Rts., 4th Sess., Agenda Item 5, U.N. Doc. A/CONF.157/PC/62/Add.18 (1993) Adopted by the Organization of the Islamic Conference in 1990, reprinted in U. N. Doc. A/Conf. 157/PC/62/Add.18 (1993) .... 23, 33n2&3, 52n21, 53, 113

Convention on the Rights of the Child, G.A. Res. 44/25, UN GAOR, 44th Session., Supp. No. 49, art. 32(1), UN Doc. A/44/49 (1989) entered into force September 2 1990 ....50n10, 56n33, 89n25, 199n50, 207n20

Declaration on the Elimination of All Forms of Intolerance and of Discrimination Based on Religion or Belief G.A. res. 36/55, 36 U.N. Doc. A/36/684 (1981) 22, 23, 40

Declaration on the Rights of Persons Belonging to National or Ethnic, Religious and Linguistic Minorities, adopted 15 December 1992, G.A. Res.47/135, reprinted in 32 ILM 911 (1993) 14 HRLJ 54 (1993). 50n12, 120

EU Guidelines on the Promotion and Protection of Freedom of Religion or Belief, adopted at the Foreign Affairs Council meeting, Luxembourg, 24 June 2013 .... 59n42, 121n37

European Convention for the Protection of Human Rights and Fundamental Freedoms, as amended by Protocol No. 11, ETS No. 5 (entered into force September 3, 1953). Protocol No. 11 (entered into force 1 Nov. 1998: E.T.S 155 ....23, 28, 221n103, 48, 221n103

General Comment 18 (37) (ICCPR) UN Doc. CCPR/C/21/Rev1/Add.1 (1989) reprinted in UN Doc. A/45/40 vol.1, Annex VI (1990) 17 .... 176n22, 185

General Comment 22, (ICCPR) UN Doc. A/48/40 vol. I (1993) 208 ....57, 118n26, 119, 130, 131, 141n95, 159, 160, 172, 174n7, 176n21, 186n15, 221n102, 224n118

General Comment 34 <www2.ohchr.org/English/bodies/hrc/docs/GC34.pdf> (2011).........195n32

Human Rights Act 1998 (U.K.) <www.legislation.gov.uk/ukpga/1998/42/contents> 65n60, 65n64, 270

ICCPR *Optional Protocol,* UNTS vol 999, p. 171, opened for signature 19 December 1966, entered into force 23 March 1976 .... 56, 58, 128

International Convention on the Protection of the Rights of All Migrant Workers and their Families, A/RES/45/158 69th adopted plenary meeting18 December 1990, entered into force on July 1st, 2003 ...... 50n11

International Covenant on Civil and Political Rights, opened for signature 16 December 1966, 999 UNTS 171 UN Doc. A/6316 1966 (entered into force March 23, 1976) 22, 24, 35, 48, 49, 249, 261, 264

Loi du Décembre 1905 Concernant la Séparation des Églises et de L'État (Law of December 1905 Concerning the Separation of Church and State) (Journal Officiel du 11 décembre 1905) 114, 212

Protocol No. 1 to the European Convention for the Protection of Human Rights and Fundamental Freedoms (1952). Opened for signature by the Council of Europe on November 4, 1950, E.T.S. No. 9, entered into force September 3 1953. .... *221*

Racial and Religious Tolerance Act 2001 (Vic) 195

Religious Freedom Restoration Act (U.S.) 1993... 117, 251

United Nations Charter, 1 UNT.S. xvi, Adopted 26 June 1945, entered into force 24 October 1945, as amended by G.A. Res. 1991 (XVIII) 17 December 1963, entered into forced 31 Aug. 1965 (557UNTS 143); 2101 of 20 Dec. 1965, entered into force 12 June 1968 (638 UNTS 308 and 2847 (XXVI) of 20 Dec. 1971, entered into force 24 Sep. 1973 (892 UNTS 119) 47, 83

Universal Declaration of Human Rights G.A. Adopted and Proclaimed by United Nations General Assembly Resolution 10 December 1948, GA Res. 217A (III), UN Doc A/810 at 71 (1948). 3, 24, 25

Victorian Charter of Rights and Responsibilities, <http://www.austlii.edu.au/au/legis/vic/consol_act/cohr-ara2006433/> 65fn62

Vienna Declaration and Programme of Action, UN GAOR, World Conf. on Hum. Rts., 48th Sess., 22d plen. mtg., part I, ¶ 5, UN Doc. A/CONF.157/24 (1993), reprinted in 32 I.L.M. 1661 (1993) 39

LIST OF CASES

(Most cases are available on the Internet)

A. R. Coeriel and M.A.R. Aurik v the Netherlands, Communication No 453/1991 (views of October 1994), UN Doc A/50/40 vol. 2 (1995) 167n53

Adelaide Company of Jehovah's Witnesses Incorporated v The Commonwealth (1943) 67 CLR 116 144,145

Ahmad v the United Kingdom, App. No. 8160/78, 22 Eur. Comm'n H.R. Dec. & Rep. 27 (1981 ....
.... 135n61; 167n54; 177

Angeleni v Sweden, App. No. 10491/83, 51 Eur, Comm'n H.R. Dec. & Rep. 41 (1986) 135, 140, 222

Applicant NABD of 2002 v Minister for Immigration and Multicultural and Indigenous Affairs, [2005] HCA 29
.... 116

Arrowsmith v the United Kingdom, App. No. 7050/75, 19 Eur. Comm'n H.R. Dec. & Rep. 5 (1978) ....
....135, 140, 152, 177, 181, 234

Attorney-General (Vic.) Ex Rel. Black v The Commonwealth (1981) 146 CLR 559................210n53; 227n8.

Başpınar v Turkey, no. 29280/95, 30 October 2001 108

Baxter v Langley (1868) 38 LJMC 1 .... 144n6

Bayatyan v Armenia, no. 23459/03, 27 October 2009 161

Boodoo v Trinidad and Tobago Communication No 721/1996/CPPR/C/74D/721/1996 .... 166n2

Braunfield v Brown, 366 U.S. 599 .... 155n2

Brinkhof v The Netherlands, Communication No. 402/1990 UN Doc. A/48/40 vol. 2 (1993), (1994) ....
.... 184n5

Burwell, Secretary of Health and Human Services, et al. v Hobby Lobby Stores, Inc., et al, 573 U.S. (2014) US Supreme Court No. 13–354. Argued March 25, 2014—Decided June 30, 2014. .. 118n23, 243n4

Buscarini and Others v San Marino [GC], no. 24645/94, ECHR 1999-I. ....
....134n58, 152n51, 166, 171n1, 178n35, 231n27

C v United Kingdom, App. No. 10358/83, 37 Eur. Comm'n H.R. Dec. & Rep. 142 (1983)......................
.... 155n1, 162n32, 163n32, 213n57

Campbell and Cosans v the United Kingdom Court judgment of 25 February 1982, Series A no. 48 ....
.... 134n2

Campbell and Cosans v the United Kingdom, 25 February 1982, Series A no. 48 (Apps. Nos 7511 /76 and 77 3/76, Report of the Commission (Adopted on 16 May 1980)) 139

Carter v. Canada (Attorney General) (2015) SCC 5 2015: February 6 ....138n80

Case Relating to Certain Aspects of the Law on the Use of Languages in Education in Belgium, ('Belgian Linguistics Case') 6 Eur. Ct. H.R. (ser. A) (1968)..139n81

Cha'are Shalom Ve Tsedek v France [GC], no. 27417/95, ECHR 2000-VII. 122n43

Chassagnou and Others v France [GC], [GC], nos. 25088/94, 28331/95 and 28443/95 .... 187n17, 197n45

Church of Scientology Moscow v Russia, no. 18147/02, 5 April 2007 151

Church of the New Faith v Commissioner of Pay-roll Tax (Vic) (1983) 154 CLR 120 ....
....143n2, 144, 146, 147n27, 215n66

City of Boerne v Flores, Archbishop of San Antonio 521 U.S. 507 ....211n42

CJ, JJ & EJ v Poland, 84-A Eur. Comm'n H.R. Dec. & Rep. 46 (1996)......................................222n111

D v France, App. No. 10180/82, 35 Eur. Comm'n H.R. Dec. & Rep.199 (1983) 135n60, 177n32

Dahlab v Switzerland (dec.), no. 42393/98, ECHR 2001-V...107n53

Darby v Sweden, 23 October 1990, Series A no. 187.....................122n39&41, 152n51, 164, 167, 168, 214

Department of Human Resources of Oregon v Smith, 494 U.S. 872 (1990) 118, 139n83

Dogru v France, App. No. 27058/05, 4 December 2008 .... 105n45, 106, 107n53, 176n24

Dudgeon v the United Kingdom, 22 October 1981, Series A no. 45 .... 132n42, 150n45

E & G. R. v Austria, App. No. 97681/82, 37 Eur. Comm'n H.R. Dec. & Rep. 42 (1984)..............214n61

Efstratiou v Greece, 18 December 1996, Reports of Judgments and Decisions 1996-VI.. 163n40-41, 164n42

Everson v Board of Education 330 U.S. 1 (1947) 117n20, 210n36

Eweida and Others v the United Kingdom, nos. 48420/10, 59842/10, 51671/10 and 36516/10, ECHR 2013 (extracts) 162, 178, 187, 188n19, 189n21, 193, 194

Faurisson v France Communication No. 550/1993 UN Doc A/52/40 1999 Vol II 194, 195

Fletcher v Salvation Army Australia [2005] VCAT 1523 (1 August 2005)..195n35

Foin, Frederic v France, Communication No. 666/1995 ICCPR, A/55/40 vol. II (views of 3 November 1999), (2000) 7(2) IHRR 354 160

Folgerø and Others v Norway [GC], no. 15472/02, ECHR 2007-VIII..................... 192n26, 221n103, 222

Freedom and Democracy Party (ÖZDEP) v Turkey [GC], no. 23885/94, ECHR 1999-VIII.........................
.... 133n50, 134n51

Gottesmann v Switzerland, App. No. 10616/83, 40 Eur. Comm'n H.R. Dec. & Rep. 284 (1984).....213n60

Grandrath v Germany, App. No. 2299/64, 10 YB ECHR (1967) 626..161n27

Griswold v Connecticut, 381 U.S. 479 (1965) 64

Groppera Radio AG and Others v Switzerland, 28 March 1990, Series A no. 173 ....133n43

Handyside v the United Kingdom, judgment of 7 December 1976, Series A no. 24, ¶48 ....
....149n39, 185n9,10

Hartikainen v Finland Communication No. 40/1978 CCPR/C/12/D/40/1978 9 April 1981..................
....221n102, 222n106

Hatton and Others v the United Kingdom [GC], no. 36022/97, ECHR 2003-VIII 185n11

Hazar, Hazar and Açik v Turkey, App. No. 16311, 16312, 16313/90 (joined) (admissibility), 72 Eur. Comm'n
H.R. Dec. & Rep. 200 (1991) .... 133n47.

Holy Monasteries v Greece, (1997) judgment of 9 December 1994, Series A no. 301-A....................123n50

Holy Synod of the Bulgarian Orthodox Church (Metropolitan Inokentiy) and Others v Bulgaria, nos. 412/03 and
35677/04, 22 January 2009 .... 173n5

Hudoyberganova v Uzbekistan, Communication No. 931/2000, UN Doc. CCPR/C/82/D/931/2000
(2004).. 174n10, 184

Iglesia Bautista "El Salvador" and Ortega Moratilla v Spain App. No. 17522/90, 72 Eur. Comm'n H. R. Dec.
& Rep. 256 (1992) 213n58, 215n71

ISKCON and others v the United Kingdom App. No. 20490/92, 76-A Eur. Comm'n H.R. Dec. & Rep.
41(1994) ....135n62& 69

Islamic Council of Victoria v Catch the Fire Ministries Inc. [2004] VCAT 2510 (22 December 2004) ...195n35

J.v K. and C.M.G. v K-S. v The Netherlands, Communication No. 483/1991 (decision of 23 July 1992), UN
Doc. A/47/40 (1994) 213n58

K.V. and C.V. v Germany, Communication No. 568/1993 (decision of 8 April 1994) UN Doc. A/49/40)
vol. 2 (1994) p. 365 ....213n58

Kalaç v Turkey, judgment of 1 July 1997, Reports of Judgments and Decisions 1997-IV 108, 177n27,
178n34

Kang v Republic of Korea, Communication No. 878/1999 (views of 15 July 2003) UN Doc. A/58/40 vol. 2
(2003), p. 152 ....159, 174

Karlsson v Sweden, no. 12356/86, 57 Eur. Comm'n H.R. Dec. & Rep. 172 ....178n33

Karnel Singh Bhinder v Canada Communication No. 208/1986 CCPR/C/37/D/208/1986 ....
.... 161, 162n29, 174n12, 185n7

Kjeldsen, Busk Madsen and Pedersen v Denmark, judgment of 7 December 1976, Series A no. 23 .... 139n81

Kokkinakis v Greece, 25 May 1993, Series A no. 260-A..... 61n51, 122n40, 123, 134, 135n63, 149n39, 150,
.... 152n51, 171n1, 175n20, 176n23, 185n10, 225, 229n17, 233n38

Kosteski v "the former Yugoslav Republic of Macedonia", App. No. 55170/00, 13 April 200 ...... 157n15, 173n6

Larissis and Others v Greece Judgment of 24 February 1998, Reports of Judgments and Decisions 1998-I 178n34, 233n38

Lautsi v Italy, (2011) [GC], no. 30814/06, 18 March 2011 .... 123, 162, 189, 190n22, 221

Lawless v Ireland (1961) Eur. Ct. H. R. (ser. B) at 408... 149n39, 185n10

Leirvåg v Norway No.1155/2003, ICCPR, A/60/40 vol. II (views of 3 November 2004) 203 ... 221n102, 222

Lemon v Kurtzman 403 (U.S.) 602 (1971)..210n36

Leyla Şahin v Turkey [GC], no. 44774/98, ECHR 2005-XI........63n56, 105, 107, 173n4, 177n27, 187n17, 197n45, 257

Locke v Davey 540 U. S. (2004) 118n24

Loizidou v Turkey (merits), 18 December 1996, Reports of Judgments and Decisions 1996-VI. 122n42

Lundberg v Sweden App. no. 36846/97, ECHR (2001) .... 214n64&65

M.A. v Italy, No. 117/81(decision of 10 April 1984), UN Doc A/39/40 (1984) p. 190 129

M.A.B., W.A.T. and J.A.Y.T. v Canada No. 570/1993, UN Doc CCPR/C/50/D/570/1993 (1994).... 129, 174n13

Maille v France (689/1996), ICCPR, A/55/40 vol. II (10 July 2000) 62...160n25

Malakhovsky and Pikul v Belarus No. 1207/2003; UN Doc. CCPR/C/84D/1207/2003 .... 174n8

Mann Singh v France (2008) ECHR, 13/11/2008/, no 4479/07 200

Mann Singh v France (2010) HRC, 26/09/2013, CCPR/C/108/D/1928/2010) 201

Manoussakis and Others v Greece, 26 September 1996, Reports of Judgments and Decisions 1996-IV 107n54, 151n50, 186n15, 231n27

McFeeley et al. v U.K., App. No 8317/78, 20 DR 44 (Dec. 1980). 134n55

Metropolitan Church of Bessarabia and Others v Moldova, no. 45701/99, ECHR 2001-XII .... 122n43&46, 270n46

Mitchell v Helms 530 U.S. 793 (2000 .... 118n23&24, 226n5, 227, 228, 230n20

Murphy v Ireland, no. 44179/98, ECHR 2003-IX (extracts)............................149, 150n40, 186, 197 210

N v Sweden no. 10410/83, 40 Eur. Comm'n H.R. Dec. & Rep. 203 (1984)................................... 173n6

Omkarananda and the Divine Light Zentrum v Sweden App. No. 8118/77, 25 Eur. Comm'n H.R. Dec. & Rep. (1981) 105 ....135n64

Otto-Preminger-Institut v Austria, 20 September 1994, Series A no. 295-A......................................149n36

Pinkey v Canada, Communication No. 27/1978, final views of 29 October 1981 (CCPR/C/OP/1 .... 63n55

Plattform "Ärzte für das Leben" v Austria, 21 June 1988, Series A no. 139..................................135n68 141

Pretty v the United Kingdom, no. 2346/02, ECHR 2002-III 137

Prince v South Africa, App. No. 1474/2006; UN Doc. CPPR/C/91/D/1474/2006 (October 2007) ....
....129n22

R (on the application of Hodkin and another) v Registrar General of Births, Deaths and Marriages [2013] UKSC
77 ....146n24

R v Registrar-General ex parte Segerdal [1970] 2 QB 697 .... 144n6

Rasmussen v Denmark Ser.A., no. 87, (1984), ¶40..186n13

Refah Partisi (the Welfare Party) and Others v Turkey (2001) nos. 41340/98, 41342/98, 41343/98 and
41344/98...110n67

Refah Partisi (the Welfare Party) and Others v Turkey ECHR 2003-II. 108n57, 122n42, 123n46, 133n49,
134n52&58, 135n74, 176n23, 187n17 197n45, 218, 219

Reformed Church of X. v the Netherlands, App. No. 1497/62, 5 Yearbook (1962) 286........................162n32

Regina ex parte Williamson and others v Secretary of State for Education and Employment and others [2005] UKHL
15 144

Roe v Wade 410 U.S. 113 (1973) 64

Ross v Canada, Communication No. 73611997 (views of 18 October, 2000), UN Doc. A/56/40 vol. 2
(2001), p. 69. ....174n15, 184, 195

S.W.M. Broeks v the Netherlands Communcation No. 172/1984 (views of 9 April 1987) UN Doc. A/42/40
(1987)..176n22

Salonen v Finland App. No. 27868/95 (Eur Comn HR) 2 July 1997 .... 135n72

Sanlés Sanlés v Spain (dec.),(2000) no. 48335/99, ECHR 2000-XI 138n79

Sanlés v Spain, (2004) UN Doc. A/59/40 vol. 2, 505 ....138n79

Schalk and Kopf v Austria, no. 30141/04, § 97, ECHR 2010...189n20

Serif v Greece, no. 38178/97 ECHR 1999IX 173n5

Sidiropoulos and Others v Greece, judgment of 10 July 1998, Reports of Judgments and Decisions 1998-IV
....233n39

Sigurður A. Sigurjónsson v Iceland, 30 June 1993, Series A no. 264. ....130n43

Sister Immaculate Joseph et al v Sri Lanka Communication No.1249/2004 (views of 21 October 200) UN
Doc.CCPR /C/85D/1249/2004...175n19

Soering v the United Kingdom, judgment of 7 July 1989, Series A no. 161, ¶102 ....132n42

Sunday Times v UK Ser. A No 30 (1979) 63n55

Svyato-Mykhaylivska Parafiya v Ukraine, no. 77703/01, 14 June 2007.................... 176n25, 186n15, 234n44

The Norwegian State Church, Knudsen v Norway App. No. 11045/84, 42 Eur. Comm'n H.R. Dec. & Rep. 247 (1985) 135n68, 167n54, 178n33, 222n107

Tsavachidis v Greece App. No. 28802/95 Eur. Ct. H.R. 1997 ....151n50

Tyrer v the United Kingdom, judgment of 25 April 1978, Series A no. 26............................ 132n37, 150n46

United Communist Party of Turkey and Others v Turkey, 30 January 1998, Reports of Judgments and Decisions 1998-I .... 133n47&50, 135n74, 140n89, 176n25, 187n17, 197n45, 233n39

United Grand Lodge of Ancient Free and Accepted Masons of England v Holborn Borough Council [1957] 1 WLR 1080 .... 144n6

United States v MacIntosh 283 U.S. 605 (1931) 144n7

V. v the Netherlands, App. No. 10678/83, 39 Eur. Comm'n H.R. Dec. & Rep. 267 (1984) 162n34

Valsamis v Greece, judgment of 18 December 1996, Reports of Judgments and Decisions 1996-VI........... .... 135n63, 163n40, 164n42

Van Den Dungen v the Netherlands, App. No. 22838/93, 80-A Eur. Comm'n H.R. Dec. & Rep. 147 (1995) 155n1

Venier and Nicolas v France (690/1996 and 691/1996), ICCPR, A/55/40 vol. II (10 July 2000) 75............ ....160n25

Vereniging Rechtswinkels Utrecht v Netherlands (1986) 46 DR 200 (ECHR) 134n53, 155n1

Waldman v Canada, Communication No. 694/1996, UN Doc. CCPR/C/67/D/694/1996 (5 November 1999) 118n26, 222n105

Walz v Tax Commission of the City of New York, 397 U.S. 664 (1970) 227

Wemhoff v Germany, 27 June 1968, Series A no. 7. 132

Westerman, Paul v The Netherlands, Communication No. 682/1996 UN Doc CCPR/C/67/D/682/1996 (13 December 1999) 160n24,184

Wingrove v the United Kingdom, 25 November 1996, Reports of Judgments and Decisions 1996-V........... .... 149n37, 196, 197n41

Wisconsin v Yoder, 406 U.S. 203 (1972) 164n43, 198, 199

X & Y v United Kingdom, 31 Eur. Comm'n H.R. Dec. & Rep. 210 (1982).................................221n104

X and Church of Scientology v Sweden, App. No. 7805/77 16 Eur. Comm'n H.R. Dec. & Rep (1979) 68.... .... 135n66, 186n13

X v Austria App. No. 1747/62, 12 Collections (1963) 42, 53-4 133

X v Austria, App. No. 8652/79, 26 Eur. Comm'n H.R. Dec. & Rep. 89 (1981) 177n32

X v Denmark, App. No. 7374/76, 5 Eur. Comm'n H. R. Dec. & Rep. 157 ....167n54

X v Germany, App. no 8741/79, 24 Eur. Com'n H.R. Dec. & Rep. 137 (1981 ....
....134n52&56, 178n33

X v Italy, App. No 6741/74 5 Eur Comm'n H. R. Dec. & Rep. (1976) 83................................... 133n46

X v the Federal Republic of Germany, App. No. 445/70, 37 Collection 119, 122, (1970) 139n84

X v the Netherlands (1962), App. No. 1068/61, 5 Yearbook (1962) 278... 162n30

X v the Netherlands (1967), App. No. 2988/66 10 Yearbook (1967) 472 ....162n33

X v the United Kingdom (1977), App. No. 7291/75, 11 Eur. Comm'n H.R. Dec. & Rep. 55 (1977) ....
....140n85

X v the United Kingdom (1981), no. 8160/78, Commission decision of 12 March 1981, Decisions and
      Reports (DR) 22 ....167n54

Yanasik v Turkey, no. 14524/89, Commission decision of 6 January 1993, DR 74 ....167n54

Young, James and Webster v the United Kingdom, 13 August 1981, Series A no. 44 ... 135n59, 187n17,197n45

Table 1: Belief rights as set out in the Belief Provisions of International Treaties

UNIVERSAL DECLARATION OF HUMAN RIGHTS (1948)*	INTERNATIONAL COVENANT ON CIVIL AND POLITICAL RIGHTS (1966)**	DECLARATION ON THE ELIMINATION OF ALL FORMS OF INTOLERANCE AND OF DISCRIMINATION BASED ON RELIGION OR BELIEF (1981)***	EUROPEAN CONVENTION FOR THE PROTECTION OF HUMAN RIGHTS AND FUNDAMENTAL FREEDOMS (1950)****
ARTICLE 18	ARTICLE 18	ARTICLE 1	ARTICLE 9
Everyone has the right to freedom of thought, conscience and religion; this right includes freedom to change his religion or belief, and freedom, either alone or in community with others and in public or private, to manifest his religion or belief in teaching, practice, worship and observance.	1. Everyone shall have the right to freedom of thought, conscience and religion. This right shall include freedom to have or to adopt a religion or belief of his choice, and freedom, either individually or in community with others and in public or private, to manifest his religion or belief in worship, observance, practice and teaching.	Everyone shall have the right to freedom of thought, conscience and religion. This right shall include freedom to have a religion or whatever Belief of his choice, and freedom, either individually or in community with others and in public or private, to manifest his religion or belief in worship, observance, practice and teaching.	1. Everyone has the right to freedom of thought, conscience and religion; this right includes freedom to change his religion or belief and freedom, either alone or in community with others and in public or private, to manifest his religion or belief, in worship, teaching, practice and observance.
ARTICLE 29			
In the exercise of his rights and freedoms, everyone shall be subject only to such limitations as are determined by law solely for the purpose of securing due recognition and respect for the rights and freedoms of others and of meeting the just requirements of morality, public order and the general welfare in a democratic society	2. No one shall be subject to coercion which would impair his freedom to have or to adopt a religion or belief of his choice.

3. Freedom to manifest one's religion or beliefs may be subject only to such limitations as are prescribed by law and are necessary to protect public safety, order, health, or morals or the fundamental rights and freedoms of others. | 2. No one shall be subject to coercion which would impair his freedom to have a religion or belief of his choice.

3. Freedom to manifest one's religion or belief may be subject only to such limitations as are prescribed by law and are necessary to protect public safety, order, health or morals or the fundamental rights and freedoms of others. | 2. Freedom to manifest one's religion or beliefs shall be subject only to such limitations as are prescribed by law and are necessary in a democratic society in the interests of public safety, for the protection of public order, health or morals, or for the protection of the rights and freedoms of others. |
| | 4. …[rights of parents to determine child's religion.] | | |

*GA Res. 2200A (XXI), 21 UN GAOR Supp. (No 16) at 52, UN Doc. A/6316 (1966), 999 UNTS 171, entered into force March 23 1976.

** UNTS vol 999, p. 171, opened for signature 19 December 1966, entered into force 23 March 1976.

*** G.A. res. 36/55, 36 U.N. GAOR Supp. (No. 51) at 171, U.N. Doc. A/36/684 (1981).

**** As amended by Protocol No. 11 (1994), opened for signature by the Council of Europe 4 November 1950, ETS No. 5 (entered into force September 3, 1953). E.T.S 155, reprinted in 33 ILM 960 (1994).

GLOSSARY AND ABBREVIATIONS

Belief Also referred to as 'personal worldview, conviction', 'life-stance'

Any personal worldview or philosophy, ('comprehensive doctrines') secular or religious, that involves (a) an explanation of nature, (b) the reason for existence, and our relationship to the natural, social and political environment, and (c) a set of values or morals to govern our behaviour in everyday life. One's personal worldview or belief applies to all of life, rather than being prescriptions applying specifically to politics, business, professions, etc. Rawls refers to beliefs as *comprehensive doctrines*. They may also be referred to as 'personal convictions' or 'life stances'. **The words 'belief' and 'beliefs', unless otherwise indicated, will be used to indicate a personal worldview.**

Belief Declaration

Declaration on the Elimination of All Forms of Intolerance and of Discrimination Based on Religion or Belief (1981).

Belief provisions

See Table 1

Belief rights

The liberties and responsibilities set out in the belief provisions of international treaties (see Table 1). **To express more accurately the purport of Article 18, the term 'belief rights' is used rather than '(the right to) freedom of belief', to indicate that the rights permitted by Article 18 are specific, conditional and limited.**

Belief tribunals

Those bodies set up by the ICCPR and ECHR to hear allegations of breaches of the rights they proclaim. They consist of the *United Nations Human Rights Committee* and the *European Court of Human Rights* (as well as the former European Commission on Human Rights).

Burdens of Judgment

Rawls's term for factors that 'burden' the process of judgment and lead to reasonable difference on philosophical, moral or religious matters. (*PL* 56-7) They include the following factors:
evidence in relation to a case is often conflicting and complex;
*   there is disagreement about the weight of different relevant considerations;
*   concepts are often vague, and indeterminate, requiring reliance on judgement and interpretation;
*   different individual experiences affect the assessment of evidence; and
*   differences occur in setting priorities and making adjustments.

Cairo Declaration

Cairo Declaration of Human Rights in Islam (1993).

Comprehensive Doctrines

Rawls's term for 'beliefs' (see above).

ECHR

European Convention for the Protection of Human Rights and Fundamental Freedoms, (1953).

ECtHR

European Court of Human Rights

European tribunals

The European Commission on Human Rights and the European Court of Human Rights.

Human rights	John Rawls distinguishes what he defines as essential 'human rights' from rights listed in the *Universal Declaration of Human Rights*. He calls the latter *basic liberties*. See Table 4 p. 56.
Human rights tribunals	United Nations Human Rights Committee ('UNHRC'), the European Commission on Human Rights ('European Commission') and the European Court of Human Rights ('European Court').
ICCPR	*International Covenant on Civil and Political Rights*, (1976).
Justice as fairness	(Rawls) Action in accordance with what is morally right or proper according to a political conception of justice, with equal conditions for all: Rawls (2003) 3, 39ff.
OIC	Organisation of the Islamic Conference.
Overlapping Consensus	(Rawls) A political conception of justice affirmed by citizens irrespective of the strength of their comprehensive doctrines: Rawls, (2003), 193.
Personal worldview	See 'belief'.
Philosophical Secularism	A worldview and ethical code based on the present life, rooted in non-belief in the existence of the metaphysical or supernatural, akin to the ideologies of humanism and rationalism.
Political (or structural) Secularism	Indifference to, or the discounting of, religion or religious considerations by the state in the exercise of its power, resulting in the separation from state authority of belief considerations.
Political Virtues	(Rawls) Ideals of good citizenship in a democratic regime. These include civility, tolerance reasonableness and cooperation. (*PL* 194ff.)
Primary Goods	(Rawls) Goods necessary for the realisation of one's capacity for a sense of justice and for a conception of what is good. They include 'rights and liberties, powers, opportunities and positions of office, income, wealth and the bases of self-respect' (Freeman, 2007a) 478.
Public Political Culture	Rawls's term for 'the political institutions of a constitutional regime and the public traditions of their interpretation (including those of the judiciary) as well as historic texts and documents that are common knowledge'. (*PL* 13,14). Religious or other comprehensive doctrines may be introduced into public political culture, *subject to the proviso of 'proper political reasons'* for their justification in governance (public reason). 'When these doctrines accept the proviso and only then come into political debate, the commitment to constitutional democracy is publicly manifested': Rawls,(2005d) 463. Justice as fairness is based on this political tradition (*PL*, 14, 8, 175).
Public Reason	(Rawls) The *idea* of public reason is reasoning that accords with the democratic interests of free and equal citizens, based on reasonable political conceptions of justice. The *ideal* of public reason is the exercise of public reason by government officials in making policy and legislation, and by citizens in voting for their representatives. (*PL* Lecture VI)

Reasonable 'comprehensive doctrine' or belief	A belief based on the exercise of theoretical and practical reason covering the major religious, philosophical and moral aspects of human life in a more or less consistent and coherent manner. It gives certain values primacy and weight, and only changes according to what, in its view is a tradition of thought and doctrine (see [[3.28]]).
Reasonable person	(Rawls) One who is 'willing to propose and honour fair terms of cooperation' and 'govern their conduct by a principle from which they and others can reason in common': (*PL* 49 fn1;[[3.28]]).
Reciprocity	Rawls uses this term in two relevant ways. At the political level reciprocity requires justification of governance in terms reasonably acceptable to all citizens. It also involves cooperation between citizens for mutual advantage, but on fair terms where any benefits bestowed on those who are already most socially or economically advantaged must simultaneously benefit the least advantaged more than an alternative benefit: Freeman (2007) 374.
Reflective Equilibrium (Rawls)	(Rawls) The 'mutual adjustment and readjustment between our pre-reflective intuitive specific convictions of justice and general, abstract principles of Justice': Sadurski (2005) 212. See also *PL*, 8, 28.
UDHR	*Universal Declaration of Human Rights* (1948).
UNHRC	United Nations Human Rights Committee.

Table 2: Membership of the United Nations

There are 193 members as at May 2013. All except those shaded (175 nations) are signatories or parties to ICCPR (non-members are Taiwan, Kosovo and the Vatican):

s = signature (endorsement and intention to ratify); *a* = accession or *r* = ratification (state agrees by either to be legally bound); *d* = succession (new state remaining bound by treaty obligations of the state from which it separated).

Sources: http://www.un.org/en/members/ http://treaties.un.org/Pages/ViewDetails.aspx?src=TREATY&mtdsg_no=IV-4&chapter=4&lang=en.

Afghanistan *a*
Albania *a*
Algeria *r*
Andorra *r*
Angola *a*
Antigua Barbuda
Argentina *r*
Armenia *a*
Australia *r*
Austria *r*
Azerbaijan *a*
Bahamas *r*
Bahrain *a*
Bangladesh *a*
Barbados *a*
Belarus *r*
Belgium *r*
Belize *a*
Benin *a*
Bhutan
Bolivia *a*
Bosnia & Herzegovina *d*
Botswana *r*
Brazil *a*
Brunei
Bulgaria *r*
Burkina Faso *a*
Burundi *a*
Cambodia *a*
Cameroon *a*
Canada *a*
Cape Verde *a*
Central African

Republic *a*
Chad *a*
Chile *r*
China *s*
Colombia *r*
Comoros *s*
Congo *a*
Congo, D R *a*
Costa Rica *r*
Côte d'Ivoire *a*
Croatia *d*
Cuba *s*
Cyprus *r*
Czech Republic *d*
Denmark *r*
Djibouti *a*
Dominica *a*
Dominican Republic *a*
Ecuador *r*
Egypt *r*
El Salvador *r*
Equatorial Guinea *a*
Eritrea *a*
Estonia *a*
Ethiopia *a*
Fiji
Finland *r*
France *a*
Gabon *a*
Gambia *a*
Georgia *a*
Germany *r*

Ghana *r*
Greece *a*
Grenada *a*
Guatemala *a*
Guinea *r*
Guinea-Bissau *r*
Guyana *r*
Haiti *a*
Honduras *r*
Hungary *r*
Iceland *r*
India *a*
Indonesia *a*
Iran *r*
Iraq *r*
Ireland *r*
Israel *r*
Italy *r*
Jamaica *r*
Japan *r*
Jordan *r*
Kazakhstan *r*
Kenya *a*
Kiribati
Korea, North
Korea, South
Kuwait *a*
Kyrgyzstan *a*
Laos *r*
Latvia *a*
Lebanon *a*
Lesotho *a*
Liberia *r*
Libya *a*
Liechtenstein *a*

Lithuania *a*
Luxembourg *r*
Macedonia *d*
Madagascar *r*
Malawi *a*
Malaysia
Maldives *a*
Mali *a*
Malta *a*
Marshall Islands
Mauritania *a*
Mauritius *a*
Mexico *a*
Micronesia
Moldova *a*
Monaco *r*
Mongolia *r*
Montenegro *d*
Morocco *r*
Mozambique *a*
Myanmar
Namibia *a*
Nauru *s*
Nepal *a*
Netherlands *r*
New Zealand *r*
Nicaragua *a*
Niger *a*
Nigeria *a*
Norway *r*
Oman
Pakistan *r*
Palau *s*
Panama *r*

Papua New Guinea *a*
Paraguay *a*
Peru *r*
Philippines *r*
Poland *r*
Portugal *r*
Qatar
Romania *r*
Russian Fed'n *r*
Rwanda *r*
St. Kitts & Nevis
St. Lucia *s*
St. Vincent, Grenadines *a*
Samoa *a*
San Marino *a*
São Tomé & Príncipe *s*
Saudi Arabia
Senegal *r*
Serbia *d*
Seychelles *a*
Sierra Leone *a*
Singapore
Slovakia *d*
Slovenia *d*
Solomon Islands
Somalia *a*
South Africa *r*
Sth Sudan
Spain *r*
Sri Lanka *a*
Sudan *a*

Suriname *a*
Swaziland *a*
Sweden *r*
Switzerland *a*
Syria *a*
Tajikistan *a*
Tanzania *a*
Thailand *a*
Timor L 'Este *a*
Togo *a*
Tonga
Trinidad/ Tobago *a*
Tunisia *r*
Turkey *r*
Turkmenistan *a*
Tuvalu
Uganda *a*
Ukraine *r*
United Arab Emirates
U.K. *r*
U.S. *r*
Uruguay *r*
Uzbekistan *a*
Vanuatu *r*
Venezuela *r*
Vietnam *a*
Yemen *a*
Zambia *a*
Zimbabwe *a*

INTRODUCTION

Making sense of the natural world and our relationship with others defines being human. We are impelled to understand where we come from, the problems that beset us, and why we are here.[1] This leads to the adoption by individuals of a *personal worldview*, which involves (a) an explanation of nature, (b) the reason for existence, and one's relationship to the natural, social and political environment, and (c) a set of values or morals to govern our behaviour in everyday life. One's personal worldview or belief applies to all of life, rather than being prescriptions applying specifically to politics, business, professions, etc. Personal worldviews thus can be distinguished from *political worldviews*, which are the political principles and values adopted by (or imposed on) a society, e.g. democracy, dictatorship or theocracy. **The words 'belief' and 'beliefs', unless otherwise indicated, will be used to indicate a personal worldview.**

Individuals and groups can become so dependent on their personal beliefs that they hold them to be self-evident and incontestable. They then feel threatened by the presence of incompatible or contradictory personal worldviews of others. There may even be a deep interconnection between religion, ethnic and at times nationalist identity.[2] In the Middle East, religion is linked with national identity. For example, 'in Saudi Arabia all citizens must be Muslims and in Iran, Kuwait and the UAE citizenship is strongly linked to Islam'.[3]

In any given society, beliefs may be based on values very different from, and even contrary to, those governing public activities. For example, in liberal democracies human rights apply generally, but these may be different from the dictates of particular religious doctrines (such as discrimination against women and restrictive sexual regulations). Therein lies the basis of some the most divisive aspects of our society. It is thus not surprising that history is full of stories of intolerance between those with different worldviews. Acceptance of the adoption and practice of diverse beliefs equally and for everyone, whether religious or non-religious, has been one of the oldest controversies in the annals of society, and a longstanding source of conflict, repression and inequality.

The one hundred and ninety-three nations that are members of the United Nations (Table 2) have signed the *Universal Declaration of Human Rights* (UDHR – see Table 1) and, with it, the promise (in Article 18) of an equal right for all individuals to 'freedom of thought, conscience and religion', and to have and to follow ('manifest') a 'religion or belief' of their choice. **Unless otherwise indicated 'Article 18' refers to Article 18 of the UDHR.**

---

1   See, e.g., van Krieken et al (2000), 481.
2   Little (1996), 68ff. See also Fox (2008), 354.
3   Fox, ibid, 355.

A similar provision, Article 9, exists in the *European Convention for the Protection of Human Rights and Fundamental Freedoms* ('ECHR'), which applies to nations in the European Union. These provisions are also set out in other international Treaties and Declarations. They are referred to as the 'belief provisions'. The belief provisions and their institutional settings are discussed in Chapter 2.

The very term 'freedom' means lack of restraints, but Article 18 itself sets out restraints to the 'freedom' it promises. This freedom thus applies to *identifiable liberties* associated with manifesting belief. Critical to the belief provisions is the specification that the right to manifestation of belief is to be subject to limits necessary for public order, health and welfare, and protection of the rights of others. Belief rights are thus not unbridled or unconditional, as will be seen in later Chapters. Despite these limitations, the 'freedom' aspect of the belief provisions is generally perceived as a justification for priority treatment of particular religious beliefs and practices by government and society. This has been detrimental to minority religious groups and non-believers alike. It has allowed individual churches and self-appointed spiritual guides (including leaders of cultic groups) to enhance political, economic and social benefits and influence through special favours, by demanding 'freedom' of religion.[4] **To express more accurately the purport of Article 18, the term 'belief rights' is used rather than '(the right to) freedom of belief' to indicate that the rights permitted by Article 18 are specific, conditional and limited.**

Even this qualified promise of freedom to follow personal worldviews in a populace consisting of many varied, and even contradictory personal worldviews, is an impossible one to realise in full, and nations make little effort at seeking to do so. I will argue that, while commendable in spirit, Article 18 is misleading in language and interpretation. In addition, its ambiguous and undefined terms, as well as its generality, have led to misuse and failure to deliver its promise. It is here argued that the United Nations, despite its splendid efforts in promoting human rights, is a major contributor to this failure in its attempts to reconcile many diverse political cultural and religious interests.

Article 18 expresses the right to 'freedom of religion or belief' (thus apparently bestowing the freedom to act according to the dictates of one's beliefs). Prohibition of particular beliefs is widespread, as is persecution of believers. However, it is argued that inherent in the meaning of Article 18 is also the right to freedom *from* the dictates of the beliefs of others. Its intention is not to *privilege* the liberty to act according to one's beliefs, but to ensure that governments restrict their policies and legislation subject to their adopted *political* worldview. They should separate their decision-making from the dictates of belief.

---

4   Mutch (2013).

Instead, governments have either tolerated religious or other groups ignoring the law, or provided privileges and specific exemptions for such groups from secular laws that are otherwise applicable to everyone. There is a consequent widespread expectation by, e.g. religious followers, that they have unmitigated freedom to follow religious practices, and are thus immune from the law.[5] Such groups can have access to government resources and policy resulting in financial benefits and legislation to impose their beliefs on others (see Chapter 12).

Even in societies where individuals are not prevented from having and practising their beliefs, those beliefs are privileged through government endorsement, funding and policy. Freedom *from* 'religion or belief' of others is thus an unfulfilled promise of Article 18 throughout the world. This influence can be insidious, as it often is in liberal democracies.

Article 18 is related to other liberties set out in the UDHR (e.g. autonomy, speech and association). Far from guaranteeing the unbridled liberty to follow the dictates of one's belief, it delineates and protects those personal liberties relating to them. For this reason, it is argued, the efficacy and relevance of the wording of Article 18 requires rethinking.

The theories of John Rawls

Given the diversity of beliefs in most societies, and often their conflict with each other, exacerbated by increased globalisation, how do we maximise the nominal right for everyone, not only to practise their belief, but to have equal opportunity to do so? In attempting to answer this question, I looked for a theoretical model of democratic pluralist liberal society. This I found in the concept of political liberalism developed by John Rawls, the celebrated twentieth-century political theorist.[6]

I have chosen Rawls because he aimed to develop a theory of justice based on what he calls *political liberalism*, one that is compatible with the two fundamental principles of democratic society: freedom and equality. Rawls's later works in particular were devoted to considering how we can ensure full and equal freedom regarding beliefs (he calls them 'comprehensive doctrines') in pluralist societies. In *Political Liberalism (PL)* he set out to investigate:

---

5   See Hamilton, (2005), 32 and (2007), who gives examples from the U.S.

6   There is a voluminous amount of literature by and about Rawls. See, e.g. the Bibliography in Freeman (2007a). While he has sparked a lively debate within political and legal academia, his influence is extensive. For example, Freeman states that 'Rawls is the foremost political philosopher of the twentieth century, and is recognised by many as one of the great political thinkers of all time' (ibid, x). Richard Arneson, says 'Rawls's achievements continue to set the contemporary terms of debate on theories of social justice' Arneson (2006), 45. See also Amitrajeet Batabyal (2000).

- how it is possible to have, over time, 'a stable and just society of free and equal citizens profoundly divided by reasonable though incompatible religious, philosophical and moral doctrines';

- how people with such 'deeply opposed though reasonable doctrines may live together and all affirm the political conception of a constitutional regime' through the adoption of an 'overlapping consensus'; and

- the structure and content of a political conception 'that can gain the support of such an overlapping consensus'.[7]

For Rawls, a 'reasonable' doctrine is based on consistent and coherent philosophical and moral aspects of human life (see [3.27]).

Rawls saw the benefit in quarantining personal morality (generated, I argue, by one's personal beliefs) from political morality. Personal morality is based on our private worldviews (Rawls calls them 'comprehensive doctrines'). It belongs to the individual as an *individual* who has no business imposing it on others.

Political, or public morality, (generated from one's political worldview) on the other hand, is based on values belonging to the political realm of government. It defines the individual as *citizen,* subject to the principles of public morality. In a liberal democracy, public morality shapes the political structure that sustains a stable society based on justice and fairness (such as human rights and the rule of law). Public morality informs a 'political conception of justice': a 'freestanding political conception that is not tied to any comprehensive doctrine or general moral conception'[8]. These values are framed by recognised principles of justice, and acceptable to everyone, whatever their personal worldview, through an 'overlapping consensus' based on the democratic process. Individuals can determine their lives according to their beliefs within the constraints of this generally accepted political structure.

This model of society means government must separate itself from belief organisations, and justify policy purely on political values. It seeks to provide that as *citizen* (a) everyone has equal entitlements to participate in political life; (b) everyone must exercise restraint when personal behaviour encroaches on the rights of others. As *individual,* everyone has the maximum opportunity to seek personal fulfilment, free to follow his or her personal worldview constrained only by the need to accommodate the political entitlements of others.

7   *Political Liberalism (PL),* (2005b), xviii.
8   Freeman (2007b), 186. See *PL* 10-12.

Rawls's model involves objectivity, reason and reciprocity on the part, both of government and citizens, rather than self-interest and the pursuit of power for its own sake. An impossible task, you might think, but Rawls describes his theory as 'realistically utopian, that is, probing the limits of practicable political possibility. The problem is, 'the limits of the possible are not given by the actual' due to 'prevailing social and political circumstances and influences'.[9] But the idea is that if we use this model as a benchmark for a truly effective liberal democracy, we can work towards maximising the chances for equal enjoyment of belief rights for everyone.

In examining belief rights in the light of Rawls's work, the idea of human rights and the principles that underlie them is considered in Chapter 1. The 'right to freedom of belief' as set out in the international treaties (Covenants and Declarations) is described in Chapter 2. Rawls's approach to belief rights is outlined in Chapters 3 and 4. An added consideration central to these freedoms that is missing from Rawls is the nature and importance of secularism in considering personal worldview liberties. This is dealt with in Chapter 5.

After basic concepts are established, Chapter 6 deals with the approach of the UN and European Council to state-belief entanglement, which is considered inadequate. Chapter 7 considers the indeterminacy of the belief provisions, pointing out the confusing references to such terms as 'religion', and 'conscience', with their lack of definition. Chapter 8 asks why there is a special reference to 'religion' at all, and argues that this diverts attention from non-religious beliefs. Chapter 9 points to the confusion in interpretation of the belief provisions between thought and action, adopting a clear division between the two. Chapter 9 examines what is meant by 'manifesting' one's personal worldview, and the different and contradictory interpretations adopted by the human rights tribunals, and this is followed by Chapter 11, which recognises individual circumstances and how they are dealt with by the tribunals. Chapter 12 considers have these issues have led to the many ways that the promise of belief rights has failed. An answer to this dilemma is offered in Chapters 13, which argues that state neutrality is necessary, but this must be through state-belief separation, not accommodation. The conclusion involves questioning the clarity and effectiveness of Article 18 itself, and in Chapter 14 sets out specific constitutional provisions aimed at maximising belief rights, and fulfilling the promise of Article 18.

---

9   Rawls (2003), 4-5.

CHAPTER 1
INTERNATIONAL HUMAN RIGHTS: A REVOLUTION

Human Rights as a revolutionary idea

[1.1] Under our legal system the Magna Carta of 1215 gave form (albeit to a limited degree) to the principle of equality through the rule of law (a fair trial for all), and the Bill of Rights of 1688 extended this to establish the supremacy of Parliament over the king. However, it was not until 1776 with the American *Declaration of Independence*, and 1789, the year of the French *Declaration of the Rights of Man and of the Citizen* that the idea of general equality for all citizens was formally recognised, at least in terms of dignity and specified rights.

[1.2] This development gave expression to the Enlightenment rejection of social status, birth and kinship as the determinants of particular entitlements, replacing those criteria with citizenship. Thus, the mere status of 'citizen' endows a person with those entitlements. Equality in its terms was linked to the right to pursue fulfilment in life, albeit initially racist, sexist and exclusive of slavery in Northern America. Every person was to have equal status and liberty.

[1.3] The idea of *political* equality does not demand universally equal social or economic outcomes within society, as it is impossible to develop one form of personal fulfilment that would equally suit every individual. Otherwise, it was recognised, that this would lead to a 'collectively imposed definition of happiness'.[1] However, the Enlightenment gave birth to the principle that the status of humanity in itself is one granting strict equality of *political* freedoms and responsibilities, including freedom from persecution based on personal belief. There should thus be an equal entitlement to enjoy political liberties, regardless of physical ability, talents, social circumstances and resourcefulness.

Human rights and civil liberties

[1.4] The 'human' source of human rights is not always accepted. As currently used, 'human rights' are attributed variously to one of three possible sources. One source exists outside human nature (be it through religious faith or some other external source), such as a god or other supernatural entity from which right and wrong are revealed.[2] A second source is nature itself, held to contain the essence of humanity from which truth and direction ('natural law') arises. This truth

---

1   Schwarzschild (2000), 158.
2   E.g., the *Cairo Declaration on Human Rights in Islam* (1993), ('Cairo Declaration'), signed by the Organisation of Islamic Conference that sources all rights in Allah, and requires interpretation of the Declaration to accord with Islamic Shari'ah law.

and direction is said to be universal, superior to human law and discoverable by 'natural' rather than 'artificial' (common law) reason.[3]

[1.5] A third possible source can, however, be explained as the inevitable development of those liberties that underscore liberal representative democracy. These liberties result from the acquisition by humans of the capacity to *know* (therefore understand), to *empathise* (therefore to feel, and appreciate another's point of view or suffering), and to *reason* (therefore to judge and evaluate courses of action, including appreciation of the principle of reciprocity, that is, treating others as one would wish to be treated).[4] These human capacities lead to the development of principles for governance, and result in recognition of the interests of each individual in equal citizenship and equality before the law, with each person having an equal voice in the governance of their society. These capacities have led us to democracy.[5]

[1.6] Central to democracy is the civil right of each citizen to vote. The right to cast a vote, however, is not enough. There must be genuine choice in the vote one casts. Democracy cannot exist without the liberty all citizens to an autonomous vote. It is an 'entitlement without which no country can properly describe itself as democratic'.[6]

[1.7] Choice in how we are governed implies the positive freedom to seek information, to express both personal beliefs and opinions, to associate with others, and to assemble and enjoy equality before the law. It also requires a degree of personal security, privacy and the rule of law. It implies the equality of all citizens. It also implies legality, i.e. that no citizen can be subjected to invasion of personal autonomy through arbitrary execution, assault, torture[7], unlawful detention or punishment. Nevertheless, within all these freedoms are contained the seeds of their own limitation, as it follows that each person must also respect the same liberties for others.

[1.8] Rights created by civil liberties differ from human rights. Civil liberties exist only as the consequence of legislation or case law accepted by the government of a particular nation. As such, they may be 'qualified, removed, restored, truncated or expanded'.[8] They are contingent on the political and legal processes in place at any given time. They are also technically only applicable to citizens of the particular society that creates them. Human rights, on the other hand, are

---

3   See e.g., Davies (1994), Chapter 3.
4   Reciprocity, incidentally, is a fundamental principle formally underlying most established religions): see Tahzib (1996), 15–16.
5   See, e.g., Gearty (2006), 66-8. These capacities could be considered the basis for Rawls's idea of moral personhood: *PL* 81.
6   Gearty (2001), 12.
7   Under human rights instruments freedom from torture, along with freedom of thought, conscience and religion, have been designated absolute rights. Under civil liberties, strictly speaking, the democratic process can limit such liberties.
8   Gearty (2001), 12.

recognised as due to all individuals by virtue of their human nature alone, regardless of national identity, personal attributes or circumstance. Human rights circumscribe the power of the state to change or modify them. They may be modified only when necessary for the protection of the state or the rights of others, but they can never be completely denied.

[1.9] Human rights thus place the source of personal power simply in the status of humanity, rather than in the beneficence or otherwise of the state. Rather than being a set of liberties granted by a ruler or government, human rights apply to all human beings, regardless of nationality, citizenship or location.[9] All individuals create within themselves, by their simple existence, the obligation of states to recognise equal rights in the face of counterclaims of society or the state. Human rights are meant to supplant policy and legislation of governments that disregard them. Thus, while civil liberties law sets the parameters of freedom in specific detail, human rights law draws on a set of fundamental principles that underlie liberty and responsibility, leaving the details to be determined according to the circumstances of individual societies.[10]

[1.10] After the Second World War, the UN was created to bind member states to the principle of global peace and mutual consideration. It aimed to bring into being recognition of the universal standards and practice of human rights, so that war on such a scale, based as it was on religion, racism and nationalism, would never recur. The UDHR was signed by member states, with later international treaties providing for the implementation of the rights set out in the UDHR. One hundred and seventy-five states have signed the *International Covenant on Civil and Political Rights* ('ICCPR' – see Table 2) which commits states more specifically to accountability for the implementation of political rights, including rights associated with belief.

[1.11] The ICCPR, then, expands the principles underlying the civil liberties that helped to define liberal democracy, establishing 'bottom line' guidelines for ensuring the self-realisation of all individuals as compared with more state-specific civil rights. Human rights documents, drawn up in a world where governments had lost sight of civil liberties, thus assume and amend civil liberties in a form that is universally accepted.[11] They specify each freedom and nominate:

- those that must never be limited – 'non-derogable' - e.g. freedom from slavery or torture; or

---

9 Humphrey (1975), 209. Martin and Nickel (1980). See also Galleoti (2002), 6.
10 See, e.g., Gearty (2001); (2004), 33ff., esp. 35.
11 Indeed, Humphrey ((1975), 209 considered universal acceptance as a 'revolutionary' aspect of the UDHR.

- whether and when rights may be subject to limitations, restrictions, conditions, or derogation (e.g. freedom of speech, assembly, association or privacy).[12]

[1.12] Cultural relativism means acceptance of the values and customs of all cultures and religions as bearing equal moral worth, no matter how diverse or contrary to ours. The universal nature of human rights means that cultural relativism is rejected in favour of universally accepted values of autonomy and equality. Before 1945, international law was based on the right to recognition of the sovereignty (i.e. unfettered power) of each nation. The individual and his or her status, liberties and often religious affiliation were defined by the particular society and government endowed by chance to govern them. Now, every human being is the subject of human rights simply through his or her status as a human being, regardless of physical, mental, social and economic or any other status. The UDHR proclaimed that the 'inherent dignity and....equal and inalienable rights of all members of the human family is the foundation of freedom, justice and peace in the world'. This notion of universal human rights has been called 'a revolution in international law', as it has both created the individual as universal, and held that 'it is no longer necessary to appeal to either a divine or natural law as a basis for human rights, for they now have a positive existence in law'.[13]

[1.13] On paper, at least, most nations of the world that have signed the UDHR, agree. Only three states were not signatories at the time of writing: Taiwan, Kosovo and the Vatican.

[1.14] The placing of the individual as the universal subject of human rights laid the foundation for the principle of equal application of such rights to all individuals equally.[14] But human rights are far from accepted across the globe, with much criticism despite their formal acceptance. Tore Lindholm issues a challenge to critics of universally applicable human rights to:

> ...come up with feasible alternative political, legal, and institutional measures that are arguably superior to what we already have as a globally entrenched regime: universally applicable human rights protection (though often inefficient and non-evenhanded) against pressing threats and impending perils to human freedom and dignity in the present-day world.[15]

---

12   The ICCPR Article 4(2), sets out non-derogable rights as being those contained in Article 6 (life), 7 (torture, cruelty), 8(1), (slavery), 8(2), (servitude), 11 (imprisonment for debt), 15 (fair trial), 16 (equality before the law), and 18 (Freedom of belief). Articles 6 and 18 are subject to limitations contained within the articles themselves.

13   Yeatman (2000), 1504.

14   Articles 26 ICCPR, and Article 14 ECHR proscribe discrimination with regard to the rights and freedoms set out in the Conventions on *inter alia*, 'religion, political or other opinion', race or ethnicity. Protocol No. 12 to the ECHR provides that 'the enjoyment of any right set forth by law shall be secured without discrimination on grounds that include religion and 'political or other' opinion. The majority of members of the European Union have not yet ratified it: see <http://conventions.coe.int/Treaty/Commun/ChercheSig.asp?NT=177&CM=1&DF=10/02/2010&CL=ENG>.

15   Lindholm (2004), 50.

[1.15] This book is based on the understanding that no feasible superior measures have been identified.

Rights and obligations

[1.16] Rights are freedoms that can be claimed by the rights-holder against a third party. In fact they are the expression of an obligation, not of the rights-holder, but of others towards the rights-holder. No one is ever *obliged* to exercise their rights, but someone else is obliged to ensure that if they wish, they can do so. One can follow this rule of thumb: to determine whether something is a right, one asks 'whether it has a legal duty correlative to it'.[16] A right, then, is the expression of an obligation, enforceable by the rights-holder, on a third party. A right is expressed in a triadic formula. It identifies, either specifically or by implication:

a) *the rights-holder, or person to whom the obligation is owed* (e.g. 'everyone', 'those charged with a crime');

b) *the rights-giver, or person or persons having the obligation* (e.g. 'everyone', or identifiable individuals such as the government);

c) *what the rights-giver is obliged to do or not do* (either refrain from activity that impedes a person exercising their right (e.g. prohibit the practise of their belief) or undertake action necessary to protect the exercise of that right(e.g. ensure a fair trial);

[1.17] Thus the statement that someone has the right to practise their beliefs is really a statement that others have the obligation to allow them to do so. The same triadic formula is used when stating the duty of third persons to the rights-holder.[17] No obligation is placed on the rights-holder to exercise their right, nor is there, in Article 18, an obligation to practise one's personal beliefs. A more effective way of expressing the right would be to indicate the obligation of third parties: what one is to be free *from* (i.e. the obligation not to prevent the manifestation of belief, or to enforce the dictates of the beliefs of others).

[1.18] Under the relevant human rights instruments, duties created by human rights are generally aimed at promoting human dignity, autonomy and self-realisation by either (a) preserving personal safety or integrity;[18] or (b) facilitating fair and equal participation in civil and political

---

16   See Williams (1968), 139.

17   Ibid. The relationship between human rights and correlative and non-correlative duties is discussed in Lazarus et al (2009), esp 26ff. See also Nickel (1993).

18   E.g., right to life, freedom from arbitrary arrest, cruel and unusual punishment, belief, speech and assembly.

life through the provision of adequate resources.[19] States thus have 'positive duties' to provide facilities necessary for the exercise of personal autonomy or integrity as equal citizens (for example, provision of information, public health and security, and the means for participation in the public political process) and negative duties (such as refraining from undue interference in the rights-holder's private life). This means that the state is not obliged to actively assist individuals or organisations in the practice of their personal beliefs, but it is obliged not to actively intervene in their doing so.

[1.19] Rawls points out that, at the political level, freedom generates a legal or constitutional structure of institutions when people are free from certain constraints either to do or not to do something 'and when their doing it or not doing it is protected from interference by other persons'.[20] It follows that liberty of conscience as defined by law, means that

> individuals are free to pursue their moral, philosophical or religious interests without legal restrictions requiring them to engage or not to engage in any particular form of religious or other practice, and when other men have a legal duty not to interfere.[21]

[1.20] Jeremy Waldron expresses this in another way when he says that someone has a right whenever the protection or advancement of some interest of his is recognized as a reason for imposing duties or obligations on others.[22] This applies whether or not the duties are specified.

[1.21] The international human rights treaties define liberties associated with personal beliefs as 'rights', with implied correlative duties. This means that the 'right' to manifest one's beliefs, is in effect the creation of an obligation, addressed to those other than the person who holds the right. It requires third parties to refrain from action that will prevent or restrict the exercise of nominated liberties by the rights-holder. The obvious task, then, is to identify the metes and bounds of that duty, while recognising that it involves the need to ensure that:

- personal beliefs are neither enforced nor privileged; and

---

19 E.g. fair trial, participation in government and education:

> A right is fully implemented or has high quality implementation when all of the major threats to the right have been adequately blocked or neutralized through actions such as gaining recognition and compliance with the right's associated moral and legal duties, providing protections and other services, and providing legal and other remedies for noncompliance with the right (Nickel (2008), 992).

20 *TJ*, 177. This accords with Glanville Williams's idea of a 'right', as opposed to a 'liberty', in that a liberty is an abrogation by the state of any duty on the part of a person to do the opposite: a legal right is a duty on the part of third parties not to prevent that person from doing it: Williams (1968), 132ff. In other words, 'every right in the strict sense relates to the conduct of another, while a liberty and a power relate to the conduct of the holder of the liberty or power', at 139.

21 *TJ*, 177.

22 Waldron (1984), 10.

- everyone enjoys the right equally.

The idea of belief rights

[1.22] Over time, there have been worldwide attempts to allow individuals the right to their own particular belief system through more tolerant societies. This has led to the twentieth century recognition (in principle at least) of the belief rights ('freedom of religion or belief') as set out in Article 18.

[1.23] This right has been held to be one of the rights designed to:

> …enable man to develop his own intellectual and moral personality, to determine his attitude towards natural and supernatural powers, and to shape his relations to his fellow creatures as well as his position in the social and political order.[23]

[1.24] In a liberal, representative democracy, the liberty of all individuals to act according to their perceived interests feeds all liberties such as those involving speech, association and assembly. These liberties are interdependent, and have been declared indivisible.[24] However, they can be restricted in the interests of the liberties of others. It is thus recognised that liberal democracy contains within itself the need to limit the very liberties it promotes. This creates what Rawls calls one's 'duty of civility'.

[1.25] This model applies to belief rights. For example, the right of children to state protection may well outweigh an individual's freedom to refuse medical treatment of their child on religious grounds. However, some governments have accepted harmful practices, such as refusal of medical treatment, child sexual abuse, domestic violence and female circumcision, as a consequence of a policy of 'respect' for, and even encouragement of, diversity of culture and religion (multiculturalism, or cultural relativism). In the US as at 2005, for example, Marci Hamilton claims that:

---

23   Partsch (1981), 209.
24   The UN has declared all human rights to be indivisible, both civil/political rights and social/economic rights. This principle is supported by the General Assembly and by the Office of the High Commissioner for Human Rights. The 1993 Vienna Declaration declares that 'All human rights are universal, indivisible and interdependent and interrelated': *Vienna Declaration and Programme of Action* (1993). Indivisibility requires that the two categories of rights be mutually indispensable as opposed to the more flexible relationship of interdependence: Nickel (2008), 991. Nickel argues that 'United Nations statements about indivisibility are broad overstatements of more modest truths': ibid, 1001, and that total indivisibility of all rights is not really a practical option, particularly for developing nations. His analysis points to a more realisable focus on supporting relationships of interdependence and interrelationship, based on particular rights and circumstances of realisation.

A total of 32 states provide a defense for felonious child neglect, manslaughter or murder where the child's life was sacrificed for religious reasons, as well as a religious defense for misdemeanours arising from physical harm to children resulting from medical neglect.[25]

[1.26] Across the world, human rights are compromised in relation to the right to change one's personal worldview, and the role of women and children based on personal worldview. Government acquiescence, either formally or informally, plays a part in their continuance.[26] Disagreement on these issues helps to explain the failure of UN membership to agree on a Covenant that would turn the *Declaration on the Elimination of All Forms of Intolerance and of Discrimination Based on Religion or Belief* (1981) – see Table 1 – a detailed declaration of belief rights signed by member states – into a legally binding Covenant.[27] Lindholm *et al* point out that

> the 1993 Vienna World Conference on Human Rights [which considered such a Covenant] did not succeed in crafting a new understanding on the universality or particularity of human rights. It merely acknowledged disagreement through its compromise language, giving continued recognition to the universality of human rights while accepting cultural and religious particularities as well.[28]

Special treatment for Religion?

[1.27] The aim of this book is not to denigrate religion, but to argue that belief rights apply to the adoption and manifestation of any personal worldview, religious or otherwise. The special attention given religious belief cannot be justified in the twenty-first century, especially given the increasing diversity of such beliefs, and their changing nature due to the influence of social mobility, global governance and the ideology of human rights.

[1.28] This proposal is supported by other considerations. Firstly, the stated intention of the international expressions of these liberties is to include a wide conception of the term to include beliefs of all kinds.

[1.29] Secondly, personal worldview liberties overlap and interrelate with other liberties, such as liberty of speech and association, personal autonomy, and liberties expressing the rule of law. The

---

25   Hamilton (2005), 32, Ch 2.
26   E.g., in Afghanistan, '[n]umerous reports demonstrate that authorities systematically fail to investigate and prosecute perpetrators of sexual violence…police and judicial officials are not aware or convinced that rape is a serious criminal offence': United Nations (2009), 24-5. 'In some countries police and judiciary help to preserve and protect harmful traditional practices, for example, in covering up murders dressed up as crimes of honour. Judges may fear interference with custom or culture': United Nations (2002), ¶197.
27   Lindholm et al , xxviii.
28   Ibid.

European Court often considers an alleged breach of Article 9 ECHR as more appropriately addressed as a breach of, e.g. freedom of speech or assembly.

[1.30] Thirdly, as soon as one accepts a broad definition of 'belief' to include both religious and non-religious worldviews, as well as relating to other freedoms, the question arises - *why should there be any special reference to, or treatment of, religious belief?* There is a lack of agreement on how to identify a distinctive nature for religion – is it religion's belief in the supernatural, its faith-based, rather than rational, basis, or the imperative nature of its dictates, with fear of eternal damnation?[29] Other worldviews are based on ethical imperatives, albeit for different reasons. They may or may not be based on faith or reason. If we believe in equal liberties for all, we need to consider all worldviews equally, whatever their basis. We would focus on the common factor of liberty in relation to whatever worldview is being considered, by grounding religious liberty in generic liberties of speech, association and expression rather than establishing some special right of its own.

[1.31] By doing this we would actually enhance the ability of all individuals to exercise more equally their liberties to have and manifest their worldview and their right to dignity and self-realisation. The liberty to hold and express worldviews would become one element, albeit essential, of liberal democratic society, with its focus on autonomy and equality. The question would then be, not, why are you acting this way, but rather, are you harming anyone else, or unjustifiably restricting their liberty in acting this way?

[1.32] It thus seems unhelpful to conceive of religion as other than a way of believing, given that 'religion or belief' connotes the acceptance of particular propositions.[30] In this case, it means propositions about personal meanings and values for living.

[1.33] So, based on a commonly accepted approach to the term 'religion or belief' as it appears in the belief provisions, 'religion' is just another form of what Article 18 terms 'belief'. However, all beliefs, religious or otherwise, are fundamental to self-identity and perception of the cosmos for all human beings. Because of this critical role in individuals' and communities' perception of the nature and meaning of their lives, different worldviews, whether religious or otherwise, have been the cause of much intolerance through discrimination, persecution and warfare for centuries,[31] and continues through to the present, particularly in Africa and the Middle East.

---

29   Richard Dawkins considers that one can sum up the functions attributed to religion as explanation, exhortation (to do right), consolation and inspiration, all of which he says are provided by science: Dawkins (2006), esp p. 347.

30   Concise Oxford Dictionary, Oxford, OUP 1985.

31   See, e.g., Malcolm Evans (2004); Ranan (2006), Ch 4; Heywood (2003), Ch10, esp 302ff.

How do we deal with 'religion or belief' in a pluralist society?

[1.34] Several approaches to dealing with pluralist society have been developed. These range from cultural relativism on the one hand, to a universalist (or 'cosmopolitan') notion of human rights governing all societies on the other. While I do not purport to examine these paradigms in depth, I will briefly discuss them and relate them to the argument of this book.

Cultural relativism and human rights

[1.35] Cultural relativism is based on the principle that culture is the sole source of validation of morality.[32] It eschews the notion of judging the actions of a particular group, and tends toward the toleration of all communities, regardless of the concern with which others might observe their practices. Most writers advocating toleration of others' cultural values, however, draw the line at some practices perceived to violate the decency of humanity.

[1.36] Cultural relativists argue that the egalitarian, individualist approach of human rights places emphasis on the individual and personal autonomy. They decry the fact that egalitarianism does not countenance other philosophical traditions that give the group priority over the individual, and where salvation depends on public conformity with the decrees of one's religion rather than a personally reasoned relationship with one's god[33], or alternative personal worldview.

[1.37] The relativist stance gives little scope for the expression of intellectual autonomy, to the extent that adoption or manifestation of worldviews is involuntary, through, e.g. indoctrination, acculturation, coercion or fear, or the perception that 'truths' cannot be questioned. Critics of cultural relativism hold that it creates an unjustified limitation of freedoms as outlined in the internationally adopted instruments, which are integral to democratic regimes.

[1.38] A major theoretical problem with cultural relativism is its absolutist claim that no reasonable person would criticise other cultures. This leads to a certain 'moral rectitude' that allows cruel and inhumane practice in the name of 'culture', as if culture is the single source of moral acceptability.[34] Further, relativism reifies culture, as if each culture is internally uniform, uncontested and unaffected by social differences, such as age, caste, gender, or by the influence of other cultures or increased awareness of human rights. Different cultures are not fixed in their practices, nor are they unaffected by transnational political and judicial processes. They are also increasingly

32   Wilson (1997), 2.
33   See, e.g. Langlois (2001) .
34   Wilson (1997), 2.

turning to human rights principles and law to further their own interests.[35] Cultural relativism tends to non-egalitarian and repressive political systems'.[36]

[1.39] Brian Barry points to fallacies he sees in moral relativism.[37] He claims that while diversity is a good thing, and society is the richer for allowing even 'nonliberal' regimes,[38] some cultural and religious practices cause harm to members of different groups.[39] He argues that there is 'some universal requirement of value, which is precisely what the premise of the [cultural-relativist] argument denies'. He also maintains that something is only good to the extent that people benefit from it, not because of social acceptance. As recognised, minority groups (particularly women and children) do not benefit from the values of many cultures and religions.[40] Barry adds that cultures are not static, and 'we should also attribute to all human beings an equal capacity for cultural adaptation'.[41]

[1.40] Another writer, Jeremy Waldron, argues that relativism is a flawed basis for acceptance of others' values, as acceptance is based solely on their expression, rather than on the *worth* of the values themselves.[42] He gives the example of Iranian clerics who justify banning pornography because it is just not acceptable in their society ('the way we do things around here') and claims that this reasoning is not sufficient to establish a general moral value that cannot be criticised. However, if the cleric justifies banning pornography because it is degrading and irredeemably corrupts *any* society, the argument goes to the content of the value espoused. '[I]f we cannot answer [this argument], and answer it adequately, we are not entitled to regard our toleration of pornography as valid even for us', let alone inflict it on anyone else.[43] He points out the responsibility of universalists is thus to 'address whatever reservations, doubts, and objections there are about our positions *out there*, in the real world, no matter what society or culture or religious tradition they come from'.[44] Thus, it seems, it is the effect of a value on society, not its source. That is the relevant consideration.

---

35   Ibid, 9-10.
36   Ibid, 8-9.
37   See generally Barry (2001), 131ff.
38   Ibid, 133-4.
39   Ibid, 134. For an examination of the harmful effects of tolerating religious and cultural values on women and girls in Afghanistan, despite in principle human rights values enunciated by the Government, see, e.g., United Nations (2009). Numerous references to the 'harm' religion causes women can be found in Litcher (2009).
40   Barry (2001), 134.
41   Ibid, ch 7.
42   Waldron (1999).
43   Ibid, 312.
44   Ibid (emphasis original).

[1.41] Globalisation has reached into almost every corner of the world to the extent that indigenous people themselves resort to the language of human rights due to expanded communication and trade.[45] There is now a global inter-connectedness allowing indigenous people to exchange information and promote their interests in a global environment.[46]

[1.42] For the above reasons, it is concluded, diversity should not be protected at any price, especially when many indigenous peoples themselves may contest former customs and rituals and seek the protection of human rights.

The 'perfectionist' paradigm

[1.43] In contrast to moral relativism, perfectionism is a teleological paradigm, based on the perception that the 'good' society can be objectively determined through excellence in art, culture and science rather than through reason.[47] Because such principles are considered inherent in human nature, it is said, they can be considered to generate principles on which government is to be based. Right conduct, expressed in culture and religion, is 'out there', says perfectionism, and not founded on individual perception of what is right. 'Strict' perfectionism says that governing institutions should use the law to encourage the 'good' society through conduct that is based on its intrinsic worth, rather than on worth that is bestowed on it through individual or social acceptance. More moderate forms of perfectionism are the result of the influence of liberalism, which balances what is considered objectively right against other non-teleological principles to determine questions of what is both right and just.[48]

[1.44] Such perceptions that the source of what is right is somehow prior to human reasoning may be suitable for individual conviction, but are not the appropriate basis for government in a just society of diverse personal life stances.

The 'neutralist' paradigm

[1.45] This approach is also referred to as the 'cosmopolitan solution'.[49] Each person, through freedom of speech, association and assembly, lives according to the cultural and other mores of his or her choice in private life, but the state remains neutral in respect of belief, neither favouring nor disfavouring belief organisation or creeds. Variations on the neutralist paradigm, in their

---

45   Wilson (1997), at p.9 notes this has occurred in diverse contexts including Central America, Africa and Canada.
46   See articles in ibid, which are summarised in the 'Introduction', 18ff.
47   For discussions on perfectionism see, e.g. *TJ* 285ff; Galeotti (2006); Sher (1997); Raz (1986), (1998).
48   Freeman (2007a), 476.
49   See, e.g., Kukathas (2006), 585.

rejection of cultural relativism, are based on the premise that egalitarianism has universal validity, albeit they diverge in the rigor with which they apply their approach.[50]

[1.46] One common thread in the egalitarian/cosmopolitan paradigm as opposed to cultural relativism and perfectionism is the recognition of the need to obey the law that is developed through a sense of co-operation and equality, expanding to a form of overall consensus for governance among belief systems in liberal democracies.[51]

[1.47] However, the perception of what government neutrality means differs. Some writers see neutrality as meaning what is described as 'accommodation' of different personal worldviews by the state without imposing any particular worldview on the populace. I consider this is in fact a regime of inequality (see [13.5]). Others say it means that governments can take measures to favour different belief systems, so long as all belief systems are favoured equally, which I shall argue is impossible (see [13.25]).

[1.48] I conclude in Chapter 13 that equal belief rights for everyone require full separation of state governance from the dictates of belief. While this could be considered a variation of the neutralist position, neutralism has often come to be seen as implying some sort of consideration of individuals or groups on the basis of their belief, that is, government attempts to privilege all (or many) beliefs equally. Instead, the idea of a neutral state needs to be clearly distinguished from the ideas of 'neutralism' outlined above, by emphasising that it requires *impartiality or detachment* of the state from any considerations founded in belief, not some degree of accommodation.

[1.49] Any connection that is made between perfectionist or neutralist liberalisms tends towards acceptance of the values different beliefs, and is potentially arbitrary and discriminatory in the political recognition of these values in government. Further, in the expression of cultural and religious values, it is most likely that leaders of cultural groups become the voice of communities, and minorities within the groups are powerless – rights thus become communally dictated, rather than belonging to the individuals within them.[52]

Conclusion

[1.50] This, then, is the background to the argument I make in this book. Freedom to adopt personal convictions and to express them is inherent in the freedom and equality to which all individuals are entitled. It leads to the conclusion that belief rights, as with other human

---

50   See, e.g., Galeotti (2006), 564.
51   See, e.g., Waldron (1995), 93; Kymlicka (1995a), 210ff; Barry (2001), 132, 136, 138ff.
52   For example, belief systems are usually male-dominated, depriving women of power and voice in the determination of values and practices, affecting their identity and autonomy within the group and in relation to others: Sheen (2004), 513, 515.

rights, express a universal value that foundational to the principles of democracy. These principles transform civil liberties (freedoms and obligations applying to individuals as a feature of their citizenship of a particular nation) into human rights (freedoms and obligations applying to all individuals because of their membership of the human race).

[1.51] Models based on cultural relativism and 'perfectionist liberalism' (with their various degrees of toleration of diverse cultures) do not provide equal opportunity for all to experience belief rights. I claim that the most appropriate paradigm, in the light of the belief provisions, is the political liberalism model, along the lines of Rawls' recognition of pluralism as detailed in Chapters 3 and 4.

[1.52] Human rights provisions are in effect both moral and legal prescriptions. As a moral statement, the UDHR establishes principles for promoting the dignity and self-realisation of all individuals. As legal prescriptions, the ICCPR, *Belief Declaration* and ECHR must be considered somewhat differently, setting the parameters of acceptable behaviour required for the realisation of liberal democratic society, and establishing obligations on participant nations. Consequently, governments must consider the nature and goals of human rights, and determine the principles underlying them, including the origin and nature of civil liberties, and the relationship of human rights with democracy.

Human rights, including belief rights, should not be subject to the whims of individual state governments, like civil liberties, but apply to all individuals because of their membership of the human race. At the very least, they apply to all individuals residing in those nations that have ratified the international treaties on human rights. These treaties provide a road map of general directions to guide interpretation for effective realisation of human rights (though imprecise and open to differing interpretations, as will be argued). These directions point to personal integrity through physical security from arbitrary government interference and equality before the law, personal development through belief rights, rights to thought, inquiry, communication, expression, association and assembly, and privacy in family and lifestyle. In short, human rights should be read in light of the principles that underlie a liberal democratic society.

CHAPTER 2:
BELIEF RIGHTS

Introduction

[2.1] Despite the diversity of conceptions of what human rights involve, all members of the United Nations have pledged themselves to uphold 'human rights and fundamental freedoms for all without distinction as to race, sex, language or religion'.[1] This has become accepted 'almost universally' as imposing moral and political, if not legal, obligations on member states.[2] By joining the United Nations, over 190 nations, almost every nation in the world, have adopted the *Universal Declaration of Human Rights* ('UDHR'),[3] the foundational statement of human rights which sets out, *inter alia,* belief rights.

The belief provisions

[2.2] This Chapter considers the provisions in international treaties that set out belief rights – what are referred to as the 'belief provisions'. These are set out in Article 18 of the UDHR, henceforth referred to as 'Article 18'.

[2.3] Article 18.1 UDHR provides:

> Everyone has the right to freedom of thought, conscience and religion; this right includes freedom to change his religion or belief, and freedom, either alone or in community with others and in public or private, to manifest his religion or belief in teaching, practice, worship and observance.

[2.4] However, the exercise of human rights may be limited by the state to respect the rights and freedoms of others, for public order and general welfare to be found in a democratic society. Article 29 UDHR says:

> In the exercise of his rights and freedoms, everyone shall be subject only to such limitations as are determined by law solely for the purpose of securing due recognition and respect for the rights and freedoms of others and of meeting the just requirements of morality, public order and the general welfare in a democratic society.

---

1   United Nations Charter (1945).

2   Tahzib (1996), 68.

3   Article 3 of the UDHR says that 'Everyone is entitlted to all the rights and freedoms set forth …without distinction of any kind, such as race, colour, sex, language, religion, political or other opinion, national or social origin, property, birth or other status.' Notably, there were no votes against the UDHR among member states at the time, Saudi Arabia, South Africa and six Eastern European states abstaining. All Muslim states present except Saudi Arabia voted for the UDHR: ibid, 76-7.

Binding nations further: the ICCPR and ECHR

[2.5] One hundred and seventy-five nations are also party to the *International Covenant on Civil and Political Rights* ('ICCPR'), the international human rights treaty that sets out specific measures by which states undertake to ensure civil and political rights established by the UDHR (see Table 2). Article 18 as it appears in the ICCPR is repeated almost word-for-word in Article 9 of the *European Convention for the Protection of Human Rights and Fundamental Freedoms* ('ECHR'), which applies to member States of the European Union.

[2.6] Those who signed the ICCPR ('states parties') include members of the Organisation of the Islamic Conference ('OIC'), an organisation to promote Islamic solidarity among member states. The UDHR and European Convention provide specifically for the right to change one's 'religion or belief'. In the UN, the Islamic nations successfully pressed for this provision to be omitted in the ICCPR and *Belief Declaration*, to accord with their religious prohibition of apostasy.

[2.7] Article 18.3 ICCPR also specifically limits the right to manifest religion or belief through laws that are necessary to protect public safety, order, health or morals, or the fundamental rights of others.

[2.8] Freedom to practise one's belief is thus not boundless, but is constrained by the need to observe essential public interests, and foster reciprocity towards others to ensure they enjoy similarly equal freedom. This, I argue, is consistent with the principles of political liberalism based on democracy.

Belief rights as part of the overall aim of Human Rights

[2.9] Natan Lerner says of the UDHR that

> [T]he critical role of the Universal Declaration in the development of the legal and political philosophy of the second part of the twentieth century is beyond controversy. It is the most important single legal document of our time, and most of its contents constitute present customary international law.[4]

[2.10] The conception of human rights as a coherent interrelationship of principles demands that their goals are reasonably specifically identified. It is proposed that the principles can be classified as follows:[5]

---

4   Lerner (1996), 88.
5   This is based on James Nickel's 'basic liberties': Nickel (2005), 943.

- *personal integrity and dignity* (e.g. belief rights, freedom from arbitrary deprivation of life or liberty, freedom from slavery, torture or inhuman or degrading treatment or punishment, and the right to a fair trial and rule of law);

- *personal development* (e.g. belief rights, freedom of thought and inquiry; communication and expression; association and peaceful assembly);

- *privacy and autonomy in personal life* (e.g. belief rights, freedom from arbitrary interference in private and family life, home and correspondence; marriage, sexuality and reproduction). This principle can be expanded to include freedom to follow an ethic, life-stance, lifestyle or traditional way of living; [6]

- *non-discrimination* on the basis of such characteristics as race, sex, ethnicity, and belief, in the application of these principles.

[2.11] Seen in this way, and taking 'belief' to include all kinds of personal convictions, belief rights can be interpreted in broad, rather than black and white, absolutist manner. This reasoning points to the conclusion that we should interpret human rights, including belief rights, in a way that gives effect to the principles on which they are founded.

Other international declarations on belief rights

[2.12] There is no shortage of human rights declarations in one form or another throughout the world. Numerous human rights treaties, Declarations, Charters and Agreements – both 'universal' and regional – proclaim the right to freedom to have and manifest 'religion or belief', and/or prohibit discrimination on the ground of 'religion or belief'.[7] Most are based on, and worded similarly to, Article 18 UDHR.

The UN International Covenant on Civil and Political Rights (ICCPR)

[2.13] The ICCPR is an international agreement on the implementation of the civil and political rights (as opposed to the economic and social rights) contained in the UDHR. It sets out the belief rights in similar terms to the UDHR.

---

6   Ibid. As mentioned above, the terms 'rights' and 'freedoms ' are used in the international instruments to cover both absolute and potentially limited freedoms. This has contributed to various perceptions of these terms. The freedom to hold personal convictions and the freedom to express them have often both been held to involve absolute rights. Consequently, claims are made, and consequent provision afforded, for preferential treatment of personal convictions, most particularly those considered religious convictions.

7   E.g., see Lindholm et al (2004), Appendix A 873; Fox (2008).

[2.14] As with the UDHR, the right to manifest belief in the ICCPR is not absolute. Unlike the UDHR, however, the ICCPR has a specific limitation clause prescribing the grounds on which the state may curtail the exercise of belief, which implies specific emphasis on them. The nominated grounds for limiting manifestation of belief are exclusive. Article 18.3 ICCPR states:

> Freedom to manifest one's religion or beliefs may be subject only to such limitations as are prescribed by law and are necessary to protect public safety, order, health, or morals or the fundamental rights and freedoms of others.

[2.15] Many attempts were made to institute a stand-alone Convention on elimination of intolerance based on religion or belief, to implement more specifically principles of belief rights and hold states party to account. However, due to the diversity of views of delegates, these came to a standstill in 1967, and no significant progress has since been made.[8] The closest the United Nations has come to agreement on elaboration of the 'right to freedom of religion or belief' is the *Belief Declaration,* which is not binding on signatories.

[2.16] For this reason, the belief provisions, as in all human rights treaties, cannot be properly understood without placing them in their political context. Member states of the UN who were party to formulating the various international instruments sought to accommodate the interests of their many diverse constitutional regimes. The pressing of divergent interests posed a fundamental obstacle to what I argue is a proper recognition of belief rights, and ended the stage of 'standard setting' in favour of compromise.

[2.17] The significance of this critical fact is evident throughout the implementation of belief rights by the UN and European Union bodies as discussed in later Chapters. The drafters the *Belief Declaration* turned their attention to measures for promoting belief rights rather than standard-setting.[9]

[2.18] Several other international instruments have included provisions to ensure belief rights for such groups as children,[10] migrant workers and their families[11] and ethnic, religious or linguistic minorities,[12] but these provisions are similar in form to the Articles described above.

---

8   Malcolm Evans (2000), 36.
9   See, e.g., van Boven (2004), 173, 174.
10   *Convention on the Rights of the Child,* (1990).
11   *International Convention on the Protection of the Rights of All Migrant Workers and their Families* (2003).
12   *Declaration on the Rights of Persons Belonging to National or Ethnic, Religious and Linguistic Minorities,* (1993).

The United Nations Human Rights Council

[2.19] Formerly the United Nations Commission on Human Rights (until 2006), the Human Rights Council is an inter-governmental body within the UN consisting of 47 members, elected by the UN General Assembly, representative of the different regions of the world. It is responsible for promoting human rights throughout the world, deals with all aspects of human rights, and considers issues relating to the general implementation of human rights. It can also consider complaints of 'reliably attested violations of all human rights and all fundamental freedoms occurring in any part of the World and under any circumstance'.[13] The strongest action it can take against violators, however, is to 'recommend to the Office of the High Commissioner for Human Rights to provide technical cooperation, capacity-building assistance or advisory services to the State concerned'.[14] The Council sends resolutions to the General Assembly for its acceptance and endorsement.

[2.20] In its overview of the status of human rights in member states, the UN Human Rights Council appoints special *rapporteurs* to examine specific human rights issues in member states and receives submissions by non-government organisations. Malcolm Evans argues that the Reports of the Special Rapporteur on Freedom of Belief are of limited guidance in determining the extent of freedom to manifest belief. This is because there is a tendency to 'relate to the ability of believers to enjoy the practice of their religion in a fairly narrow sense', as well as the need to direct resources to 'more pressing, and basic, needs'.[15] There is a

> reluctance to move beyond the forms of manifestation either set out in, or directly flowing from, the [Belief] Declaration and address wider and more controversial questions concerning the ability of believers to act in accordance with the dictates of their religious beliefs.[16]

[2.21] However, he states that what Reports there are 'provide a depressing catalogue of the infinite variants surrounding the restriction of even the most basic form of manifestation [of belief]'.[17]

The Limited Recognition of Human Rights Treaties

[2.22] As will be seen in the following Chapters, the human rights treaties have a limited effect. Despite the overwhelming subscription by nations to the UDHR, and the ICCPR, one factor

---

13   Human Rights Council Resolution 5/1: *Institution building* (18 June 2007).
14   Ibid.
15   Malcolm Evans (1997), 253-4.
16   Ibid, 254; See, e.g., the UN Special Rapporteur's report of 1988, E/CN.4/1987/35, ¶63. Evans discusses the role and work of the Special Rapporteur on the Right to Freedom of Religion and Belief at ibid, 245ff.
17   Ibid, 254.

that has encouraged nations to defy these treaties is UN forbearance in relation to recalcitrant nations, no doubt adopted with the intention of winning them over, but with little effect, as religious hostility and intolerance is increasing globally, not decreasing.[18]

Alternative human rights Declaration

[2.23] Notwithstanding the purported universal agreement on the UDHR, some nations have rejected adopting belief rights outright. For example, the majority of the constitutions of the Middle East and North Africa promise religious freedom but state that this freedom is subordinate to Islam, local customs, public order or some similar qualification, which effectively allows significant restrictions on religious freedom.[19] The Organisation of the Islamic Conference (56 member states) in 1996 adopted an alternative version of human rights, while most remain nominally States Parties to the ICCPR.[20] Under its *Cairo Declaration of Human Rights in Islam* ('Cairo Declaration'), all human rights are to be subject to 'Islamic Shari'ah', thus establishing state-enforced religious practice.

[2.24] The Cairo Declaration, which its proponents maintain is complementary to the UDHR, proclaims that all rights are derived from God. The preamble states that

> no one as a matter of principle has the right to suspend [the nominated rights] in whole or in part or violate or ignore them in as much as they are binding divine commandments, which are contained in the Revealed Books of God....making their observance an act of worship and their neglect or violation an abominable sin....

[2.25] The Declaration is inconsistent with the ICCPR in that all rights and freedom it stipulates are 'subject to the Islamic Shari'ah', which is to be the 'only source of reference for the explanation or clarifications of any of the articles' (Articles 24 and 25). Shari'ah is based on the holy books of the Islamic religion, as well as interpretation of these by imams, or ministers of religion. This makes the Cairo Declaration a religious document, despite some liberal language.[21] It is based on inequality between men and women (Article 6), denies belief rights (Article 22) and limits free speech (Article 22).

---

18   Pew Research Center (2014).
19   Fox (2008), 248.
20   E.g, Afghanistan, Bahrain, Bangladesh, Cameroon, Chad, Djibouti, Egypt, India, Indonesia, Iran, Iraq, Jordan, Kuwait, Lebanon, Libya, Mali, Morocco, Somalia, Sudan, Syria, Thailand and Algeria, Tunisia, Turkey, Yemen. Egypt declared accession to the ICCPR only to the extent that its provisions do not conflict with Islamic Shari'ah, while Saudi Arabia, Pakistan and UAE are not parties: Clarke (2007), 94.
21   A detailed consideration of the provisions of the Cairo Declaration can be found in Guichon (2007), 185ff. and Artz (1990). For critical comment by the Civil Liberties Alliance see <http://www.libertiesalliance.org/education/cairo-declaration/>.

[2.26] Strangely, the Cairo Declaration was included in an official volume of human rights documents by the Office of the High Commissioner for Human Rights, providing quasi-official recognition by the UN.[22] By recognising the Cairo Declaration, the UN appeared to give credence to contradictory statements of rights, thus undermining the integrity of the UDHR. The Cairo Declaration is considered to be a valid statement of human rights by its signatories, presumably supplanting contrary principles of the UDHR and ICCPR.

[2.27] Membership of countries on the United Nations Human Rights Council that do not accept the provisions of the UDHR in their lawmaking is also a hurdle to the advancement of belief rights. In December 2013 the International Humanist and Ethical Union released a report that assesses every country in the world for observance of belief rights, taking into particular consideration the legal treatment of the non-religious (although the religious are also affected). Bob Churchill considered the membership of the United Nations Human Rights Council.[23] He found that of the 47 members of the Council,

- nine states "severely discriminate" directly against belief. Examples include states that have laws restricting inter-religious marriages, laws which prohibit "blasphemy" or "insult to religion" (punishable by prison) and laws taking children away from fathers who are 'apostates';[24] and

- eight states that commit "grave violations" directly against belief.[25] Examples include states that punish apostasy or blasphemy with death; states restricting government office to members of one religion; and state complicity in violence against atheists.

[2.28] Four of those states punish leaving (the Muslim) religion with death (Maldives, Morocco, Saudi Arabia and UAE). This is not to mention member states that tolerate human rights violations against women and children through practices based on belief.[26]

[2.29] One can wonder at the acceptance of these countries as members, given the Council decree that 'members elected to the Council shall uphold the highest standards in the promotion and protection of human rights'.

[2.30] One can also wonder at the result of pressure by OIC resulting in the adoption of a series of resolutions on 'combating defamation of religion' by the UN Human Rights Coun-

---

22   Human Rights: *A Compilation of International Instruments: Volume II: Regional Instruments* (1997), 477.

23   Bob Churchill (2013). For an updated version see International Humanist and Ethical Union (2013).

24   Nations named as criminalising blasphemy or insultng religion are Algeria, Austria, Brazil, Chile, Germany, India, Ireland, New Zealand, Russia and the UK: International Humanist and Ethical Union (2013).

25   Indonesia, Morocco, the Maldives; United Arab Emirates, Pakistan, Kuwait, Saudi Arabia, and China.

26   See, e.g., Ida Lichter (2014); Tom Gross (2013).

cil since 1999.[27] Laws prohibiting 'defamation of religion' have been used as a way by religious organisations to silence the expression of adverse opinion, and can lead to forced conversion or oppression of minority religions and beliefs.

[2.31] Australia, along with approximately one third of the UNHRC, refused to support the adoption of the resolution, *Combating Defamation of Religions* in 2010.[28] The resolution was passed with a narrow majority.

[2.32] The General Assembly has passed a similar version of the Resolutions each year from 2005.[29] Ironically, these resolutions are comprehensive in their language regarding belief rights, which are at odds with many government policies and legislation. A long history of contention has led to the OIC recently recasting its approach, expressing opposition to religious incitement to hostility or violence against believers in general, rather than 'combating defamation of religion'.

[2.33] By its recognition of nations that so blatantly reject belief rights, the UN seems to have left the door to theocracy ajar, muddying the waters in respect of the relationship between state and belief, and the meaning of belief rights itself.

The European Convention on Human Rights and Freedoms (ECHR)

[2.34] Article 18 was the model used to create similar freedoms in the ECHR adopted by the Council of Europe in Article 9 of the ECHR.

[2.35] Article 9 retains the freedom to change one's religion or belief, whereas Article 18 ICCPR dropped any mention of that right at the request of the Islamic member states that disapprove of conversion from Islam to another religion, apostasy, or proselytism by those of another religion. However, it has been argued that non-specification of the right to change one's belief does not eliminate that right anyway, as it is inherent in the right to have a belief (see [7.25]).

---

27   Wikipedia offers a hisory of resolutions regarding 'defamation of religion' at <http://en.wikipedia.org/wiki/Defamation_of_religion_and_the_United_Nations>.

28   '[T]he reasons given for this refusal to support the resolution was that it over-referenced Islam and did not adequately address all religions. Further, it confuses issues around defamation and human rights – humans, not religions, have human rights' and also 'the terms 'combating' and 'defamation' lack clarity and the way they are used in the resolution are confusing': Australian Human Rights and Equal Opportunity Commission (2008), 55. Recently (in 2010), the Gay and Lesbian Human Rights Commission was refused "consultative status" at the UN Economic and Social Council (ECOSOC), by the Committee on Non-Governmental Organizations although it fulfilled all the requirements for recognition. The refusal was pursuant to a majority vote by such countries as Egypt, Sudan, Qatar, Pakistan and China: Charbonneau, (2010).

29   **UN General; Assembly resolutions condemning Defamation of Religion:** (2006), A/RES/60/150; (2007) A/RES/61/164; (2008), A/RES/62/154; (2009) A/RES/63/171(2010) A/RES/64/156 (2011) A/RES/65/224. **Resolutions condemning all forms of incitement to discrimination, hostility or violence:** (2012) A/RES/67179; (2013).A/RES/69/170.

[2.36] The limitation provision in Article 9 ECHR is slightly different to the ICCPR by specifically tying governments to democratic principles in relation to belief rights (whereas the UDHR ties them to democracy indirectly). Article 9.2 states that

> Freedom to manifest one's religion or beliefs shall be subject only to such limitations as are prescribed by law and are necessary in a democratic society in the interests of public safety, for the protection of public order, health or morals, or for the protection of the rights and freedoms of others.

The human rights monitoring bodies and their role

[2.37] In discussing the implementation of human rights, this book will focus on what are called the 'human rights tribunals'. These are the bodies within the UN and the EU that deal specifically with complaints about breaches of human rights. They are

- the Human Rights Council and Human Rights Committee of the UN, and

- the European Council, European Human Rights Commission and European Court of Human Rights.

The UN Human Rights Council ('HR Council')

[2.38] The Human Rights Council is a Charter-based body: that is, it is established under the UDHR. It reports to the Economic and Social Council (ECOSOC), which in turn reports to the UN General Assembly. The Human Rights Council examines complaints pertaining to 'situations which appear to reveal a consistent pattern of gross and reliably attested violations of human rights and all fundamental procedures occurring in any part of the world and under any circumstances'.[30] Such violations include torture, genocide, apartheid, racial or ethnic discrimination, forced mass migrations and mass imprisonment without trial. Investigations do not require the consent of the country involved. ECOSOC incorporates the information it receives in its recommendations to the General Assembly.

[2.39] The HR Council can also carry out fact-finding missions (with a country's consent), pass resolutions condemning human rights violations, appoint Special Rapporteurs[31] and provide educational and informational assistance to states.

---

30   Human Rights Council, Resolution 5/1: *Institution Building* (18 June 2007).
31   Complaints of breaches of human rights of general effect can be made to the Special Rapporteur.

[2.40] Decisions and recommendations of the HR Council are not legally enforceable. However, they may have effect through pressure on the offending nation by the imposition by member states of economic or diplomatic sanctions.

The United Nations Human Rights Committee ('UNHRC')

[2.41] The Human Rights Committee ('UNHRC') is a treaty-based body established under the ICCPR Part IV. It has 18 members who are experts in their fields, acting independently of their states, assisting the United Nations Centre for Human Rights and reporting to ECOSOC.[32] The Committee is one of nine human rights treaty bodies set up to monitor compliance of Member States with the various United Nations human rights treaties.[33] The Committees receive State Party reports on measures they have taken in compliance with the relevant Covenant, which are to be submitted every five years. It then conducts an examination of each state's report in public meetings with representatives of that state. Representatives from non-government organisations can also make submissions. The Committee then issues 'Concluding Observations' on its inquiry, expressing views and making recommendations to the State Party concerned. From the questions it asks of the state whose report is being examined, and its concluding observations, one can glean indirectly the views of the UNHRC on the meaning of the belief provisions.[34]

[2.42] Under the first ICCPR *Optional Protocol* (1976), the UNHRC 'receives and considers Communications from individuals subject to its jurisdiction who claim to be victims of a violation by that State Party of any of the rights set forth in the Covenant' (Article 1). There are 115 States that have ratified or acceded to the Optional Protocol and 35 signatories.[35] *Communications* are complaints to the UNHRC by individuals who allege they are the victims of human rights violations by their state government, and who have exhausted all available domestic avenues of appeal. The UNHRC releases its *Views* after consideration of the matter.[36] As there is no court for considering breaches of human rights attached to the UN, this is a way of seeking a remedy for individual victims of human rights abuses. The first *Optional Protocol* entered into force on 23 March 1976.

---

32   Tahzib (1996) 250; Steiner and Alston (2000), 707ff. (the authors give a detailed examination of the work of the UNHRC in chapters 8 and 9).

33   The other five Committees are the Committee Against Torture, Committee on Economic, Social and Cultural Rights, Committee on Elimination of Discrimination Against Women, Committee on the Elimination of Racial Discrimination and Committee and the Committee on the Rights of the Child.

34   For a discussion of the reasons that the UNHRC cannot effectively perform similarly to adjudication by a court, see Steiner (2000b), 15.

35   Details can be found at <https://treaties.un.org/Pages/ViewDetails.aspx?src=TREATY&mtdsg_no=IV-5&chapter=4&lang=en>.

36   These are updated and available at < http://www1.umn.edu/humanrts/undocs/undocs.htmwebsite>.

[2.43] The UNHRC also considers reports written by Non-Government Organisations and issues *General Comments* on their respective treaties for adoption by the General Assembly. *ICCPR General Comment 22* sets out the official UN interpretation of the ICCPR.[37]

[2.44] Treaties are backed by the norms regulating international law. They are thus formally legally binding, as International law takes precedence over the domestic law of a state. When a nation signs a treaty it undertakes to adopt the provisions set forth within the treaty into the domestic law of a state.[38] This differentiates treaty-based mechanisms from Charter-based ones, which are unenforceable. It is relevant to any consideration of the Committee's views that enforceability by armed intervention or diplomatic action is subject to political pressures within the UN General Assembly and Security Council. A current example is the blocking by Russia and China of any resolution by the Security Council for UN intervention in the current Syrian civil war.

[2.45] The State Party subject to a ruling by the UNHRC must recognise its competence to determine whether there has been a violation of the ICCPR, and undertake to ensure its citizens are all subject to its jurisdiction. States sometimes deny the legitimacy of proceedings, or register reservations to particular provisions, and so hold themselves exempt from compliance with views and opinions of UN bodies. The procedure the Committee undertakes is simple and involves only consideration of paperwork in a closed meeting, without the appearance of the parties concerned. There is no prescribed procedure for ensuring compliance.[39] There may be economic or political sanctions imposed on a non-compliant state by the General Assembly (e.g. current economic sanctions against Myanmar or North Korea in relation to human rights breaches), or even more direct intervention in the state by a resolution of the Security Council. In extreme cases, the Security Council may approve military action. These actions are all subject to a vote by members of the UN, and so are influenced by political and diplomatic considerations.[40]

[2.46] A simple outline of the functions of the UNHR Council and the UNHRC is as follows:

---

37   See for text, < http://www1.umn.edu/humanrts/gencomm/hrcom22.htm>; for information on procedure, etc., <http://co-guide.org/interpretation/general-comment-22-article-18-iccpr>.

38   See, e.g. <http://www.hrea.org/index.php?base_id=163>.

39   See, e.g., Steiner and Alston (2000), 738 ff.

40   The lack of enforcement powers is considered in some detail in ibid, 740ff.

Table 3: The UN Human Right Council and the UN Human Rights Committee

UN Human Rights Council (Established by UN Charter)	UN Human Rights Committee (Established by ICCPR)
• Oversees all nations; • Carries out fact-finding missions; • Receives complaints of state violations of human rights; • Issues decisions and recommendations; • Reports to ECOSOC; • May result in sanctions, diplomatic action or other action by resolution of General Assembly.	*Under ICCPR generally:* • Receives reports from member states on human rights; • Issues 'Concluding Observations' with recommendations; *Under Optional Protocol* • Receives complaints from individual citizens of signatory states ('Informations'); • Issues decisions, which may be repudiated by the respondent state.

[2.47] Additionally, the UN develops programs for the promotion of human rights at both the institutional and civil society levels. It works globally towards bridging the gap between Western and other societies by seeking to overcome prejudices, misconceptions and polarisations that potentially threaten world peace.

[2.48] Because the UN is a universal body, with widely diverse societies represented by the member states, embracing many different kinds of regimes and beliefs, a more binding, judicially oriented approach to human rights would be difficult, if not impossible, to achieve, this being more appropriately undertaken by regional complaints systems such as the European, African and American regional human rights systems, which 'offer several advantages in the areas of logistics, local trust, and homogeneity'.[41]

The European Human Rights tribunals

[2.49] The Council of Europe is the main European human rights organisation open to states claiming a commitment to European integration, democracy and fundamental human rights and freedoms. There are 47 member states, 28 of which are members of the European Union (a separate body). The Commissioner for Human Rights is an independent institution within the Council of Europe, charged with promoting awareness of, and respect for, human rights in the member states.

[2.50] Unlike the European Union, the Council of Europe cannot make binding laws. Its work includes developing legal standards in the areas of human rights, democratic development, the

---

41   Opsahl (1992), 421, 421. See also Merrills (1988), in relation to other nations.

rule of law and cultural co-operation. It has produced standards, charters and conventions to facilitate cooperation between European countries.[42]

[2.51] The Council of Europe is also the administrating body of the ECHR. All member states of the Council have signed up to the ECHR, which establishes the European Court of Human Rights ('ECtHR'), the judgments of which *are* binding on states parties and supervised by a Committee of Ministers (Article 46). The sheer number of cases as well as complexities and difficulties in executing judgements, is a matter of ongoing consideration by the Council.[43]

[2.52] Until 31 October 1998 there were two tribunals established by the ECHR. These were the European Court of Human Rights (a part-time court), and the European Commission of Human Rights. These had jurisdiction to hear complaints between states, and between individuals and a concurring State.

[2.53] Due to the growth in matters brought under the Convention, Protocol 11 was brought into effect on 1 November 1998, fusing the Commission and the Court into a full-time and enlarged European Court of Human Rights. The Court assumed the Commission's task of determining matters of admissibility and merit. The new Court has three tiers:

- Committees, each consisting of three judges;

- Chambers, each consisting of seven judges; and

- a Grand Chamber of seventeen judges, including the President, Vice-President and Presidents of the Chambers.[44]

[2.54] The restructured Court has jurisdiction to hear complaints between States as well as complaints brought by individuals against a State. If a Committee accepts a matter as admissible, a Chamber of the Court will then decide the case.

[2.55] Before rendering judgment, the Chamber may relinquish jurisdiction in favour of the Grand Chamber if the matter raises a serious question about the interpretation of the Convention, or if the case involves departing from principles previously expressed by the Court. In addition, any party to the case may, for the same reason, request that the case be referred to the Grand Chamber, which will hear the case. In addition, a decision of the Chamber may be taken

---

42   Its latest guidelines on human rights is *EU Guidelines on the Promotion and Protection of Freedom of Religion or Belief* <https://www.consilium.europa.eu/uedocs/cms_data/docs/pressdata/EN/foraff/137585.pdf>.
43   De Schutter (2010), 903ff.
44   ECHR Art. 27.

on appeal to the Grand Chamber. As a result, each case is heard by at least one convocation of the court.

[2.56] The ECHR Article 46 provides that:

1) The High Contracting Parties undertake to abide by the final judgment of the Court in any case to which they are parties.

2) The final judgment of the Court shall be transmitted to the Committee of Ministers, which shall supervise its execution.

[2.57] In comparison with the UNHRC, it has been said:

What makes the Strasbourg [ECHR] legal system a more thorough-going international legal system than say, United Nations human rights law, is that Strasbourg displays a much more settled and accepted system of secondary rules and institutions. Moreover, the actors within the system, both governments and individual litigants, as well as their lawyers, recognize the Strasbourg rules and the Strasbourg institutions as legitimate.[45]

[2.58] The deliberations of these monitoring bodies are useful as they implement human rights treaties with similar wording. Between them, they have developed a body of case law and commentary aimed at establishing the metes and bounds of belief rights.

[2.59] In addition, case law and commentary from other jurisdictions recognising the human rights principles, mainly the UK, can fill gaps where this case law is wanting, and provide some useful examples for comparison.

Non-Discrimination principle

[2.60] Both the ICCPR and ECHR provide that all rights, including belief rights, apply without:

- 'distinction of any kind, such as race, colour, sex, language, religion, political or other opinion, national or social origin, property, birth or other status' (Article 26 ICCPR); or

- 'discrimination on any ground such as sex, race, colour, language, religion, political or other opinion, national or social origin, association with a national minority, property, birth or other status' (Article 14 ECHR).

---

45   Janis, et al (2000), 87.

Belief rights require democracy

[2.61] A society that best gives effect to human rights principles is one that accepts democratic standards of liberty and equality applying to all individuals.[46] While the UDHR appears to espouse a 'democratic society' by implication from its terms, this has not been defined as such by the UNHRC.[47] The 'notion of a democratic society is firmly embedded in the Statute of the Council for Europe'.[48] Jonathon Fox has concluded, from an intensive study of religion throughout the world, that there is a 'clear correlation between democracy and [separation of religion and the state],'[49] while, conversely, there has been an overall global increase in government involvement in religion by means of regulation over recent years.[50] In relation to belief rights, the European Court has stated:

> As enshrined in Article 9 [ECHR] (art. 9), freedom of thought, conscience and religion is one of the foundations of a "democratic society" within the meaning of the Convention. It is, in its religious dimension, one of the most vital elements that go to make up the identity of believers and their conception of life, but it is also a precious asset for atheists, agnostics, sceptics and the unconcerned. The pluralism indissociable from a democratic society, which has been dearly won over the centuries, depends on it.[51]

[2.62] These principles express the lofty but elusive ideal of freedom for individuals to investigate and develop a frame of reference for establishing identity and relationship to the world around them. While some may argue this ideal is unattainable, the principle at least provides a 'roadmap' for maximum realisation of personal fulfilment through belief rights.

[2.63] Based on human autonomy, dignity and equality, the freedom to hold and manifest worldviews is entrenched in such fundamental rights as liberty of the person, freedom of speech, assembly and association, as well as the right to family privacy. If this is so, then it follows that

---

46   Article 29(2), UDHR, on which the ICCPR and the *Belief Declaration* are based, provides that

   In the exercise of his rights and freedoms, everyone shall be subject only to such limitations as are determined by law solely for the purpose of securing due recognition and respect for the rights and freedoms of others and of meeting the just requirements of morality, public order and the general welfare in a democratic society.

   Article 25 ICCPR provides for equal participation of all in public affairs and universal suffrage, Article 26 provides for equality before the law for all. The preamble of the ECHR that human rights are 'best maintained...by an effective political democracy', and notes specifically that the rights to a fair trial, (Art. 6); privacy (Art. 8), manifestation of belief (Art. 9), expression (Art. 10); and assembly and association (Art. 11), are dependent on what is necessary for a democratic society. See McCarthy (1998), ch 3.

47   McCarthy (1998), 109; Steiner (2000a).
48   McCarthy, ibid, 120.
49   Fox (2008), 345ff.
50   Ibid, 100. For a more recent survey of global government regulation of religion see Pew Research Center (2014).
51   *Kokkinakis v. Greece*, (1993), §31.

freedom to deliberate and debate, to adopt opinions and personal convictions and express them (whether by word or action) or even to criticise them, are all equally deserving of protection by the law. On this reasoning, the extent of protection of manifestation of beliefs, is dependent, not on whether the belief in question is religious or not, but the effect of its manifestation on other individuals or society in general.

Are the international human rights treaties moral or legal pronouncements?

[2.64] The human rights treaties are at least statements of political principles. Some commentators argue that they are moral rather than legal edicts, having persuasive rather than coercive power. Others maintain that case law indicates that the ICCPR and ECHR *are* intended to create obligations on states subscribing to them. As noted, states parties to the ICCPR agree to UN scrutiny and accountability. As early as 1975 John Humphrey argued that the UDHR had been invoked so many times both in and outside the UN that it has become part of international customary law and thus binding on all nations.[52] States party to the ECHR are subject to judicial review by the European Court of Human Rights. Both treaties thus expose States party to them to recognised legal processes and sanction by those bodies, indicating that both the ICCPR and ECHR are statements of some form of legal obligation.

[2.65] Further, the ICCPR and the ECHR require the signatories to implement human rights through domestic policies and legislation. This is intended to institute a legal framework offering a degree of certainty, clarity and predictability with the parameters of dignity and autonomy established by acknowledged human rights. It is of note that Australia does not have a Bill of Rights, and there is pressure within the UK government to rescind theirs.

[2.66] Some commentators argue that to translate human rights statements into a language that will create precisely detailed entitlements and duties for nominated individuals could undermine the pluralism essential to universality that is said to be the essence of human rights. Nevertheless, the purpose of human rights treaties is to be more than just a pious wish-list. Those entitled to a nominated right and the objectives of that right must be clearly identified, and what is allowed or prohibited, together with methods of accountabity, and any sanction involved, clearly defined. They must be set out with

---

52   Humphrey (1975), 207.

enough precision to provide a meaningful balance between freedom and equality within the parameters of human rights and democracy.[53]

Human rights at the state level

[2.67] While human rights apply at all times, some are absolute (such as freedom from arbitrary execution and freedom from torture) regardless of public emergency. Others can be legitimately restricted.[54] As will be discussed more fully in later Chapters, although the UNHRC case law is somewhat more indefinite in its language than that of the European Commission and Court, both jurisdictions invoke the principle of legality regarding states imposing limits on the exercise of human rights. This means that any restrictions on manifestation of belief by government or courts must:

- be subject to established law of general application (apply to everyone equally);

- be expressly neutral in respect of belief (no special provision for personal worldviews);

- be adequately accessible to, and understandable by, the public; and

- provide adequate protection against arbitrary use of discretion. [55]

[2.68] 'Established law' includes regulatory measures taken by regulatory bodies as part of their rule-making powers delegated to them by Parliament, as well as judge-made law.[56]

[2.69] The United Nations Human Rights Commission (UNHRC) and Special Rapporteurs, as well as the Council of Europe, have provided interpretations of the various human rights documents. These set out the scope of specific rights, when they should apply and when limitation of those rights is appropriate. Whilst these measures are intended to ensure that human rights are not applied in an arbitrary or unqualified

---

53   As argued above, democracy is the fundamental principle on which human rights are built, thus informing the belief provisions (see e.g. Gearty (2004), Ch 4, esp. 68). Human rights give expression to principles of legality: Gearty, ibid, 60; Anna-Lena McCarthy (1998), 54 ff. This is reflected in the fact, for example, that any limitation or interference with a right must have basis in domestic law (see below, Ch 10).

54   See e.g., Anna-Lena McCarthy (1998), 54 ff., 93.

55   UN (1984); *Sunday Times v UK* (1979), ¶39; *Pinkey v Canada,* (1978); C. Evans (2001), 136; M. Evans (1997), 319; Plowden and Kerrigan (2002), 34ff. esp 36; De Schutter (2010), 294

56   *Leyla Şahin v Turkey* (2005), ¶88. See, for discussion on legality, De Schutter (2010), 288ff.

manner, the dangers of political influence from member nations affecting their application have been noted.[57]

[2.70] In the application of human rights at the state level, the intention of the human rights treaties is that they are to be implemented, preferably with constitutional status, taking precedence over non-constitutional legislation. Objections that the human rights treaties are too general have at times been met by governments and courts adopting a narrower (or, at times, broader) meaning to general expressions of rights in their Constitution or rights legislation. An example of a narrow approach can be seen in the US Government's implementation of the provision that 'Congress shall make no law…abridging the freedom of speech'. Congress has excluded, *inter alia,*incitement to violence and defamation. An example of courts adopting a broader meaning to constitutional provisions than was arguably originally intended is *Roe v Wade* (1973) and *Griswold v Connecticut* (1965) where the US Supreme Court held that prohibition of first and second trimester abortion and contraception breaches the Constitutional right to privacy.

[2.71] Opinions differ on the question of which body, the legislature or the judiciary, is most appropriate for determining whether a particular law or policy is consistent with the rights accepted within a jurisdiction.

[2.72] One view favours the legislature as a representative body (or at least argues that judges are no better at moral decisions than are legislators). This approach points to the legislature potentially addressing the views of all citizens. It is based on the argument that the legislature allows consideration of a broader range of issues than those permitted a court in a specific matter. Proponents prefer what they see as Parliament's ability to deliberate and act according to the democratic process of debate, and to determine appropriate rights for the society in question.[58]

[2.73] The other view holds that whereas the legislative process can be captured by vested interests and political expediency, it is not a pure process of democracy. Rather, this view holds, it is the judiciary who can best do so in a specialist, nominally impartial environment of reflective deliberation. The judiciary, in this view, is free from the pressure of vested interests experienced by politicians and can deliver an authoritative ruling

---

57   See, e.g. Gearty (2006), ch 3.
58   See, for a discussion of the arguments regarding preference for legislative or judicial determination of rights, Jeremy Waldron (2009); Wojciech Sadurski, (2009), 24.

on the meaning of the rights in question.[59] Both views present the best examples of their favoured body's working, and the worst of their opponent's.

[2.74] Recognising the generality of human rights language, English-speaking jurisdictions among others seek to mitigate the disadvantages of both the above approaches (e.g. the UK[60], the Australian Capital Territory (ACT)[61] and Victoria, Australia[62]). They have passed what amount to bills of rights as ordinary legislation, which can be amended or repealed by Parliament, as opposed to consitutional provisions which require a referendum for creation, change or repeal. The government is required to act according to the human rights principles set out in the legislation, so that all other legislation and government policy must be compatible with those principles. Government legislation and policy is subjected to review by an independent body before implementation (or on review where already implmented) and alleged incompatibility is subject to judicial review. The court may issue a Declaration of Incompatibility where incompatibility is found to be the case. [63] The court does not strike down the legislation, as happens with Constitutional rights provisions, but the matter returns to Parliament, which then must determine whether to amend the legisaltion, or justify retaining it notwithstanding the finding of incompatibility.

[2.75] In the U.K., once the court has issued a declaration of incompatibility and an appropriate Minister of the Crown considers that there are compelling reasons for action, he or she may, by a 'remedial order', make such amendments to the legislation considered necessary to remove the incompatibility. Remedial orders are at the government's discretion, and a failure to act on a declaration of incompatibility cannot itself be challenged under the *Human Rights Act*.[64]

[2.76] In the ACT and Victoria, a declaration of incompatibility must be tabled in the legislature, requiring a response from it within a set period. The matter then becomes a political issue. The legislature may decide to amend the legislation or defend its retention in terms of the grounds for limiting the rights set out in the Act.

---

59   Sager (2002), 11.
60   *Human Rights Act 1998* (U.K.), – ('HRA').
61   Human Rights Act 1994 (ACT).
62   Victorian Charter of Human Rights and Responsibilities.
63   This generally only applies to 'primary legislation'. While the various Acts are silent on delegated legislation, a declaration that subordinate legislation is incompatible with the U.K. *Human Rights Act* would impliedly be invalid to the extent the primary and secondary legislation is incompatible, the secondary legislation being ultra vires the parent Act: see Plowden and Kerrigan (2002), 198 ff. Acts of public authorities that are incompatible with the HRA may be the subject of an action for compensation.
64   *Human Rights Act 1998* (U.K.), s. 6(6)(b).

[2.77] The approaches of these jurisdictions is to leave the ultimate decision in the hands of the legislature rather than the courts. The issue becomes a matter, to be debated through democratic procedures, but one made with the benefit of impartial and expert judicial examination.

[2.78] Consideration of human rights as the end result of human deliberation and reasoning leads to the conclusion that human rights are a very human creation. It is suggested that if we view human rights as stemming from human nature rather than an external, supernatural force, human rights are necessarily based on a secular understanding of governance. Conversely, personal conviction, both religious and non-religious, can lead to breaches of human rights, through, for example, discrimination against women, 'sinners', non-believers and apostates. To avoid this happening, as will be argued, belief rights are subject to limitations that accord with liberal democratic society.

Conclusion: the globalisation of human rights

[2.79] Olivier De Schutter describes the positive possibilities of the human rights treaties:

> Whether they are adopted at the universal or at the regional levels, all human rights treaties are derived from the UDHR, from which they borrow, sometimes quite literally, much of their language. It is therefore quite natural for international courts or quasi-judicial bodies, whether they belong to regional or universal systems, to cite one another, and to entertain a dialogue with national courts applying human rights recognised in constitutional instruments, where the wording is similar or identical.[65]

[2.80] He points out that the internet, increasing number of data bases and proliferation of NGOs – who agitate for human rights and act as *amici curiae* (advisers to courts) – has promoted a 'global interjurisdictional conversation' (a '*jus commune*' of human rights) which judges perceive will give them increased legitimacy. This has led to potential negative outcomes, such as an unrealistic view of human rights, which holds that interpretations that are desirable in one jurisdiction or situation must be replicated albeit inappropriately in others, thus undermining the legitimacy of human rights themselves.[66]

[2.81] Human rights treaties are based on a model of liberal democracy, involving representative government, political pluralism, impartial exercise of government power and equality before the law. They promise the means of maximising freedom to have or adopt a belief, and to practise its tenets – subject to restrictions that preserve the integrity of the (democratic) state and the

---

65   De Schutter (2010), 31.
66   Ibid, 30ff.

rights of others. This, I suggest, includes appropriate protection of culture and belief within such a society.

[2.82] As can be seen, the 'right to freedom of religion and belief' is to be widely construed, and is not confined to religion, as the wording seems to imply. That is why the term 'belief rights', rather than 'freedom of religion or belief' is used throughout this book.

[2.83] But belief rights, along with other rights, will not flourish where there is no consensus on what it means among those involved. That is why consensus is an essential component of political liberalism. This is outlined in Rawls's authoritative model of political liberalism and is described in the following Chapters.

CHAPTER 3
RAWLS AND BELIEF: LIBERTY

[3.1] To simplify Rawls's elaborate and detailed model of political liberalism as an ideal model for recognition of belief rights, it is perhaps instructive to consider first his bifurcated model of rights and liberties.

Rawls and non-liberal 'decent' societies: essential human rights

[3.2] In *The Law of Peoples* ('*LoP*'), Rawls addresses the fact that not all societies are liberal and democratic, despite subscribing to the liberties of a democratic society. These societies may be what he calls **'decent but illiberal' societies.** 'Decent but illiberal' societies are non-aggressive and have a conception of the common good through consultation with all groups. They subscribe to what Rawls describes as *human rights.* For Rawls, 'human rights' are distinct from those listed in the UDHR. For him, they are limited to the minimal freedoms, powers and protections 'necessary for any system of social cooperation, whether liberal or nonliberal',[1] and are entitlements no one can take away. Rawls said that the human rights he lists are essential for acceptance by the international community (and encourage liberalism). Anything less is tyranny or dictatorship (which may be based on hardline theocracy[2]) and a potential justification for intervention by other states.

[3.3] Rawls's essential human rights, then, do not include all the rights as we know them in Western democracies, and those included are not as broad. They are the default conditions, if you like, for 'decent' living.

Rawls and liberal democratic society: 'basic liberties'

[3.4] If we want to provide for truly equal autonomy, dignity and the opportunity for self-realisation as an individual and citizen, as prescribed for liberal democracy, we need the add-ons provided by what Rawls calls *basic liberties*. For Rawls, 'basic liberties' are similar to those listed as universal human rights in the UDHR and ICCPR (he did not address these documents in his works). 'Basic liberties' form the foundation of *political liberalism*. This model of society, involving the human rights add-ons of the UDHR and set out in his book *Political Liberalism* ('*PL*'), is the one with which I am concerned.

---

1   Freeman (2007a), 436; *LoP* 68.
2   I use the term 'hardline thocracy' to denote government that is in effect an instrument of a particular religious belief. Max Wallace uses the term 'soft theocracy' to describe 'a state where church and government purposes coincide to garnishee taxpayers' money and resources, strucurally through tax exemptions and functionally through grants and priveleges.' Wallace (2010), 72.

[3.5] The difference between Rawls's concepts of *human rights* and *basic liberties* (or *liberal rights*) are set out in the following table:

Table 4: Rawls's difference between Human Rights and 'Basic Liberties'

HUMAN RIGHTS	BASIC LIBERTIES
The minimum to qualify as a 'decent society'	Basis of liberal democracy ('political liberalism')
LoP 65ff.	*PL*, 291; Freeman (2007a), 464.
May not apply equally to all citizens	*Apply equally to all citizens*
• The right to life (means of subsistence and security);	**Rights listed by Rawls:**
• Personal freedom (freedom from slavery, serfdom, forced occupation);	• Freedom of thought and liberty of conscience;
• Freedom of thought and expression;	• Political liberties, such as the right to vote, hold office, form and join political parties, express views and enjoy fair opportunity to take part in political life;
• A 'sufficient measure' of liberty of conscience, though not an equal liberty;	• Freedom of association;
• Respect for the rights of women in 'just consultation' (while not necessarily resulting in equality with men); and	• Freedoms associated with the liberty and integrity of the person;
• Formal equality as expressed by the rule of law, that is, similar cases treated similarly, although there may be inequality among members of society.	• Right to hold personal property;
	• Rights and liberties covered by the rule of law.
	Rights that may be inferred from the above list, set out in the ICCPR:
	• The right to privacy (Art. 17);
	• The right to marry, family privacy and protection of children (Arts 23, 24)
	• The right to participate in public affairs, vote and access to public service: (Art. 25);
	• The right to equal protection of the law and non-discrimination (Art. 26);
	• The right to enjoyment of culture, language etc. (Art. 27)

[3.6] For Rawls, a statement of basic liberties is not a legally binding statement, but a political one. Where states are party to the human rights treaties, however, one can argue that what Rawls treats as basic *liberties* – permissions that can be withdrawn – when adopted by government, become recognised liberal *rights* – enforceable entitlements, imposing legal duties on others not to impede the exercise of the freedoms they prescribe.

[3.7] A basic liberty is necessary, says Rawls, when it is an 'essential social condition for the adequate development and full exercise of the two powers of moral personality over a complete life'.[3] These two powers are (a) individuals can rationally pursue a coherent set of values and (b) they can cooperate with others on fair terms to pursue these.[4] Consequently, in a society that undertakes to provide for the realisation of the two powers of moral personality, what may otherwise be a 'liberty' becomes a 'right'.

[3.8] According to Freeman, Rawls's *'human rights'*, are the minimum rights required for the most basic expression of the moral powers needed for social cooperation in any society. *'Basic liberties'* are necessary for *full* expression of the moral powers in a liberal democratic society. Liberal rights 'depend on an ideal of persons and of citizens - as free, self-reflective, and self-governing agents with a good of their own that they have freely accepted':[5]

> However important and inspiring this liberal ideal of the person, for a person to be denied specifically liberal rights and freedoms is not as egregious as the failure, implied by a denial of human rights, to recognize that one is a person who is due moral respect and consideration for the essential conditions of existence.[6]

[3.9] Rawls stated that people normally have a sense of justice, including mutual respect, that is, a desire to justify their actions to others in terms others can reasonably accept.[7] However, essential human rights will prevail only to the extent that the gravest of injustices are eliminated. These injustices include 'unjust war and oppression, religious persecution and the denial of liberty of conscience, starvation and poverty, not to mention genocide and mass murder').[8]

Equal basic liberties in a pluralist society

[3.10] In *A Theory of Justice* (*'TJ'*) Rawls recognised that some individuals may accept the need for a social order that is just and fair for all, but wish to follow diverse religious, philosophical and

---

3   *PL* 293.
4   Freeman (2007a), 54.
5   Freeman (2007b), 436.
6   Ibid.
7   Freeman (2007b), 179; *TJ*, 414–19.
8   *LoP*, ¶1, esp. 78. See generally, Sadurski (2005).

moral views that conflict with those of others, potentially jeopardising the stability and durability of their society.[9]

[3.11] A particular social or political order is stable and durable, he said, if

a) there is a measure of agreement in conceptions of justice;

b) individuals' activities are congruent, to permit the exercise of anyone's legitimate expectations;

c) social cooperation will be regularly and willingly exercised; and

d) stabilising forces are available to control any deviations or infractions that threaten this stability.[10]

[3.12] Rawls's conditions for a stable non-liberal decent society are pushed further in a liberal democratic 'well-ordered' society,[11] elaborated in *PL*. They require the basic elements of justice:

- a 'political conception of justice'. This is based on public reasoning, i.e. democratic values and ideals that provide justice and fairness for all and are independent of beliefs ('comprehensive doctrines');

- an 'overlapping consensus' on justice. The public political conception of justice is accepted by followers of different beliefs and as compatible with their tenets (making them 'reasonable'); and

- government impartiality regarding matters of basic justice. A public conception of justice is non-discriminatory, with no special treatment of anyone based on, *inter alia*, his or her belief.[12]

Justice: the basic Principles

[3.13] Individuals, Rawls argued, have the capacity to 'form, revise and pursue a conception of the social 'good', and the capacity for a sense of justice, and can 'understand, apply and follow requirements of principles of justice' through cooperating with others.[13] This is the source of a

---

9   Freeman ibid, 185.
10   *TJ*, 5-6.
11   In a 'well-ordered society' 'the public conception of justice provides a mutually recognized point of view from which citizens can adjudicate their claims of political rights on their political institutions or against one another': Rawls (2003), 9.
12   Freeman (2007a), 329.
13   Ibid, 294.

fair system of social cooperation over time from one generation to the next, based on an 'overlapping consensus' across society.[14] Rawls saw adopting the principle of 'justice as fairness' as a form of social contract entered into by all citizens, designed to treat everyone the same in relation to their political rights, regardless of individual characteristics such as race, religion, gender, social status and circumstances.[15] It explains how liberty and equality are to be understood.

[3.14] Consensus in liberal society, as Rawls and neutralists see it, does not involve a need to adopt a uniform religion or other belief. The 'good' in liberal democracy involves the *general conditions* for social and physical advantage of all that are in accordance with political liberalism, based on government advocacy of reciprocity and mutual respect.[16] Consensus accords with the basic principles underlying differing beliefs. In that sense, the overlapping consensus is not about a consensus of personal beliefs. It is limited to the domain of the political, to provide the constitutional structure that is the 'best solution to the problem of finding the most appropriate conception of justice for a democratic society'. Rawls argues '[w]hat makes an overlapping consensus "stable for the right reasons" is that, from the standpoint of all the reasonable comprehensive doctrines, there is no better conception of justice'.[17] By 'stable for the right reasons' he means stable because of mutual and overall acceptance through free will, not authoritarianism, even if it is benign authoritarianism.

'Justice as fairness'

[3.15] 'Justice as fairness' involves what Rawls calls the two Principles of Justice.[18] The First Principle of Justice ('First Principle') provides for equal basic political liberties. The two fundamental components of the First Principle are *freedom* and *equality* in relation to political rights. It states that:

> Each person has an equal claim to a fully adequate scheme of equal basic rights and liberties, which scheme is compatible with the same scheme for all; and in this scheme the equal political liberties, and only those liberties, are to be guaranteed their fair value.[19]

[3.16] 'Basic rights and liberties' have been described above.

---

14 Rawls (2003), 5. For a more in-depth discussion, see *PL*, 11ff.

15 *TJ*, Chapter 1; see esp p.10ff. The basic principles of justice as fairness are based on the idea of individuals participating in a social contract. The contract is founded on the hypothetical individual viewed from a 'veil of ignorance', that is, stripped of such characteristics as gender, social class, race ethnic origin, belief and personal or social history. Only general facts about human nature and social and economic institutions are applied: *TJ*, Ch.3.

16 Freeman (2007a), 217. For discussion see Rawls (2003) esp. 198ff.

17 Freeman (2007a), 366ff, esp 369-70.

18 These Principles were first described in *TJ*, 52. They are revised in *PL* 5.

19 As revised in *PL*, 5, 291. First enunciated as requiring a 'most extensive scheme of equal basic liberties' in *TJ*, 52 ff..

[3.17] The Second Principle of Justice ('Second Principle') addresses social and economic inequalities. The Second Principle states that:

> Social and economic inequalities are to satisfy two conditions: first, they are to be attached to positions and offices open to all under conditions of fair equality of opportunity; and second, they are to be to be to the greatest benefit of the least advantaged members of society.[20]

[3.18] A distinction is thus drawn between political equality (the First Principle) and what I call 'distributive' equality (the Second Principle), a distinction I consider more fully in Chapter 4. Belief rights come squarely under the category of political equality.

[3.19] Where the two Principles of Justice conflict, the First Principle 'trumps' the Second Principle, by which Rawls means that the 'equal right to fully adequate scheme of equal basic liberties' must not be sacrificed for other economic or social advantages, even to achieve social or economic equality.[21] Thus, for example, less prosperous social groups should not be denied equal political liberties (such as the right to vote) in exchange for greater economic prosperity.[22] This would trade the power of self-determination for dependence on whatever government, benevolent or otherwise, is in power. On the other hand, some special social and economic measures may be required to ensure political equality (e.g. physical/economic resources to maximise the opportunity for all to fairly participate in the political process through access to information, education, voting facilities, etc.).

[3.20] For Rawls, justice in liberal democracy is established through a 'four-stage sequence' for ensuring political institutions, such as the legislature, executive and judiciary, operate in accordance with his notion of a just and fair society based on political liberalism. After (1) the conditions for a political conception of justice have been determined, (2) appropriate governmental institutions have been established, and (3) rules are adopted through policy and legislation, then (4) judicial and other government officers apply these rules according to the established principles.[23]

[3.21] In sum, I suggest in Rawls's terms 'justice' means an outcome that is in accordance with what is considered *politically* morally right (for example, basic liberties), and 'fairness' requires justice to be applied under equal conditions for all. This is the understanding with which I use these words.

---

20   *PL*, 6, also discussed at 291.
21   *PL*, 294 ff.
22   Freeman (2007a), 66; Lop 295.
23   *TJ*, 171ff. For discussion see also Van Wyk (2001), Ch 3, 80; Kymlicka (2001), 328 ff.

Determining a 'political conception of justice'

[3.22] Given society ascribes to the principle of belief rights, how, and to what extent, should it inform a political conception of justice? Should the government ensure that every individual proclaiming a belief has the resources to act in accordance with his or her belief? Should there be special treatment through legal provisions or financial or other assistance to provide special treatment for individual beliefs? Should there be provisions for every individual to worship, practice or teach according to his or her belief unimpeded,[24] or should the state completely distance itself from any recognition of one or all beliefs altogether? What is a fair and just outcome? These are some of the questions addressed by a political conception of justice.

[3.23] A political conception of justice, says Rawls, has three elements. Firstly, it applies to the basic structure of society; secondly, it is freestanding of any 'comprehensive doctrine', and thirdly, its content 'is expressed in terms of certain fundamental ideas seen as implicit in the public political culture of a democratic society' (such as a constitutional regime and the basic principles of liberal democracy).[25] It is 'a module' adopted generally within a society as an 'overlapping consensus', which can be supported in principle by different comprehensive doctrines that agree to be regulated by it'.[26] It provides that people:

- as individuals have their personal understanding of what life is all about and order their lives accordingly; but

- as citizens, dealing with each other, accept a set of principles for living that allow others their personal beliefs and refrain from encroaching on their rights and liberties.

[3.24] The political conception of justice forms the basis for procedures aimed at ensuring a fair and equitable government that is acceptable to all citizens, regardless of their personal beliefs ('procedural justice': see below).

---

24   These practices are called 'unimpaired flourishing' by Eisgruber and Sager (1996), 599. One major proponent of 'unimpaired flourishing' is McConnell (1990a); (1992), (esp. 169ff.); and (1990b). In the last-cited article McConnell says 'Even the almighty democratic will of the people is, in principle, subordinate to the commands of God, as heard and understood in the individual conscience' (at 1516). Another proponent is Laycock (1990).

25   *PL*, 11ff.

26   Ibid, 12.

[3.25] Justice as fairness is not inexorably fixed.[27] Firstly, there may be differences as to just how principles of justice are to be implemented. At this level, one asks, how are rights to apply in this particular society? A liberal democracy requires that any reasonable political conception of justice aims to protect at least the basic liberties Rawls describes. As noted, the UDHR lists those liberties.

[3.26] Secondly, the principles of justice having been accepted, it must be determined how to put them into practice within a given society. At this level one asks, how do we rank entitlements where rights conflict? How do we apply those entitlements in the particular circumstances existing at the time? There may be differences of opinion on these matters, as '[r]easonable political conceptions of justice do not always lead to the same conclusion'.[28] A decision on how to proceed 'is to be seen as reasonable provided all citizens of a reasonably just constitutional regime sincerely vote in accordance with the idea of public reason'.[29] This principle applies to politicians, judges and citizens alike. But what is 'reasonable'?

Justice and reason

[3.27] Rawls uses the term 'reasonable' a lot in his consideration of justice, referring to reasonable people, reasonable comprehensive doctrines, and reasonable political conceptions. With the aid of his discussion of the reasonable,[30] and Freeman's glossary.[31] I will set out my understanding of the notion of reasonableness.

[3.28] *Reasonable people* are 'ready to propose principles and standards as fair [just and equal] terms of cooperation and to abide by them willingly, given the assurance that others will likewise do so'.[32] Reasonable people thus:

- subscribe to principles and beliefs compatible with a political regime of justice and equality;

---

27 Schwartzman (2004), discusses in detail arguments that public reason fails to generate agreement on fundamental issues and/ or fails to provide sufficient reasons for making important political decisions. He concludes that public reason is not *meant* to end reasoned disagreement, but rather to provide a suitable framework for values and principles, by which citizens may resolve moral and political differences and eliminate indeterminancy through the democratic 'second order decision-making strategies' he outlines.

28 *PL* liv.

29 Ibid.

30 Ibid, Lecture II, esp. p 48-58.

31 Freeman ((2007a), 480-9.

32 *PL* 49.

- recognise that other reasonable people may nevertheless differ on aspects of the interpretation and application of the principles of fairness;[33] and

- want to cooperate with like-minded others who are also reasonable on terms they can accept. They are 'willing to govern their conduct by a principle from which they and others can reason in common' and 'take into account the consequences of their actions on others' well-being'.[34] This is Rawls's idea of 'reciprocity'.

[3.29] *Reasonable political principles* accord with the principles of justice as fairness, and are based on a conception of what is good (such as political liberalism).

[3.30] *Reasonable beliefs* (1) consider aspects of human life in a consistent and coherent manner; (2) assess the relative importance of values and how to balance them, and (3) belong to a tradition of thought that develops according to what they see as good and sufficient reasons, based on those values.[35]

[3.31] As a result, those in a liberal democracy who are 'reasonable' can accept others' diverse but reasonable beliefs, subscribing to an overlapping consensus of values that all can agree to as in accordance with a liberal conception of justice. Government is based on these commonly agreed principles, rather than an irreconcilable conflict between them.[36]

[3.32] Although Rawls does not specifically discuss the UDHR, in effect, his idea of a reasonable political conception of justice for liberal democracy is enshrined in the international human rights treaties, and the idea of constitutional government and the rule of law. The UDHR is a purportedly political conception of justice recognised by all member states of the UN. One must recognise that a perfect consensus across society based on Rawls's conception of justice can be contentious and difficult to achieve, given human nature and the vagaries of politics. However, setting out the ideal of a political conception of justice and procedure for attaining it provides

---

33   Reasonable difference of opinion on philosophical, moral and religious issues can arise from what Rawls calls the 'burdens of judgment':

These are the facts other than conflicts of interest that lead even reasonable and rational persons to have different judgments regarding philosophical, moral, and religious issues. They include (among other things), complexity of evidence; assigning different weight to considerations agreed to be relevant; vagueness of concepts and differing interpretations of them; different ways of assessing evidence due to different experiences; complexity of normative considerations of differing forces on both sides of issues; pluralism of values and the fact that many hard decisions may seem to have no answer. (Freeman (2007a), 465. See also *PL* 54ff.

34   *PL* 49 n1.

35   Freeman (2007a), 481.

36   As stated above, individuals may bring into the public sphere values and reasoning for public policies based on comprehensive doctrines. It is up to them to argue that such policies are reasonably acceptable within a secular democratic regime for proper political reasons, informed by a political conception of justice. See, e.g., Rawls (2005d), 462.

a useful yardstick for improving the ability of all to enjoy equally the liberties incorporated in belief rights. It is also a helpful contribution to understanding how the promise of these rights has failed, and how we can work towards fulfilling it.

Fairness = procedural justice, or one law for all

[3.33] A fully adequate scheme of equal basic rights and liberties requires processes for legislative and judicial decision-making considered just and fair by the standards of the society that creates them. Rawls calls these processes *'procedural justice'*.[37] With the idea of a political conception of justice as its basis, the aim of a liberal government should be to develop procedures that are objective, based on a public conception of justice and applied to everyone. In other words, being true to what is morally acceptable means there should be one law for all. A just and fair society is determined by the extent to which minority groups can exercise their human rights.[38]

[3.34] *Perfect procedural justice* according to Rawls is exemplified by a well-run lottery. The intention of the exercise is to indiscriminately award a prize to a ticket-holder. Both the procedure (the 'rules of the game') and the outcome (substantive justice) are designed to be fair. There is no objective way of determining the fairness of the process, other than by the procedure itself, where every ticket has the same value, and the winning ticket is objectively selected without any conditions. 'Perfect' procedural justice can also be assured when external objective criteria, that can demonstrate fairness, can be applied to the result. The procedural justice for the cutting of a cake in equal portions for those wanting to eat it is an example given by Rawls. A fair result, and 'perfect' procedural justice, is evidenced through demonstrating the equal size of portions by comparing the size of each piece. Perfect procedural justice ensures that each person has the same chance at achieving the desired outcome.[39]

[3.35] Rawls recognised that the complexity of human life is such that perfect procedural justice is neither practicable nor necessarily desirable. Because of different individual circumstances and needs, the same chance at achieving the desired outcome should not be equal for everyone, and cannot be perfectly so. While procedural justice aims at a fair outcome, it is impossible to provide for multiple, diverse and changing social conditions. Circumstances cannot be judged in isolation from historical and social context. The different conditions in which people find themselves mean that governments are unlikely to develop procedures that can ensure the same chance at the achieving the desired just outcome for every individual.[40] But we can attempt to develop

---

37   See, e.g., *TJ*, 74ff; 173.
38   *PL*, Lecture VII ¶9, 281ff.
39   See *TJ*, 74ff; Rawls (2005c), 421ff.; Freeman (2007a), 480.
40   *TJ*, 316-7

procedures that maximise the possibility of achieving this result. The process thus becomes one of *imperfect procedural justice.*

[3.36] An example of imperfect procedural justice is criminal legal procedure. This is designed to provide just and fair criminal procedures, but may fail to provide a morally acceptable result (such as a true finding of guilt or innocence) in a particular instance, because of the vagaries of accompanying circumstances, such as the composition of the jury, availability of evidence and expertise of counsel.[41] We can at best use public reason to establish procedures to apply to everyone. It does not guarantee a perfectly fair outcome (what is morally right according to a public conception of justice) in every particular situation, and cannot be expected to do so, but it does provide procedural *rules* that are morally acceptable to all. This means that in the dispensing of justice, citizens and legislators are not to take a narrow or group-interested standpoint and then alter their procedure so that it leads to a predetermined outcome, even if it satisfies the legitimate interests of those involved.[42] That would lead to the allegation of one law for some but not for others.

[3.37] Imperfect procedural justice thus means that the *process* of governance, accepted through democratic processes, must be considered equitable ('procedural justice'), although the outcome may result in some individuals being denied an equitable outcome ('substantive justice').[43] However, as substantive justice is the aim, procedures (such as criminal trials) should not be considered acceptable unless they result in what is considered substantive justice in at least the vast majority of cases.[44] The aim is indeed to *maximise* the chances of justice as fairness through equitable procedures. Where just outcomes are not attained, the procedure may require reconsideration.

[3.38] Given the complexity of pluralist society, then, the best we can do is to practise democracy through imperfect procedural justice: 'a system that strengthens the achievement of democracy's foundational values', although it cannot guarantee perfect justice in every instance.[45] A just society means individual circumstances are taken into account to the extent that they do not compromise the fairness of the procedure. It is not perfect, but it minimises corruption through exceptional treatment of favoured people or causes. While substantive justice (as accepted by society) is the desired outcome, it is the *procedure* that characterises a just and fair society.

---

41   *TJ*, 74, Freeman (2007a), 480.
42   Ibid, 317.
43   *TJ*, 75; Freeman, ibid 480. See discussion of procedural justice and its implications for fairness in Sadurski (2008a), 22ff.
44   Rawls (2005c), 422.
45   Sadurski (2008a), 24.

Liberty and the 'worth of liberty'

[3.39] It is critical to Rawls's theory to draw the distinction between the *status* of liberty: the 'complete system of the liberties of equal citizenship' and the *worth* of liberty to individuals, that is, whether they actually have the *opportunity* to enjoy those liberties.[46] It is the distinction between formal recognition of the status of liberty ('nominal liberty') and the means for ensuring the realisation of that liberty ('substantive liberty'):

> ...liberty is represented by the complete system of the liberties of equal citizenship, while the worth of liberty to persons and groups depends on their capacity to advance their ends within the framework the system defines.[47]

[3.40] Martha Nussbaum gives the example of women in India being legally entitled to education, but denied the opportunity because of lack of resources and government interest. The worth of a liberty, she says, is determined not simply by government declaring it exists, or even if people accept being deprived of it. A liberty is worthwhile only if they have the wherewithal to enjoy it, whether they do or not.[48]

[3.41] The worth of liberty, in relation to democracy, is expressed in somewhat similar terms by Robert Post,[49] who argues that the self-determination fundamental to democracy involves more than the casting of a vote. It requires meaningful involvement in the making of political decisions. He refers to the example of North Korea, where the apparent freedom to vote is undermined by limited choice elections. Self-determination, according to Post, means rather the autonomous authorship of decisions.[50] Rawls would agree with Post, I think, when he says that, in a democracy, citizens must perceive the process by which decisions are made

> as responsive to their own values and ideas...[I]f citizens are free to participate in the formation of public opinion, and if the decisions of the state are made responsive to public opinion, citizens will be able to experience their government as their own, even if they hold diverse views and otherwise disagree.[51]

[3.42] The requirement of a meaningful individual participation in the process of governance through international and regional human rights ideology is also adopted by such writers as

---

46   *TJ*, 179.
47   *TJ*, 179 .
48   Nussbaum, (2000), esp p. 71ff.
49   Post (2006), 24.
50   Ibid, 25.
51   Ibid, 27.

Henry Steiner[52] and Thomas Franck.[53] Wojciech Sadurski adds that equal political opportunity in the process of decision-making includes an opportunity to convey one's message to the audience one wants to reach.[54]

Conclusion

[3.43] Rawls addressed the fact that people hold different, often incompatible understandings of their relationship with the world and consequent moral, philosophical and social values. He asked the question, how we can have a stable liberal and democratic society, while ensuring equal opportunity for everyone to adopt and practise their personal religious or other beliefs?

[3.44] To answer this question, he developed a model of society whereby the state operates, not on the dictates of any personal convictions or vested interests, but on principles drawn from a consensus of *political* values that all citizens, regardless of their beliefs (religious or otherwise) can endorse. These principles are used to develop a system of procedural justice, which is necessarily 'imperfect' to take account of the diversity of social and individual circumstances.

[3.45] Two important contributions to political practice are made by Rawls in what he sees as stable, enduring, democratic and liberal society.

[3.46] Firstly, there is a need to separate personal morality from political morality, with the latter based on an agreement to the values that all can accept for governance in public life. This consensus, a 'public political conception', arises from the need, in a democracy, for citizens to act co-operatively, exercising restraint where pursuing personal agendas is contrary to the public interest (e.g. public health and security, the rule of law, or the rights of others including their belief rights).

[3.47] The positive language in the term 'freedom of religion or belief' emphasises the license to act, in relation to personal conviction, and tempts proponents to downplay the responsibility of reciprocity. It is used to claim privilege for, and tolerate government favouring of, religious or other groups. Acting as individuals or members of families, societies and religious or other groups

---

52 Henry Steiner argues that the minimum right of political participation expressed by Article 25 ICCPR and government by the 'will of the people' in Article 21 UDHR 'should never require less than provision of meaningful exercise of choice by citizens in some form of electoral process permitting active debate on a broad if not unlimited range of issues. But it could require more': Steiner (1988), excerpted in Steiner and Alston (2000), 899.

53 See, e.g., Franck (1992), who points to the international and regional human rights documents to argue that there is 'a large normative canon for the "democratic entitlement" of peoples'. This, he says, creates the opportunity through processes of self-determination, freedom of expression and electoral rights, 'for all persons to assume responsibility for shaping the kind of civil society in which they live and work': Franck (1992), excerpted in Steiner and Alston (2000), 900, 901.

54 Sadurski (2008b), 61.

that have a common set of values and goals, people may follow their personal or communal ideals, morals and beliefs: they have a right to 'freedom *of* religion or belief'. Adequate recognition of the corollary right to freedom *from* the principle and practices of beliefs would acknowledge the equal value of their right to be free from unwarranted influence of the beliefs of others.

[3.48] Secondly, one must draw a distinction between procedural justice and substantive justice. The recognition that stable society relies on cooperation and fairness leads to reducing corruption and promotion of freedom for everyone to further their interests by reasonable consideration of the interests of others. The reins are drawn on the promotion of personal freedoms at the expense of the freedom of others. That is, freedoms imply responsibilities.

[3.49] This brings us to consideration of Rawls's second main characteristic of political liberalism: *equality*. This concept has already been discussed at some length, but the nature of political equality, as opposed to social and economic equality, needs elaboration. Rawls's approach to equality is explored in the next Chapter.

CHAPTER 4
THE IMPORTANCE OF EQUALITY

Equality essential to human rights

[4.1] The second half of the human rights equation is equality. Freedom is not just freedom, but *equal* freedom. The United Nations Charter affirms 'faith in fundamental human rights' in its Preamble, which provides for 'the dignity and worth of the human person in the equal rights of men and women…'. The principles of equality and non-discrimination 'constitute the dominant single theme of the ICCPR'.[1] Sir Hersch Lauterpacht has proclaimed that '[t]he claim to equality is in a substantial sense the most fundamental of the rights of man. It occupies the first place in most written constitutions. Equality of respect is the starting point of all other liberties'.[2] Conor Gearty argues that the phrase 'human rights' hinges on equality of respect and this is the idea that is in turn the 'lynchpin of democracy'.[3] Many people want freedom, but not necessarily on equal terms with others.

[4.2] The ICCPR specifically applies the principle of equality in six general provisions. They are:

- the inherent dignity and equal and inalienable rights of all members of the 'human family' (Preamble);

- equal enjoyment of rights for all without distinction of any kind (Article 2.1.);

- equality of enjoyment of rights for both men and women (Article 3);

- prohibition of discrimination on such grounds as race, colour, sex, language, religion, political or other opinion, national or social origin, property, birth or other status (Article 4.1);

- prohibition of advocating national, racial or religious hatred that constitutes incitement to discrimination (Article 20.2.);

- equality before law and the court and equal protection of the law (e.g. Article 26).

[4.3] The ECHR also gives priority to equality. Article 1 ECHR states that '[t]he High Contracting Parties shall secure to everyone within their jurisdiction the rights and freedoms defined

---

1   Ramcharan (1981), 246.
2   Lauterpacht (1945), 15 (cited in ibid, 247).
3   Gearty (2006), 55; See also, in relation to democracy and the European Court, Gearty (2000), 381-2.

in…this Convention'. The ECHR relies on each right being applied to everyone, or by stating that no one shall be deprived of a right. Article 14 then states that ['t]he enjoyment of the rights and freedoms set forth in this Convention shall be secured without discrimination on any ground such as sex, race, colour, language, religion, political or other opinion, national or social origin, association with a national minority, property, birth or other status'.

[4.4] The priority of political equality can be seen in Rawls's public conception of justice. However, as stated, he recognised that not everyone can be equally satisfied in all circumstances; this is inevitable in a diverse society. Rather, he advocated what he called a 'fair equality of *opportunity*' to benefit in their political liberties, regardless of individual circumstances. Through his First and Second Principles, Rawls also implies an important distinction for political liberalism between:

- the *absolute* nature of political rights for everyone, and the state's duty to provide the means for everyone to enjoy these rights equally;

- the *discretionary* nature of social and economic equality through enhancing opportunities for enjoyment of the material benefits of society by all.

Political equality versus social and economic equality

[4.5] This is similar to the approach of Robert Post,[4] whose description of democracy clarifies this distinction between participation in the democratic process and life chances. Post calls these 'democratic equality' and 'distributive equality' respectively. Post, like Rawls, sees democracy as ensuring that every citizen is entitled to be treated 'equally in regard to the forms of conduct that constitutes autonomous democratic participation' – that is, political equality.[5]

[4.6] The right to political equality – equal participation in political rights – is absolute in this sense. The right itself cannot be taken away, however the opportunity for an individual to exercise that right may be compromised because of personal or social circumstances. In an ideal society, the government has an obligation to work towards *maximising the opportunity* for everyone to participate in the democratic process.

[4.7] Provision of social or material goods or benefits beyond those required for equal political rights is secondary to this. Equality is thus an essential determinant of whether there is appropriate liberty to participate in the public conception of justice. The two concepts of political liberty and equality are interdependent.

---

4   Post (2006), 29. Political equality requires 'only those forms of equal citizenship that are necessary for the project of collective self-determination to succeed' (at. 32). It does not require rectification of other, albeit unfair, inequalities, through equal allocation of social or economic resources for its own sake – what Post calls 'distributive equality' (at. 24).

5   Ibid 29.

[4.8] Equal opportunity for non-political life chances, on the other hand, is a separate issue to full enjoyment of political liberalism. It focuses on the moral, humanitarian consideration of providing material benefits, and is based on a combination of social, religious and cultural beliefs, as well as social and economic circumstances at the time. Rawls argues that this means

> the provision of distributive benefits should be arranged so as to distribute income, wealth, and powers and positions of office so as to maximise the share that goes to the least advantaged members of society'[6] (Second Principle: see above [3.17]).

[4.9] While highly desirable, social and economic distributive equality is concerned with benefits beyond those required for the exercise of equal political rights, with material benefits of societies themselves being the major consideration. It can involve redistribution of resources such as health, welfare and prosperity, or such potentially problematic practices as affirmative action, quotas for position in employment or education, or even reverse discrimination.

[4.10] It should be apparent that many measures involving social and economic well-being are essential for ensuring political equality, so perceptions as to where political and distributive equality intercept are matters of debate. Tension is caused between those whose life chances are enhanced from the re-allocation of benefits, and those whose life chances are consequently narrowed. For example, affirmative action programs might be seen as taking job opportunities from qualified males and giving them to less suitable women. Also important is the fact that what constitutes a desirable lifestyle varies between individuals, being relative and often self-contradictory (an often-used example is the distinction between the claims of those with gourmet tastes compared to those with less expensive tastes). Difference in needs and desires prevents universal agreement on the benefits of re-allocation for this purpose in the first place. Accordingly, distributive equality must be considered with caution.[7] Rawls did not generally advocate preferential treatment such as affirmative action, however he did indicate in lectures that this may be acceptable as a temporary means of remedying past (unfair) discriminatory treatment.[8]

[4.11] While distribution of resources can mean some people benefit while others may lose out, it is critical to Rawls's model of political liberalism that those who are advantaged from the distribution of social and economic benefits 'are not to be better off at any point to the detriment

---

6   Freeman (2007a).

7   Sadurski (2008a), 90 makes a similar point:

> ... the very adoption of a democratic procedure reveals a prior acceptance of a strongly egalitarian premise; a premise weighty enough to prevail over the arguments (whatever they may be), for a non-democratic system of government.

See also Sadurski (2008b).

8   Freeman (2007a), 90-91.

of the less well off'.[9] 'No one *deserves* his greater natural capacity or merits a more favourable starting point in society'.[10] People should be free to use their good fortune to their best ability, and accept society's support in their endeavours. But justice as fairness demands that they use their advantage only on terms that favour those who are less fortunate.[11]

[4.12] By separating the idea of equality into political and distributive equality, the tension between liberty and equality described above is confined to considerations of distributive equality. This separation provides guidelines for when limits can be placed on freedoms in the name of equality. Rawls cites the examples of granting state resources that favour the exercise of religious practices (e.g. for a pilgrimage to a holy place, or for building grand places of worship). Granting such resources can create an inequity in the 'worth' of the right to manifest belief between citizens, negating opportunities for equal participation of all in the exercise of their political liberties. This favouring of one belief over others could be considered unjust and divisive, as 'some receive more than others depending on…their [sectarian] conceptions of the good'.[12]

Equality in the 'private sphere'

[4.13] What are the implications of Rawls's theories on equality for the exercise of personal beliefs? This equality is negated if we see democracy as based simply on factors such as the proclaimed right of everyone to vote, without recognising the inequalities that can arise from influences within the private world of social organisations (e.g. the family and the church). Constraints on the enjoyment of political freedom and equality – through missed opportunities for autonomy or participation in public discourse – are accepted because of one's allocated position within the domestic sphere, or the dictates of religion.

[4.14] Constraints on the enjoyment of the worth of political freedom and equality are thus falsely deemed legitimate in the name of religious freedom. The influence and power that may be wielded over minority groups by those with majority acceptance, government recognition and approval is concealed:

> The domestic division of labour has direct consequences for the nature and degree of political involvement and because of this should be regarded as a political and not just social concern…the point of universal suffrage is that it treats each person as of equal weight to the next: if so, that point is far from being reached.[13]

---

9   Rawls (2003), 124;. *TJ*, 86ff., esp 87.
10   *TJ*, ibid (emphasis added).
11   Ibid. See, also Sandel (2009), 156.
12   *PL* 330.
13   Phillips (1999a), 193.

[4.15] Feminism has resulted in the acknowledgement that values of democracy extend beyond formally decreed gender equality alone, to more a wide-ranging interest in how people relate to each other.[14] Gender discrimination (like social and economic inequality) is also relevant to the question of political equality.

[4.16] Feminists and others claim Rawls's theory only provided for equality in the public sphere of government, and therefore did not consider inequity that can occur among individuals (particularly women and children) as members of associations and families. In response, Rawls explained how his theory provides for principles of justice to extend into associations and families in his paper *The Idea of Public Reason Revisited*.[15]

[4.17] Rawls acknowledged there that belief communities may subscribe to doctrines that are incompatible with basic liberties. They may practise inequality or patriarchy, or refuse certain medical treatment to women and children, and disown those who break the rules. However, he holds that members of groups, religions and associations are all equal citizens, and that essential human rights should nevertheless apply to everyone. Every member of society is entitled to demand the enjoyment of fundamental human rights such as equality before the law, and personal autonomy:[16]

> As citizens we have reason to impose the constraints specified by the political principles of justice on associations; while as members of associations we have reason for limiting those restraints so that they leave room for a free and flourishing internal life appropriate to the association in question.[17]

[4.18] Whilst his approach seems somewhat imprecise at times, it is proposed that, keen to provide flexibility and width in his treatment of belief, Rawls is stating that political liberties apply throughout society in all its parts. Family, churches and associations must adjust to the requirements of justice,[18] recognising such rights as personal autonomy and dignity, voluntary membership, mutual tolerance and recognition of the law. Members should be at liberty to reject or question the religious (or other) group to which they may belong, without retaliation,[19] as well as to enjoy other political rights, described above, that apply to all citizens.[20] Subject to this,

---

14   Ibid, 194.
15   Rawls (2005d), 466ff.
16   Ibid, 469ff.
17   Rawls (2005d), 469.
18   *PL* 261.
19   The exercise of this freedom is suppressed in some religious groups, for example, Muslims (see, e.g., Jordan (2002); Exclusive Brethren: (see e.g., Bachelard (2008), esp. Chapter 10).
20   Rawls (2005d), 468-9.

however, the association may apply its own notions of justice in any given instance (such as rules, forms of worship and ethical doctrines).

[4.19] In this sense, for Rawls, reference to public and private spheres of life can be misleading. A domain or sphere of life is not a 'kind of space' but rather 'a difference in how the principles of justice are applied, directly to the basic structure and indirectly to the associations within it'.[21] He thus makes an important point about democratic society that has been undervalued by many commentators: the public and private 'spheres' of society are

> not…two separate, disconnected spaces, each governed solely by its own distinct principles…the principles of justice still put essential restrictions on the family and all other associations. *The adult members of families and other associations are equal citizens first; that is their basic position. No institution or association in which they are involved can violate their rights as citizens.*[22]

[4.20] Citizens' rights, then, trump individual rights. The individual as citizen, with all the attendant rights and freedoms resulting from the principles of justice, carries those rights and freedoms into the family and associations to which he or she belongs. This means, for example, that individuals are protected from sanctions against alleged apostasy or heresy, or against disassociating themselves from any belief or questioning its tenets.

[4.21] It follows that some principles of what may be considered to constitute *political* justice need not apply to the internal life of churches, or other non-political organisations, 'nor is it desirable, nor consistent with liberty of conscience or freedom of association, that they should'.[23] Gender discrimination, for example, is an integral part of many religions. While the principle of political 'equality' applies to all, it must be read down to mean 'equality before the law'. Reading it more broadly would be to accept the discriminatory practice of beliefs (which include the mainstream religions) as a legitimate part of government policy.

[4.22] Authority over personal lifestyle (saying of prayers, support of children or the disabled, residence and duties) may be mandated by clerics or other recognised sources. However, denial of personal autonomy and slavery are not permitted. Belief rights are based on the essential con-

---

21   Ibid, 471.
22   Ibid, 470-1 (emphasis added).
23   Ibid, (2005d), 468.

dition that the individual is a *voluntary* subscriber to any doctrine.[24] Problematically, children have belief rights 'consistent with the evolving capacities of the child'.[25]

[4.23] Rawls makes it quite clear: those who want to belong to a liberal democracy – recognising the principles of justice as fairness inherent in such societies – must make a commitment. They must be prepared to give priority to those principles over the demands of their belief when these demands clash with the principles of liberal democracy.[26] Otherwise, they must abandon the claims of belief rights, and admit a tendency to theocracy.

[4.24] Justice as fairness, then, 'affirms [equal] political freedom for all but leaves the weight of ethical freedom to be decided by citizens severally in light of their comprehensive doctrines'.[27] This means that the strength with which one holds a particular belief, while making it personally right, does not automatically make it politically right.[28] Both political and ethical values may be compatible in a liberal democracy, but where they are not, the principles of political freedom take precedence according to the political conception of justice (i.e. the law).

[4.25] This is the promise of Rawls's First Principle, a promise that is necessary for the establishment of just legislation and an effective process for democracy.[29] Accordingly, Rawls sees belief rights as primarily a political freedom, established by the First Principle, the 'lexical' antecedent of the Second Principle, which enhances its practical effect. I have noted that Rawls's model is the expression of an ideal, but ideals are what we strive for.

[4.26] The lexical priority of political freedoms underscores Rawls's concept of 'civic duty': reasonable citizens in a liberal democracy accept the need for, and outcome of, procedural justice, even where it may result in a denial of substantive justice in individual cases. In liberal democracy, procedural justice is fair by its very definition.

---

24   Ibid, 471-2. Rawls proposes that actions are voluntary when they are 'rational': chosen solely to achieve an end, even when conditions are unfair; or 'reasonable': chosen between more than one option when surrounding conditions for any are fair (at 472 n 68).

25   *Convention on the Rights of the Child* (1989), Article 14.

26   They must be 'devoted to the ideal of public reason.' Ibid 485ff.

27   *PL*, 78.

28   See Rawls (2003), 192-3. Sadurski (2008a), agrees with this view (at p. 52), stating that to favour one value over another based on the strength with which it is held would involve irrelevant considerations. But overall social implications of action are a relevant consideration (e.g., the social effects of legislating for some form of voluntary euthanasia). Consequently, 'all that counts for the political process…is the fact that each of us espouses a particular judgment and not how strongly we espouse our respective values'.

29   See, e.g., Rawls (2003), esp. p 45–47.

Reconciling liberty and equality

[4.27] Rawls puts it this way: '[f]reedom and equal liberty is the same for all; *the question of compensating for a lesser than equal liberty does not arise*'.[30] This is because a 'lesser than equal liberty' is a contradiction in terms. No-one loses the freedom itself. However, the very freedom each of us has is self-limiting by the equal opportunity to exercise that same freedom open to others. It is modified by what allows them, also, that opportunity.

[4.28] There is no question, then, that all citizens enjoy the *status* of equal belief rights; the extent to which they can *exercise* that freedom, however, is dependent on political, social, physical and economic circumstances. While freedom as equal liberty is in theory the same for all, in reality the *worth* of liberty is not. Some have greater authority and wealth than others, and so have more ability to experience the worth of their liberties.

[4.29] It follows that to attain equal enjoyment of the 'worth' of belief rights, some circumstances require 'compensation'.[31] Compensation can be rendered, for example, through addressing poverty, ignorance and a lack of access to social goods generally. Those who are intellectually or physically disadvantaged are assisted through reallocation of resources to 'maximise' first, their opportunity to exercise their political rights, and only then their right to social and economic parity. This is where the Second Principle of Justice becomes relevant.

[4.30] Rawls is clear on his distinction between the absolute liberty that applies to everyone without exception, and the worth of liberty, which is variable, depending on social and economic circumstances:

> Compensating for the lesser worth of freedom is not to be confused with making good an unequal liberty…the basic structure is to be arranged to maximise the worth to the least advantaged of the complete scheme of equal liberty shared by all. This defines the end of social justice.[32]

[4.31] Accordingly, whereas many people see a potential conflict between liberty and equality, for political liberalism they coalesce. Indeed, both are essential for the full exercise of belief rights by everyone. Rawls differentiates between a liberty itself (such as the right itself to manifest one's belief) which applies to everyone, and the *worth* of that liberty (the value it holds for a particular individual, considering access to resources and opportunity, and government regulation, etc.), which not everyone may enjoy.

---

30   *TJ*, 179 (emphasis added).
31   Ibid.
32   Ibid.

Public political culture recognised

[4.32] Rawls recognises the 'public political culture' of societies as part of their political conception of justice. He adopts a 'wide view' of public political culture, which 'comprises the political institutions of a constitutional regime and the public traditions of their interpretation (including those of the judiciary) as well as historic texts and documents that are common knowledge'.[33] He thus allows for variations in societies of how people experience their freedoms, depending on history and culture.

[4.33] Public political culture as part of a liberal democratic conception of justice, however, is subject to the overlapping consensus on principles that can be accepted generally, regardless of belief.

[4.34] Liberal democracies should not tolerate dictatorships, tyrannies and other outlaw regimes that refuse to comply with essential human rights, in Rawls's view. However, they *should* tolerate 'decent but illiberal' societies, although he does not endorse them. Full personal self-fulfilment requires at least the enjoyment of basic liberties. 'With confidence in the ideals of constitutional liberal democratic thought', Rawls says, 'the Law of Peoples respects decent peoples by allowing them to find their own ways to honour those ideals'.[34] Liberal democracies should refrain from exercising military, diplomatic or economic sanctions to make them change their ways: these are methods they may consider for outlaw states. Comprehensive doctrines are to be respected, 'provided that these doctrines are pursued in ways compatible with a reasonable political conception of justice and its public reason'.[35] Respect for human decency 'is a condition of justice, but not all decent societies are just in a liberal democratic sense'.[36]

[4.35] Rawls's aim in *Law of Peoples* is to draw a limit on tolerable regimes through an idealised classification of nations. His description of illiberal but decent societies is archetypal, and general in its terms. Given the complexity of society, perhaps no society neatly fits into this idealised category of governance.

State, belief and equality

[4.36] In relation to a 'decent' but illiberal society — one which recognises his essential human rights and governs according to them — Rawls holds that it may have a state religion or belief and politically endorse a particular kind of comprehensive doctrine, 'as long as it provides an

---

33   *PL* 13,14 (my emphasis).
34   *LoP* 122.
35   Ibid, 59.
36   Freeman(2007), 429.

appropriate degree of freedom to practise dissenting religions'[37] and recognise rights for women [despite their discriminatory nature] through a process of consultation.[38] These are carefully chosen words that indicate his insistence that women, for example, are consulted about their rights, not just subject to male-dominated doctrine.

[4.37] When he considers basic liberties, however, the situation changes, and we are lead to understand that Rawls advocates 'separation of church and state': 'It protects religion from the state and the state from religion; it protects citizens from their churches, and citizens from one another.'[39] However, he does not elaborate on this statement, which must be read along with his rejection of special treatment (favourable or otherwise) of comprehensive doctrines by the state. One can only presume this means he would not countenance establishment of state religion in a liberal democracy as part of such separation. He does not specifically express a view on liberal democracies such as that of the UK or Denmark, or of those nations that have established or legislated for special recognition of one or more religion, such as Germany, where the state exacts taxes on behalf of recognized religious institutions from their members. This is an important omission in Rawls's theory, but the presumption is that he would disapprove. The case for state-belief separation is made in Chapter 13.

Conflicting rights and 'reason'

[4.38] As noted above, Rawls is flexible as to precisely how liberties are to be specifically defined in each liberal democratic society, allowing, in individual cases, for consideration of circumstance, history and culture, provided individuals affirm the same conception of themselves as free and equal citizens, enjoying the 'same basic rights, liberties and opportunities'.[40] He sees the basic liberties as a whole, 'as one system', with the worth of one liberty weighed against the other liberties in any given circumstances, so long as the essential objective of each liberty is preserved.[41]

[4.39] Consequently, Rawls does not provide a list of basic liberties in order of merit, relying on the two principles of justice to determine priorities when liberties are in conflict in particular cases (the human rights treaties establish some rights as absolute, while others are subject to potential limitation ([1.11]). This lack of specificity may not be a serious disadvantage, however. By avoiding particularity at the stage of constitutionally defining rights and responsibilities, there is room for a particular society to determine in more detail how to regulate and adjust basic lib-

---

37   Ibid, 430. See, e.g., *LoP* 75.
38   *LoP* , 110.
39   Rawls (2005d), 476.
40   *PL* 180, 185.
41   *TJ*, 178.

erties to maintain an adequate scheme of equal basic rights and liberties for all.[42] This is to occur at the stage where the legislature sets out in more detail rules and policies to take account of historical, cultural, technological and economic circumstances (so long as this is done with 'sufficient exactness to sustain [the] conception of justice'). While they may never be extinguished altogether, basic liberties are to be interpreted in a way that maintains a 'coherent scheme of liberties' (presumably justice as fairness).[43]

[4.40] An example of the difference public political culture can make within a liberal democracy is the diversity between the English system of trial by jury and the European inquisitorial system, for dealing with criminal trials. The diverse procedures can be seen to be in accord with justice as fairness to the extent that they facilitate the principles underlying the political conception of justice recognised by those countries.

[4.41] The absence of prioritising liberties may thus be appropriate, given the abstraction at which Rawls is working, as the resulting generality allows for the establishment of a particular society's individual set of values, priorities, and understanding of the 'good'. In a liberal democracy, however, this flexibility is necessarily constrained within the secular structure of political liberalism.

[4.42] By the political conception of justice, based on the idea of public reason and not a conception of the person as conceived by any comprehensive doctrine, Rawls seems to be developing the idea of the citizen as a construct of the state 'an ideal implicit in democratic political culture'.[44] The individual as a *private being* may claim rights and responsibilities based on a personal worldview accepted by him or her, influenced by sources such as family, church or other associations. The individual as a *political being* (citizen), however, is subject to the publicly recognised rights and responsibilities relating to autonomy, equality and liberty, and these apply to how he or she must act towards others.[45]

[4.43] Rawls acknowledged that a strict approach to separation of beliefs from public reason may erode personal freedom, e.g. in cases involving the wearing of religious apparel or refusal

---

42   Rawls's four-stage process of establishing procedural justice are (1), determination of the good based on the First and Second Principles; (2), formulation of a constitution based on these Principles; (3), establishment of the legislature and rules forming the social structure of society; (4), Implementation of legislation by judicial and other officials.

43   *TJ*, 54; 295. See also Van Wyk, Chap 4, 80. Rawls says that

> ...this indeterminancy is not in itself a defect. It is what we should expect. Justice as fairness will prove a worthwhile theory if it defines the range of justice more in accordance with our considered jugdments than do existing theories, and if it singles out with greater sharpness the graver wrongs a society should avoid. (*TJ*, 176).

44   *LoP* 15; Freeman (2007a), 211–12, Freeman (1994), 664–5. (This article is reproduced in Freeman (2007b). Douzinas (2000), Chap. 9, makes the argument that rights create the person, not vice-versa.

45   *PL*, 12ff.

of immunisation, based on religious belief. Where actions impinge on others, he relies on the 'reasonableness' of liberal democracy, where citizens are 'willing to govern their conduct by a principle from which they and others can reason in common' for the general benefit of society.[46]

[4.44] Thus, in the case that liberties are themselves regulated, this must be within what Rawls calls the 'central range of application' of the basic liberties,[47] to preserve the fundamental aim of each liberty. Rawls does not define the term 'central range of application', but explains it by referring to freedom of speech. Rules of order are required for regulating free discussion (e.g. rules of debate and procedures of enquiry), and for social cohesion and prevention of harm such as defamation, incitement to crime or restriction of others' rights.[48] Otherwise, speech should not be curtailed.

[4.45] In relation to belief rights, the 'central range of application' can plausibly be explained by referring to the statement of the United Nations Human Rights Committee (UNHRC) that 'although a state might defend its culture and national religion, in doing so, it could not deviate from the fundamental common values elaborated in the Covenant'.[49]

Rawls: Perfectionist, Neutralist or neither?

[4.46] Perfectionist and neutralist paradigms were outlined in Chapter 1 ([1.43]ff.). Rawls considered the perfectionist paradigm a 'comprehensive doctrine', and draws a clear distinction between it and the narrower doctrine of justice as fairness.[50]

[4.47] Accordingly, political liberalism admits 'only those conceptions of the good...the pursuit of which is compatible with the principles of justice'.[51] Thus, there is a distinction between the comprehensive moral doctrine of perfectionism (in either the strict or the moderate sense) and the political paradigm of justice as fairness.

[4.48] Regarding neutrality, Rawls agreed with a neutrality where

> ...institutions and policies are neutral in the sense that they can be endorsed by citizens generally as within the scope of a public political conception....Justice as fairness is not pro-

---

46   *PL* 49 n 1.
47   Ibid, 295-6.
48   Ibid, 296.
49   UN Human Rights Committee, *Report of the Human Rights Committee Concluding Observations,* Sudan (UN Doc. CCPR/A/46/40, 1991), 517.
50   Rawls (2003), 14.
51   Ibid.141. For a fuller discussion see also Freeman (2007a), 147.

cedurally neutral. Principles of justice are substantive and express far more than procedural values and so do its political conceptions of society and person.[52]

[4.49] Neutrality, then, does not mean government is devoid of any moral values at all, or only values that regulate fair procedures. This, I conclude, means that while procedures for judgement and decision-making based on public reason aim to be neutral in effect respecting belief, public reason (and thus justice as fairness) is not devoid of values. It reflects a morality based on its public political culture, as opposed to morality based on personal worldviews.

[4.50] As most nations in the world have formally subscribed to a set of universal moral values as human rights, however, their acceptance means they are a political issue as well as a moral one.[53] Nations have purportedly accepted, as their public political culture, the principles and specific requirements spelt out in the Universal Declaration of Human Rights (UDHR). Rawls's view of political liberalism is based on these requirements.[54] As noted above, however, human rights have not been recognised in practice by all nations at all historical times, 'but only when development occurs to the extent that they can be effectively exercised'.[55]

Conclusion

[4.51] How, then, can we sum up Rawls's treatment of equality of freedom in relation to belief? As noted, Rawls formulated two Principles that underlie justice in a liberal democracy (see [3.15]). Through the development of a public political concept and its consequent overlapping consensus (discussed in Chapter 3), society has the makings of the 'adequate scheme of equal basic liberties'. The acceptance of the UDHR as an overlapping consensus for liberal democracy means that what Rawls says about essential human rights can be applied to the expanded list of rights it enumerates.

[4.52] Where the Principles of justice conflict, the First Principle 'trumps' the second. That means that while inequalities in wealth and power may limit the *extent* to which we can exercise our basic political rights, they never negate the *possession* of those rights themselves, or our entitlement to their full enjoyment. These are our political rights. They involve the maximisation of social and economic conditions for their exercise. Social and economic conditions that simply enhance prosperity and self-fulfilment are secondary to these.

---

52   *PL*, 192.
53   The political (as opposed to philosophical approach of Rawls is examined in Nickel and Reidy (2010), 61.
54   Arneson, et al (2006), 52.
55   Ibid, 47.

[4.53] Whilst the First Principle has been recognised as promoting liberty, it can be argued that this principle is as much about equality as liberty, as equality describes the liberty it promotes. It could be argued that the interrelationship between the two principles in fact makes it impossible to give preference to 'liberty' (which is also a term that depends for its meaning on its context) over 'equality'. Both factors depend, in their formulation, on each other. Rawls takes the principle of equality beyond equality of opportunity (which requires that all have an equal opportunity to acquire the goods of society despite being constrained by natural, social or economic differences). He proposes that those who are naturally advantaged through status, ability or circumstance should not benefit from their advantage to the detriment of those less fortunate. 'No one deserves his greater natural capacity nor merits a more favourable starting point in society.'[56] He thus recognises social and economic difference in society, and does not intend to eliminate it, but argues that it should he dealt with by the 'merit principle', so that

> no one gains or loses from his arbitrary place in the distribution of natural assets or his initial position in society without giving or receiving compensating advantages in return.[57]

[4.54] It is to be noted that Rawls did not see his theory as offering a pre-existing, inherent principle, like that of natural law, but rather a practical approach to the establishment of a just social order. It depends on objectivity, reason and reciprocity on the part of both government and citizens, rather than either the dictates of personal belief, or self-interest and the pursuit of power for its own sake. While this might be seen as impracticable, given the countervailing pressures of political ambitions and social circumstance, Rawls describes his model as 'realistically utopian,' that is, probing the limits of practicable political possibility.

[4.55] In this 'realistically utopian' model of society, the government is separate from belief. In other words, government should be secular. I consider the nature of state secularism in the following Chapter.

---

56   TJ 87.

57   *TJ,* 87. Rawls believed that all would be better able to 'improve their lot' in a society that places liberty above equality because various 'social primary goods (such as rights, liberties, powers, opportunities, income wealth and especially self-respect), are more likely to be attained in a free society. However liberty should be subject to the 'difference principle' that requires it to be modified by equality. He says this approach is preferable to its two chief competitors:

- •   natural liberty (presumably untrammelled freedom): because people benefit from morally irrelevant factors such as wealth and position; and

- •   equal opportunity: preferable, but still relying on morally irrelevant factors such as talent and opportunity to develop it.

His concession to equality, however, is that those who gain from natural talents or resources would not do so without contributing to the benefit of those not so fortunate.

CHAPTER 5
SECULARISM AND BELIEF

[5.1] Rawls argues that the state, in its policymaking and laws, should remain aloof from considerations of personal beliefs. I argue that the position he takes is one that implies a form of secularism – that is, state governance that is wholly disassociated from 'comprehensive doctrines'. Rather than purporting to favour them equally, the state doesn't favour them at all.[1] Religious and cultural considerations may be considered in the formulation of government policy, with the proviso that the fundamental principles of government are based on the liberal conception of justice.

What is secularism?

[5.2] The terms 'secular' and 'secularism' have been given various meanings and connotations that are significantly different in their implications.[2] Generally speaking, they have been used in one or more of the following three senses:

a) temporal or worldly considerations and activities undertaken by religious bodies or personnel, such as charitable works and the administration of church financial affairs;

b) a worldview and ethical code based on the present life, akin to the ideologies of humanism and rationalism, rooted in non-belief in the existence of the metaphysical or supernatural (Bielefeldt calls this '*doctrinal* secularism'[3]); or

c) indifference to, or the discounting of, religion or religious considerations by the state in the exercise of its power (Bielefeldt calls this '*political* secularism'[4]).

[5.3] Many authors have reviewed these three broad approaches in a variety of ways. Elizabeth Hurd[5] identifies two general uses of the term 'secularism' in modern democratic society. One (similar to (c)) she calls 'laïcism', which requires the separation from state prescriptive authority of religious considerations. Secularism in this sense is thus a structural notion. It embeds impartiality

---

1   See, e.g., *PL* 194.
2   See, e.g., An-Na'im (2005), 60ff, esp. 62-3, who canvasses the different meanings and applications of the concept of 'secular' and 'secularism'. See also, Mortensen (1995), 33ff; Barbier (2005); McKinnon (2007); Hurd (2008); Julian Baggini (2006); Anders Berg-Sørensen (2007); Weller (2006); Lindholm (2004), Ferrara (2009); 36ff, Muriel Fraser, 'Secularism' (2008), Concordat Watch ('Secularism'), <http://www.concordatwatch.eu>; András Sajó (2008); Wilkins (2010).
3   Bielefeldt (2012), 19.
4   Ibid.
5   Hurd (2008), 23ff.

in the governmental structure of society. Hurd (although wrongly, I will argue) associates this view of secularism with attempts to actively eliminate religion from public discussion.

[5.4] Hurd calls the second form of secularism, (b), 'Judeo-Christian secularism'. This form of secularism seeks to 'claim and reinforce the "secular" as a unique Western achievement that both distils and expresses the essence of Euro-American history'.[6] By adding a (Western, Christian) normative element to the nominal neutrality of the state, it infuses a specifically theological content. In this more qualified approach to state neutrality, 'secularism' purports to thwart sectarianism by nominally creating a level playing field between all religions, while identifying (whether formally or otherwise) with those of Judeo-Christian heritage.

[5.5] The evolution of international protection of belief rights in modern Europe has been described in terms of three successively realized, but partially overlapping, models of the state-religion relationship.[7] These are:

- the mono-religious model ('*cuius regio, eius religio*') model, when state sovereignty over religion was recognised, and one's religion was determined by the leadership of one's region or country (beginning in the sixteenth century);[8]

- the minority protection model where formally ethnic or religious states provided some protection of minority groups (in the 17th-19th centuries); and

- the twentieth century human rights model ensuring belief rights for all.

[5.6] While the first two models of government can exist in states that provide official privileged status to a particular religion, the last model requires the presence of a structurally secular government.

[5.7] The 'emancipation of positive law', then 'rupture of religious hegemony' and, finally, public schooling indifferent to religion, rendered religions free to blossom and specialise and differentiate in their own independent realm.[9] This freeing of religion from state intervention meant that

---

6   Ibid.
7   See, e.g., Lindholm (2004), 27-30; Malcolm Evans (2004), 11ff . Evans (1997), gives a comprehensive historical view of the development of the right to belief at Chaps 2-9.
8   This principle focused on the freedom of religion of the state, rather than the individual. See Evans (2004), 4ff.
9   Lindholm (2004), 36ff.

in a mature secular society no particular religion, life stance, or ideology is encumbered with the status, roles and liabilities of premodern hegemonic and more or less coercively implemented religion.[10]

[5.8] The international human rights treaties invoke a (modified) secular political structure based on humanitarian, rather than religious, values, albeit these values are compatible with some religions, as those values were agreed upon by the many nations ratifying them. These factors form the criteria for assessment as to their effectiveness.

Weller's four forms of secularism

[5.9] Paul Weller has pointed to what he sees as four different ways in which secularism appears in practice in modern nations.[11]

'Separation of Religion and State (with religiosity)'

[5.10] Weller identifies this model as the form that secularism takes in the US. It could be argued that a reason for the call in the early years of the newly forming American nation for separation of religion and state arose from problems associated with establishing a particular religion, reinforced, presumably, by the experience of establishment of a particular religion in England.

[5.11] However, there is a strong, albeit, multi-faceted, religious tradition in the US, with Christianity seen by a (diminishing) majority as deserving a privileged place in a society. A strong religious tradition means that separation of religion from the state has come to be seen as protection of religion from intervention by the state, with an emphasis on personal liberty over equality. This is based on a functional model of secularism, which sees religion as an integral part of society and thus of government, whose role is to facilitate its flourishing in the name of liberty. In Western nations, 'secularism' is skewed toward Judeo-Christian values, expressed as the form of Judeo-Christian model of secularism outlined by Hurd and described above.

'Pillarisation'

[5.12] A second form taken by secularism is 'pillarisation' ('*Verzuiling*')[12], which has been most evident in the Netherlands. 'Pillarisation' is a social structure that allows an individual to live his or her life wholly within a particular religious or secular social bloc, or 'pillar'. One can be educated, marry, find employment, subscribe to print and electronic media and participate in sport

---

10   Ibid, 38. This depends on the presence of other differentiated autonomous institutions such as positive law and democratic system of government.
11   Weller (2006), 32.
12   Weller (2006), 29; see also Rath (1999), 53.

and leisure activities solely within institutions established and regulated within one's religious bloc, independent of government. This approach can be socially divisive, with 'ghettoisation' and concentration on allegiance to the individual community rather than the nation as a whole. Weller argues that certain notorious murders and persecutions perpetrated by members of religious groups have shown some disadvantages of this model.[13] Pillarisation is considered by some to be no longer a current general practice in the Netherlands, as Dutch society changed from being 'vertically and hierarchically organised and pillarized' to being more horizontal and democratic from the 1960s.[14]

'Communalism'

[5.13] A third form of secularism noted by Weller is communalism, adopted in India by the Congress Party, in the face of violent sectarian uprisings. This involves the self-government of communal political units that arose from the hostile polarisation of politics between Hindus and Muslims.[15] Communal politics based on religious groups is the politics of religious identity, but communalism is not necessarily based on religion. It can just as easily be based on caste, culture or region.[16] Religious communalism in India, according to Achin Vanaik, is divisive:

> ...a process involving competitive de-secularization (a competitive striving to extend the reach and power of religions), which – along with non-religious factors – helps to harden the divisions between different religious communities and increase tensions between them.[17]

[5.14] The central Indian government is meant to be a bulwark against communalism, but it is interventionist and insufficiently discriminating: 'it has all too often lapsed readily into a posture of actively balancing communalisms'.[18] It appears to vacillate between contradictory policies of promoting no religion and promoting them all equally, though not always effectively.[19]

'Secularist Secular Tradition'

[5.15] While they are based on constitutional provisions for secularism, in practice the Dutch and Indian models of secularism are less well delineated than that of the US, with its formal, constitutional non-establishment of religion. However, Weller's fourth model is less ambiguous, and one that can be compared and contrasted directly with that of the US. Weller argues that the

---

13   See e.g., Weller (2006), 29ff.
14   van Mierlo (1996). Vink (2007), also refutes the idea that pillarisation lasted past the 1970s.
15   McLean and McMillan, *The Concise Oxford Dictionary of Politics* (Oxford, Oxford University Press 2003), 96.
16   Vanaik (1992), 48.
17   Ibid, 50.
18   ibid, 61.
19   Weller (2006), 33.

secularist secular tradition is found in the French revolutionary republican tradition that has given rise to the current use by that Government of the separationist principle of *laïcité*.

[5.16] In contrast to the US, where 'separation is combined with a high degree of religiosity in public life',[20] in France separation is associated with an ethos that is strongly opposed to 'contamination' of the state by religion.[21]

[5.17] In Europe in the 18th Century, particularly in France, the momentum for secularism came from movements against the state-established power of the Church[22] (specifically, in France, the Catholic Church).[23] Secularism has there been invoked to mean independence of political authority from religious and other ideologies or worldviews. In the US and the Northern European countries (which inherited a Protestant culture), the emergence of modernity was associated with state promotion of religion (albeit not dictating any particular one). Conversely, in France, modernity was pitted *against* state promotion of religion, particularly the Catholic Church. Consequently, the Enlightenment proved more radical in France than in surrounding countries.[24] Most importantly, this has led to the more robust view of secularism as separation of religion and state ('*laïcité*') in France than in other countries, including the US, despite its Constitutional provision for non-establishment. I would argue that Rawls's view of the relationship between religion and the State is closer to the French approach of *laïcité*, with a stricter separation than that of the US.

Secularism as Political Structure

[5.18] Both the US and France have adopted forms of political structure consistent with what Allessandro Ferrara[25] and Heiner Bielefeldt[26] call 'political secularism'. This Ferraro defines as 'the fact that all citizens can freely express their religious freedom and worship one God, another God or no God at all, and the fact that the churches and the state are neatly separated'. Religions must 'never invoke support from the state's coercive power, never pretend to turn sin into crime and always allow their believers to turn to another religion or no religion'.[27] Rawls's public political culture is based on this idea of political secularism, without which equal enjoyment of belief rights cannot be ensured.

---

20   Ibid, 26.
21   Ibid, 27.
22   Lindholm (2004), 19, 26ff.
23   See, e.g., Pena-Ruiz (2005), esp ch. 2, 3.
24   Jean Baubérot (2004), 441, 441-2.
25   Ferrara (2009).
26   Bielefeldt (2012), 18ff.
27   Ibid, 78.

[5.19] Ferrara claims that secularism seen from this political perspective allows us to perceive our erstwhile blindness to where supposedly secular governance is subject to religious influence or unjust historical contexts.[28] We become aware of government symbolism (iconic or linguistic), rituals (such as religious rituals as part of formal government proceedings), policies that have arisen in religious or other belief customs and teachings, or privileged treatment based on belief. By insisting that government recognition of social history and culture (including religion) is subject to the proviso that these comply with the liberal conception of justice, and his advocacy of state-church separation, I argue that Rawls attests to his agreement with this approach.

[5.20] Maurice Barbier writing on *laïcité*, claims that in attempting to be fair by actively treating all beliefs equally, Government impartiality may be ruled out by sleight of hand – and become even non-existent – in the cause of tolerance and harmony.[29] It is thus not a form of neutrality at all (indeed, I argue in Chapter 13 that a neutral outcome is not feasible). Barbier maintains that, where government adopts a policy of state-belief separation, values such as freedom of religion and conscience, pluralism and tolerance follow naturally, and are necessary (and more stable) consequences of it.[30] He concludes that, for the sake of a clear and general understanding, the term secularism should maintain a negative character, being a political structure in which religion is irrelevant.[31] In other words, '*Laïcité* is not an opinion; [or belief] it is the freedom to have one'.[32] This is its one simple principle.

[5.21] Two main consequences arise when secularism is operative as this one principle. Firstly, individuals as citizens have the right to express their beliefs, whatever they may be, through worship, observance, practice and teaching. Secondly, that right is matched by a duty to maintain the secular structure of the state, by (a) recognising the same right for others, restricting their own actions to provide for this, and (b) ensuring a politically secular mechanism for state governance.

[5.22] Bielefeldt points out that political secularism is a 'second order' principle, deriving its persuasiveness from 'something superior', a 'first order principle': in this case that of belief rights.[33]

[5.23] The difference in their history has meant that in the US 'religion has been integral to the emergence of modernity', whereas in France 'modernity erected itself against religion'.[34] In

---

28   Ibid, 79.
29   Barbier (2005), 4.
30   Ibid, 7, 14.
31   Ibid, 14. See also Troper (2000), 1267.
32   '*La laïcité n'est pas une opinion, c'est la liberté d'en avoir une.*' Matisson (2003), 3. See also Bielefeldt (2012), 12.
33   Bielefeldt (2012), 12.
34   Baubérot (2004), 441.

other words, in the US, the emphasis is on protecting religion from the state, whereas in France, the emphasis is on protecting the state from religion.[35]

[5.24] The understanding of secularism as a political structure – not a philosophy in itself but a means for freedom to adopt any philosophy – is, I believe, to be preferred in the consideration of belief rights. András Sajó describes secularism in these terms:

> Secularism is a form of ordered political coexistence that does not admit of according preference to, or allowing domination by, religious, social, or political groups. This requires that citizens be somewhat loyal to the state or, at least, not stand actively against it.[36]

[5.25] This approach paves the way for full recognition by the state of the right of individuals to provide their own moral agenda through the adoption of religious and philosophical doctrines, with the proviso that they are in accordance with the obligations of citizenship:

> Without equality in the sense of non-discriminatory implementation, rights of freedom would amount to freedom for the happy few.[37]

Secularism and Rawls

Rawls fails to recognise his endorsement of political secularism

[5.26] When asked in an interview with Bernard Prusak in 1998, Rawls emphatically denied that he was making a veiled argument for secularism.[38] But it is important to note that *Rawls considered secularism as being similar to other philosophies and doctrines as 'reasoning in terms of comprehensive non-religious doctrines'*.[39] Consequently, he said '...a central feature of political liberalism is that it views all [secular arguments] as philosophical in the same way it views religious ones, and therefore these secular philosophical doctrines do not provide public reasons [for justifying public policy and legislation]'.[40] As I have argued, the philosophical conception of secularism as a belief, with a set of moral values similar to religious doctrines, is only one interpretation among many that have been given to the idea of 'secularism'.

[5.27] While he may have considered 'secularism' to denote a philosophy, Rawls's approach to the political conception of justice has endorsed a political structure akin to political secularism: government institutions and procedures that ensure separation of the state from the influence of

---

35   Scott (2008), 2.
36   Sajó (2008), 619.
37   Bielefeldt (2012), 9.
38   Prusak (1998).
39   Rawls (2005d), 452 (emphasis added).
40   Ibid, 458.

personal beliefs. I maintain that his was a clear argument for political secularism, and his model of society is the poorer for its failure to unveil this tacit endorsement.

[5.28] Consequently, Rawls's approach can be usefully compared with the position on secularism adopted by the French Government – *laïcité* – that gives precedence to the separation from belief of government through public reason. As a result, both the relevance of Rawls's work concerning (a) secularism as a structural foundation of democratic and pluralist societies and (b) its usefulness in understanding belief rights, may not have been fully appreciated.

[5.29] My argument, then, is that Rawls in effect assumes a similar, though perhaps not identical, position on the relationship between the citizen and the state as that held by the French:

> Reasonable comprehensive doctrines, religious or non-religious, may be introduced in public political discussion at any time, provided that in due course proper political reasons… are presented that are sufficient to support whatever the comprehensive doctrines introduced are said to support.[41]

[5.30] The proviso rules out the use of religious and other comprehensive doctrines in the political forum to support measures not supportable by public reason.[42] This is the foundation of the citizen's 'duty of civility', the moral duty of citizens and political officials to make their case for the policies and laws they advocate in accordance with public reason.

The belief tribunals and secularism

[5.31] The belief tribunals are the bodies set up by the ICCPR and ECHR to hear allegations of breaches of the rights they proclaim. They consist of the United Nations Human Rights Committee, and the European Court of Human Rights, (as well as the former European Commission on Human Rights). The UNHRC has not specifically described secularism as necessary for ensuring belief rights, nor has it held constitutional secularism a reason for the government to limit manifestation of belief. There is no formal UN interpretation of the word 'secular' or 'secularism' for the purposes of belief rights. The meaning of 'secularism' has not been definitively described by the European Court either, and remains very general and imprecise. However, the Court has considered the importance of secularism in the French and Turkish context, where secularism is constitutionally guaranteed, and considered in terms of *laïcité*.

---

41   Rawls (2005d), 462ff. People who argue and vote for their views only on the basis of their religious and other comprehensive doctrines without regard to the requirements of public reason are being unreasonable and violating a moral/political duty. Freeman (2007a), 412.

42   'Citizens must vote for the ordering of political values they sincerely think the most reasonable. Otherwise they fail to exercise the political power in ways that satisfy the criterion of reciprocity': Rawls (2005d), 479.

Secularism and Religious Apparel

[5.32] A particularly controversial issue arising from claims that prohibition of the wearing of the Islamic hijab, niqab or burqua restricts manifestation of belief. In the case of *Leyla Şahin v Turkey* (2005), the Court said that 'secularism, as the guarantor of democratic values', is 'the meeting point of liberty and equality'…it prevents the state from 'manifesting a preference for a particular religion or belief' guiding the state in its role as 'independent arbiter', and 'necessarily entailing freedom of religion and conscience'.[43]

[5.33] The applicant in that case, Leyla Şahin, a university student, alleged that regulations prohibiting the wearing of the 'Islamic headscarf' in the university she attended violated her belief rights under Article 18. The European Court upheld findings by the national court that the constitutional system attached prime importance to the protection of women's rights. It noted the national court's opinion that for those who favoured secularism, the Islamic headscarf had become the symbol of a political Islam, risking undermining order and causing unrest on campus, and that each Contracting State may, in accordance with the Convention provisions, take a stance against such political movements, based on its historical experience.[44]

[5.34] The European Court agreed that secularism was one of the fundamental principles of the Turkish State, and is in harmony with the rule of law and respect for human rights and democracy. Secularism in Turkey, it held, exemplified democratic values and the principle that freedom of religion is inviolable. It was based on the principle that citizens are equal, and protected the individual not only against arbitrary interference by the State but also from external pressure from extremist movements. Consequently, freedom to manifest one's religion could be restricted in order to defend those values. The Court concluded that this notion of secularism was consistent with the values underpinning the ECHR. Upholding that system could be considered necessary to protect the democratic system in Turkey.[45]

[5.35] Further, the Court approved the Turkish Constitutional Court ruling that allowing pupils to wear the Islamic headscarf is incompatible with the principle of secularism since the headscarf is in the process of becoming 'the symbol of a vision that is contrary to women's freedom and the fundamental principles of a secular state'.[46]

---

43   At ¶ 113. For a detailed argument along these lines see Hammond and Mazur (1955).
44   *Leyla Şahin v Turkey*, ¶¶115ff.
45   *Leyla Şahin v Turkey* ¶114; See also *Dogru v France* (2008), ¶66.
46   Ibid ¶¶37, 93.

[5.36] The Court did not state that secularism or laïcité is *mandated* by the ECHR. Rather, it is currently mandated by the Constitution of Turkey. It is noted that the political climate in Turkey is changing, so further judgments as to the state-belief relationship may take a different approach.

[5.37] The wearing of the Islamic head coverings in educational institutions first became an issue in France in 1989.[47] The responsible French Minister referred to 3,000 such cases when addressing the Senate in 1994. He produced a report for the President of the Republic on 11 December 2003. The picture it presented of the perceived threat to secularism, it said, 'bordered on the alarming'.[48] It claimed that instances of behaviour and conduct that run counter to the principle of secularism are on the increase, particularly in public society. The reasons for this were said to be difficulties experienced by Islamic immigrants to France in integrating, the living conditions in many suburbs, unemployment and feelings of alienation and discrimination. Consequently, the immigrants were responsive to encouragement to reject the values of the Republic and were consequently considered a threat to Republican authority that called for its reinforcement, especially in schools. The Report went on to say:

> [F]or the school community…the visibility of a religious sign is perceived by many as contrary to the role of school, which should remain a neutral forum and a place where the development of critical faculties is encouraged. It also infringes the principles and values that schools are there to teach, in particular, equality between men and women.

[5.38] In the case of *Dogru v France*, the applicant, a schoolteacher in charge of a class of small children, wore a veil that covered her face except for the eyes. In considering her right to do so, the Court questioned what a 'powerful external symbol such as the wearing of a headscarf might have on the freedom of conscience and religion of young children, who were more easily influenced, and its proselytising effect',[49] as it appeared to be imposed on women by religious authority. Moreover, it held, it is hard to reconcile with the principle of gender equality.[50] A further consideration, not mentioned by the Court, is the absence of visibility of the teacher's mouth, which eliminates a source of learning for young children in pronunciation and aids those with hearing deficits.

[5.39] The Court elsewhere said:

---

47   *Dogru v France*, (2008) ¶21.

48   Conseil D'État : *Commission de Reflexion sur l'application du Principe de Laïcité dans la Republique*, November 2003 (Commission to consider the Application of the Principle of Secularity in the Republic), (the 'Stasi Commission'), cited in *Dogru v France* (2008), ¶21.

49   *Dogru v France* (2008), ¶40.

50   Ibid, ¶64.

[T]he principle of secularism is certainly one of the fundamental principles of the State which are in harmony with the rule of law and respect for human rights and democracy. An attitude which fails to respect that principle will not necessarily be accepted as being covered by the freedom to manifest one's religion and will not enjoy the protection of Article 9 of the Convention.[51]

[5.40] It is important to note that neither tribunal found that wearing of religious symbols such as headwear is contrary to democratic society *per se*. Whether and how a state regulates this is a matter of discretion dependent on the domestic context, as action to protect the principle of secularism 'falls squarely within the margin of appreciation [discretion] of the state', as the state is best placed to evaluate local needs and conditions and educational requirements.[52] This discretion is considered by the Court to be particularly appropriate in dealing with the wearing of religious symbols in educational institutions, as there is no uniform European conception of 'public order' or 'protection of the rights of others', and must be left up to the State concerned. A balance must be found between protection of belief rights, recognition of the rights of others, and preservation of public order .[53]

[5.41] Accordingly, the Court has accepted that regulation of educational institutions may vary in time and in place according to the needs and resources of the community and competent authorities must be left some discretion in this sphere.[54] Rawls's term 'imperfect procedural justice' comes to mind (see above [3.33]ff.).

[5.42] In the case of *S.A.S. v France* (2014), just decided at time of writing, the European Court considered government prohibition of identity-concealing head covering in public places. It agreed with the government that concealment of the face is incompatible with the civility required for social interaction necessary for living together. This interaction between individuals, in the government's view is an essential expression of tolerance and broadmindedness essential for democratic society. Barriers to equitable social interaction result from a large portion of the populace wearing identity-concealing face covering. The Court held it was a legitimate ground for government prohibition of identity-concealing headgear in public places, whether or not there is also a need to do so for security measures.[55] In the *S.A.S.* case, the Court ruled that the government was entitled to a 'margin of appreciation', in this instance meaning discretion in

---

51   Ibid, ¶72.
52   Ibid ¶75. For further discussion of the margin of appreciation see below.
53   *Leyla Şahin v Turkey* (2005), esp, ¶109-110; *Dahlab v Switzerland* (2001), esp. p.12 electronic copy; *Dogru v France* (2008), esp., ¶¶71-5.
54   *Leyla Şahin v Turkey* (2005), ibid. The ECHR has held that public order 'varied on account of national characteristics'. *Manoussakis and Others v Greece* (1996), ¶39. Yourow, esp. 188ff.
55   *S.A.S. v France* (2014) at [140]ff..

determining what is necessary for living in a democratic society such as France. The 'margin of appreciation' is considered more fully below at [11.9].

Public Service

[5.43] Cases referring to limitation of religious activity for the purpose of upholding secularism have involved duties relating to public service. Examples are the military, government institutions, or political parties in states where the principle of secularism is constitutionally established, and where the government's principle of secularism is compromised. In the military, for instance, cases such as *Kalaç v Turkey* (1997) and *Başpinar v Turkey* (2001) involved the removal of personnel for their involvement in a fundamentalist sect that promoted the pre-eminence of religious rules. The court found that the applicants were not dismissed for their religious opinions and beliefs, or their performance of religious duties (which was allowed) but because their conduct in promoting their religion 'breached military discipline and infringed the principle of secularism'.[56]

[5.44] In equating secularism with democracy, the European Council and Court have thus indicated that consideration can be given to promotion of secularism by the state in deciding what is 'necessary in a democratic society'. This presupposes that government denominational impartiality is a valid basis for limiting manifestation of belief. Nevertheless, the European Court has also recently emphasised that intervention by the state to preserve the secular nature of the political regime must be considered necessary in a democratic society.[57]

[5.45] Despite warnings that failure to respect secularism potentially violates Article 9, Malcolm Evans, among others, lamented what he saw as increasing breadth allowed by the Court for government discretion.[58] Evans holds that while the formal structure within which belief rights operate does not predetermine a particular outcome, the European Court has shifted its approach from allowing the state 'no direct role in the religious life of believers'. Instead of emphasising 'that the state could only intervene to ensure a level playing field between believers', the Court has 'come to see the role of the state as being to ensure that the playing fields were level in the first place'.[59] He argues that it now countenances a more proactive, interventionist

---

56   In *Kalaç v Turkey* (1997), the court found that the applicant (1), belonged to and participated in the activities of the Süleyman community, which was known to have unlawful fundamentalist tendencies; (2), had given it legal assistance, taken part in training sessions and had intervened on a number of occasions in the appointment of servicemen who were members of the sect; (3), carried out instructions from the leaders of the sect (¶30). In *Başpinar v Turkey* (2001), the applicant, a non-commissioned officer, was a member of the Nakşibendi sect. He adopted extreme religious ideology and his superiors considered him an undisciplined and insubordinate soldier.

57   *Refah Partisi (the Welfare Party), and Others v Turkey* (2003), ¶93.

58   Malcolm Evans (2008), 300ff. See also Taylor (2005), 184ff.; Harris, et al (1995), 479ff.

59   Evans, ibid, 300.

and restrictive approach by engaging with religions as institutions, rather than dealing only with individuals claiming their rights had been interfered with.

> Thus in parallel with the cases concerning the rights of individuals, the court was also facing series of cases concerning the registration and official recognition of religious leaders, communities and churches.[60]

[5.46] Evans seems concerned that the Court has moved too far towards requiring religious manifestation to be 'compatible with the underpinnings of the ECHR system, these being democracy and human rights'. This, he says, means that the principles of respect, pluralism and tolerance are no longer understood to mean so much as 'respect by others *for* religion but respect *by* religions for others.[61] Thus, he concludes, the Court construes any forms of manifestation that do not exhibit respect for religion as a threat to the values of the ECHR system. Consequently, the Court endorses secularism as a 'tangible manifestation of neutrality'.[62]

[5.47] This, Evans argues, 'amounts to an attempt to brush aside the reality of church–state relations and with it a foundational element of national identity in member states of the Council of Europe'.[63] This differs from the more individualist former approach, which

> did not prevent the privileging of a form of religion in the public life (or of excluding all religions from public life) provided that all individuals were in fact capable of enjoying their freedom of religion or belief.[64]

[5.48] 'Indeed', Evans maintains,

> one might be tempted to conclude that such an approach makes Article 9 as much a tool for restraining the manifestation of religion or belief as it is a means of upholding it.[65]

[5.49] My argument is that this is *precisely* the purpose of Article 9. The limitations expressed by the belief provisions form an essential part in defining the liberties they express. Evans misreads the purpose of political secularism, it seems, seeing it as somehow restrictive of religious practice. Instead, as this book contends, it is the most effective way of ensuring equal belief rights for all. Moreover, despite Evans's view that the Court discriminates against religion, the Court has in

---

60   Ibid, 301.
61   Ibid, 303.
62   Ibid, 306.
63   Ibid, 303.
64   Ibid, 305.
65   Ibid, 308

fact sometimes taken a more conciliatory approach to the 'national identity' of states through recognition of religious sensitivities (see, e.g. Chapter 11).

[5.50] One can appreciate the argument Evans puts forward when one considers the contrasting approaches of the cosmopolitan-leaning European Court and more religion-favouring UNHRC as illustrated by the approach of *Shingara Mann Singh,* ([11.70]) and *S.A.S v France* ([5.42]). Nevertheless, while individual decisions of the Court may lead to controversy, preservation of a balance between the liberties and limitations of Artifle 9 is a concern of the Court. Lindholm[66] disagrees with Evans's argument that there has been a diminution in the importance of achieving belief rights by its incorporation into human rights.[67] He states that it instead 'constitutes an elevation of internationally binding protection of freedom of religion or belief so as to properly fit the structural constraints and cultural dynamics of modern societies'.[68] Binding protection of belief rights, it is argued, accords with Rawls's idea of procedural justice.

[5.51] Evans appears to be proposing an approach that privileges religion and presumes a special bond between Church and State.[69] One may disagree with the Court's ruling in individual cases, arguing that its approach to limitation of manifesting belief provides too much or too little discretion to the state (which may occur particularly in those cases relating to the wearing of religious symbols and allegedly offensive speech). However, it is proposed that *procedural justice,* borne of true state impartiality ('separation') as proposed by Rawls, is not incompatible with a just and fair recognition of belief. Individual outcomes may cause disagreement, but the rules for getting there, in a liberal democracy, should be rules that are acceptable to, and apply equally to, everyone.

Conclusion

[5.52] While many states claim to be 'secular', the terms 'secular' and 'secularism' have been given different connotations in different contexts. I have proposed the term 'political secularism', to what I argue should be the model of secularism as practised by the state. This involves a separation of the state from the dictates and practices of religious or other belief. It requires indifference to, or the discounting of, religion or religious considerations by the state in the exercise of its power. It requires a separation between the political conception of what is right, that is, values that apply to government, and personal moral values, that one applies generally to the conduct of

---

66   See, Lindholm (2004), esp. Parts C and E.

67   Evans (2008), 312ff. He criticises the Court's holding in *Refah Partisi (the Welfare Party), v Turkey (2001),* that Shari'ah is 'difficult to reconcile with the fundamental principles of democracy' as itself 'difficult to accommodate ...within an approach which focuses on the neutrality of the state in matters of religion, and endorses secularism as a tangible manifestaton of neutrality. My argument is that structural secularism, which denies the institutional inequality which sharia and other religions would enforce, is in fact wholly *compatible* with democracy: see ibid 305ff.

68   Ibid.

69   See Malcolm Evans (2008).

personal activities. Political secularism is in line with Rawls's stipulation that the coercive power of the state is to be justified on the grounds of compliance with the public political conception of justice. Separation, as opposed to neutralism, as the basis of state-belief relations, is considered in Chapter 13.

[5.53] As demonstrated, the European Court has considered constitutionally guaranteed secularism is consistent with the principles of citizen equality and autonomy, the rule of law, respect for human rights and democracy. Secularism, says the Court, prevents both arbitrary interference by the State and the unwanted influence of religious sects and belief-influenced movements. While freedom to manifest one's belief should be modified in order to defend secularism, however, it does give states some discretion in line with the social context of the action in question (see Chapter 11).

[5.54] Given the above groundwork for a secular state-belief relationship, however, consideration of how states currently deal with belief organisations and their members generally is called for. This is considered in Chapter 6.

CHAPTER 6
BELIEF PROVISIONS AND STATE-BELIEF ALLIANCE

[6.1] Given that all 197 members of the UN have subscribed to the basic liberties set out in the UDHR, one can ask, well, *shouldn't the enjoyment of basic liberties be universal?* Sadly, as indicated, this is not the case. Despite the International treaties on human rights, and their establishment of what is in effect an overlapping consensus throughout the world, there is little evidence of the realisation of the promise of belief rights, anywhere near the ideal form outlined by Rawls.

[6.2] This is the case even where states provide for secularism and/or belief rights, either in their constitutions or other legislation, be it in terms of separation of Church and state, state secularism, or freedom of religion or belief. Some of these states are members of the OIC, with its perverse adoption of the Cairo Declaration. There is a wide variety of state involvement with religion.

[6.3] Relying on sources,[1] it is estimated that of the world's nations there are about 10 theocratic states that mandate, prohibit, or interfere with the practice of alternative beliefs.[2] Over 40 states have a specific religion officially established by government with varying toleration of others[3] and, where relevant, these generally require the monarch, head of state or government to be of a given religion.[4] There are at least 113 states (nominally secular or otherwise) without an established religion or belief, with varying state accommodation of religion such as the US, France and Turkey). Some states show varying degrees of hostility to religion or belief, or subject particular beliefs to state control or suppression.[5] State-belief relationships are hard to categorise, as they are volatile, changing over time, as witnessed by the recent Middle East political disturbances, so these figures are generalisations only.

[6.4] Thus, states may be nominally secular but blend the roles of religious institutions and beliefs with those of the state. They may establish a state church while formally permitting free-

---

1   The following draws on information from O'Brien and Palmer (2007), 47; Carolyn Evans (2001), 20-21 and Kuru (2007), 570.

2   E.g., Iran, Saudi Arabia, Jordan, the Holy See.

3   E.g., Greece, U.K., Iceland, Holy See, Denmark, Scotland, Bulgaria, Bolivia, Paraguay and Argentina (Christianity); Iran, Iraq, Algeria, Libya, Morocco and Bangladesh (Muslim); Nepal (Hinduism), Bhutan (Buddhism). The U.K. has established the Church of England to the extent that the monarch is the supreme governor of the Church, the House of Lords includes bishops from the Church and no other Church, certain public ceremonies such as coronations follow Church ritual and the law specifies the religious affiliation of Royalty. Barro and McCleary (2005) at p. 1336 state that of 188 countries surveyed, 113 had a state religion in 2000.

4   E.g., Algeria, Argentina, Norway, Denmark, Libya Pakistan, Greece.

5   E.g., China, Vietnam, Myanmar, North Korea, Turkmenistan.

dom of religion,[6] or provide constitutionally that there will be no state church, but nevertheless involve themselves with religion.[7] States may have exclusive legislation setting out special financial, property or other conditions and/or privileges for one or several denominations, whether or not they establish the particular denomination as a state religion.[8] They may provide special privileges to a particular church through agreement, as in Spain, which has a concordat with the Catholic Church providing for a number of financial or other special privileges not provided to other religious institutions.[9]

[6.5] Finally, there are countries with a strong separation of religion and state, at least in principle. For example, despite recent leanings in government towards religion, Turkey has a strong secularist constitution of which the preamble states 'as required by the principle of secularism, sacred religious feelings shall in no way be permitted to interfere with state affairs and politics'. Section 24 allows freedom of religion but prohibits the use of religious beliefs for personal or political influence to any extent 'basing the fundamental social, economic, political, and legal order of the State on religious tenets'. Article 68 prohibits programs that conflict with the 'principles of the democratic and secular Republic'.

[6.6] France's Constitution in its preamble [Article 1] describes France as a Republic, 'indivisible, secular, democratic and social'.[10] Legislation, after providing for belief rights, states in section 2 that the state does not 'recognise, salary nor subsidise any religion'.[11] Fiji has recently (November, 2013) installed a constitution that provides for a secular state, with strongly worded separation provisions. These prohibit government privileging of religion, and preferment of 'other beliefs' besides religious beliefs in appointment of officials. It is proposed that this is the preferred approach to establishing belief rights in Chapter 14.

---

6   The 'Evangelical Church of Iceland shall be the National Church in Iceland and shall, as such, be supported and protected by the State': *Constitution of the Republic of Iceland* No. 33, 17 June 1944 (as amended), art 63, cited in Carolyn Evans (2001), 20.

7   Ibid. The Basic Law of Germany (1949), states that 'there shall be no state church' (however its preamble refers to 'responsibility before God and humankind', and the state enforces church taxes). The Constitution of Ukraine also, while invoking 'responsibility before God' states that the church and religious organisations are to be separate from the state and school (though the Ukrainian Constitution has been, and is currently, in a state of flux). Ireland, has no formally established religion but establishes religion de facto by invoking religion in the Constitution and enforcing religious values.

8   Legislation has established particular Churches as institutions, granting property rights, exclusive financial or unconventional corporate arrangements.

9   For a current commentary on Concordats see <http//www.concordatwatch.eu>.

10   Carolyn Evans (2001), 20.

11   *Loi du Décembre 1905 Concernant la Séparation des Églises et de L'État* (Journal Officiel du 11 décembre 1905). Article 2 abolishes all state spending on religious activity.

[6.7] Despite the ubiquity of governments' involvement in religion, most states (with the notable exception of Islamic nations) have some form of legislative prohibition on discrimination on the grounds of religious belief. Despite this, as Carolyn Evans points out, in respect of European countries, there is no consensus that this commitment requires the separation of church and state or necessarily leads to disestablishment.[12] This also applies across the world.

State-belief relationships Compared

[6.8] W. Cole Durham has developed taxonomy for classifying different state-belief approaches to freedom of religion that is a useful reference point in setting out my argument for a secular government.[13] This description is set out in the following list of possible regimes:

Table 5: State-belief Regimes

'Established-church' regimes	Include theocracies; state monopoly of religious affairs, with limited or no toleration of minority groups (e.g. some Islamic states); state church, but theoretical belief rights for all (e.g. U.K., Greece).
'Endorsed-church' regimes	Include states with formally endorsed (but not established) particular religion, which is favoured and politically influential.
'Cooperationalist' regimes	Include states that fund and favour particular religion(s) without constitutional or other formal endorsement. May be through concordats (e.g. Spain, Italy and Poland) or policies (e.g. German 'church tax' of members of mainstream religions).
'Accommodationist' regimes	Include states with formal state-belief separation, but '[N]o qualms about recognizing the importance of religion as part of national or local culture, accommodating religious symbols in public settings, allowing tax, dietary, holiday, Sabbath and other kinds of exemptions, and so forth'.
'Separationist' regimes	Clearer and rigorous separation of roles. Prohibit state support or funding of any religious activity, as well as any appearance of influence over, or identity with, any religious group. The same applies for religious groups *vis-à-vis* the state. Religion considered a strictly private matter, and totally divorced from public affairs.

[6.9] Because church-state relationships are flexible and can change over time, Durham recognises a continuum between total theocracy and total separation of church and state. He points out, however, that in practice the situation cannot be expressed in a simple single scale from

12   Carolyn Evans (2001), 22.
13   Durham (1996), 21-25.

theocracy to separation. Repression of religion can occur even where there is constitutional separation of church and state where it takes the form of intolerance of religion, such as occurred under USSR state atheism.[14]

[6.10] Establishment or endorsement of a religion by a state will very often result in any freedoms being nevertheless exercised within the *shadow* of the majority values and beliefs. Nations may identify themselves, whether formally (as has the UK) or by implication (as has Australia[15]), as 'Judeo-Christian'. They may identify themselves formally (as has Iran) or by implication (as has Indonesia) as 'Islamist'. There may be either subtle or more overt marginalisation of those who do not belong to the majority belief. Where there is no clear separation of state and belief, any freedom is nevertheless exercised under the influence of state-endorsed or majority religious or ethical beliefs. In some countries, people have to 'quietly' and covertly practise their religion.[16]

[6.11] Durham outlines state patterns of inadvertent legislative or bureaucratic hostility, subtle or not-so-subtle privileging of mainline or dominant groups, and overt persecution. These can occur within the different regimes listed above.[17] Western nations, for example, mostly include features of 'endorsed', 'cooperationalist' and 'accommodationist' regimes.

[6.12] Of his models set out above, Durham prefers the 'accommodationist regime', claiming that history shows this to provide maximum belief rights. He maintains that 'substantial' belief rights can be achieved in 'cooperationalist' or 'endorsed-church' regimes, but concedes that minority groups will be marginalised and lack resources for functioning where funding goes to major churches, which members of the minority groups may feel thus coerced to support.

---

14   See, e.g., Bowman (1996), 289.

15   See, e.g. the Speech by his Excellency the then Governor-General of Australia to the Anglican Synod, Government House Canberra, 24 October 2007, at <http://www.gg.gov.au/speech.php/view/id/290/title/reception-for-anglican-synod>; Maddox (2010), 16.

16   In the case of *Applicant NABD of 2002 v Minister for Immigration and Multicultural and Indigenous Affairs* (2005), a refugee applicant was returned to his home country despite the need to hide his religious beliefs for fear of persecution. Kirby J, dissenting, said at, ¶113:

> Reading the [ICCPR] in the context of international human rights law, specifically as that law defends freedom of religion, helps to demonstrate why the imposition of a requirement that a person must be "discreet", "quiet", "low profile" and not "conspicuous" is incompatible with the objects of the Convention, properly understood. True, the human rights of the applicant for protection must be accommodated to the human rights of other individuals, both in the country of nationality and in the country in which protection is sought. Violent, aggressive or persistently non-consensual conduct "for reasons of … religion" are not protected by the Convention, any more than by other instruments of international law. Yet neither is it an answer to an assertion of a "fear" of being "persecuted for reasons of …religion" that such "fear" is not "well-founded" because it can be avoided by the behavioural expedients of discretion, quietness, maintaining a "low profile" and so forth. Such an approach is incompatible with the inclusion of religious freedom in the Convention.

17   Durham (1996), 23.

[6.13] Durham rejects a stronger separationist approach, dismissing its argument that religious beliefs should not receive special treatment on the ground that 'differential treatment does not necessarily violate equality norms if there is a rational basis for the differentiation'.[18] His approach appears to be based on the view that there is not merely a rational basis, but a *compelling justification* for some form of accommodation in the case of religious belief. His conclusion states: 'On the religious freedom gradient, history has demonstrated that a "rule of law" constraint on permissible limitations on manifestations of religious freedom is not adequate'.[19] He quotes with approval James Madison, to emphasise this point: 'One of the most important features of religious liberty – one that makes it a fundamental and inalienable right – is that it is prior, "both in order of time and in degree of obligation, to the claims of Civil Society"'.[20] In the context of his writing, Durham would appear to be giving religious expression a pre-eminence over other rights and arguably the rule of law because of an inherent quality it possesses.[21]

[6.14] No doubt religion can provide social benefits to individuals, such as giving meaning to life, inspiring charitable works and providing values to live by, identity among significant others and solace to peoples' lives in times of crisis. The benefits they experience are recognised. However, Durham does not cite any demonstrable and unique contribution religion makes to society (as opposed to, say, non-religious humanitarian practices) that earns it a pre-eminent claim to protection over other rights, such as those of freedom of expression, assembly and association. Whilst religious beliefs may contribute to social cohesion, harmony and good order, non-religious beliefs can be just as effective.[22] My argument is about favouring religion *per se,* not charitable works.

[6.15] Durham's reference to 'compelling' justification invokes the test set out in the US *Religious Freedom Restoration Act* ('RFRA') of 1990. That Act provided that the Government was not

---

18   Ibid, 24. See also Ahdar and Leigh (2004), who argue, for example, that a 'weak' form of establishment is consistent with religious freedom, and that 'an historic religion supported by a majority of citizens performing valuable social, educational and cultural functions might well be more 'deserving' in a broad sense of state assistance than a recent, tiny, insular community' (at pp. 671-2). This is to confound religion with social welfare, and to grade the merits of a religious belief on such welfare.

19   Durham (1996), 24, 43-44.

20   Ibid, 44 fn 89, quoting Madison "Memorial and Remonstrance Against Religious Assessments", reprinted as an Appendix to *Everson v Board of Education* (1947). However, Boston points out that Madison was 'stricter on separation than any other president, including Jefferson': Boston (2003), 81.

21   This argument is also made in detail by Garry (2005), 37ff.

22   Marshall (2000), considers the many reasons given for favouring religion and argues that these all of these features can apply to secular groups and individuals. There are, e.g., many secular charities and humanitarian-inspired programs as well as non-religious leaders who have demonstrated their concern for their work in promoting the social good. Paul (2005), demonstrates that 'non-religious, pro-evolution democracies contradict the dictum that a society cannot enjoy good conditions unless most citizens ardently believe in a moral creator' and shows a correlation between high religiosity and social dysfunction in the U.S.

to substantially burden a person's exercise of religion unless it could demonstrate (a) a compelling state interest to do so, and (b) it used the least restrictive means for protecting that interest.

[6.16] This law was enacted to overrule the then prevailing approach of the US Supreme Court in *Department of Human Resources of Oregon v Smith* (1990). In that case a law prohibiting the use of marijuana was held not to violate belief rights for a sect that wished to consume marijuana as part of religious ceremonies. The Court held that criminal laws that have the 'incidental effect' of restricting religious conduct did not offend the First Amendment (freedom of Religion clause of the Constitution). It was suggested that a law under which marijuana could be consumed which was religion-neutral and applied to everyone would not offend belief rights.

[6.17] The two principles of free-exercise (freedom) and non-establishment (equality) in relation to belief rights can thus come into conflict. This is evident in the differences in this case between the US Congress (favouring freedom through exception to the law) and the Supreme Court (favouring equality through one law for all). The US Supreme Court has, however, sought to soften the effect of rigid state-belief impartiality when it leads to restriction on the practice of religious or other personal convictions.[23] This has led to ambivalence in interpretation of the principles, and inconsistency in the Court's approach.[24]

State and belief: Approach of the UN

[6.18] The absence of more detailed consideration of state-belief separation in Rawls's work leaves a gap in his model of belief rights. The international human rights instruments do not close this gap.[25] While they are directed at defending belief rights, the UN international human rights treaties do not require either separation of the state from belief systems or organisations, nor do they prohibit establishment of a state religion, church or belief organisation.[26]

---

23   See, e.g., the recent cases of *Mitchell v Helms* (2000); *Burwell, Secretary of Health and Human Services, et al. v Hobby Lobby Stores, Inc., et al* (2014).

24   For example, the term 'play in the joints' has been invoked by the U.S. Supreme Court in permitting indirect state financial support for religious study. In *Locke v Davey* (2004), it ruled the state could refuse a university scholarship to the respondent to pursue a devotional theology degree when he was otherwise eligible to receive it. The scholarship could nevertheless be awarded for attendance at universities that required students to undertake Bible and other studies in the pursuit of a degree in other subjects. The Court determined that this was a case that involved the 'play in the joints' between the establishment and the free-exercise clauses of the Constitution's First Amendment. The link between government funding (non-establishment), and religious training (free-exercise), was broken by the choice allowed the recipient – it did not require the applicant to choose between the scholarship and his religion. See also Monsma (2002) *Mitchell v Helms* (200); Monsma, (2002); Marshall (1993); Durham (1996).

25   *Travaux préparatoires.* See Bossuyt (1987), 360. See UN Doc. A/2929, 48 (¶108); *General Comment No. 22,* and decisions by human rights tribunals as described above. However, while *General Comment No. 22* makes it clear that not only is discrimination against those not belonging to the state-sponsored religion to be avoided, but cautions against 'giving economic privileges to them,' this principle is more honoured in the breaking than the observance.

26   *Waldman v Canada* (1999), esp. the concurring judgment by Martin Scheinin, ¶1, who points to ICCPR *General Comment 22,* ¶9.

[6.19] The *travaux préparatoires* for Article 18 UDHR and ICCPR indicate a clear intention of the framers that this was to be the case, the most likely reason being the desire to maintain the support of nations that did not want to relinquish historical or cultural institutions or practices.[27]

[6.20] Additionally, *ICCPR General Comment 22* (1993) indicates that the state may establish an official or traditional religion, so long as it does not

> …result in any impairment of the freedoms under article 18 or any other rights recognized under the Covenant nor in any discrimination against persons who do not accept the official ideology or who oppose it.[28]

[6.21] Provisions preventing discrimination on the ground of 'religion or other opinion' (UDHR Article 2, ICCPR Article 26) appear to indirectly require some degree of separation of the state from personal conviction. Article 2(2) of the *Belief Declaration*, explicit in what it means in prohibiting discrimination on the grounds of religion or other belief, provides indirectly for state neutrality:

> For the purposes of the present Declaration, the expression "intolerance and discrimination based on religion or belief" means any distinction, exclusion, restriction or preference based on religion or belief and having as its purpose *or as its effect* nullification or impairment of the recognition, enjoyment or exercise of human rights and fundamental freedoms on an equal basis (emphasis added).

[6.22] The UN Special Rapporteur on Freedom of Religion or Belief, as well as the UNHRC have expressed concern over what they see as institutionalised discrimination that accompanies state endorsed or established religion.[29] Discrimination may also result from the use and effects of requiring registration of religions and the criteria and regulations imposed on registration.[30] Further, the UNHRC has inferred by its questioning of state activities that it considers separation of church and state a desirable feature of belief rights.[31] Activities questioned include payment by the state of salaries and pensions of ministers of religion; regulation by the state of church affairs; the requirement that religions register with the state; and registration of members of religious groups.[32]

---

27   See, e.g., Evans and Thomas (2006), 706. Bossuyt (1987), 360.
28   ICCPR *General Comment 22*, ¶¶10, 11.
29   See, e.g., Bielefeldt (2011), ¶59ff; Taylor (2005), 197.
30   Durham (2004).
31   Tahzib (1996), 260ff.
32   Ibid.

[6.23] Jonathon Fox claims that of the six Western democracies with an active state religion, all but one, Malta, place some restrictions on minority religions, and five give some religion preferential treatment.[33] This raises the issue of the influence and pressure for social and occupational acceptance that result from a state-established religion.

[6.24] Special consideration for religion and culture are enshrined in the *Declaration on the Rights of Persons Belonging to National or Ethnic, Religious and Linguistic Minorities*, but with narrower limitations than the belief provisions. Article 4(2) states that:

> States shall take measures to create favourable conditions to enable persons belonging to minorities to express their characteristics and to develop their culture, language, religion, traditions and customs, except where specific practices are in violation of national law and contrary to international standards.

[6.25] Articles 1 to 4 specify that this is to be through government measures that include protection and encouragement of conditions for the promotion of group identities. These measures involve granting special competence to these minorities to participate effectively in decision-making affecting them, non-discrimination against them, and positive steps to provide equality by and before the law.[34] *General Comment No. 23* on Article 27 ICCPR points out that that such measures must respect the non-discrimination and other clauses of the Convention.[35] This, I suggest, results in significant ambiguity as to the UN perception of the state-belief relationship.

[6.26] There is thus an overall failure on the part of those interpreting and implementing Article 18 to fully recognise that 'freedom *of* belief' necessarily requires the corollary 'freedom *from* belief'. Case law of the UNHRC clearly indicates a focus by the Committee on the individual citizen and his or her freedom to manifest belief in particular situations. This neglects consideration of the overall state-belief relationship by governments invoking 'neutrality' to justify granting benefits on the basis of belief (albeit nominally 'equal' benefits), rather than no benefits at all.

---

33   Fox (2008), 111. 'Active state religion', for Fox, involves, e.g., government administered church taxes, mandatory religious education or church involvement in government activity. Fox lists other countries with active state religion such as Denmark, Finland, Iceland, Greece and Norway. He also lists other countries with preferred treatment of a particular religion as Ireland Italy, Luxemburg, New Zealand and Portugal. He describes Australia as having 'moderate separation' (at 114).

34   This raises the issue of boundaries between state and belief: van der Vyver (2004), 87ff.

35   CCPR/C/21/Re v 1/Add.5, 26 April 1994 ¶6.2, 8.

State and belief: European organisations

[6.27] The ECHR does not specify separation of the state from belief. Framers were aware of the constitutional separation in states such as the US and France, but were also conscious of the need to retain support of those nations that desired to retain historical, religious and cultural practices. Further, they, and later the European Commission and Court, were of the opinion that appropriately restrained state involvement with religion would render separation not necessary to ensure belief rights.

[6.28] Much more has been said on state-belief relations by European organisations overseeing the ECHR. Resolution 1804 of the European Parliamentary Assembly[36] expresses an ambivalent approach to the idea of 'separation of church and state'. Paragraph 4 states that '[t]he Assembly reaffirms that one of Europe's shared values, transcending national differences, is the separation of church and state', a 'principle that prevails in politics and institutions in democratic countries'. On the other hand, paragraph 5 says that states can organise relationships between the state and the church 'in compliance with the provisions of the European Convention on Human Rights' and 'member states today show *varying* degrees of separation between government and religious institutions *in full compliance with the Convention*' (emphasis added).

[6.29] The EU has adopted Guidelines on how its nations are to promote belief rights, including in their relationships with other nations.[37] Modelled on *ICCPR General Comment No 22*, the Guidelines expound the international human rights standards on belief rights. They give direction to officials of EU institutions and EU Member States, to be used in contacts with third countries and with international and civil society organisations. They provide that religion is personal, and does not protect a religion or belief as such (clause 18).

[6.30] The EU Guidelines protect 'acts integral to the conduct by religious groups of their basic affairs'. 'Integral acts' involve, but are not limited to, matters dealing with legal personality and internal affairs, including the right to establish and maintain freely accessible places of worship or assembly, the freedom to select and train leaders or the right to carry out social, cultural, educational and charitable activities (clause 31). Finally it says that its protection of freedom of speech applies to persons rather than religion or religious organisations (clause 19). However, the EU Guidelines do not specifically *prohibit* state involvement in religion or other belief.

[6.31] A European Parliament resolution of 27 February 2014 on the situation of fundamental rights in the European Union stated that

---

36   Council of Europe Recommendation 1804 (2007), text adopted by the Assembly on 29 June 2007 (27th Sitting).
37   *EU Guidelines on the Promotion and Protection of Freedom of Religion or Belief* (2013). Adopted at the Foreign Affairs Council meeting, Luxembourg, 24 June 2013

secularism defined as the strict separation between non-confessional political authorities and religious authorities, as well as the impartiality of the State, are the best means of guaranteeing non-discrimination and equality between religions and between believers and non-believers.[38]

Despite this endorsement of state-belief separation, it would seem that establishment of an active state church or religion is thus not in itself considered a breach of the ECHR.[39] While not specifying the boundaries of the relationship between the state and belief, the case of *Kokkinikas v Greece* entrenched the democratic basis of belief rights in European human rights case law. It stated this freedom as being, as well as protection of religious belief, is

> a precious asset for atheists, agnostics, sceptics and the unconcerned. The pluralism indissociable from a democratic society, which has been dearly won over the centuries, depends on it.[40]

[6.32] The European Commission summarized the issue in this manner:

> A State Church system cannot in itself be considered to violate Article 9 (Art. 9) of the Convention. In fact, such a system exists in several Contracting States and existed there already when the Convention was drafted and when they became parties to it. However, a State Church system must, in order to satisfy the requirements of Article 9… include specific safeguards for the individual's freedom of religion.[41]

[6.33] Nevertheless, the European Court has frequently emphasised the State's role as a neutral and impartial overseer of the exercise of various religions, faiths and beliefs, and stated that this role is 'conducive to public order, religious harmony and tolerance in a democratic society'.[42] It also considers that the State's 'duty of neutrality and impartiality is incompatible with any power on the State's part to assess the legitimacy of religious beliefs,'[43] or interfering with their internal affairs.[44]

[6.34] An exception is made where internal differences involve property rights, or to ensure an association is required to fulfil certain requirements for entitlement to state recognition for ben-

---

38 *European Parliament resolution of 27 February 2014 on the situation of fundamental rights in the European Union (2012) (2013/2078(INI)),* ¶34.
39 *Darby v Sweden* (1990).
40 *Kokkinakis v Greece* (1993), ¶31.
41 *Darby v Sweden* (1990), ¶45.
42 *Refah Partisi (the Welfare Party), and Others v Turkey* [GC] (2003).
43 Ibid, ¶92. See also *(Cha'are Shalom Ve Tsedek v France* (2000), ¶4. *Metropolitan Church of Bessarabia and Others v Moldova* (1999), ¶123.
44 Minnerath (2004), 311, 311-314.

efits such as tax exemptions, or financial support such as social services.[45] Additionally, the Court also requires the State to ensure mutual tolerance between opposing groups to ensure everyone's beliefs are respected.[46]

[6.35] In sum:

> The state itself, therefore, must be democratic and pluralistic in order to fit within the requirements of the ECHR, and it must respect religious freedom, but within those boundaries, there is no requirement or prohibition of establishment between church and state.[47]

[6.36] Notwithstanding this, the provisions of the international instruments have even been interpreted as specifically endorsing state involvement in the establishment of state religions and the favouring of specific religious groups. Thus, say Javier Martínez-Torrón and Rafael Navarro-Valls:

> Not even privileged collaborations between states and certain churches, in the form of hidden confessionality of the state (as in Greece), or in the form of state churches (as in England or in some Scandinavian countries), have been considered contrary to the European Convention.[48]

[6.37] The aim of Article 9 ECHR, they conclude, is to provide only an 'adequate' guarantee of the right to freedom of religion and belief. Its purpose

> is not to establish certain uniform criteria for church-state relations in the Council of Europe member states nor – even less – to impose a compulsory secularism (laïcité). The background of this approach is the idea that the state's attitude towards religion is primarily a political issue and is the result, to a large extent, of the historical tradition and the social circumstances of each country. [49]

[6.38] Thus, for example, in the case of *Kokkinakis v Greece* the European Court did not question that the close connection of the Greek Orthodox Church with the state was a legitimate political choice.[50] In the recent decision of *Lautsi v Italy* (2011) the Grand Chamber of the European Court accepted a close connection between the Christian religion and the Italian State. It overturned a Chamber decision that mandatory display of a crucifix in government classrooms is

---

45   Durham (2004).

46   *Refah Partisi (the Welfare Party), and Others v Turkey* [GC] (2003), ¶91. See also *Metropolitan Church of Bessarabia and Others v Moldova* (1999), ¶¶123, 128.

47   Evans and Thomas (2006), 700 (footnotes omitted). See also Martínez-Torrón and Navarro-Valls (2004), 217.

48   Martínez-Torrón and Navarro-Valls, '(2004), 216.

49   Ibid, 216-217.

50   Martínez-Torrón and Navarro-Valls, (2004), 217. See also Commission's report in *Holy Monasteries v Greece*, (1997).

a breach of the ECHR. Nine countries joined in appealing this decision to the Grand Chamber, which recognised, *inter alia,* the state's right to exercise a 'margin of appreciation' based on its judgment of community interest. Two judges dissented, arguing that the 'positive' duty of tolerance and mutual respect means the margin of appreciation is limited (see discussion [11.31]ff.).

Conclusion

[6.39] Despite frequent use of language indicating the contrary, the monitoring bodies of the human rights treaties, and indeed the framers of the treaties themselves, accept state involvement in religious and other beliefs and associated organisations. This approach complements and aids the threshold interest of states (for whatever reason) in privileging historical religious and non-religious practices of their citizens. The power struggles between those holding different philosophies and life-stances ensures that no government is free from the influence of some religion or life-stance or another in the guise of promoting freedom to exercise religion, and in reality promoting freedom for *some* to exercise their religion.

[6.40] As András Sajó says:

> Even where "secularism" is mentioned as an accepted concept having constitutional value, it is often subject to the unprincipled wishy-washiness of balancing — or disregarded in the name of proportionality — for the sake of free exercise of religion.[51]

[6.41] The result has been, as Fox concludes, a substantial involvement of government in the advancement of some beliefs (most notably religion), to the detriment of others.[52] It means that, while both the UN and the European tribunals espouse 'state neutrality' towards belief, they have (due to this power struggle within their ranks) permitted state-belief entanglement. This is the political reality of the belief provisions.

[6.42] We need to go further, however, in investigating the challenges facing implementation of belief rights. The following Chapters investigate the language of the belief provisions themselves.

---

51   Sajó (2008), 605, 617.
52   Fox (2008), 364 (see below Chapter 12.

CHAPTER 7
BELIEF PROVISIONS AND INDETERMINACY

Introduction

[7.1] In addition to the politically-driven nature of state-belief relations, further undermining the belief provisions is their language. In the next three Chapters I will attempt to show how these provisions themselves fall short of the model Rawls developed. This Chapter begins by considering in more detail what the belief tribunals and commentators have said about the meaning of the words 'thought', 'conscience', 'religion' and 'belief'.

[7.2] There are three main rights set out in the wording of the first paragraph of each of the belief provisions:

- The first is a right, to thought, conscience and religion, which means you can form your own values and guidelines for living. This right, says the UDHR, is absolute, that is, it cannot be denied under any circumstances.[1]

- The second is a right to have, adopt and expressly or impliedly allows you to change, your 'religion or belief', which is also absolute;[2] and

- The third is a right to follow your religion or belief in 'worship, observance, practice and teaching', which is not absolute, but 'subject only to such limitations as are prescribed by law and are necessary to protect public safety, order, health, or morals or the fundamental rights and freedoms of others'.[3]

Terminology

[7.3] The use of the words 'conscience' and 'religion' seem to imply that the provisions apply to religion only. As noted, this interpretation has been demonstrated in the almost universal and exclusive association of the belief provisions with religion in the general conception of the provisions, discounting consideration of the rights of non-religious minorities to practice their beliefs independent of dominant religious culture. The implications of giving special recognition to religion are significant, and are dealt with in Chapter 8.

---

1   There is to be no derogation from Article 18 (taking into account its limitation provisions), even in times of emergency (Article 4 ICCPR). The ECHR does not exempt Article 9 from derogation, but derogation from freedom of thought would seem to be unjustifiable in any circumstances: Malcolm Evans (1997), 317.

2   Article 18.2 ICCPR; Evans, ibid.

3   ICCPR Article 18.3, ECHR Article 9.2 and *Belief Declaration* Article 1.3.

[7.4] Malcolm Evans suggests that it would make more sense, considering the ICCPR as a whole, if Article 18 were to refer only to religion.[4] He suggests that freedom to manifest non-religious belief is more appropriately dealt with by Articles 19 and 20 (freedom of speech and association).[5] By implication, this reasoning would also apply to Articles 9 and 10 ECHR respectively. This approach, while it may be superficially attractive, has not been generally accepted (nor should it be, as is argued below).

[7.5] Considering Article 18 as it stands, then, the use of the words 'conscience', 'religion' and 'belief' may be considered generally applicable to both religious and non-religious beliefs, but generalisation are not enough when it comes to considering just how provisions are to be put into practice, and especially if there is disagreement as to how they are to be applied. Legal scrutiny requires a more literal approach and those who want to question entitlements before tribunals will turn to dissecting the wording and hair-splitting.

[7.6] The first right excludes reference to 'belief'. What are we to make of the fact that the provisions introduce the word 'belief' only in terms of adoption and manifestation, where the words 'thought' and 'conscience' are missing? Does this mean that you can adopt and manifest a religion or belief, but not individual 'thought' or 'conscience'? Are we to draw a distinction between religion and belief (and if so, what is it)?

[7.7] Carolyn Evans proposes that there is a 'legally important distinction' indicated by the terms 'thought and conscience' and 'religion or belief'.[6] In legal provisions, the choice of words always is meant to indicate important distinctions. While this conclusion may be drawn from the wording of the belief provisions (disregarding the view that 'thought' includes all ideas, thus including non-religious beliefs) there is no indication of just what the distinction could be. However, she concludes that this interpretation would 'seem to suggest the strange outcome that an atheist has the right to manifest [live by] his or her belief…but his or her right to hold this belief is not protected'.[7]

[7.8] Recognising the difficulty in reconciling the terminology of the belief provisions, Carolyn Evans concludes that to make sense of understanding the untouchable mental processes that are covered by the freedom of 'thought, conscience and religion', presumptions as to the intention of the Articles must be made. Consequently, she argues, 'beliefs' should be considered a 'subset'

---

4   See, e.g., Malcolm Evans (1997), 203; see also Malcolm Evans (2000), 43.
5   Malcolm Evans (1997), 203.
6   Carolyn Evans (2001), 52. Her view appears to be based simply on the choice of different words: there is no formal justification of the different terms.
7   Ibid, 53.

of the broader category of 'thought and conscience' for the purposes of freedom of 'thought, conscience and religion'.[8]

[7.9] On their face, then, these three expressions of freedom in the belief provisions are ambiguous, and the human rights tribunals have so far not explained the implications of their use. Specific emphasis on their reference to 'conscience' and 'religion' appears to apply selective protection to accepted mainstream religious beliefs, and cast doubt on the protection provided for religious or other beliefs.

[7.10] Given what has been argued previously, and according to Rawls's model of what is in effect structural secularism, we don't need special reference to, or treatment of, religious beliefs – or indeed any other particular personal worldview – in understanding belief rights. There is no difference in the freedom of both religious and other beliefs (i.e. life-stances): all are given equal consideration.

Muddying the waters: drafting of the belief provisions

[7.11] What was the intention of those who actually wrote the human rights treaties? It is useful to consider both the *travaux préparatoires* (preparatory deliberations by those writing the provisions) and interpretation by major international bodies.

[7.12] One of the difficulties in determining the meaning of the belief provisions is the lack of consensus among the drafting bodies. There is an apparent broad formal consensus on non-theism and inclusiveness, but 'little insight into what the terms meant beyond this'.[9]

[7.13] The debate around what to include is described by Malcolm Evans, who outlines the drafting process of Article 18 both as part of the UDHR (where initially it was Article 16) and as adopted in the ICCPR.[10] He points out that in the initial drafting stage of the UDHR the 'discussions reveal widely divergent views concerning the relationship between the freedom of thought and conscience, and the freedom of religion and the meaning of belief'.[11] Evans concludes that '[t]o put the matter briefly, the essential difficulty was that it was entirely unclear what [Article 18] was meant to imply, and the discussion surrounding its adoption provides no clarification'.[12] Thus, the agreement of members of the drafting Committee of the UDHR to the

---

8   Ibid.
9   Carolyn Evans (2001), 61.
10 Malcolm Evans (1997), ch 8. See also Malcolm Evans (2000), 39ff; Bossuyt (1987), 351ff.
11 Malcolm Evans (1997)190. Paul Taylor outlines the concerns expressed by the Muslim countries: see Taylor (2005), 27ff.
12 Malcolm Evans (1997), 189.

wording of the Articles 'reflected a willingness to compromise rather than insist on a common agreement on what should be embraced by such a right'.[13]

[7.14] The Drafting Committee of the ICCPR was also divided between those who wanted the provision to include adoption and manifestation of non-religious belief, and those who wished to restrict it to 'religion', thereby effectively excluding reference to other beliefs.[14] No consensus on this matter was reached, although, according to Evans, 'the discussion leant towards the inclusive interpretation that had received mild endorsement from the Secretariat'.[15] Records show that while freedom of religion was a priority for the majority of delegates to the bodies tasked with framing the belief provisions, they nevertheless formally expressed the intention that belief rights were to include non-religious beliefs.[16] The UN Commission on Human Rights reported that, in relation to Article 18 ICCPR, '[n]o restrictions of a legal character, it was generally agreed, could be imposed on man's inner thought or moral consciousness, or his attitude towards the universe or its creator'.[17] There was no reference to *manifestation* of thoughts and attitudes.

[7.15] Despite the ambivalence noted above, there is a repeated inference by both the UN and the European human rights drafting sessions that 'belief' is to include non-religious beliefs, and be given a broad interpretation. Even if it were to be considered a necessary preliminary for protecting particular liberties, the difficulty of attempting to identify religion distracts from the purpose of the relevant Articles – that is, that both religion and non-religious convictions are equally valued.

Approach of the United Nations Human Rights Committee (UNHRC)

[7.16] The UNHRC tended, especially in earlier decisions, to avoid a reasoned explanation for its findings, thus leaving any definition of the words 'thought', 'conscience', 'religion' and 'belief' undefined and open to conjecture.[18] The UNHRC considered of the meaning of 'religion or belief' under Article 18 ICCPR in only one communication under the ICCPR First Optional Protocol, which provides for individuals to bring complaints of human rights provisions to the

---

13   Ibid, 183.
14   Ibid, 203.
15   Ibid, 204.
16   Ibid, 190ff. See also Ch 8; Tahzib (1996), examines the process of deliberation in framing belief rights, Ch 3, esp 70ff. See also Malcolm Evans (2000), 39ff.; Bossuyt (1987), 351ff.
17   Commission on Human Rights, 5th Session (1949), 6th Session (1949), 8th Session (1952): A/2929 Chap VI, ¶106, cited in Bossuyt (1987), 355.
18   Peter Radan points out that the UNHRC in its earlier decisions consisted of 'a short recitation of the relevant facts, an account of the efforts of the author(s), to seek domestic remedies, an account of the submissions made before the UNHRC, followed, finally, by the decision' (Radan (2005), 13). This is also the case with the European Commission, and, particularly in its early days, the European Court.

Committee.[19] The complainants *M.A.B., W.A.T. and J.A.Y.T.*, were leaders of the 'Assembly of the Church of the Universe', whose beliefs and practices 'necessarily' involved 'the care, cultivation, possession, distribution, maintenance, integrity and worship of marijuana'.[20] The UNHRC held the communication to be inadmissible, stating simply that 'a belief consisting primarily or exclusively in the worship and distribution of a narcotic drug cannot conceivably be brought within the scope of Article 18 of the Covenant'.[21] No indication of why this was so, or what *could* conceivably be brought within the scope of Article 18 ICCPR was provided.

[7.17] The matter remained unresolved by a more recent consideration by the Committee of the use of cannabis sativa by members of the Rastafari sect in South Africa.[22] The author of the communication alleged that prohibition of the possession or use of cannabis restricted the manifestation of his religious beliefs. The Committee accepted Rastafarianism as a religion without explanation, as well as the use of cannabis, as 'inherent in the manifestation of the Rastafari religion'.[23] It distinguished *M.A.B., W.A.T. and J.A.Y.T.* because the latter 'concerned the activities of a religious organization whose belief consisted primarily or exclusively in the worship and distribution of a narcotic drug'.[24] However, it dismissed the Rastafarians' complaint, stating that prohibition of certain drugs was justified based on potential harmful effects, and that a general prohibition on drug use was not discriminatory, as it applies to all individuals, regardless of religion or other belief.[25]

[7.18] A further example of uncertain reasoning by the UNHRC as to what is covered by Article 18 ICCPR can be seen in the case of *M.A. v Italy*.[26] In that case, the UNHRC ruled inadmissible a communication from a person convicted for attempting to re-establish the Fascist Party in Italy. The Committee considered restriction of his actions was

> justifiably prohibited by Italian law having regard to the limitations and restrictions applicable to the rights in question under the provisions of articles 18 (3), 19 (3), 22 (2) and 25 of the Covenant.[27]

[7.19] This suggests that the UNHRC left open consideration of fascism as a 'belief' under Article 18 ICCPR, taking the idea of belief into the political sphere and potentially embracing

---

19   *M.A.B. W.A.T. and J.A.Y.T. v Canada* (1994).
20   The "Sacrament" ["God's tree of life"] of the Church' ibid, ¶2.1.
21   *M.A.B. W.A.T. and J.A.Y.T. v Canada* (1994), ¶4.2
22   *Prince v South Africa* (2007).
23   ibid, ¶¶6.5, 7.2.
24   ibid, ¶6.5.
25   ibid, ¶7.3.
26   *M A v Italy* (1984).
27   Ibid ¶13.3.

Nazism, communism and other non-democratic ideologies. Questions then arise as to what protection should be granted to political and allegedly anti-social beliefs (presumably the manifestation of such beliefs could be limited according to Article 18.3).

The UN and the Belief Declaration

[7.20] The *Belief Declaration* was adopted by the UN in 1981. It implied the intention to give a broad definition to 'beliefs'. The right to change the religion or belief of one's choice was omitted from Article 1 at the behest of some Islamic states. In the final document, however, a broad approach to 'religion or belief' was established. This occurred by the inclusion of the word 'whatever' before 'belief', to stipulate that freedom of thought, conscience and religion 'shall include freedom to have a religion or *whatever* belief of his choice'. Again 'belief' is not defined, but the Preamble describes 'religion or belief', for anyone who professes one, as constituting 'one of the fundamental elements in his conception of life'. Article 8 of the *Belief Declaration* goes on to provide that

> Nothing in the present Declaration shall be construed as restricting or derogating from any right defined in the Universal Declaration of Human Rights and the International Covenant on Human Rights.

By invoking the ICCPR, the UN has adopted interpretations that apply to it (widened by *ICCPR General Comment 22*: see below) and by invoking the *Belief Declaration*, the UN has included the right to adopt and change one's 'religion or belief', which is omitted in the ICCPR.

The UN and ICCPR General Comment 22

[7.21] The UN then clarified its intention to cover convictions other than religious beliefs in *ICCPR General Comment 22* of 1993 (*General Comment 22*). It stated there that the right to freedom of thought, conscience and religion (which includes the right to 'have or adopt a religion or belief') 'is far-reaching and profound; it encompasses freedom of thought on all matters, personal life stance and the commitment to religion or belief…'[28] Moreover, the General Comment states that Article 18 ICCPR 'protects theistic, non-theistic and atheistic beliefs, as well as the right not to profess any religion or belief' and is 'not limited in its application to traditional religions or to religions and convictions with institutional characteristics or practices analogous to those of traditional religions'.[29] The terms 'belief' and 'religion' are to be broadly construed',[30] and Article 18 'does not permit any limitations whatsoever on the freedom of thought and conscience or on

---

28   General Comment 22, ¶1.
29   Ibid, ¶2.
30   Ibid.

the freedom to have or adopt a religion or belief of one's choice'. Further, '[t]hese freedoms are protected unconditionally, as is the right of everyone to hold opinions without interference…'.[31] It is contended here that the strength of the language used does express the overall intention to give equal protection to all personal life stances as defined above.

[7.22] The view that the UN intends equal protection for all 'beliefs' as personal life stances gains further credence from its preparatory deliberations on the *General Comment 22* in the UNHRC. There it noted the UN's intention, firstly, that freedom of religion did not have a higher status than freedom of thought, conscience and belief, and, secondly, that the freedoms in Article 18 ICCPR include all personal convictions, religious or otherwise.[32] Paragraph 5 of the ICCPR *General Comment 22* reinforces the equality of all personal life stances by emphasising that the right to change from one religion or belief to another is covered by Article 18 ICCPR, and applying Article 18 equally to religious and non-religious belief.

[7.23] So freedom of 'religion or belief' includes non-religious beliefs, but uncertainty remains.

[7.24] Malcolm Evans points out that while the case law of the UNHRC provides little assistance for forming a definition of 'religion or belief', it has adopted *General Comment 22* as an authoritative statement of its understanding of Article 18. However, he goes on to argue that the Committee has failed to adequately determine the substance of the right to 'freedom of thought, conscience and religion' and how that relates to the question of discrimination on these grounds.[33] The result is that the 'core meaning of Article 18' has not been clearly established.[34] As a result, attempts to give effect to Article 18 risk consequent discrimination between one recognised 'religion or belief' and another, as well as denial of the rights of those of minority religions and beliefs.[35]

[7.25] Odio Benito, one-time Special Rapporteur on the Right to freedom of Religion and Belief sought to clarify one issue. She has stated that the relevant provisions of the UDHR, ICCPR and the *Belief Declaration* all provide that individuals have the right to 'leave one religion or belief and to adopt another or to remain without any belief'. She goes on to claim that this right is 'implicit in the right to freedom of thought, conscience, religion and belief, regardless of

---

31   Ibid, ¶¶2, 3.
32   Tahzib (1996), 313 quoting UN Doc CCPR/C/SR.1162, ¶ 37 (Müllerson), ¶35 (El-Shafei), ¶37 (Chanet), ¶39 (Lallah). It is perhaps also instructive to note that in the original French version of drafts of Article 18, the French term *croyance* was used – a term that is associated with religion or faith. However later versions adopted the French term *conviction*, which, as does its English counterpart, allows for the inclusion of other matters.
33   Malcolm Evans (1997), 208.
34   Ibid, 209.
35   Ibid, 210.

how that concept is presented'.[36] This still leaves the question open to interpretation in the light of the social environment of the day. I use the case of Diane Pretty (see [7.37]) as an example of the potential arbitrariness of determining what is to be considered a belief.

Approach of relevant European bodies

[7.26] The general approach to interpretation of the Convention by the European Commission and Court has also led to an expansive approach to what is protected by Article 9 ECHR. From its earliest judgments, the European Commission considered the Convention to be a 'living document', to be interpreted according to the conditions and social standards of the time of consideration of each case.[37] The European Commission and subsequently the European Court have adopted what Merrills calls the 'effectiveness principle' in their approach to interpretation of treaties. That is, an approach that gives the provisions of a treaty 'the fullest weight and effect consistent with the language used and with the rest of the text and in such a way that every part of it can be given meaning'.[38] This would supplant pedantic argument over the meaning of words.

[7.27] This 'effectiveness principle' was expressed by the European Court in *Wemhoff v Germany*, in which it held that any interpretation of the ECHR should be 'most appropriate' in order to 'realise the aim and achieve the object of the treaty, not that which would restrict to the greatest possible degree the obligations undertaken by the parties'.[39] The European Court's approach is one of the 'most judicially active in the field'.[40] In effect, George Letsas has argued, 'The Court has instead opted, albeit not consistently, for the moral reading of the Convention rights'.[41]

[7.28] The Court has consequently considered prevailing social values in Europe[42] and referred to texts adopted by other Council of Europe organisations, as well as practice of the International

---

36   Benito (1989), ¶21 quoted in Tahzib (1996), 168, n342.
37   *Tyrer v the United Kingdom* (1978), ¶31; Letsas (2010), 541.
38   Merrills (1988), 89, Ch 10.
39   *Wemhoff v Germany* (1968), p 19, ¶8 Series A no. 7. This case involved the need to choose between different interpretations of Article 5(3), ECHR (providing for prompt appearance before the court on arrest and trial within a reasonable time), where the complainant had been arrested in November 1961 and held on remand until his trial in April 1965.
40   Merrills (1988), 229: 'Judicial activism' is used to describe an approach that eschews strict construction of the law and seeks to produce the most desirable result envisaged by the underlying principle of a law – 'doing justice in individual cases and, more generally, keeping the law up to date', at 210. Letsas (2010), states that the Court has rejected originalism, and rather than following the textual meaning or determining the drafters' intentions, has 'paved the way for the development of the doctrines of autonomous concepts and evolutive interpretation': 520 (emphasis original). He calls this a 'moral reading' of the ECHR (at 512).
41   Letsas (2010), 512 (footnote deleted).
42   E.g., it considered the operation across European countries of enforcement procedures in *Loizidou v Turkey* (1996); attitudes to homosexuality in *Dudgeon v the United Kingdom* (1981), ¶60; and the death sentence in *Soering v the United Kingdom* (1989), ¶102, Series A no. 161.

Labour Organisation,[43] to promote conformity with related international tribunals. This has also led to the Court allowing wide discretion on the part of governments ('margin of appreciation' see [11.9]). While the result in individual cases might be disputed, the use of this approach is an attempt to find a principled and fair decision. However, there is a danger: the circular nature of trying to draw a balance between principle and result, with consequent partiality is inescapable. Hence Rawls's appeal to procedure, with uniformity of approach, rather than outcome, with its inequity and uncertainty.

[7.29] In most cases where breach of Article 9 of the ECHR has been invoked, the European tribunals have tended to avoid considering whether the applicant's actions were actually based on a 'religion or belief' (and what, indeed, that means) by presuming they were. They thus proceeded immediately to consider whether, as manifestations of such belief, any demonstrated state interference in them was permissible under Article 9.2. Critics argue that this has bypassed the perceived need for clarification of what actions constitute manifestations of a belief[44] (see below Chapter 10).

[7.30] The European Commission's early judgments nevertheless lacked a clearly enunciated meaning of 'belief'. This can also be seen in the case of *X v Austria*,[45] which involved prosecution of the claimant for promotion of neo-Nazism. The Commission, without setting out reasons, treated the conviction as an interference with the informant's rights under Article 9 ECHR and went on to hold that the government was justified in suppressing the applicant's activities under Article 9.2. Similarly ambiguous were cases dealing with applications relating to State suppression of fascism [46] and communism.[47]

[7.31] While the European Court has later considered specifically applying the protections of Article 9 to the expression of beliefs that involve political parties,[48] it rather dealt with these issues under other ECHR Articles,[49] such as Article 10 (freedom of expression),[50] Article 11 (freedom

---

43   *Sigurður A Sigurjónsson v Iceland* (1993), (a case dealing with freedom of association). See also *Groppera Radio AG and Others v Switzerland* (1990), esp. ¶¶36–42 (a case dealing with freedom of speech).
44   See, e.g., Gunn (1996), 315; Martínez-Torrón and Navarro-Valls (2004), 215.
45   *X v Austria* (1963), 53–4.
46   *X v Italy* (1976).
47   *Hazar, Hazar and Açik v Turkey* (1991), 212; *United Communist Party of Turkey and Others v Turkey* (1998).
48   Taylor, (2005), 79–80.
49   See, e.g., ibid; also *Refah Partisi (the Welfare Party), and Others v Turkey* [GC], (2003).
50   See, e.g. *United Communist Party of Turkey and Others v. Turkey*, (1998); *Freedom and Democracy Party (ÖZDEP), v. Turkey*, (1999), §§42–3.

of assembly and association),[51] and Article 17 (destruction of rights and freedoms of others). This would accord with the view, as expressed by Rawls, that political philosophies and practices are different from personal worldviews. The Court later established that the notion of 'belief' in Article 9 ECHR 'includes non-religious convictions that attain a certain level of cogency, seriousness, coherence and importance'.[52]

[7.32] In another case, the aim of accessing prisons to give free legal advice to prisoners, although it was idealistic, was held not to be manifestation of a 'belief' for purposes of Article 9 ECHR.[53] Where an individual claims undue constraint of a non-religious life stance, the matter is most likely to be held to fall outside Article 9 ECHR.[54] Accordingly, the European Commission has avoided direct consideration of the question and declared the refusal to wear prisoner garb by applicants considering themselves political prisoners as unrelated to Article 9 ECHR.[55] It addressed the issue more directly where it held an applicant's wish to have his ashes scattered in his garden was not a 'coherent view on fundamental problems'.[56]

[7.33] The European Court's seminal statement in *Kokkinakis v Greece* (1993), that Article 9 applies to not only the religious, but to 'atheists, agnostics, sceptics and the unconcerned as part of 'a pluralism indissociable from a democratic society'[57], has been entrenched in ECHR law (it has been acknowledged by the UNHRC as well), and the dimensions of Article 9 ECHR have been further established in later cases.[58]

[7.34] Jean-François Renucci, in an official Council of Europe publication on Article 9 ECHR, has stated (albeit enigmatically), that Article 9 applies to 'all personal, political, philosophical, moral and of course religious beliefs and life stances'. It includes, he argues, 'philosophical ideas and conceptions of all kinds, with specific reference to an individual's religious conception and

---

51   Cases involving political parties considered under Article 11 ECHR include *Refah Partisi (the Welfare Party), and Others v. Turkey* (2003) esp, §§90ff. 'The fact that their activities form part of a collective exercise of freedom of expression in itself entitles political parties to seek the protection of Articles 10 and 11 of the Convention': *Freedom and Democracy Party (ÖZDEP), v. Turkey* [GC], (1998).

52   This was the term used by the European Court in *Campbell and Cosans v the United Kingdom* (1982), ¶36 Series A no. 48. The European Commission held that the wish to have one's ashes scattered in a certain place is not a 'religion or belief' under Article 9 because it is not a 'manifestation of any belief in the sense that some coherent view on fundamental problems can be seen as being expressed thereby': *X v Germany* (1981), 138.

53   *Vereniging Rechtswinkels Utrecht v Netherlands* (1986).

54   See, e.g., Malcolm Evans (1997), 292.

55   In *McFeeley et al v U K* (1980), 76. The Court did not address the issue of whether the applicant had a 'belief' under Article 9, but held that he had not shown that not wearing prison clothes was required by his belief.

56   *X v Germany* (1981).

57   *Kokkinakis v Greece* (1993) ¶31. See [2.61].

58   See, e.g., Buscarini and Others v San Marino (1999), recently referred to in *Refah Partisi (the Welfare Party), and Others v Turkey* (2003).

his own way of perceiving his social and private life'.[59] Despite his reference to preferential treatment of religion, his language is unmistakably inclusive, while again ambiguous.

[7.35] As well as automatically including mainstream Christian religions, the ECHR bodies have held the following to be protected: Judaism,[60] Islam,[61] Hinduism,[62] Jehovah's Witnesses,[63] the Divine Light Zentrum,[64] the Salvation Army[65] and the Church of Scientology,[66] while avoiding exhaustive consideration of their religiosity – possibly because of the inclusiveness assigned the term 'religion or belief'.[67] Among the non-church-based beliefs that have been held admissible for consideration have been ethical or philosophical life stances such as opposition to abortion,[68] pacifism,[69] membership of the Communist Party,[70] atheism[71] and choice of children's forenames.[72]

[7.36] The European Court has ruled out cultural or language preferences as part of belief, stating that '[b]y religious and philosophical life stances are meant those ideas on the world in general and human society in particular that each man considers the most true in the light of the religion he professes and the philosophical theories he adopts'.[73] As noted, political ideologies have generally been dealt with as issues of freedom of speech or assembly.[74] Freedom to manifest belief protects specific activities, that is, worship, observance, practice and teaching, the first three of which are usually, but, it is suggested, not exclusively, activities most likely to apply to religion.[75] Freedom of expression (Articles 19 ICCPR and 10 ECHR), and freedom of assembly and association (Articles 21 and 22 ICCPR, and 10 and 11 ECHR) are more likely to be applied to non-religious beliefs, or complaints involving breach of several rights that include belief rights.

---

59   Renucci (2005), 12 (footnotes deleted). In the context of this statement, and of the European bodies' decisions, it is suggested that Renucci means that the ideas and conceptions are to constitute personal convictions. He refers to *Arrowsmith v the United Kingdom* (1978), which dealt with pacifism, as an example of a 'philosophical' conviction, and describes the term as applying to 'an individual's conception of life and, more specifically, of man's behaviour in society"(at 12, n 13). He refers to *Young, James and Webster v the United Kingdom* (1981), in relation to private life.

60   *D. v France*, App. No. 10180/82 (1983), 35 D&R 199.

61   *Ahmad v the United Kingdom* (1981).

62   *ISKCON and others v the United Kingdom* (1994).

63   E.g., *Kokkinakis v Greece* (1993); *Valsamis v Greece* (1996).

64   *Omkarananda and the Divine Light Zentrum v Sweden* (1981).

65   *The Moscow Branch of the Salvation Army v Russia* (2006).

66   *X and Church of Scientology v Sweden* (1979).

67   See Knights (2007), 41.

68   *The Norwegian State Church Knudsen v Norway* (1985); *Plattform "Ärzte für das Leben" v Austria* (1988).

69   *ISKCON and others v the United Kingdom* (1994).

70   *Hazar Hazar and Açik v Turkey* (1991).

71   *Angeleni v Sweden* (1986).

72   *Salonen v Finland* (1997).

73   *Case "relating to certain aspects of the laws on the use of languages in education in Belgium"* (1968).

74   *United Communist Party of Turkey and Others v Turkey (1998); Refah Partisi (the Welfare Party), and Others v Turkey* (2003).

75   However, non-religious groups have 'civil ceremonies' such as ceremonies for naming, coming of age, marriage and funerals. These are yet to be legally recognised as 'manifestations' of belief.

There is little difference between grounds for permitted limitation in these Articles, thus making belief, expression and association interdependent elements of a holistic means of self-realisation based on thought, worldview and their manifestation. As a result, the adjudicative bodies often prefer to consider it as a matter of freedom of speech, assembly or association, rather than belief.[76]

Table 6: Permitted Limitation of Belief, Expression and Association

When Limitation permitted:	Freedom of Religion, Belief, Association, Assembly	Freedom to manifest belief		Freedom of expression		Freedom of assembly and association	
	UDHR Article 29	ICCPR Article 18	ECHR Article 9	ICCPR Article 19	ECHR Article 10	ICCPR Articles 21, 22	ECHR Article 11
Prescribed by law	✓	✓	✓	✓	✓	✓	✓
Necessary in democratic society		✓	✓		✓	✓	✓
Public safety		✓	✓		✓	✓	✓
Protection of public order	✓	✓	✓	✓		✓	
Protection of (public) health		✓	✓		✓	✓	✓
Protection of (public) morals	✓	✓	✓	✓	✓	✓	✓
Protection of others' rights and freedoms	✓	✓	✓	✓	✓	✓	✓
National security				✓	✓	✓	✓
For territorial integrity					✓		
For prevention of disorder or crime					✓		✓
Protection of reputation				✓	✓		
Protection of privacy					✓		
Maintenance of judicial authority & impartiality					✓		
General welfare in a democratic society.	✓						

---

76   Eg, *Refah Partisi (the Welfare Party) and Others v. Turkey* [GC], nos. 41340/98, 41342/98, 41343/98 and 41344/98, ECHR 2003-II. When the state dissolved a political party that espoused the imposition of theocracy, the complainant members alleged, *inter alia,* breach of freedom of belief, expression, association and assembly (Articles 9, 10 and 11 ECHR). Because their aims were political, albeit based on religious belief, the Court considered the case primarily as one of freedom of association. Finding no breach of Article 11 ECHR, the Court declared unnecessary a separate examination of complaints under other Articles of ECHR.

[7.37] A recent example of the uncertainty that results from the European Court's use of terminology, and failure to provide reasons for its approach to the meaning of 'belief' can be found in *Pretty v The United Kingdom* (2002). The applicant, Diane Pretty, was suffering from the final stages of motor neurone disease. She was effectively paralysed from the neck down, with an electronic device with which to communicate, and was being fed by a tube. Nevertheless, she had retained her intellectual capacity and very strongly indicated her wish to end her life with the aid of her husband. As the Court noted, the final stages of the disease, with increasing respiratory failure, are 'exceedingly distressing and undignified' leaving her 'frightened and distressed'.[77] Her fear and distress was extreme, as a film made on her behalf has shown.

[7.38] Ms Pretty sought the DPP's undertaking not to prosecute her husband should he assist her to commit suicide in accordance with her wishes. The DPP refused, and this refusal was supported by all the domestic courts. Ms Pretty applied to the European Court for a ruling that her human rights under the ECHR had been violated, including her belief rights. The European Court, in relation to the alleged violation of Article 9 ECHR, simply stated that

> [t]he Court does not doubt the firmness of the applicant's views concerning assisted suicide but would observe that not all opinions or convictions constitute beliefs in the sense protected by Article 9.1 of the Convention. Her claims do not involve a form of manifestation of a religion or belief, through worship, teaching, practice or observance as described in the second sentence of the first paragraph [of Article 9].[78]

[7.39] The Court did not elaborate. It did not explain *why* Ms Pretty's convictions did not attain the requisite level of cogency, seriousness, coherence and importance for the purposes of Article 9 ECHR. It therefore missed the opportunity to specify just what 'opinions' or 'convictions' *do* constitute a 'belief' in the sense protected by Article 9 ECHR. Arguably, given her circumstances, Ms Pretty's beliefs in assisted suicide met these criteria, at least for her, as they involved belief about the meaning of life and consequent ethical norms, but the Court gave no reason for holding otherwise. Instead, it held that if the law against murder generally exempted even voluntary euthanasia, this could be abused (Ms Pretty was not asking for such a law, but the right to exercise a well-established belief). This raises the unanswered issues of (1) what is a belief, and legitimate criteria for determining the required level of cogency, seriousness, coherence and importance for a belief; (2) whether the test is an objective, rather than a subjective, one; and (3) and why assisted suicide on compassionate grounds where volition and determination has been clearly established is an offence, while unassisted suicide (under any circumstances) is not.

---

77 *Pretty v The United Kingdom* (2002), ¶8.
78 Ibid, ¶82.

[7.40] This finding is all the more perplexing because, while disallowing Ms Pretty's claim to a belief, the Court nevertheless went on to address the claim that voluntary euthanasia would be a form of manifestation of a religion or belief, and reject it without discussion. This infused further complexity into the issue. If Ms Pretty's beliefs were not a 'belief', and therefore not eligible for consideration under Article 9 ECHR, it surely follows that such consideration of manifestation would be irrelevant. Without supporting justification, it seems the Court has inappropriately applied religionist reasoning to the meaning of 'worship, observance, practice or teaching' to her non-religious views. Ms Pretty's assisted demise could be seen as a manifestation of what to her was a 'coherent view on fundamental problems'.[79] The Court did not elaborate on why it thought otherwise.

[7.41] In contrast to the *Pretty* case, it is noted that in a decision of February 2015, the Supreme Court of Canada determined that legislation prohibiting assisted suicide was a breach of the right to life, liberty, and security of the person (Article 7 of the Canadian Charter of Rights).[80] It held that the current law denied to some individuals rights that are intended to apply to everyone (in this case life, liberty and security of the person). It does so in a manner that in no way furthers the object of these rights. In other words, the right to assisted dying, as part of the right to life, liberty and security, should not be removed from some people 'in order to make enforcement more practical'. It is a universal right. Societal issues, such as concern to protect vulnerable persons, 'slippery slopes', coercion and reluctance of physicians to assist, the Court said, were a separate matter, that should not impinge on the basic right to assisted dying. This implies (in Rawlsian-like fashion) that while social circumstances may be considered, at the end of the day, good government must be compatible with the principles that underlie our democratic society, rights should not be unduly interfered with, and lawmakers should vote accordingly.

[7.42] The view that Article 9 ECHR applies to a broad range of beliefs is to be found to in the European Court's approach to Protocol 1, Article 2 ECHR ('P1-2'). P1-2 provides that:

> No person shall be denied the right to education. In the case of any functions that it assumes in relation to education and teaching, the State shall respect the right of parents to ensure such education and teaching in conformity with their own religious and philosophical life stances.

---

79   Both the European Court and the UNHRC were required to consider the right to assisted death with dignity in the matter of *Ramón Sampredo*. Sampredo's daughter, Manuella Sanlés Sanlés, sought a finding that he had been denied the right, inter alia to manifestation of belief. In both instances the tribunals rule the matter inadmissible (given that Sampredo had in fact committed suicide by this time): *Sanlés Sanlés v Spain* (2000), European Court; *Manuela Sanlés v Spain* (2004), UN.

80   *Carter v. Canada* 2015.

[7.43] The relationship of P1- 2 and Article 9 ECHR has created difficulties for the European tribunals, as there is a potential conflict between the right of children to an education provided by the state (including, for example, an understanding of their human rights), and the right of parents to determine the nature of education (which may exclude such information).[81]

[7.44] Nevertheless, the use of the term 'conviction' in respect of Article 9 ECHR is supported by the European Commission's interpretation of the term 'philosophical convictions' in the case of *Campbell and Cosans* (1980). There the Commission was dealing with the meaning of the term 'philosophical convictions' for the purposes of P1-2. It stated in its Report to the European Court that

> as a general idea, the concept of "philosophical convictions" must be understood to mean those ideas based on human knowledge and reasoning concerning the world, life, society, etc., which a person adopts and professes according to the dictates of his or her conscience. [82]

[7.45] This approach was endorsed by the European Court decision in the case, which related 'convictions' with 'beliefs' in the following way:

> In its ordinary meaning the word "convictions", taken on its own, is not synonymous with the words "opinions" and "ideas", such as are utilised in Article 10 (art. 10) of the Convention, which guarantees freedom of expression; it is more akin to the term "beliefs" (in the French text: "*convictions*") appearing in Article 9 …which guarantees freedom of thought, conscience and religion – and denotes views that attain a certain level of cogency, seriousness, cohesion and importance.[83]

[7.46] It is argued that this is not a critical distinction, and convictions are not in effect different from opinions and ideas (which are protected in the right to freedom of speech). The term convictions is meaningful, but only to indicate those opinions that are so strongly held that they are fundamental to determining how we conduct our life.

[7.47] The European Commission and Court may have thus inclined towards an *inclusive* rather than an *exclusive* focus on what is considered admissible for consideration as a belief. However, while it held that while a light worshipper failed to provide adequate evidence of his beliefs[84] and

---

81   See, e.g., the discussion on this issue in Taylor (2005), 165ff; *Kjeldsen Busk Madsen and Pedersen v Denmark* (1976); *Case "Relating to Certain Aspects of the Law on the Use of Languages in Education in Belgium" ('Belgian Linguistics Case'),* (1968).

82   *Campbell and Cosans v the United Kingdom* (1980), ¶92.

83   Ibid,¶36 (emphasis added). Steven Smith, in discussing the importance of protecting belief, draws the distinction between 'inert or unacted upon belief' and 'living, active, embodied belief'. It is the latter, he argues, that 'makes U.S. the persons we are' and it is that personhood which is protected by the belief rights: Smith (2005).

84   *X v the Federal Republic of Germany* (1970).

a self-proclaimed Wiccan failed to satisfy the Commission of the existence of the Wiccan religion,[85] the Commission did not clearly set out just what evidence is required in such cases. The European Court has tended to leave the domestic courts to determine this. The House of Lords in *Regina, ex parte Williamson v Secretary of State for Education and Employment* (2005), for example, has ruled that so long as a claimant holds a belief, no matter how unreasonable, they should be 'given the benefit of the doubt'.[86]

[7.48] Additionally, where beliefs are non-religious, the situation is not quite so clear. The European Commission and Court have required that they relate to well-established schools of thought, such as pacifism[87] atheism,[88] and communism.[89] A personal conviction is more likely to be accepted if it is supported by an established association.[90] Even so, the European Commission has applied a narrow, mainstream religion-based distinction between permissible and non-permissible associations.[91]

The European Council and the ECHR

[7.49] The intention behind Article 9 ECHR has been expressed as similarly broad. In drafting the ECHR, the Council of Europe used the UDHR as the model for the ECHR, adopting the same wording. The *travaux préparatoires* of those responsible for drafting the ECHR (the Consultative Assembly) are of limited assistance, as published records are incomplete.[92] From the evidence available, it seems that religion was a specific focus of discussion, with the Christian religion given predominance.[93]

[7.50] Notwithstanding this, the final wording in the consultative Assembly's recommendation to the Council of Ministers was to include in the Convention a 'right to freedom of thought, conscience and religion as laid down in Article 18 of the Declaration of the United Nations'.[94] This proposal was accepted without discussion in the debate before the Assembly. While the

85   *X v the United Kingdom* (1977).
86   Knights (2007), 42.
87   *Arrowsmith v the United Kingdom* (1978).
88   *Angeleni v Sweden* (1986).
89   *Hazar Hazar and Açik v Turkey* (1991); *United Communist Party of Turkey and Others v Turkey* (1998).
90   Malcolm Evans (1997), 289ff. There is little guidance on this issue: see, e.g., Ibid, 289ff.
91   Ibid, 292ff.
92   See Carolyn Evans (2001), 38ff.
93   Ibid.
94   Council of Europe (1956), European Commission of Human Rights *Preparatory Work on Article 9 of the European Convention on Human Rights Information Document Prepared by the Secretatiat of the Commission.* <http://www.echr.coe.int/LibraryDocs/Travaux/ECHRTravaux-ART9-DH%2856%2914-EN1338892.pdf; also at vol 1, p 174 of the Collected Edition of the *Travaux Préparatoires* of the European Convention on Human Rights. The official version of the *travaux préparatoires* are published in 8 volumes from 1975-1985 by Martinus Nijhoff in the Hague.

Committee of Experts then charged with drafting the Convention accepted the belief rights as set out in the UDHR,[95] the question of limitation was subject to some dissension and debate.[96]

Conclusion

[7.51] What can we conclude from the above discussion? Firstly, it is suggested, the specific expression of a 'right to freedom of religion and belief', and specifically the wording of the belief provisions, has caused problems with the interpretation and implementation of that right. For those states that wish to apply the belief provisions to their actions there are problems with the nomination of 'religion' and 'conscience' as distinct categorisations of thought, and 'religion' as separate from 'belief' creates ambiguity and confusion as to what is intended. Attempts to unravel the nuances of language distract from the underlying principles of autonomy (the liberty to act as you will) and the qualifying requirement of equality (the obligation to ensure the same liberty for others). The provisions are subsequently open to political, economic and social pressures that detract from their effective realisation.

[7.52] It is argued here that the case of *Plattform "Ärzte für das Leben" v Austria* (1988) points to the proposition that Article 18 is in some senses redundant.[97] In that case, doctors who were prevented from demonstrating against abortion complained of a breach of freedom to manifest their belief (under Article 9 ECHR), as well as the right to freedom of expression (under Article 10). The Commission held that the right to manifest belief and the right to freedom of expression are inseparable from that of freedom of assembly (Article 11). The basic motivation for expression, assembly and association are irrelevant, where the resulting action is permissible under the Convention. As the UDHR and ICCPR also both include such rights, it held, this principle can be held to apply to them as well.

[7.53] This supports the argument that the belief provisions are in effect contained within the provisions for freedom of speech, assembly and association. As they stand, the belief provisions are commonly taken to imply for particular beliefs (mostly religion) some sort of priority, and cause difficulties by diverting inquiry into the nature of 'religion' 'belief', and of 'manifesting' belief, etc. Speech, assembly and association are subject to similar limitations to freedom to manifest belief. There is no question we need belief rights, with guidelines, resolutions and charters of freedom that address religious and non-religious self-determination. But when given the authority of internationally recognised and enforceable rights and obligations, those rights should be expressed as a function of the right to freedom of all speech, assembly and association. Freedom

---

95   It is noted that *General Comment 22* was finalised much later.
96   See, for an account of the drafting of the ECHR, see Malcolm Evans (1997), 262-272. See also Carolyn Evans (2001), 38ff.
97   At p. 71.

of expression, it is noted refers to the right to thought and belief: 'freedom to hold opinions without interference and to seek, receive and impart information and ideas'. Freedom of association refers to participating in activities with others.

[7.54] In addition, while the human rights tribunals are quite clear that Article 18 is to be 'construed broadly', to include personal life stances other than religion itself, the effect of giving special recognition to religion undermines the realisation of its promise. The next Chapter considers the problems posed by reference to religion in the belief provisions.

CHAPTER 8
WHY 'RELIGION'?

[8.1] Religion is given special reference in Article 18 UDHR because most of those who originally drafted it were religious, and/or represented a society that attributed special values to religion. Despite the inclusion of 'belief' at the insistence of a minority representation on the drafting committee, religion has been given special consideration ever since. If there were no mention of religion, the Article would still have recognised religious freedom. Instead, the door has been opened not only to the privileging of religion, but also to complex and arbitrary interpretations of what constitutes a religion.

[8.2] Many different meanings have been given to the words 'religion' and 'belief'.[1] Narrow substantive interpretations that focus solely on religion require recognition of a supernatural being or entity (e.g. in the Australian courts).[2] Functional views consider these terms jointly to refer to any convictions that play a role (similar to religion) that generates social identity and cohesion (e.g. in the US courts).[3]

[8.3] Despite the intended broadness of the term 'religion or belief', the belief provisions are generally used (either mistakenly or deliberately) to give credence to the global phenomenon of a favoured status for religion generally, and/or honouring specific religious groups. Demands for special treatment for religious groups follow, and, as noted, there is a global tendency for states to give some preference to some religions over others (see also Chapter 12). Academic discussion of belief rights overwhelmingly tends to see the issue in terms only of religion, with little attention to the right to equal consideration of other life stances.

[8.4] Attempts by courts in different jurisdictions to determine what constitutes a 'religion' indicate the difficulty in developing a legal definition. Courts have tended to take a position somewhere within two different broad approaches. The first is a 'substantive' approach, which determines the content of what makes beliefs religious, such as belief in the supernatural, life

---

1   See, e.g., Gunn (2003), 189.
2   See, e.g., *Church of the New Faith v Commissioner of Pay-roll Tax* (1983).
3   See, e.g., Horwitz (1997), 129.

after death or the possession of a soul.[4] The 'substantive' approach can be seen in, for example, Australian[5] and earlier UK[6] and US[7] case law.

[8.5] The second is a 'functional' approach, focusing 'not on what religion is, but what it does',[8] for example, answering the fundamental questions about existence or provision of comfort or sense of meaning to one's life. The United Nations High Commission for Refugees has specifically adopted what amounts to a 'functional' approach to the definition of religion in its guidelines on religion-based refugee claims, released in 2004.[9] It stated that 'religion' can include non-religious convictions (which are centred around the developed life stance and/or values of the person), religion as identity (which is represents membership of a group or community) and religion as a way of life. Functional approaches have been more recently adopted in the UK (reflecting the ratification of the ICCPR and adoption of ECHR provisions in the Human Rights Act 1998 (UK))[10] and the US.[11]

[8.6] Notwithstanding the nature of religion, the principles underlying the belief provisions indicate that the appropriate concern of government in a liberal democracy is not *why* one acts, but rather the *effect of that action on others*, and its compatibility with public reason.[12] This further supports the argument that the need to determine whether what one believes is a religion or not is simply beside the point. The issue for the state is the functional effect of belief: what you do, whatever your motivation, and how your actions impact on the rights of others. Manifestation of belief is considered in Chapters 10 and 11.

Religion as belief in the supernatural

[8.7] The difficulty in identifying 'religion' is demonstrated by the approach of the Australian High Court when it had the opportunity to determine what constitutes 'religion' in the case of *Church of the New Faith v Commissioner of Pay-roll Tax* (Vic).[13] In that case it rejected theism as a

---

4   Roberts (1984), 3.
5   See, e.g., *Adelaide Company of Jehovah's Witnesses Incorporated v The Commonwealth* (1943), 116; *Church of the New Faith v Commissioner of Pay-roll Tax* (1983), 120.
6   See, e.g., *Baxter v Langley* (1868), 38 LJMC 1, 5; *United Grand Lodge of Ancient Free and Accepted Masons of England v Holborn Borough Council* (1957), 1 WLR 1080, 1090; *R v Registrar-General ex parte Segerdal* (1970), 707.
7   See, e.g., *United States v MacIntosh* (1931): 'One cannot speak of religious liberty, with proper appreciation of its essential and historic significance, without assuming the existence of a belief in supreme allegiance to the will of God' (Chief Justice Hughes at 634).
8   Ibid, 7.
9   United Nations (2004), 501.
10 See, e.g., the rejection of a 'substantive' approach to belief in *Regina ex parte Williamson and others v Secretary of State for Education and Employment and others* (2005), (Lord Nicholls of Birkenhead at ¶24).
11 See, e.g., Horwitz (1997), 129.
12 See discussion of state neutrality in U.S. and Australian courts in Sadurski (1990).
13 *Church of the New Faith v Commissioner of Pay-roll Tax* (1983).

necessary basis for a belief to be considered 'religious'. However, it indicated that belief in the 'supernatural' generally plays a central role in religion.

[8.8] The Court was seeking a definition of religion in order to consider whether Scientology was a religion for the purposes of Victorian payroll tax legislation. Four out of five judges agreed in the centrality of a supernatural being or entity in religious beliefs, but differed in how belief in such an entity constitutes a religion.

[8.9] Mason A.C.J. and Brennan J. applied a twofold test: 'first, belief in a supernatural Being, Thing or Principle; and second, the acceptance of canons of conduct in order to give effect to that belief', while allowing for variations of emphasis on each of these characteristics.[14]

[8.10] Wilson and Deane JJ. held that there is no single characteristic that can be applied to a religion. They preferred 'to formulate the more important of the indicia or guidelines that must be derived by empirical observation of accepted religions'.[15] The indicia they nominated were a belief in the supernatural, absence of which makes a belief unlikely to be a religion; ideas that 'relate to man's nature and place in the universe and his relation to things supernatural'; codes of conduct; constitution of an identifiable group; and self perception as a religion. These, they said, 'are no more than aids' in determining whether a belief is a religion. However, '[i]t is unlikely that a collection of ideas and/or practices would properly be characterized as a religion if it lacked all or most of them'.[16]

[8.11] Murphy J., in a minority judgment, differed from his fellow judges. Quoting Latham J. in *Adelaide Company of Jehovah's Witnesses Inc. v Commonwealth* (1943),[17] he adopted the approach that each person chooses the content of his own religion.[18] On this reasoning, the categories of religion are not closed,[19] and while a belief in the supernatural would indicate a belief is religious, also included is 'any body which claims to be religious and offers a way to find meaning and purpose in life'.[20] This is akin to the stated UNHRC and ECtHR approach to the belief rights.

[8.12] An after-effect of this case provides an example of the inconsistency that can arise from attempts to classify beliefs by whether they are 'religious' or not. It also shows the inequality of treatment of different belief groups when some are given favourable treatment based on personal

---

14   Ibid, 136.
15   Ibid, 173.
16   Ibid, 174.
17   At p. 124.
18   Ibid, 150-151.
19   Ibid, 150. He stated at p. 151 that anybody believing in a supernatural being or beings 'whether physical and visible, such as the sun or the stars, or a physical invisible God or spirit, or an abstract God or entity, is religious'.
20   Ibid, 150.

convictions. The case has been interpreted to require a belief in some sort of supernatural phe-nomenon to be granted the special status of 'religion' (and thus exemption from taxation) by the Australian Tax Office ('ATO'). Thus, when the Raelian organisation (a self-nominated religion) sought tax exemption as a religion, the ATO refused to classify it as a religion for tax purposes, as its extra-terrestrial but material masters "Elohim" were held to be not supernatural.[21] Pointing to the Court's findings in the Church of the New Faith case, the ATO stated in a letter to the Raelian Bishop of the Australian Raelian Movement, Jean François Aymonier, that the 'two main criteria' for beliefs to count as a religion are:

- a belief in a supernatural Being, Thing or Principle; and

- the acceptance of canons of conduct in order to give effect to that belief.

[8.13] The letter went on to state that the ATO considered that Book Two of the Raelian writings, setting out the doctrines of Raelian belief, *The Messages of the Elohim*, indicates that the concept of an immaterial God is incorrect and that there is no soul to fly out of the body after death. The Raelians were thus not considered a religious institution.[22] In contrast, the ATO considers the Church of Scientology a religion, holding as it does a belief in supernatural inter-galactic beings.[23]

[8.14] The Australian approach was cited with approval in a recent case concerning Scientology in the UK. Lord Toulson, speaking for the majority in the UK Supreme Court, defined religion 'in summary' as

a spiritual or non-secular belief system, held by a group of adherents, which claims to explain mankind's place in the universe and relationship with the infinite, and to teach its adherents how they are to live their lives in conformity with the spiritual understanding associated with the belief system.[24]

[8.15] He emphasised the 'spiritual or non-secular' element:

---

21 Elohim are extra-terrestrial beings who are 'our creators' who first made contact with Earth through the leader of the Raelian religion, Rael.

22 Correspondence from the Australian Tax Office to Mr Aymonier, quoted with permission by him.

23 Church of Scientology teachings, it is alleged, include, among stories of other intergalactic activities, the belief that intergalactic beings space-shipped their galaxy's surplus population to Earth millions of years ago and disposed of them by burying their frozen bodies in volcanoes and blowing them up with nuclear weapons. Their 'souls', known as 'thetans' clung to the survivors causing personal problems in all subsequent human generations. These problems can only be resolved by Scientology 'auditing', a ritual of interview and confession undertaken with the use of an 'E-Meter', a lie detector device. Until the subject is 'clear' of their problems they cannot realise their full potential. See, e.g., Rothstein (2009), 365.

24 *R (on the application of Hodkin and another), v Registrar General of Births, Deaths and Marriages* (2013), ¶ 57.

By spiritual or non-secular I mean a belief system which goes beyond that which can be perceived by the senses or ascertained by the application of science…Such a belief system may or may not involve belief in a supreme being, but it does involve a belief that there is more to be understood about mankind's nature and relationship to the universe than can be gained from the senses or from science. I emphasise that this is intended to be a description and not a definitive formula.[25]

[8.16] Where the law is concerned only with whether doctrines are 'religious', it loses focus on the broader goals of promoting individual autonomy, dignity and freedom through belief rights as applying to religious *or* non-religious worldview. The result is a special, or privileged, approach to such doctrines, which would be protected solely because they are labelled 'religious'. This devalues the life stances of atheists, agnostics and others who are not perceived as 'religious'. It also impedes the means to deal with life stances inspired by a mixture of tradition, 'spiritual beliefs' (whatever these may be) and religious doctrines. The broader goal of individual autonomy, dignity and self-realisation would be lost to the priority granted to exclusively religious beliefs so designated.[26]

[8.17] It is noteworthy that in the Australian case, Mason A.C.J. and Brennan J invoked the idea of political secularism while not recognising it as such:

Protection is not accorded to safeguard the tenets of each religion; no such protection can be given by the law, and it would be contradictory of the law to protect at once the tenets of different religions which are incompatible with one another. Protection is accorded to preserve the dignity and freedom of each man so that he may adhere to any religion of his choosing or to none. The freedom of religion being equally conferred on all, the variety of religious beliefs which are within the area of legal immunity is not restricted.[27]

[8.18] They added:

Conduct in which a person engages in giving effect to his faith in the supernatural is religious, but it is excluded from the area of legal immunity marked out by the concept of religion if it offends against the ordinary laws, i.e. if it offends against laws which do not discriminate against religion generally or against particular religions or against conduct of a kind which is characteristic only of a religion.[28]

---

25   Ibid.

26   This is the thrust of the argument proposed by Edge (2006), 27–34.

27   *Church of the New Faith v Commissioner of Pay-roll Tax* (1983), 132.

28   Ibid, 136. This view was also implied by Wilson and Dean JJ. at 176.

[8.19] Thus, 'canons of conduct which offend against the ordinary laws are outside the area of any immunity, privilege or right conferred on the grounds of religion'.[29] There was no specific ruling, however, that laws must not discriminate against a religion. Nevertheless, it appears that religiously inspired activity is clearly 'trumped' by the laws of the land if it conflicts with them. The circuitous judicial language above, however, does not specify separation of religion and the state.

Special treatment of religious belief

[8.20] Despite the formal recognition of non-religious beliefs by the human rights bodies discussed above, conceptions and biases have resulted over time with religion being given special significance, both in terms of state endorsement of particular religious values and financial assistance to state-recognised 'religion(s)'. One example of this is the inclusion by most Western nations of 'advancement of religion' in the definition of what constitutes a charity, and religions are therefore eligible for government tax relief, government subsidies and other benefits. This is a relic of the 17th century, and religion and charity have been considered synonymous characteristics ever since, despite the fact that religious organisations need not carry out any charitable work to qualify for such benefits.

[8.21] Most commentators, despite conceding that the belief provisions refer to a broad range of personal convictions, discuss 'belief' either exclusively or generally in terms of religion only.[30] Paul Rishworth goes further in his discussion of the incorporation of similar wording to the belief provisions in the New Zealand *Bill of Rights Act* 1990. He states that '[i]t is conceivable that a bill of rights drafted for the modern secular age would not include freedom of religion' but would treat all beliefs as equal.[31] However, he notes that the belief provisions appear to establish a right to manifest 'religion' and 'belief', but not a right to manifest non-religious 'thought' and 'conscience' (presuming one can draw a distinction between these). That distinction, he argues, 'simply reflects the values of the bill of rights tradition, which has long put religion in a special place'.[32]

[8.22] This appears to place the 'bill of rights tradition' at odds with his view of the US Courts' approach to the US Constitution First Amendment ensuring freedom of belief, which he says has 'understandably' been concerned to avoid 'wholesale exemptions from secular laws so as to place

29 Ibid.
30 E.g., Malcolm Evans (1997); Carolyn Evans (2001); Taylor (2005). In researching this book, the author found little result in response to searching the word 'belief' either online or in indexes. Reference to 'freedom of belief' was almost invariably referenced as 'religion'. No books characterising the right as one simply to 'belief' in their title was found.
31 Rishworth (1995), 257 n 37.
32 Ibid, 230.

adherents of religion in a favoured position over others'.[33] The intention that religion is to have a pre-eminent or special role in the application of the right to 'freedom of belief' is also suggested by the words of Jean-François Renucci, writing for the Council of Europe, who argued that Article 9 ECHR 'concerns religion in particular' and points out that it makes 'specific reference to an individual's religious conceptions'.[34]

[8.23] The view that religion is to be given special treatment is supported by religious adherents who claim that their personal convictions *per se* are superior to others. Eduado Peñalver, for example, argues religious convictions are superior to others because it is both based on a 'higher authority' than the state, and is seen as having a 'singularly all-encompassing, meaning-conferring nature'.[35]

[8.24] Moreover, notwithstanding the *Pretty* case (see above [7.37]), the European Court itself has shown some ambivalence toward giving special treatment to religion. In a case involving state prohibition of showing of an allegedly religiously offensive film, the Court declared that Article 9 ECHR guarantees 'respect for the religious feelings of believers'.[36] This differs from its approach in a later case dealing with suppression of an allegedly religiously offensive film, in which the issue was regarded as one of freedom of speech, thus avoiding consideration of Article 9 altogether.[37]

[8.25] In the more recent case of *Murphy v Ireland*,[38] the European Court upheld the suppression of an advertisement for a meeting to discuss the evidence of the Resurrection of Christ. It endorsed the State's right to exercise some discretion ('margin of appreciation',[39] i.e. recognition of social attitudes current in the relevant country) as to what is 'necessary to protect public safety, order, health or morals' under Article 9.2 ECHR. The Court concluded that 'a wider margin of appreciation is generally available to the Contracting States when regulating freedom of expres-

---

33   Ibid, 234.

34   Renucci (2005), 12. Indeed, despite the general acceptance of the framers of the ICCPR that Article 18 was to include non-religious convictions, 'some still took the view that the Article was principally concerned with freedom of religion and should be read in that light' (Malcolm Evans (1997), 40, footnote deleted).

35   Eduardo Peñalver (2006), esp. 2249ff. Also favouring the view that religious belief is 'special' are Fish (1997); McConnell (2000); Greene (1994). Those specifically rejecting it include Smith (2005b); Eisgruber and Sager (1994a); Nickel (2005).

36   *Otto-Preminger-Institut v Austria* (1994).

37   *Wingrove v the United Kingdom* (1996).

38   *Murphy v Ireland* (2003).

39   *Kokkinakis v Greece* (1993), ¶47, Series A no. 260-A 1993. See also *Handyside v the United Kingdom* (1976), ¶ 48 ff, Series A no. 24; *Lawless v Ireland* (1961). Margin of appreciation is dealt with in more detail at [11.9].

sion in relation to matters liable to offend intimate personal life stances within the sphere of morals or, especially, religion'.[40]

[8.26] Another source of ambivalence lies in the fact that while the UN calls for Article 18 ICCPR to be 'broadly construed' and treats with concern discrimination against any 'religion or belief', it fails to say what a 'religion or belief' is, and tends to equate 'belief' with 'religion'.[41] This further encourages a narrowed focus on traditional religions with institutional characteristics.[42] The call for the terms 'religion' and 'belief' to be 'broadly construed' thus loses its initial apparent broad scope in practice. Rather than conclude, as does Malcolm Evans, that the failure to clarify the meaning of the terms underlies the need for setting boundaries between them,[43] it makes more sense if both terms are considered together to amount to personal life stances. This is surely in line with the egalitarian liberal democratic society that Rawls describes.

[8.27] It is perhaps not surprising that a frequent result of the emphasis on traditional religions is that governments and adjudicators may favour particular social and cultural attitudes towards or against particular religions, even if they do so unintentionally. Different 'ideologies' can inform judicial reasoning,[44] including personal ideologies based on social, religious or other life stances (for example views on homosexuality as 'unnatural and immoral',[45] or the expression of personal opinion and experience of corporal punishment in schools.[46]

[8.28] An extreme example of an unfavourable view of the manifestation of a particular belief is the disfavour in which Judge Valticos held a non-state religion in the Case of *Kokkinakis v Greece* (1993). This case involved a member of the Jehovah's Witnesses (a religion the judge disfavoured) who visited a household to discuss his religious views and was subsequently convicted of unlawful proselytism (attempting to undermine a person's religious beliefs through inducement, fraud or unfair advantage). The alleged 'victim', the wife of a cantor in the Greek Orthodox Church, stated that the 15-minute discussion did not influence her beliefs. Judge Valticos in his dissenting judgment at ¶10 described the accused's actions as those of a

---

40   *Murphy v Ireland* (2003), ¶67. The Court dealt with the matter under Article 10 ECHR (freedom of speech. It said 'a wider margin of appreciation is generally available to the Contracting States when regulating freedom of expression in relation to matters liable to offend intimate personal convictions within the sphere of morals or, especially, religion'.

41   Ibid, ¶2.

42   Malcolm Evans (1997), 41ff.

43   Ibid, 43.

44   As regards the European Court, this is considered in detail in Merrills (1988), Ch 10.

45   See, e.g., the dissenting judgement of Judge Zekia in *Dudgeon v the United Kingdom* (1981).

46   See, e.g., dissenting judgment of Sir Gerald Fitzmaurice, in *Tyrer v the United Kingdom* (1978), who applies his own personal opinion and experience of corporal punishment by saying that he suffered it and it did him no harm.

militant hardbitten adept of proselytism…an experienced commercial traveller and cunning purveyor of a faith he wants to spread…whose earlier convictions [for proselytism of religion other than the state established Church] have served only to harden him in his militancy' who 'swoops' on his victim, 'trumpets' good news…expounds to her his intellectual wares cunningly wrapped up in a mantle of universal peace and radiant happiness…

[8.29] Other examples are not so extreme, and include, inter alia, preference for traditional religious beliefs such as Christianity, Islam, Judaism, Buddhism and Hinduism, over other personal life stances.[47]

[8.30] Decisions that favour specific groups such as religions are made by state administrations for the purpose of special treatment, notably tax and other legal exemptions, and government grants.[48] Preference of one personal life stance, such as religion, over another can become a judgment on whether the particular beliefs or actions are acceptable to the government or the legal system. There is evidence of state bias in favour of state-endorsed religions through suppression of non-established religions.[49] An example of the state persistently and arbitrarily refusing to register an association as a religious association can be found in the case of *Church of Scientology Moscow v Russia* (2007). In 1996 the European Court pointed out that 'numerous' cases showed that the Greek State tended to impose 'rigid, or indeed prohibitive conditions on practice of religious beliefs by particular non-Orthodox movements, in particular Jehovah's Witnesses', and that

> the extensive case-law in this field seems to show a clear tendency on the part of the administrative and ecclesiastical authorities to use these provisions to restrict the activities of faiths outside the Orthodox Church.[50]

---

47   See, e.g., Gunn (2003).

48   Gunn points out examples of purposes for identifying religions, such as

- whether an entity is a 'religion' or 'religious association' for purposes of granting legal personality, obtaining tax benefits, or limiting the personal liability of the organizers;

- whether someone has 'religious' beliefs for the purpose of obtaining conscientious objector status; or

- whether someone should be exempted from a law of general applicability on the grounds of religious belief (e.g., a Sikh motorcyclist being exempted from a requirement to wear a helmet or a Muslim or Jewish slaughterhouse being permitted to kill animals in accordance with ritual laws): at 191 fn 14.

49   Gunn (1996), 325. (Gunn believes the Court allows too wide a margin of appreciation to states in their restriction of religious practices).

50   *Manoussakis and Others v Greece* (1996), ¶41ff. See, also, e.g., *Penditis and others v Greece,* No 23238 Rep 1996, ¶34-39 and *Tsavachidis v Greece* (1997). These cases ended in a friendly settlement, with the Court finding breach of Article 9 and claimants allowed to practise their religion.

Why 'religion'?

[8.31] Religionists who don't look for power or privilege (but rather true benefit to others through its advancement) may argue that we should give religion special treatment for the general good of society. It is conceded that religion can inspire many to good works and a charitable outlook, and the argument here is not that religious institutions should be eliminated or discouraged when this is their purpose. Indeed, the whole intention is to provide an environment where no religion is favoured or suppressed for its own sake. However, it is argued that the privileging of religion *per se* leads to incoherence, inconsistency and inequity in governance through bias in implementing liberties relating to belief. The promotion of equal participation of all individuals in the liberty to live by their personal convictions is consequently hindered.

[8.32] In relation to *incoherence*, for example, there is often judicial vagueness and uncertainty towards what should be considered a religion. Should only a socially or politically recognised 'religion' be considered?[51] If so, is it to include a god, several gods, some other sort of supernatural entity, or should it rather include any belief that forms the same function as religion? If the latter, what *is* the function of religion? Is it to provide a system of enquiry, a set of rules, a comforting social support or a proud cultural heritage? Does the content of what one believes matter at all? Is it rather a matter of how one acts as a result? To be considered manifestation of religion, must protected actions be central to religion (such as church services) or merely motivated by religion (such as good works or modest dress)? Opinions and judicial deliberations differ.[52] These are all questions that are raised by the need to find a definition of 'religion'. They are, it is maintained, irrelevant to the intention of Article 18.

[8.33] If courts or tribunals are concerned as to whether a belief is 'religious', they can also be distracted by other questions of doubtful relevance, such as, is the claimant sincere in her belief, or is 'religion' being used falsely as an excuse for her actions? Is the wearing of particular dress or symbols a deeply religious act, or more one of cultural or political solidarity? Does the claimed manifestation have to be specifically mandated by relevant religious doctrine? Should adjudicators question the validity of religious tenets of a claimant against their religious community as a whole, or can the claimant's differing views from their religious community be taken into account? What if the claimant argues that his or her own unique beliefs are religious? [53]

---

51   See, e.g., discussion of this issue in, e.g., *Arrowsmith v the United Kingdom* (1978); *Kokkinakis v Greece* (1993); *Buscarini and Others v San Marino* (1999); *Darby v Sweden* (1990).

52   Durham (1996); Gunn (2003).

53   The difficulty of determining just what beliefs should be considered religious or not, and whether individual ideas of right and wrong are included is outlined by Malcolm Evans (1997), 203ff.

[8.34] *Inconsistency* occurs because Governments and courts have differed in the meaning they have given religion from one jurisdiction to another. Scientology, for example, is recognised as a religion for tax purposes in some countries but not others.

[8.35] Finally, *inequality* results from the stratification of society based on belief. Individuals rank themselves according to what they consider to be true or untrue beliefs, and good or bad behaviour. Some see themselves as entitled to privilege and power based on their religious beliefs and activity, and consider others outsiders, unworthy or deserving of punishment, again not because of breaches of the law, but of religious tenets held by the group. Examples of this are apparent throughout this book.

[8.36] On the grounds of incoherence, inconsistency and inequality, then, special mention of religion in the belief provisions is problematic, in effect undermining the principle of belief rights.

Conclusion

[8.37] Who needs freedom of religion? Answer: everyone, whether we have a religion or not. We all need freedom of thought, opinion and conviction and the freedom to articulate these in our personal activities through expression, association and assembly, without unreasonable interference by the state. The content may differ, but the freedoms themselves have the same force for everyone.

[8.38] However, a major misconception that interferes with the genuine exercise of belief rights by everyone is the persistence in granting privileged treatment to religion. The language of Article 18 with its religion-associated terminology means that those charged with implementing it are diverted by irrelevant considerations, and inclined to subvert its intentions. It seems that inconsistent, incoherent and inequitable approaches to the belief provisions, both those of the human rights tribunals and academics, lead, in practice, to the favouring of religious beliefs over other life-stance philosophies. The view that religious freedom is pre-eminent over freedom of other beliefs cannot be sustained if there is to be true freedom of, and consequently from, belief.

[8.39] As will be demonstrated, the approach of the belief tribunals has not been as clear as it should have been. It is argued, as does Carolyn Evans, that, despite their formal definition of 'religion or belief', the human rights tribunals have also adopted a religion-centred interpretation of what constitutes the practice of 'religion or belief'. This, she says, has led to protection under the Convention extending only to 'manifestations that are highly analogous to Christian beliefs', disproportionally affecting minorities 'whose practice may be less familiar to the Court'. Consequently, the recognition of belief rights 'has very limited scope and provides little protection to non-traditional forms of practice'.[54]

[8.40] Before considering the tribunals' decisions, it is considered appropriate in the next Chapter to consider another misconception that has dogged the understanding of the Article 18 promise: the appeal to conscience, and related introduction into deliberation on belief rights of the distinction between the 'public' and 'private' spheres.

---

[54]   Carolyn Evans (2001), 132. See also Malcolm Evans (1997), 291ff.

CHAPTER 9
CONSCIENTIOUS OBJECTION: THE 'FORUM INTERNUM'

[9.1] People may object to the state either preventing them acting according to their conscience, or requiring them to act contrary to their conscience. They invoke the right to 'freedom of conscience' and argue that the state is violating Article 18. There is disagreement among commentators between the line between the right to hold one's own conscientious beliefs (the *'forum internum'*) and the right to act according to one's conscience is to be drawn. This creates further ambiguity and uncertainty regarding the belief provisions.

Objection to limitation on manifestation of belief

[9.2] The second right espoused by the belief principles, the right to 'have and adopt' a belief of one's choosing, has been described by the European Commission as protecting 'the sphere of personal beliefs and religious creeds, i.e. the area which is sometimes called the *forum internum*'.[1] It then qualified its approach to the *forum internum* when it considered conscientious objection to mandatory action a matter of manifestation of belief:

> Article 9 primarily protects the sphere of personal beliefs and religious creeds, i.e. the area which is sometimes called the *forum internum*. In addition, it protects acts which are intimately linked to these attitudes, such as acts of worship or devotion which are aspects of the practice of a religion or belief in a generally recognised form.

> However, in protecting this personal sphere, Article 9 of the Convention does not always guarantee the right to behave in the public sphere in a way which is dictated by such a belief: for instance by refusing to pay certain taxes because part of the revenue so raised may be applied for military expenditure.[2]

[9.3] By introducing the concept of *forum internum* into the discussion of belief rights, a further cloud of obscurity has been introduced, creating other barriers to a clear conception of what is required. Despite the clear indication that acting according to one's beliefs is not absolute, many wishing to follow a particular belief insist that limiting the manifestation of their belief is an attack on the *forum internum*, forcing those involved to renounce or reject their belief. This creates

---

1   *C. v United Kingdom* (1983), 147. This case held that objection to payment of taxes was not protected by Article 9 ECHR; Malcolm Evans call this a 'standard recital' as it was adopted, e.g., in *V v the Netherlands* (1984). *Vereniging Rechtswinkels Utrecht v Netherlands* (1986); *Van Den Dungen v the Netherlands* (1995), ¶1 (complainant demonstrated outside abortion clinic): Malcolm Evans (1997), 294ff. See also Taylor (2005), 147.
2   Ibid. See also Chief Justice Warren, in the U.S. case of *Braunfield v Brown*, 366 U.S. 599, 607.

spurious grounds for demanding the right to practise one's belief regardless of the law or effect on the rights of others, infusing society with belief-based practices and principles. A consideration of the fallacies surrounding such claims is thus required.

What is the 'forum internum'?

[9.4] Some commentators adopt a broad definition of the *forum internum*[3]. They perceive the *forum internum* in the psychological sense of deep-seated identity in a belief, arguing that limiting the practice of a belief is tantamount to forcing a person to recant the belief itself.[4] Their views are situated anywhere along the spectrum between the narrowest and the broadest representations of the *forum internum*. This approach is based on the sense of solidarity and belonging that comes from such activities as the wearing of particular clothing, eating of particular foods and other personal means of identifying with their particular belief system – the normative, cultural and social aspect of the belief provisions. Other commentators, along with the belief tribunals, adopt a narrow approach to the idea of the *forum internum* limiting protection of the *forum internum* to protection from actions that are intended to induce a change of mind such as indoctrination and mind control.[5]

[9.5] Paul Taylor, adopting a broad definition, describes the *forum internum* as 'the internal and private realm of the individual against which no State interference is justified',[6] but goes on to say that it involves more than mere choice of religion or belief. He argues that the human rights tribunals have been inconsistent and unclear in their understanding of the *forum internum*.[7] In Taylor's view, freedom from coercion to behave contrary to one's religion or belief is protected by the *forum internum*.[8] He seems thus to include some actions, or refusal to act, as part of the unconditionally protected right to freedom of 'thought, conscience and religion'.

[9.6] However, while lamenting clarity on the part of the human rights tribunals, Taylor notes that his proffered interpretation of *forum internum* is problematic, and concedes that the human rights tribunals have not adopted it.[9] For one thing, it would not be practical or compatible with the human rights of others to allow all conscientious objections to obeying the law. The bottom

---

3   See, e.g., Taylor (2005), 115ff. Tahzib (1996), 26; Carolyn Evans (2001), 74ff. Martínez-Torrón and Navarro-Valls (2004), indicate they favour a similar approach, at p. 228.
4   See, e.g., Carolyn Evans (2001), 72ff., esp. 77-78; Taylor (2005), Ch 3; Tahzib (1996), 26.
5   See, e.g., Malcolm Evans (1997), 72ff.
6   Taylor (2005), 115.
7   Ibid, 118ff.
8   Ibid, 119.
9   Ibid

line is that belief rights comes at a cost,[10] and that cost is bound up with the requirement for reciprocity, which is specified in the limitation provisions.

[9.7] On the other hand, Bahiyyih Tazhib argues that the *forum internum* includes enforced or proscribed membership of a religion or belief, discrimination on the ground of religion or belief, enforced participation in religious practices and recanting a religion or belief or changing allegiance to or from a religion or belief.[11] However, as none of these activities necessitate the internal willingness of the individual involved, it is argued that the *forum internum* in fact remains intact.

[9.8] Similar to Taylor, others, such as Pieter van Dijk et al. describe freedom of 'thought, conscience and religion' as including the freedom to accept a religion or belief, and 'not to be obliged to act in a way that entails the expression of the acceptation of a church, religion or belief that one does not share'.[12] This goes further than actually having or adopting a belief, and suggests that they also have a broad notion of the *forum internum*.

[9.9] Malcolm Evans, takes a contrary view. He argues that the *forum internum* is restricted to internal thoughts and beliefs. He sets a threshold for the *forum internum* based on the view that 'provided that the individuals are able to continue in their beliefs, the *forum internum* remains untouched and there will be no breach of Article 9.1 [ECHR]'.[13] He points to the absolute right to thought, religion and conscience in the first sentence of Article 9 (and, by implication, Article 18 ICCPR). This right is

> 'narrowly circumscribed', and 'cannot be used to extend beyond the scope of the freedom to hold a pattern of thought, conscience or religion beyond the *forum* internum – the 'private sphere'. In particular it cannot be used to justify claims to exercise rights in the public sphere, since they are unnecessary to private belief'.[14]

[9.10] He notes that breaching this threshold would violate other rights as well, such as the right to freedom from torture, inhumane or degrading treatment or punishment, or from the forceful influence of a person's autonomy of thought.[15] If the *forum internum* refers only to private thoughts (which include thoughts related to conscience, religion and belief) without any

---

10   See, e.g. Evans (1997), 300.
11   Tahzib (1996), 26.
12   van Dijk et al (2006), 758 (emphasis added).
13   Malcolm Evans (1997), 295 and van Dijk et al (2006), 752.
14   Malcolm Evans (1997), 299. His use of the term *forum internum* is thus restrictive.
15   Ibid, 294–5. Elsewhere he points to the case of *Kosteski v "the former Yugoslav Republic of Macedonia"* (2000), where the European Court questioned the sincerity of the applicant's belief: 'What this case makes clear is that the *forum internum* is very much a sphere of inner personal conviction and offers little by way of substantive protection to those seeking to protect the lifestyle generated by their beliefs from the intrusions of the state': Malcolm Evans (2008), 293.

action or communication of them to others, then its violation would require 'external pressure sufficient to induce a forcible change in inner belief'.[16]

[9.11] Another way of violating the *forum internum* would be by indoctrination, that is, directing a person in a point of view in a manner that demands or results in uncritical acceptance (e.g. imposed attitudes to government in North Korea). It involves institutional suppression of critical thinking through interference with thought processes through educational activities or sheer violence. Indoctrination would apply at least to those who are not in a position to consider rationally the material with which they are being indoctrinated, such as children.[17]

[9.12] D. J. Harris et al. adopt a similar stance in relation to Article 9 ECHR, stating that the internal forum is limited to the choice of religion or belief only, protecting against imposition of penalties for holding beliefs and indoctrination where this involves positive action directed against the individual.[18]

[9.13] Those who take a broad view of the *forum internum* differ in their demands for its protection, some saying, for example, it applies specifically to exemption from legal obligations that conflict with individual conscience, others going further to demand acceptance by the state and fellow citizens of a whole raft of religious activities.[19] What approach one takes on this issue is important, because, as protection of the *forum internum* has been held to be absolute, extending it to (vague) aspects of manifesting belief distorts the belief provisions by allowing unhindered the following of belief, allowing people to become, in effect, a law unto themselves.

[9.14] By taking the view that belief-based activity is an integral part of holding a belief itself, and thus absolute, the principles of democratic freedom and equality are eroded. As noted, unbridled manifestation of belief (any form of worship, observance, practice and teaching) is not guaranteed by the belief provisions, but subject to limitations (discussed further in Chapter 10). The differences in opinion just confuse the issue and result in arbitrary and inconsistent approaches to manifesting belief.

[9.15] The *forum internum* is concerned with the individual as *private person* (individual), with rights to personal identity and autonomy. How one acts (the *forum externum*?) is concerned with the individual as *citizen*, a member of the body politic and accountable to fellow citizens and the state for actions that affect their interests, consistent with Rawls's idea of reciprocity.

---

16   Malcolm Evans (1997), 294; (2008), 292.
17   Parents are allowed to 'indoctrinate' children, or allow them to be indoctrinated under the belief provisions: Malcolm Evans (1997), 356ff.
18   Harris, et al (1995), 360ff.; Taylor (2005) succinctly sets out the different positions in Freedom of Religion, at 116.
19   E.g., Taylor ibid, adopts the former view, Tahzib (ibid, 26), lists proscription of many activities involving worship, observance, practice and teaching as breaching the *forum internum*.

[9.16] This leads to the conclusion, it is suggested, that the narrower approach to the use of the term *forum internum* is to be preferred, both in accordance with logic and the stated intention of the belief provisions.

The belief tribunals and the forum internum

[9.17] There is no reference to *forum internum* in United Nations treaties or decisions. As well as case law, *General Comment 22* treats customs such as diet, dress and language as observance and practice of religion or belief, thus classifying them as manifestation of belief.[20] The *Belief Declaration* has a more extensive list of what it calls inclusively the right to 'freedom of thought, conscience, religion or belief', including teaching, distributing literature, solicit funds and establish institutions (see [10.6] for a full list), however this refers to belief rights in general, applying to freedom to both have and manifest a belief.

[9.18] Contrary to this approach, the UNHRC has avoided consideration of breach of the *forum internum,* but confounded the issue in the case of *Kang v Korea* (2003). In that case a dissident was convicted and sentenced to, *inter alia,* a rehabilitation process involving changing his ideology through an 'ideology conversion system' designed to induce change in a person's political opinion by the use of favours. The Committee considered that the State had

> failed to justify [the 'ideology conversion system'] as being necessary for any of the permissible limiting purposes enumerated in Articles 18 and 19, and thus restricted freedom of expression and manifestation of belief as set out under these Articles, in conjunction with Article 26 (which guarantees equality before the law).[21]

[9.19] The basic principles established by the human rights tribunals are critical to understanding their approach to the distinction between having and manifesting beliefs. Despite any use of the term *forum internum*, the human rights tribunals and others overall appear to be clear that the right to have or adopt a belief of one's choice is to be restricted to protection from indoctrination that violates the individual's conscious control of his or her religious and philosophical beliefs.[22]

[9.20] The *forum internum*, as its name implies, must have a corollary, the *forum externum*, or 'public face' of beliefs, through behaviour that reflects personal convictions. There is no meaningful exposition of the concept *forum externum*, by either the human rights tribunals or commentators, but it presumably would involve manifestation of belief described broadly as 'worship, obser-

---

20   *ICCPR General Comment 22* Par. 4: 'The observance and practice of religion or belief may include not only ceremonial acts but also such customs as the observance of dietary regulations, the wearing of distinctive clothing or head coverings, participation in rituals associated with certain stages of life, and the use of a particular language customarily spoken by a group'.

21   *Kang v Republic of Korea* (2003), ¶7.2.

22   Malcolm Evans (1997), 294-6.

vance, practice or teaching'.[23] As noted above, Article 6 of the *Belief Declaration* sets out a list of activities it covers. These are subject to Article 1.3, which applies to manifestation of belief and its limitations, as does *General Comment 22*. Article 6 of the *Belief Declaration* does not draw a distinction between having a belief and acting on it, so the matter is not resolved there.

[9.21] One would have thought that the 'ideology conversion system' is more appropriately considered a means of indoctrination, or interference with a person's ability to exercise freedom of thought or deliberation: a true invasion of the *forum internum*. This case confuses the distinction between thought and action.

Conscientious objection to military service

[9.22] The UNHRC treats objection to mandated (or, by inference, prohibited) action that is based on one's judgment of what is right ('conscientious objection') as an issue concerning manifestation of belief. While Article 8 ICCPR prohibits forced or compulsory labour, this prohibition does not include military service, or substitute service where conscientious objection is recognised by a government. *General Comment 22* ¶11 states that conscientious objection to military service 'can be derived from Article 18, inasmuch as the obligation to use lethal force may seriously conflict with the freedom of conscience and the right to manifest one's religion or belief'. Enigmatically, whether such objection is in fact a right appears to be subject to State law.[24] Paragraph 11 goes on to provide that

> [w]hen this right is recognized by law or practice, there shall be no differentiation among conscientious objectors on the basis of the nature of their particular beliefs; likewise, there shall be no discrimination against conscientious objectors because they have failed to perform military service.[25]

[9.23] Thus, while there is no specified right to conscientious objection to military service, states may require alternative service for conscientious objectors. However, the UNHRC has pointed to the Commission on Human Rights Resolution on Conscientious Objection to Military Service. The Commission acknowledged objection to military service as part of belief rights and recommended that governments

---

23   E.g., Articles 18(3), ICCPR; 9.2 ECHR and 1 *Belief Declaration.*
24   This was the approach taken by the UNHRC in *Westerman, Paul v The Netherlands* (1999).
25   *Foin, Frederic v France* (2000), ¶10.3. See also *Maille v France* (2000), ¶10.4; *Venier and Nicolas v France* (2000), ¶10.

provide for conscientious objectors [with] various forms of alternative service which are compatible with the reasons for conscientious objection, of a non-combatant or civilian character, in the public interest and not of a punitive nature.' [26]

[9.24] The European tribunals have also not made formal concessions to conscientious objection to military service. Article 4 ECHR prohibits forced labour, except, *inter alia*, for military service, or its substitute where allowed by the state. The European tribunals have stated emphatically that conscientious objection to some form of military service is not guaranteed under the ECHR.[27] However, where conscientious objectors were convicted of draft evasion because there was no law providing for such objection, the Court found a violation of Article 9. It considered that effective alternatives for objectors exist in the overwhelming majority of European States, and that in the case of *Bayatyan v Armenia* (2011) the applicant's conviction had occurred at a time when Armenia had already pledged to introduce alternative service.[28]

Conscientious objection to other state directives

The basic principle

[9.25] While not labelling them as such, the human rights tribunals have addressed cases of what has been considered as conscientious objection to state directives other than compulsory military service. The UNHRC considered the refusal of a Sikh to wear a safety helmet at work as required by law based on his refusal to remove his turban for religious reasons in the case of *Karnel Singh Bhinder v Canada* (1986). The Government submitted that the requirement did not violate the right defined in Article 18(1) of the Covenant because it was a religiously neutral legal requirement, imposed for legitimate reasons (health and safety) and applied to all members of the relevant work force without aiming at any religious group.

[9.26] The UNHRC agreed. It held that the prohibition was not a breach of Article 18, because it was justified under the limitation provisions of Article 18.3. The Tribunal added that the law did not constitute discrimination under Article 26 ICCPR, as the author was not targeted specifically because of his religion. It stated that

---

26 UN Commission on Human Rights 54th Session, Agenda Item 22, Un Doc. E/CN.4/1998/L.93, adopted 1998, ¶¶1, 4 .

27 See, e.g., *Grandrath v Germany* (1967). The European Commission held that 'As in [Article 4] provision it is expressly recognised that civilian service may be imposed on conscientious objectors as a substitute for military service, it must be concluded that objections of conscience do not, under the Convention, entitle a person to exemption from such service', ¶32 (emphasis original).

28 *Bayatyan v. Armenia* (2011), and *Erçep v. Turkey* (2011).

applying criteria now well-established in the jurisprudence of the Committee, the legislation requiring that workers in federal employment be protected from injury and electric shock by the wearing of hard hats is to be regarded as reasonable and directed towards objective purposes that are compatible with the Covenant.[29]

[9.27] In response to the argument that the potential harm from not wearing a safety helmet was a personal risk of injury an individual takes, the point was made that government can take into account the potential effect of a person's actions on third parties. These may involve the health and safety of others at work, or personal loss, distress and injury of other individuals. There is also potential cost to society in general for associated government resources, such as rescue, medical treatment and rehabilitation.

[9.28] Regarding conscientious objection to other directives, Taylor points to early cases of the European Commission dealing with conscientious objection to legal obligations. Applicants objected to subscribing to a regulatory health program for cattle breeding,[30] to paying general taxes when some of these were used for defence expenditure,[31] or a pension scheme for the aged,[32] and a third party motor vehicle insurance scheme.[33] These objections were based on the belief that it is God, not humans, who ordains our destiny, and it is incumbent on good Christians, not the state, to care for each other. Also considered was the refusal by a doctor, who charged patients according to their ability to pay, to participate in a compulsory professional pension scheme that involved contributions based on gross income.[34] The Commission, without specific deliberation, found no breach of Article 9 ECHR in each of these cases, treating them as instances of manifestation of belief, and applying the test of Article 9.2 requiring (and finding) justification according to permitted limitations to protect the interests of the state or other individuals.[35] More recent cases, discussed elsewhere for different reasons, are *Lautsi v Italy* (2011) (see [11.31]) and *Eweida and Others v the United Kingdom* (2013) (see [11.19]).

[9.29] Again, by adopting a broad approach to the *forum internum* such as that adopted by Taylor and others, one would be in effect giving protection to acting (or refusing to act) according to individual values – becoming a law unto oneself. The reason for limitation, as pointed out by

---

29   *Karnel Singh Bhinder v Canada* (1986), ¶6.2.

30   *X. v the Netherlands* (1962).

31   *C. v United Kingdom*, 10358/83 37 D&R (1983), 14210538/83, 142.

32   *Reformed Church of X v the Netherlands* (1962).

33   *X. v the Netherlands* (1967), 476. The complainant believed that God determines one's fate, and it is up to the community to care for those who require it.

34   *V. v the Netherlands* (1984), 267.

35   See, for a detailed discussion, Taylor (2005), 119, who adopts the approach that violations of the *forum internum* include compulsion to act contrary to one's conscience, even whilst recognising that 'an express general prohibition to that effect would be unacceptable because of its breadth'.

Pieter van Dijk et al., is that the 'boundlessness of conscience' excludes the feasibility of generally applicable and clear-cut limitations.[36]

[9.30] Taylor complains that upholding a law because it applies to everyone and is not aimed at any specific belief 'would involve the fallacy that neutral laws are incapable of giving rise to issues of conscience'.[37] This is not so, it is argued. Neutral laws may indeed give rise to issues of conscience. The point is that these issues of conscience may not be matters that are protected by the belief provisions, because:

a) they do not involve manifestation of belief; or

b) if they do, they accord with the criteria for limitation under the belief provisions.

[9.31] Laws may not be morally acceptable to particular individuals, in which case one may feel personally morally justified in breaking them, but it does not follow that there is a *legal* right to do so, and the state may be justified in holding one to account.[38] The adjudicative bodies have suggested that political action is the remedy for law to which one has conscientious objection, unless one can argue the law is a wrongful limitation under the belief provisions.[39]

Errors of judgment? The European Commission and Court

[9.32] The European Court of Human Rights considered the issue of conscientious objection to mandatory behaviour in 'twin' cases each brought against the Greek Government on behalf of Jehovah's Witness schoolgirls.[40] In each case, the claimant was suspended from school for refusing to participate in a school parade marking Greek National Day. Some of the many parades throughout the country included the Greek military, marking the war with Italy. The girls' refusal to participate was founded on their pacifist religious convictions. The Court in both cases held that the suspension for refusing to participate in a parade did not amount to an interference with their right to freedom of religion, stating that it could see no reason for offence in activities to the claimants or their parents.[41] In explaining the reasoning for such an approach, the Court used the same justification in both cases:

•   the parades can serve both pacifist objectives and the public interest;

---

36   See, e.g., van Dijk et al (2006), 761ff.
37   Taylor (2005), 126.
38   See, e.g., Dworkin (1978), Ch 7.
39   See, e.g., *C. v United Kingdom* 10358/83 37 D&R (1983), 142 147.
40   *Valsamis v Greece* (1996). *Efstratiou v Greece* (1996), (1996).
41   *Valsamis v Greece*, ¶32; *Efstratiou v Greece* (1996), ¶31.

- the presence of military representatives does not in itself alter the nature of the parades; and

- they do not deprive the parents of their right 'to enlighten and advise their children', exercise parental functions of education, or guide them in accordance with their own religious or philosophical convictions.[42]

[9.33] Carolyn Evans considers that the punishment of the girls was an invasion of their *forum internum,* arguing that it is difficult, if not impossible, to divorce thought and action.[43] She says of the claimants:

> They were in effect being asked to recant, by their behaviour, their religion. This conflict between the behaviour required of them and their beliefs was such that it arguably interfered with the internal as well as the external realm.[44]

[9.34] However, she recognises that it was action that was the centre of consideration:

> In neither case did the action of the state go so far that it made impossible (or even particularly difficult) for the individuals to maintain their internal beliefs, but in each case the State *required the individuals to act* in a way they felt was in direct contradiction to the requirements of those beliefs.[45]

[9.35] Carolyn Evans also points to cases such as *Darby v Sweden*[46] (discussed below [9.46]) involving the imposition by government of church tax on a non-member of the church. She proposes that these impositions violate the holding of the individual's religion itself.

[9.36] The perception that thought and action are indissoluble may well apply to the moral imperatives associated with belief and with the consequent moral disequilibrium and stress of feeling like an involuntary hypocrite.[47] This adverse effect should not be underestimated (hence the limited restrictions on manifestation of belief) but the line is drawn between thought and its manifestation.

---

42   *Valsamis v Greece,* ¶31; *Efstratiou v Greece* (1996), ¶32.

43   Carolyn Evans (2001), 74ff. She points to Chief Justice Burger's decision in *Wisconsin v Yoder* (1972), 220, where he held that 'belief and action cannot be neatly confined in logic-tight compartments' and that that religious and other beliefs and actions are intertwined.

44   Ibid, 78.

45   Carolyn Evans (2001), 77-78 (emphasis added). See also pp 72-9 and 170-198 for discussion of compulsion. See also her argument that *forum internum* is underestimated by the European Court (at 102).

46   *Darby v Sweden* (1990).

47   'We want to enjoy our lives, and we want to enjoy them with a good conscience. People who disturb that equilibrium are uncomfortable': Blackburn (2001), 6.

[9.37] It is proposed that Carolyn Evans's criticism is misplaced. Here there is no attempt to change the girls' beliefs: their stated objections to participation indicated otherwise. The fact that one can object to external pressure to act against one's belief disproves the claim that thought and action are indissoluble.

[9.38] While one can sympathise with the claimants in these cases, as indeed they may have felt as if they were required to recant their beliefs, Malcolm Evans, expressing what I suggest is the better view, points out that:

> The freedom of thought, conscience and religion is exercised in the private sphere, the *forum internum*. Penalties, disabilities and criticism do not prevent a person holding a pattern of thought, conscience or religion. *The [European] Convention does not prevent society from extracting a degree of sacrifice from individuals who subscribe to certain forms of belief.*[48]

[9.39] To penalise a person for simply holding a belief, however, he says, 'does lie beyond the limit of acceptability'.[49] The suspension of the children for their conscientious punishment could be seen to be the imposition of a penalty. This, I suggest, became the source of error on the part of the Court. One could well argue that the children should have been excused from marching, or else the school commemorate the day in a way that would be acceptable to all. It is suggested that the Court erred in applying the judges' personal views as to whether the pacifist objection was reasonable. Rather, it should have considered whether it was necessary to demand the children march against their conscientious beliefs.

[9.40] In sum, the fact that a person can perceive their actions to be coerced means that their belief is not changed, despite their actions. A violation of a person's thought processes must involve the intention and character of involuntary mind control. Thus, it is argued, coerced action in conflict with a person's belief is not strictly a violation of the person's thought patterns itself – it is, while coerced, a breach of the right to manifest belief from abstaining from action.

[9.41] Carolyn Evans also proposes that:

> Only very narrow definitions of religion restrict it to the primarily intellectual sphere of developing a system of ideas/beliefs in one's own mind. More sophisticated definitions take note of how religion may play an important role in the way in which people live their whole lives.[50]

---

48   Malcolm Evans (1997), 304 (emphasis added).
49   Ibid. To the extent that it amounts to discrimination on the ground of belief, it would, of course be a breach of Article 14 ECHR.
50   Carolyn Evans (2001), 76.

[9.42] It is suggested that Evans is here demanding the equation of apples and oranges. Her 'narrow definitions of religion' relate to the political right to the equal exercise of one's belief in a liberal society. That is a matter of political and legal relationships. What she calls 'sophisticated definitions' relate to something quite different – the personal psychological and social experience of religion (or other beliefs). The belief provisions do recognise the social and psychological importance of belief in the way people live their lives through action and they provide protection for it. They also recognise the political importance of applying that protection equally to everyone.

Other cases of compulsion

[9.43] Objection to expressing views was held to be different from being required to swear an oath based on the Bible or other religious book, or to swear allegiance to a particular belief in the case of *Buscarini and Others v San Marino* (1999). The European Court viewed action as manifestation where the applicants, who were elected to the legislature of San Marino, were required to take the oath laid down by law swearing on the 'Holy Gospels'. When they demurred, they were refused an alternative form of words, and took the oath under protest rather than forfeit their parliamentary seats. The court treated the oath as an issue of manifestation of belief ruling that the requirement to take a religious oath was inconsistent with the thrust of the Convention. It required the applicants to commit to (rather than simply express) a belief different from their own[51] – a requirement that gave them no option (the court drew a distinction between being able to choose another job and inability to take up public office at all).

[9.44] Despite the ambiguity of language and concepts, one can conclude, from the approach of the European Commission and Court, that protection from state-mandated activity that is contrary to the dictates of conscience is subject (albeit only) to the limitations that apply to the manifestation of belief, unless they are of such a nature that they imperil the very process of thought itself. The UNHRC has taken this approach as well.[52]

[9.45] Other cases heard by the UNHRC and European Commission and Court reveal that while a name change for religious reasons may be an important part of identity, this was con-

---

51   *Buscarini and Others v San Marino* (1999) ¶39.
52   *Boodoo v Trinidad and Tobago* (1996), ¶6.6.

sidered a matter of privacy under Articles 17 ICCPR and 8 ECHR.[53] Also, the European Commission and Court have held that conscientious objection to employment duties is to be considered under Article 9.2 ECHR (freedom to manifest belief) rather than Article 9.1 (freedom of thought etc.),[54] and thus subject to the limitation clauses.

Objection to state enforcement of Church taxes

[9.46] Objection to paying taxes because some public revenue goes to defence spending has been held inadmissible, and so taxation for the purpose of funding defence is permissible under the human rights treaties. The human rights tribunals have indicated that the appropriate way to deal with objection to government use of public funds is through the political system, unless of course, it violates constitutional obligations. This principle was applied to taxation for the purposes of funding of religious bodies in the case of *Darby v Sweden*.[55]

[9.47] Darby, a Finnish citizen, was a permanent resident in Finland, but stayed and worked in Sweden during the week. While employed in Sweden he was, according to an international agreement, liable to Swedish, rather than Finnish, tax. He was subject to municipal tax law, which levied a special tax on behalf of the Lutheran Church of Sweden ('church tax') on members of the church. Non-members who were registered as residents in Sweden were eligible for a thirty percent reduction in the amount assessed for them.[56]

[9.48] Having only a temporary abode in Sweden, Darby could not apply for residency status, and thus the residency discount. He argued that his belief rights had been violated under Article 9 ECHR, and that he had been wrongfully deprived of this property (proscribed by Article 1 of

---

53 *A R Coeriel and M A R Aurik v the Netherlands* (1995). The Committee found 'that a person's surname constitutes an important component of one's identity and that the protection against arbitrary or unlawful interference with one's privacy includes the protection against arbitrary or unlawful interference with the right to choose and change one's own name', ¶10.2. The state's reasons for refusing the authors a change of surname for pursuing religious studies were 'that the authors had not shown that the changes sought were essential to pursue their studies, that the names had religious connotations and that they were not "Dutch sounding"'. This, the Committee found, was a breach of article 17, paragraph 1, of the ICCPR (at, ¶10.5).
54 See, e.g., *X v Denmark* (1976); *The Norwegian State Church, Knudsen v Norway* (1985): objection by clergy to rules of performing duties; *Yanasik v Turkey* (1993), and *Engel v Netherlands* (1976); *X v the United Kingdom* (1981): soldiers' membership of fundamentalist Muslim movement; *Ahmad v the United Kingdom* (1981): teacher forced to resign because he insisted on absenting himself on Fridays for prayer at the local mosque.
55 *Darby v Sweden* (1990).
56 The 30 per cent of the church tax that remained after the reduction was supposed to cover the costs borne by the parishes of certain administrative functions such as the keeping of population records and the maintenance of churchyards and other public burial-grounds.

Protocol 1 to the ECHR)[57]and that this amounted to discrimination (proscribed by Article 14 ECHR).[58]

[9.49] As to violation of Article 9, the European Commission, in its deliberations, held that the legal requirement to pay church tax was, in this case, a 'manifestation' of religion under Article 9. It was, in the Commission's view a compulsion 'to be involved directly in religious activities against his will without being a member of the religious community carrying out those activities'.[59] The Commission distinguished cases involving the imposition of general taxes, a portion of which may be allocated to a cause objected to by an applicant. Such taxes lay within the jurisdiction of the state, objections to be resolved through the political process. These differed from the present case, where the individual was obliged to contribute directly to the church and its religious activities. This, the Commission argued, was a breach of the right to have or adopt a religion under Article 9.1.

[9.50] While commentators see the Commission's statement as portending advent of absolute protection of some forms of conscientious objection, it appears the European Court has not opened the door to such a view. The Court, to which the Commission referred Darby's case, did not rule on the question of breach of Article 9. It followed its tendency with claims of Article 9 breaches to look to other provisions of the ECHR. It instead found for the applicant on the second argument, that there was a violation of Article 14 together with Article 1 of Protocol 1 (which protects private property[60]). As a result, it found that the church tax was an unjustified and discriminatory denial of property rights. It concluded that it did not need to deal with the alleged breach of Article 9.[61]

[9.51] What was not considered in this case was the favourable treatment through state enforced legislation of the (state) Lutheran Church.[62] More critical, however, is the failure in both the Commission and the Court to recognize state endorsement and subsidization of churches as a breach of belief rights, which is condoned under the international human rights treaties.

---

57   Article 1 of Protocol No. 1 (P1-1), provides that '…no one shall be deprived of his possessions except in the public interest and subject to the conditions provided for by law and by the general principles of international law'. However, '[t]his is not to impair the right of a State to enforce such laws as it deems necessary to control the use of property in accordance with the general interest or to secure the payment of taxes or other contributions or penalties': *Darby v Sweden* (1990), ¶29.

58   Article 14 of the Convention provides that rights and freedoms established by the Convention 'are to be secured without discrimination on any ground such as…religion'.

59   *Darby v Sweden* (1990), ¶52.

60   Article 1 of Protocol 1 ECHR provides that no one will be deprived of his possessions except in the public interest and subject to law.

61   Ibid, ¶28-35.

62   The case was referred to the European Court, which focused on the fact that the tax was administered in a discriminatory way (residents of Sweden could avoid the tax by registering as dissenters whereas Darby, a non-resident worker in Sweden could not so register).

The 'public/private sphere' dichotomy

[9.52] Along with the division drawn between the *forum internum* and the *forum externum* of individual life, theorists have drawn a structural dichotomy between the 'private' and 'public' spheres of personal, social and political activity, with each sphere independent of the other.

[9.53] As noted in Chapter 4, Rawls rejects the idea of separate 'spheres' or domains of life. He sees the idea of private and public 'spheres' as applying to the different application of the principles of justice to either the basic institutions of society, or to the associations within it, with designated basic principles of justice (such as autonomy and personal integrity) applicable to both spheres (see [4.13][4.13]ff.). This approach fosters the universal nature of human rights.

[9.54] It is proposed, then, that the 'separate sphere' approach to belief rights is, like the approach to *forum internum,* misplaced. It conflates one's personal outlook on life with the way one acts towards others in personal and social relationships. It is then presumed that one is immune from the obligation to respect the belief (and other) rights of those in this artificially designated 'private sphere' as political principals of justice are deemed not to apply. As argued at[4.19]] the individual as citizen, with all the attendant rights and freedoms resulting from the principles of justice, carries those rights and freedoms into the family and associations to which he or she belongs.

Conclusion

[9.55] The contestable concept of the *forum internum* in the writings of some commentators has confused the distinction between the absolute right to thought (including conscience and religion) and the right to act upon thought. Consequently, conscientious objection has been seen to provide the expectation of an absolute right to manifest one's belief. The human rights bodies have clearly negated this perception, and established the distinction between the internal and external aspects of belief rights. This means while citizens are free to believe what they choose and to act on that belief, when such action diminishes the democratic process or adversely affects the rights of others, the state may legitimately limit what he or she does, or refuses to do. This does not deny the integrity of the *forum internum*. Diversity must be provided for, but also according to, a conception of justice.

[9.56] As we saw earlier, a conception of justice must be one based on considerations external to comprehensive doctrines, that is, a conception that can be endorsed by those holding widely different and even irreconcilable comprehensive doctrines. It necessitates seeing people as having an interest both in (a) individual development based on a life stance and moral compass for personal living, and (b) social cohesion and harmony based on a political moral compass for societal governance. Invasion of the *forum internum* involves indoctrination or emotional manipulation to induce voluntary submission. To consider limitation on belief-based activity an invasion of the *forum internum* is to pave the way to belief-based domination of government and society.

[9.57] Issues surrounding manifestation of belief are dealt with in the next Chapter.

CHAPTER 10
WHAT'S IS 'MANIFESTING' BELIEF?

Introduction

[10.1] Besides those already covered, further issues arise in the interpretation and implementation of the belief provisions. Chapter I considered the language of the belief provisions in relation to manifestation of belief, demonstrating how they can lead to ambiguity, confusion and at times contradiction, compromising the promise of freedom of, and from, belief. In Chapter 11 I examine how the belief tribunals have viewed the state's right to restrict belief-based activity.

[10.2] The belief provisions provide that '[e]veryone has the right to freedom…either alone or in community with others and in public or private, to manifest his religion or belief, in worship, teaching, practice and observance'. Not only is there a right to practice a belief, but also a right *not* to practice it.[1] Moreover, manifestation, as indicated, is subject to limitations (see Table 1).

[10.3] Article 29.2 UDHR relies on a general limitation clause covering all rights, which are to be restricted only to secure the rights of others and 'meeting the just requirements of morality, public order and the general welfare in a democratic society'. Article 29(3) states that '[t]hese rights and freedoms may in no case be exercised contrary to the purposes and principles of the United Nations'.

[10.4] The ICCPR, *Belief Declaration* and ECHR state that freedom to manifest belief shall be subject only to limitations that are (a) prescribed by law, and (b) necessary to protect public safety, order, health, or morals or the fundamental rights and freedoms of others.

[10.5] The principle of reciprocity likewise places restraints on the actions of individuals and groups to the extent that they impede the generally accepted freedoms of others. This is based on the premises of a political conception of justice, individual reasonability and procedural justice.[2] It cannot be emphasised enough that the right to manifest belief is as much a *restraint* as a freedom. In principle at least, the human rights tribunals adopt a similar approach. Both restraint and freedom are balanced according to the principles of proportionality, or in Rawls's terms, justice as fairness, aimed at promoting the freedom of everyone to the maximum feasible extent.

---

1   *Kokkinakis v Greece* (1993), ¶31; and *Buscarini and Others v San Marino* (1999), ¶34).
2   See, e.g., *PL* II, ¶2, esp. 48ff. 'Reasonable' people want to cooperate with others on reasonable terms they can all accept; appreciate the consequences of the burdens of judgement; have a sense of justice; want to be seen as reasonable, or fair or just: Freeman (2007a), 481.

What constitutes manifestation of belief?

UNHRC

[10.6] The *UN General Comment 22* lists what can be included in the manifestation of belief, and the *Belief Declaration* sets out a more comprehensive list. As can be seen, these lists are extensive:

Table 7: Manifestation of belief: UDHR & Belief Declaration

ICCPR *General Comment 22* (Paragraph 4)	Belief Declaration (Article 6)
Worship extends to: • Ritual and ceremonial acts giving direct expression to belief ; • Various practices integral to such acts, such as: – the building of places of worship; – the use of ritual formulae and objects; – the display of symbols; and – the observance of holidays and days of rest. **The observance and practice of religion or belief may include such customs as:** • Observance of dietary regulations; • Wearing of distinctive clothing or head coverings; • Participation in rituals associated with certain stages of life; and • Use of a particular language customarily spoken by a group. **Practice and teaching of religion or belief includes:** acts integral to the conduct by religious groups of their basic affairs such as: • Freedom to choose their religious leaders, priests and teachers; • Freedom to establish seminaries or religious schools; and • Freedom to prepare and distribute religious texts or publications.	The right to freedom of thought, conscience, religion or belief shall include, inter alia, the following freedoms: c) To worship or assemble in connection with a religion or belief, and to establish and maintain places for these purposes; d) To establish and maintain, appropriate charitable or humanitarian institutions; e) To make, acquire and use to an adequate extent the necessary articles and materials related to the rites or customs of a religion or belief; f) To write, issue and disseminate relevant publications in these areas; g) To teach a religion or belief in places suitable for these purposes; h) To solicit and receive voluntary financial and other contributions from individuals and institutions; i) To train, appoint, elect or designate by succession appropriate leaders called for by the requirements and standards of any religion or belief; j) To observe days of rest and to celebrate holidays and ceremonies in accordance with the precepts of one's religion or belief; k) To establish and maintain communications with individuals and communities in matters of religion and belief at the national and international levels.

European tribunals

[10.7] The ECHR does not set out a list of what constitutes manifestation of belief, and the European Court has not considered in detail what is involved in manifesting belief. Like the UNHRC, decisions of both the European Commission and Court have indicated an avoidance of 'delving deeply into the parameters of worship, teaching and observance', so that 'the key to understanding what amounts to a manifestation for the purposes of Article 9 lies in determining the scope of 'practice''.[3] The Court has tended to give a broad interpretation of the concept of 'practice'[4] and seems to place more emphasis on whether government actions are necessary limitations of such action.

[10.8] The belief tribunals, like government, do not have the right to interfere with internal issues of religious organisations,[5] nor can they sit in judgment on the content of a citizen's inner and personal beliefs.[6] However, they can investigate (a) whether the complainant's action or refusal to act is a manifestation of that belief, and (b) whether any state restriction of that manifestation is justified under the international treaties.

'Manifestation': it's complicated

[10.9] There are numerous cases dealing with manifestation of belief, and probably just as many different approaches to what it means in practice. This results from the complexity of life, and the need to apply general terms and principles to many different circumstance and social values. There are, however, ambiguities and contradictions arising from the tribunals' interpretation of the wording of the manifestation provisions. These have compromised the promise of freedom to manifest belief, and are considered below.

---

3   Malcolm Evans (1997), 306.

4   See, e.g., *Leyla Şahin v Turkey* (2005). Malcolm Evans (2008), provides a critique of the European Court's approach (at 300ff). See discussion above [5.45] ff.

5   E.g., the UNHRC held that a teacher appointed by the Catholic Church to teach religion in a government school who advocated 'liberation theology' could, however, be disciplined by the Catholic Church: *Paez v Colombia Communication* (1990). The European Court held that the prosecution of a man who 'acted as a religious leader of a group who willingly followed him [when the state had appointed another cleric] can hardly be considered compatible with the demands of religious pluralism in a democratic society' *Serif v Greece* (1999), ¶51. See also *Holy Synod of the Bulgarian Orthodox Church (Metropolitan Inokentiy), and Others v Bulgaria* (2009). State interference in internal disputes within religious communities, and criminalising a leadership role in a religious community could not be justified.

6   However, in *Kosteski v "the former Yugoslav Republic of Macedonia"* (2000), ¶39, the Court rejected a claim that freedom to manifest religious beliefs was curtailed by the refusal of a paid religious holiday, as generally permitted by the government, to the claimant. The government claimed he was not sincere in his proclaimed belief, as he was happy to take Christian holidays, and was not known to follow other Muslim practices. In cases concerning conscientious objection the authorities may legitimately require strong evidence of genuine religious objections to justify exemption from the civil duty of military service (e.g. *N v Sweden* (1984), p. 203; *Raninen v Finland* (1996).

UN: Meaning of 'manifestation of belief'

[10.10] The UNHRC has stated that the term 'worship, observance, practice or teaching' covers 'a broad range of acts'.[7] It is notable that the UNHRC has even included enforced 'ideology conversion system' as a violation of the right to manifest, rather than hold or adopt, a particular belief (*Kang v Korea* (2003), see [9.18]). This blurs the distinction between having and manifesting a belief.

[10.11] The UNHRC has also reinforced the requirement that state limitation of belief must be *necessary* for public safety, order, health etc. (Article 18.3). For example, the Committee ruled out excessive and unnecessary requirements that hinder bodies from registering for government recognition as a religion,[8] and prevent them from operating.[9] It also found that, where the Uzbekistan government prohibited the wearing of the 'hijab',[10] and the French Government required the removal of headgear for identity photos,[11] when neither government could show evidence that it was necessary to do so, they violated Article 18(3) ICCPR.

[10.12] The UNHRC has considered objection to laws on safety apparel[12] or consuming drugs[13] as matters relating to manifestation of religion, as well as claims based on conscientious objection [9.25]. There is, however, little case law by the UNHRC on just what is allowed in 'manifestation' of belief. There seems to be some confusion when considering these complaints between the need to investigate the nature of the belief concerned under Article 18, and the appropriateness of treating the issue as one of freedom of expression or assembly whenever possible.[14]

[10.13] In one case before the UNHRC that caused a (brief) but helpful consideration of manifestation of belief and its context, a teacher, Malcolm Ross, published several books and pamphlets and made public statements, including a television interview, reflecting controversial, allegedly religious opinions concerning abortion, conflicts between Judaism and Christianity, and the defence of the Christian religion.[15] Ross claimed that his rights under both Article 18 ICCPR (freedom to manifest religious belief) and Article 19 ICCPR (freedom of speech) had

---

7   *ICCPR General Comment 22*, ¶4; See discussion by Durham (2004), 321.
8   *Malakhovsky and Pikul v Belarus* (2003). The authors were denied the right to manifest their religion, as they could register only as a religious *community* (whose administrative address was held to violate safety rules set down for congregations). The Committee held that the requirements were unnecessary for a legal address. Appropriate premises for congregation could be obtained subsequent to registration. Further examples can be found in Durham (2004).
9   Durham, ibid.
10   For example,: *Hudoyberganova v Uzbekistan* (2004), ¶6.2.
11   *Mann Singh* (2010). See further discussion on this case in relation to other matters at [11.70].
12   E.g., *Karnel Singh Bhinder v Canada* (1986).
13   E.g., *M.A.B., W.A.T. and J.A.Y.T. v Canada* (1994).
14   See e.g. C Evans, (2001) 120ff., esp. 123.
15   *Ross v Canada* (2001).

been breached. While Ross's activities were carried out separately from his teaching, a Board of Inquiry held that they contributed to the creation of a 'poisoned environment within [the school district] which greatly interfered with the educational services provided to [a parent] and his children'.[16]

[10.14] The Committee first considered whether Article 19 ICCPR (freedom of expression) had been breached. It found that Ross's comments had violated the 'rights or reputation' of persons of Jewish faith, and created a 'poisoned school environment' for Jewish children in the school district. Thus, disciplinary action against Ross was held not to have breached Article 19.[17]

[10.15] In relation to Article 18, the UNHRC found that:

- the author's activities were not manifestations of a religion, 'as he did not publish them for the purpose of worship, observance, practice or teaching of a religion';

- disciplinary action taken against the author was 'not aimed at his thoughts or beliefs as such, but rather at the manifestation of those beliefs within a particular context', thus engaging questions of freedom of speech as well as religion;

- consequently, Article 18 had not been violated by the disciplinary action taken against Ross.[18]

[10.16] Proselytising, on the other hand, is considered a legitimate form of manifestation. The UNHRC held that for numerous religions, 'it is a central tenet to spread knowledge, to propagate their beliefs to others and to provide assistance to others'.[19] The European Court has agreed that *reasonable* proselytising (e.g. 'bearing Christian witness') is not a breach of Article 9 ECHR, whereas *improper* proselytising (e.g. offering material or social benefits, exerting improper pressure, using violence or brainwashing) is.[20]

[10.17] The difficulty in specifying the scope of 'practice' can be seen by the UNHRC adoption of the principle that not all acts motivated or inspired by a belief could be considered as manifestations of belief. Added to ambiguity is the Committee's apparent distinction between what *is* included in 'worship' (e.g. ritual and ceremonial acts, and practices 'integral to such acts') and what *may* be included in 'observance or practice' (e.g. customs such as dietary regulations,

---

16   Ibid, ¶4.3.
17   Ibid, ¶¶11.5, 11.6.
18   Ibid, ¶11.8 (emphasis added). It noted that similar limitations were relevant to both Articles 18 and 19.
19   *Sister Immaculate Joseph et al v Sri Lanka* (2004), ¶7.2.
20   *Kokkinakis v Greece* (1993): "… more generally, it is not compatible with respect for the freedom of thought, conscience and religion of others' (¶48).

clothing or language).[21] Given the personal nature of belief, many interpretations, varied and contradictory, can be applied even by those professing the same belief.

[10.18] In determining what is 'necessary' to justify limiting the manifestation of belief, the UNHRC has based its decision-making on whether state action has 'reasonable and objective criteria', which is a formula for determining allowable state discretion (see below [11.5]). Limitations may be justifiable if they are 'reasonable and objective' and if the aim is to achieve a purpose which is legitimate under the Covenant.[22]

European tribunals: Meaning of 'manifestation'

[10.19] While the European tribunals have not elaborated on out what constitutes 'manifestation' of belief, the European Court has rather focused on legitimate *limits* to manifestation. It determined that provisions limiting manifestation of belief are 'exhaustive' and 'are to be construed strictly'. Limitations must 'correspond to a "pressing social need" and must be "proportionate to the legitimate aim pursued."'[23]

[10.20] Firstly, government restrictions on manifesting belief must be 'prescribed by law'. This provides the democratic principles of political participation, with the resulting overlapping consensus through public reason.[24] The UNHRC would agree with this.

[10.21] The Court said its task then is to determine whether the state's actions were justified in principle and proportionate to the legitimate aim pursued. The state's actions must be in conformity with the principles embodied in the Convention and based on 'an acceptable assessment of the relevant facts'.[25]

---

21   Paragraph 4 of *General Comment 22* provides that

> The concept of worship extends to ritual and ceremonial acts giving direct expression to belief, as well as various practices integral to such acts, including the building of places of worship, the use of ritual formulae and objects, the display of symbols, and the observance of holidays and days of rest. The observance and practice of religion or belief may include not only ceremonial acts but also such customs as the observance of dietary regulations, the wearing of distinctive clothing or head coverings, participation in rituals associated with certain stages of life, and the use of a particular language customarily spoken by a group.

22   ICCPR *General Comment 18* (37), UN Doc. CCPR/C/21/Rev1./Add.1 (1989), reprinted in UN Doc. A/45/40 vol 1 Annex v (1990), 174., ¶13; *S W M Broeks v the Netherlands* (1987), ¶13.

23   *Kokkinakis v Greece* (1993), ¶47ff. See also *Refah Partisi (the Welfare Party), and Others v. Turkey* (2003), ¶106; de Schutter (2010), 293ff, esp. 294.

24   *Dogru v France* (2008), ¶¶49, 52.

25   *Svyato-Mykhaylivska Parafiya v Ukraine* (2007), ¶138. See also *United Communist Party of Turkey and Others v Turkey* (1998), ¶ 47.

[10.22] However, not all action inspired by religious belief is acceptable. This approach was first articulated by the Human Rights Commission in *Arrowsmith v United Kingdom*,[26] and reinforced by the European Court.[27] The applicant in the Arrowsmith case had been convicted for inciting soldiers to neglect their duty. She had distributed leaflets to British soldiers, exhorting them, *inter alia*, to refuse to serve in Northern Ireland or to go absent without leave and seek asylum in Sweden. Addresses in Sweden were provided, from which legal advice or social help could be obtained.

[10.23] Her appeal rights in the UK exhausted, Ms Arrowsmith applied to the European Commission, alleging, *inter alia,* that she had been denied the right to manifest her pacifist belief as guaranteed under Article 9 ECHR, and her right to freedom of expression under Article 10 ECHR. The Commission accepted pacifism as a belief under Article 9.[28] It also accepted that this was a genuine belief held by Ms Arrowsmith at the time.[29]

[10.24] In considering the pacifist conviction of Ms Arrowsmith, the Commission determined that the thrust of the leaflet was to express opposition to government policy on Northern Ireland. It was also directed solely at soldiers who might be posted to Northern Ireland, and could have been written by non-pacifists (indeed, it contained material that could be held to infer that fighting in some circumstances could be justified).[30] Accordingly, in prosecuting and convicting the applicant, the Government was motivated, 'not by her holding particular opinions, including pacifist views, but by the fact that her action in distributing the leaflets constituted the offence of incitement to disaffection'.[31]

[10.25] The European Commission continued this distinction between actions constituting *manifestation* of a belief and those that are *motivated by* a belief in other cases, to reject some activities as religious practice.[32] In the case of *Ahmad v United Kingdom* (1981) a Muslim teacher was refused leave for 45 minutes on Fridays for prayers at a mosque. The Commission found that he had voluntarily implied by his employment contract that he did not deem it necessary to attend

---

26   *Arrowsmith v the United Kingdom* (1978).

27   See, e.g., *Kalaç v Turkey* (1997), ¶¶27-31 (no interference with the right guaranteed by Article 9 where a military officer with fundamentalist beliefs was compulsorily retired for breach of discipline); *Leyla Şahin v Turkey* (2005), ¶¶105, 212 (wearing of headscarf at school).

28   *Arrowsmith v the United Kingdom* (1978), ¶69.

29   Ibid, ¶68.

30   Ibid, ¶72.

31   Ibid, ¶103.

32   The following are examples of actions held to be merely motivated, rather than mandated, by religion: underage marriage permitted by Islamic law: *Khan v United Kingdom* (1981); Buddhist prisoner sending letter to religious publication: *X v United Kingdom* (1974); setting up a legal association: *X v Austria* (1981); refusal by a Jew to hand a gett (notice of divorce), to his ex-wife thus preventing her remarriage: *D v France* (1983).

prayers. In such cases, the human rights tribunals have been unwilling to accept claims of violation of religion or belief.[33]

[10.26] The European Court has continued the approach of the Commission, and, as with the UNHRC, the official approach is that the employment choice must be a genuine one,[34] and consistent with the values of the Convention.[35] However in the recent case of *Eweida and Others v The United Kingdom* (2013), the Court held that this principle can be overridden where the employer is a government body that adopts a non-discrimination policy in relation to gays, even after employing the applicant (the state's 'margin of appreciation' see discussion[11.19]).

[10.27] The difficulties posed by isolating religious doctrine as a basis for determining whether particular action is a manifestation of belief is raised by Carolyn Evans's criticism of its effects.[36] These involve the arbitrary division of action which, it is argued, contravenes religious dogma from one's personal conscience. Surely, if the purpose of the belief provisions is to allow freedom to practise one's *beliefs*, religious or otherwise, the issue is simply whether one's *actions* are unjustifiably prohibited or mandated by the law.

Case Study: Different approaches to limiting belief-based action

[10.28] One result of the different determinations of what are legitimate limitations on manifesting belief adopted by the UN and the European Court relates to the wearing of headgear that covers the face. Because the Article 9.2 ECHR specifies consideration of a 'democratic' society, whereas Article 18.3 ICCPR does not, the European Court's interpretation of the grounds for limiting to belief-based action has tended to be broader than the UNHRC's more restrictive approach. *In S.A.S v France* (2014) the European Court, in a comprehensive examination of the arguments for and against prohibition, of face-coverings in public demonstrated the tension between protecting freedom to manifest belief (emphasised by approaches of the UN), and protecting what is seen to be in the interest of democratic society (emphasised by the European Court).

---

33   See *Karlsson v Sweden* (1986), (clergyman taken to have agreed to adhering to state religion tenets as condition of appointment); *The Norwegian State Church Knudsen v Norway* (1985), (clergyman taken to have agreed to undertake state services – conducting marriages and keeping birth register – as part of appointment); *X. v Germany* (1981), (wish to have ashes scattered in a garden did not amount to a belief).

34   See also cases involving the military and potential lack of autonomy, such as *Larissis and Others v Greece* (1998); *Kalaç v Turkey* (1997).

35   E.g., in the case of *Buscarini and Others v San Marino* (1999), it was held incompatible with the thrust of the Convention for the position of member of parliament to be subject to commitment under oath to a particular set of beliefs. This contradicts their obligation to be impartial to different beliefs within society (at, ¶39).

36   Carolyn Evans ((2001), 120ff.

[10.29] The Islamic applicant, a French national, challenged the law prohibiting the wearing of face coverings under a range of ECHR Articles. The Court dismissed some claims, but ultimately upheld the government's prohibition under Article 9 ECHR. The legitimate grounds for limiting the manifestation of belief (protection of public safety and order in a democratic society, and the rights of others) include the right of others to live in a space of socialisation that makes living together easier. It held that the prohibition is a proportionate interference with manifestation of belief in pursuit of a legitimate aim:

> The Court takes into account the respondent State's point that the face plays an important role in social interaction. It can understand the view that individuals who are present in places open to all may not wish to see practices or attitudes developing there which would fundamentally call into question the possibility of open interpersonal relationships, which, by virtue of an established consensus, forms an indispensable element of community life within the society in question.[37]

[10.30] This introduces the idea of 'consensus' into consideration of legitimate limitations in Article 9. It is argued here that if one interprets this statement very broadly, the Court could be seen to open the door to tyranny of the majority. It rejected this allegation.[38] Rather, it took an approach more in line with 'consensus' in the Rawslian sense, invoking the international consensus of democracy based on the human rights principles of autonomy and equality.

[10.31] The Court recognised the possibility that by prohibiting clothing that conceals the face in public places, the state has 'restricted the reach of pluralism, since the ban prevents certain women from expressing their personality and their beliefs by wearing the full-face veil in public'. It also saw the danger of the potential opposite effect by prohibiting those women who want to wear the burqa or niqab in public and manifesting their beliefs, the Court nevertheless gave priority to the State's interest in protecting 'the ground rules of social communication and more broadly the requirements of 'living together' by

> seeking to protect a principle of interaction between individuals, which in its view is essential for the expression not only of pluralism, but also of tolerance and broadmindedness without which there is no democratic society.[39]

---

37 *S.A.S v France* (2014), ¶122.

38 Ibid ¶128: '…a balance must be achieved which ensures the fair treatment of people from minorities and avoids any abuse of a dominant position… pluralism and democracy must also be based on dialogue and a spirit of compromise necessarily entailing various concessions on the part of individuals or groups of individuals which are justified in order to maintain and promote the ideals and values of a democratic society.'

39 Ibid ¶153.

The Court recognised a duty on the part of those manifesting their belief: the barrier raised against others by a veil concealing the face was legitimately perceived by the government as breaching the right of others to live in a space of socialisation which makes living together easier. It was not out of proportion to the 'harm' it was designed to prevent.

[10.32] The court also observed that public safety is a legitimate reason for the government to restrict belief-based activity. It said that apparel designed to conceal the face could be legitimately prohibited to prevent danger for the safety of persons and property, and to combat identity fraud.[40] In the light of recent threatened attacks by religious extremists not only in current 'hotspots' in Iraq and Syria, but also against individuals in Western nations, one could argue that prohibition of face-coverings may need reconsideration. Legislation to do so would a need to be carefully crafted to ensure it belief-neutral, applies to everyone and is proportional to any perceived danger.

Conclusion

[10.33] The limitation clause of the belief provisions seems to foster a form of political liberalism along the lines proposed by Rawls. The clause specifies maximum freedom curtailed only by the necessity to ensure the integrity of a democratic society and preserve the rights of all. The differences in the language used makes it difficult to rule there is a direct correlation between Rawls's model and the belief provisions. However, there is, as indicated throughout this Chapter, a significant degree of similarity between the two. Like Rawls, the provisions promote a form of structural secularism as the basis for any society seeking to advance belief rights.

[10.34] Despite this, the diverse interpretations of the limitation provisions by the monitoring bodies can lead to ambiguity, confusion and, at times, contradiction, compromising the promise of both freedom 'of', and 'from', belief. When Article 18 is seen to protect action based on religious belief only, irrelevant questions are raised that divert from the purpose of the belief provisions: must religion *oblige* particular action (once it is determined what a 'religion' is in the first place)? How is this determined? Does it require fear of religion-based punishment if a person acts otherwise, or is religious inspiration reason enough for action to be protected? Must there be a recognised belief system with a set of rules to be recognised? What if there isn't such a system, or no universal acceptance of a set of rules within a particular religious organisation? It is concluded that these questions are irrelevant to the Article 18 promise of belief rights for everyone. The more relevant question, then, is rather how 'necessity' for a limitation is to be determined: is it to be based on, e.g. the probability/certainty of widespread death or illness, riot, or merely social orderliness and facility of governance?

---

40   Ibid ¶115.

[10.35] Case law considers individual situations, and provides only incremental, and often seemingly confusing or contradictory principles. If Ms Arrowsmith had been simply expressing views on the involvement of soldiers in Northern Ireland, be it for religious, philosophical, political or financial grounds, surely her rights to do so would have been the same. In fact she was prosecuted for promoting disaffection. Adoption of the *Arrowsmith* principle has at least emphasised that the European tribunals' do not treat action as part of the *forum internum*.[41]

---

41 See, e.g., CarolynEvans (2001), 115. Evans argues that the result is a lack of clarity and difficulty in maintaining coherence in applying this approach, and the Commission has neglected the specific facts of later cases, but has cited the test in *Arrowsmith v the United Kingdom* (1978) and used it to dismiss cases.

CHAPTER 11
RECOGNITION OF INDIVIDUAL CIRCUMSTANCES

Cultural and religious background

[11.1] Added to the complexity arising from actual interpretation of terms in the belief provisions, however, is a further ground for uncertainty. Despite the declarations that the provisions on limiting manifestation of belief are to be construed strictly, it is accepted by the belief tribunals that governments can use a degree of discretion in placing limitations on manifesting belief. Discretion is based on the social and cultural circumstances of individual countries, based on the presumption that states are best placed to determine what is necessary to protect them.

[11.2] In this way, one can argue that the belief tribunals recognize a similar principle to Rawls's 'justice as fairness', in allowing for 'reasonable' recognition of social, cultural and religious customs (the 'burdens of judgement': see Glossary).

[11.3] Many individual decisions of the human rights tribunals have been criticised for their recognition of state discretion, on the ground that it can lead to privileging religious or other belief-based practices. For example, relying on 'public morals' as a ground for limiting behavior is the 'least clear and most controversial of all the legitimating grounds for justifying restrictions on the freedom to manifest one's religion or belief'.[1] The cases based on religious offense outlined below bear this out.

[11.4] Allowing state discretion means that vested interests may influence the outcome of a tribunal's rulings. Religious groups may use undue pressure on the political or judicial process and majority religions may dominate social customs that are accepted by government. Nowak and Vospernik argue that case law shows the 'difficulties of striking a fair balance between the manifestations of a freedom of religion on one hand and protection of public interests as well as human rights of private persons on the other'.[2] They give a succinct account of some decisions they believe skew this balance, thus inhibiting manifestation of belief. Considerations of individual/societal circumstances will always be a source of controversy. The challenge is to maximise equality of opportunity to exercise belief rights, unhampered by illegitimate political and personal interests.

---

1   Nowak and Vospernik (2004), 159.
2   Ibid, 172. See also Evans (2008).

The UN: 'specifics of the context' of particular cases

[11.5] The UNHRC has indicated that in considering alleged state interference with belief rights, it is appropriate to consider the context of the particular case at hand. The case of *Hudoyberganova v Uzbekistan* (2004) for example, involved a university student wearing a headscarf (referred to by both parties as a 'hijab') on campus, a practice that was prohibited by the university authorities. In this case, neither party offered sufficient detail on the specific attire that was worn, nor did the state give justification for the prohibition. In its findings, the Committee indicated that it was to take into account, *inter alia*, the 'specifics of the context' of a case, and, it was unable to do this here through lack of information by both parties. It found a violation of Article 18 on the part of the State.[3]

[11.6] The case of *Ross v Canada* (2001) considered the religious opinions expressed by a teacher out of school and their alleged creation of a poisonous environment within the school district (see above[10.13]). The Committee weighed the circumstances of the case, such as the makeup of the local society, the influence and responsibilities of teachers and the social ramification of communicating ideas.[4]

[11.7] The willingness to allow a degree of state discretion in determining what is 'necessary' includes the growth of particular practices in surrounding countries. In *Westerman v The Netherlands* (1999) the UNHRC held that conscientious objection to military service is 'a clear manifestation' of belief.[5] In so doing, the Committee pointed to the growing acceptance by other states of alternative service for conscientious objectors. It also pointed to the then Commission on Human Rights draft resolution on conscientious objection to military service,[6] accepting conscientious objection to military service as a legitimate manifestation of belief, sponsored by the Netherlands and 11 other European States.

[11.8] Thus, while tying manifestation to the particular forms set out in Article 18(3) ICCPR, the UNHRC indicates a preparedness to consider developing policy of states-parties in some circumstances. It has initially taken the view that belief rights only comprise freedom from state interference with the manifestation of belief, and there is no positive obligation for states to provide special assistance through dispensation from legislative obligations to members of religious

---

3   *Hudoyberganova v Uzbekistan* (2004), ¶6.2.
4   *Ross v Canada* (2001), ¶11.4ff.
5   *Westerman, Paul v The Netherlands* ¶9.3. The UNHRC has taken a more liberal approach to recognizing conscientious objection than the European bodies: whereas the latter have required evidence of membership of a recognised belief organisation, the UNHRC has insisted on no differentiation between particular groups: *Brinkhof v The Netherlands* (1994), ¶9.3. For a comparison of the two jurisdictions, see Taylor (2005), 192ff.
6   E/CN.4/1998/L.93. Text adopted by the Assembly on 29 June 2007 (27th Sitting).

groups.[7] This, however, does not prohibit providing special measures to ensure freedom to practise one's belief. *General Comment 18(37)* provides that:

> the principle of equality sometimes requires States parties to take affirmative action in order to diminish or eliminate conditions which cause or help to perpetuate discrimination prohibited by the Covenant. For example, in a State where the general conditions of a certain part of the population prevent or impair their enjoyment of human rights, the State should take specific action to correct those conditions.[8]

The European tribunals: 'margin of appreciation'

[11.9] In determining whether restriction of manifesting belief violates Article 9.2 ECHR, European case law has taken a similar perspective to the UNHRC. While recognising the need for the restraints set out in the belief provisions, in its consideration of individual circumstances the European Court has often granted a 'margin of appreciation' in its decisions. That means allowing a degree of discretion on the part of states in accordance with local needs and conditions, as individual states are considered to be in a better position than the international court to evaluate them.[9] Judicial decisions of a domestic court may be considered.[10] The national authorities' actions are nevertheless subject to review by the Court for conformity with the requirements of the Convention,[11] which, it is said must be construed strictly.

[11.10] The use of a 'margin of appreciation' has been described by Judge Robert Spano of the European Court as restrained by the ECHR. Where limitations on rights are possible under the Convention, whether explicitly or implicitly, national authorities are to take the general principles of case law into account in their domestic assessment of a case. They then apply those principles to the facts of the case, within the core of their margin of appreciation. Recent Court decisions have ruled that in deciding whether, and to what extent, the Court should grant a Member State a margin of appreciation, the Court is to examine the quality of decision-making, both at the legislative stage and before the national courts.[12]

[11.11] Following the ECHR requires consideration of various factors, such as:

- the nature of the right involved;

---

7   E.g., *Karnel Singh Bhinder v Canada* (1986), ¶4.5.
8   UN Doc. CCPR/C/21/Rev1/Add.1 (1989), reprinted in UN Doc. A/45/40 vol.1, Annex VI (1990), 17, ¶10.
9   See, e.g., *Handyside v the United Kingdom* (1976), ¶48.
10   *Kokkinakis v Greece* (1993), ¶47. See also *Handyside v the United Kingdom* (1976), ¶48 ff; *Lawless v Ireland* (1961), 408.
11   *Hatton and Others v the United Kingdom* (2003), ¶101.
12   Spano, (2014).

- the degree of interference involved (i.e. whether it was proportionate to the intended aim);

- the nature of the public interest; and

- the degree to which that interest requires protection.[13]

[11.12] Malcolm Evans argues that

> [b]ecause they are so interdependent, none of these aspects can be examined convincingly in isolation. Nor does any one [aspect] have sufficient prominence to justify its use as the primary framework for analysis.[14]

[11.13] Somewhat confusingly, then, the human rights tribunals, (the European ones in particular) have indicated two potentially incompatible provisions in determining limitations on manifestation of belief:

a) there is a permissible 'discretion' or 'margin of appreciation in determining the legitimacy and extent of an interference' in manifestation of belief,

b) the limits that can be placed on this interference must be strictly constrained according to the belief provisions.[15]

[11.14] The European Court tends to deal with religious speech under Article 19 ECHR, where the margin of appreciation is widely applied. In the case of *Murphy v Ireland* (2003) the Court upheld the suppression of an advertisement for a meeting to discuss the evidence of the Resurrection of Christ. The Court upheld the State's right to exercise a margin of appreciation as to what is 'necessary to protect public safety, order, health or morals' under Article 9.2 ECHR. It concluded that

> a wider margin of appreciation is generally available to the Contracting States when regulating freedom of expression in relation to matters liable to offend intimate personal life stances within the sphere of morals or, especially, religion'.[16]

[11.15] Some state discretion is in line with Rawls. The Court has held that

---

13   *X and Church of Scientology v Sweden* (1979), 73; *Rasmussen v Denmark* (1984), ¶40.

14   Malcolm Evans (1997), 322.

15   *Svyato-Mykhaylivska Parafiya v Ukraine* (2007), ¶137; *Manoussakis and Others v Greece* (1996), ¶44. For the UN prescription for strict adherence to these requirements see, e.g., *ICCPR General Comment 22*, ¶8.

16   *Murphy v Ireland* (2003), ¶67. The Court dealt with the matter under Article 10 ECHR (freedom of speech).

a balance must be achieved which ensures the fair and proper treatment of people from minorities and avoids any abuse of a dominant position…Pluralism and democracy must also be based on dialogue and a spirit of compromise necessarily entailing various concessions on the part of individuals or groups of individuals which are justified in order to maintain and promote the ideals and values of a democratic society…It is precisely this constant search for a balance between the fundamental rights of each individual which constitutes the foundation of a "democratic society".[17]

[11.16] The concepts of 'necessity' and allowing for a 'margin of appreciation' can be ways of instituting what Rawls calls justice as fairness. They allow for consideration of the circumstances of the case, the beliefs of those involved and the social and cultural environment. Establishing the fairest balance between the individual's right to freedom to manifest belief and the public good and fundamental rights and freedoms of others is potentially a foundation for substantive justice.

[11.17] The catch lies in the fact that discretion is subject to political pressure and judicial subjectivity, which will always attract contention, as can be seen in any consideration of the tribunals' decisions.

Examples: recognition of circumstances

[11.18] The ambivalence and potential for different results from applying the margin of appreciation has resulted in different and sometimes conflicting and controversial Court decisions. Some cases have led to the *privileging* of religion or other belief, rather than the 'levelling of the playing field',[18] while other cases the result is the invocation of a margin of appreciation to limit the practice of belief, as the following cases demonstrate.

Relationships counselling

[11.19] The European Court recently invoked the margin of appreciation in restricting the manifestation of religion in the case of *Eweida and Others v the United Kingdom* (2013). In this case involving four applicants, two of them, Ms Ladele and Mr McFarlaine were dismissed by their respective employers for their objection to providing services to same-sex couples, based on their religious beliefs. Ms Ladele, a Registrar of Births, Deaths and Marriages, refused to participate in the registration of same-sex unions as part of her responsibilities. Mr McFarlane, a counsellor with a private counselling body, refused to provide psycho-sexual therapy to same-sex couples.

---

17 *Leyla Şahin v Turkey* (2005), ¶108. See also *Young, James and Webster v the United Kingdom* (1981), ¶63; *Chassagnou and Others v France* (1999); *United Communist Party of Turkey and Others v Turkey* (1998), pp. 2122, ¶45; *Refah Partisi (the Welfare Party), and Others v Turkey* (2003), ¶99.

18 Indeed, the provision of a 'level playing field' is what Malcolm Evans advocates (2008), 299ff.

Both alleged that their beliefs should have been accommodated, and that by insisting on their providing the services, their employers violated their belief rights.

[11.20] The Court considered that the policies of the applicants' employers required employees not to discriminate in providing services. This included the legitimate aim of securing the rights of same-sex couples, which were also protected under the Convention. In particular, the Court pointed to previous cases where it had held that particularly serious justification was required for differences in treatment based on sexual orientation, and that same-sex couples were entitled to similar legal protection of their relationship to different sex couples.

[11.21] Although Ms Ladele's employer introduced presiding over civil partnerships after Ms Ladele entered into her contract of employment, the Court held that this did not ensure her right to manifest her religious belief by objecting to involvement in them. It took into consideration the fact that allowing Ms Ladele to avoid conducting civil partnerships would create difficulties in rostering staff, and place an unreasonable burden on others.

[11.22] The Court invoked the margin of appreciation. It said that the local authority's policy aimed to secure the rights of others, which are also protected under the Convention:

> The Court generally allows the national authorities a wide margin of appreciation when it comes to striking a balance between competing Convention rights. In all the circumstances, the Court does not consider that the national authorities, that is the local authority employer which brought the disciplinary proceedings and also the domestic courts which rejected the applicant's discrimination claim, exceeded the margin of appreciation available to them.[19]

[11.23] Thus, it held, there was no violation of Article 9 ECHR.

[11.24] Mr McFarlane was aware, on taking up his position, that his employer had a non-discrimination policy. Despite also enrolling in a training program in psycho-sexual therapy, his religious beliefs led him to object to providing same-sex couples with psycho-sexual therapy (while he was agreeable to counselling them on other matters). His attitude caused dissension among staff.

[11.25] An additional issue was the fact that the option of his avoiding providing same-sex couples with psycho-sexual therapy was considered not a reasonable option by his employer, due to difficulty in filtering clients on the ground of sexual orientation.

---

19   *Eweida and Others v. the United Kingdom* (2013), ¶106.

[11.26] The Court held an individual's decision to enter into a contract of employment and to undertake responsibilities which he knows will have an impact on his freedom to manifest his religious belief is not necessarily determinative of whether Article 9 ECHR has been violated. Rather it is a matter to be considered when deciding whether a fair balance between competing interests has been struck.

[11.27] The most important factor to be taken into account in this case was that the employer's action was intended to secure the implementation of its policy of providing a service without discrimination. The State authorities, therefore, benefitted from a wide margin of appreciation in deciding where to strike the balance between Mr McFarlane's right to manifest his religious belief and the employer's interest in securing the rights of others. In all the circumstances, the Court did not consider that this margin of appreciation was exceeded.

[11.28] The Court also held that

> same-sex couples are in a relevantly similar situation to different-sex couples as regards their need for legal recognition and protection of their relationship, although since practice in this regard is still evolving across Europe, the Contracting States enjoy a wide margin of appreciation as to the way in which this is achieved within the domestic legal order.[20] Against this background, it is evident that the aim pursued by the local authority was legitimate.[21]

[11.29] The Court concluded that the right balance had been struck between the employer's right to secure the entitlements of others and the right of both Ms Ladele and Mr McFarlane to manifest their religion, and therefore that there had been no violation of Article 9.

[11.30] As the employer in Mr McFarlane's case was a private body, the extent of the state's obligation to secure rights under the belief provisions (in this case Article 9 ECHR) required consideration. The Court held that the state's obligation required that a fair balance is struck between the competing interests of the individual and the community as a whole, determined in light of the margin of appreciation afforded the state. The Court decided that in both cases the state had not overstepped its margin of appreciation.

Religious symbols in the classroom

[11.31] This privileging of religion was endorsed in the case of *Lautsi and Others v Italy* (2011). Parents in Italy objected to the presence of crucifixes in public school classrooms, placed there by ancient (1920s) decree and influenced by agreement with the Catholic Church. They argued that

---

20   The Court referred to *Schalk and Kopf v. Austria* (2010).
21   *Eweida and Others v. the United Kingdom* (2013), ¶105.

the presence of crucifixes was contrary to the Italian constitution that all religious creeds are to be equal before the law. They also argued that their presence was a breach of Article 2 of Protocol No 1 to the ECHR, to which Italy was a party. That Article provides that 'the state shall respect the right of parents to ensure…education and teaching in conformity with their own religious and philosophical convictions'. The Italian courts found against the applicants, so they took their argument on the Protocol to the European Court. The Chamber of the European Court found in their favour. It held that the placement of crucifixes was a violation of Article 2 of Protocol No. 1. The Court reasoned that:

- The State is obliged to refrain from imposing beliefs, even indirectly, in places where persons are dependent on it, or where they are particularly vulnerable. The schooling of children is a particularly sensitive area in that respect.

- The compulsory and highly visible presence of crucifixes in classrooms clashes with the secular convictions of parents whose children attend a State school. It is also emotionally disturbing for pupils of non-Christian religions or those who profess no religion.

- The "negative" freedom of religion is not limited to the absence of religious services or religious education: it extends to practices and symbols expressing, in particular or in general, a belief, a religion or atheism.

- The state has a duty to uphold confessional neutrality in public education. School attendance is compulsory regardless of religion, which had to seek to inculcate in pupils the habit of critical thought.

- The crucifix is a symbol that it is reasonable to associate with the majority religion in Italy. It could not serve the educational pluralism, which was essential for the preservation of "democratic society" within the Convention meaning of that term.[22]

[11.32] The matter was referred to the Grand Chamber, which reversed the Chamber's decision, presenting a different perception of the facts. It held:[23]

- As to imposing beliefs, while states must respect the rights and freedoms enshrined in the Convention and its Protocols, contracting States enjoy a margin of appreciation in the functions they assume in relation to education and teaching, and whether or not to perpetuate tradition and Italy's historical development. The Court must

---

22   *Lautsi and Others v Italy* (2011), ¶¶ 30, 31.
23   Ibid, ¶63ff.

recognise the great diversity of cultural and historical development in Europe. The organisation of the school environment is a matter for the public authorities, of the state.

- As to clashes with the secular convictions of parents, the crucifixes are fixed symbols and not an active form of manifestation of belief. They do not clash with parental beliefs, or the right to educate children in one's religion.

- As to harm to children, while students are young persons whose convictions are still in the process of being formed, the Court had received no evidence that the display of a passive religious symbol on classroom walls may have an effect comparable to that of didactic speech or participation in religious activities. The applicant's subjective perception is not in itself sufficient to establish a breach of Article 2 of Protocol No. 1.

- While the regulations confer on the country's majority religion preponderant visibility in the school environment, that is not indoctrination and thus not a breach of the requirements of Article 2 of Protocol No. 1. The crucifixes cannot be deemed to have an influence on pupils.

- As to respect for the right of parents to ensure such education and teaching in conformity with their own religious and philosophical convictions, other courts have accepted the granting of a larger share of the curriculum to knowledge of a particular religion. This is within the margin of appreciation without offending pluralism and objectivity.

- As to confessional neutrality, the Grand Chamber implied that, beyond its religious meaning, the crucifix is justified because it 'symbolised the principles and values which formed the foundation of democracy and western civilisation'. [24]

[11.33] Judge Malinverni, joined by Judge Kalaydjieva, dissented. They said:

Whilst the doctrine of the margin of appreciation may be useful, or indeed convenient, it is a tool that needs to be handled with care. This is because the scope of that margin will depend on a great many factors: the right in issue, the seriousness of the infringement, the existence of a European consensus, etc… The proper application of this theory will thus depend on the importance to be attached to each of these various factors. Where the Court decrees that the margin of appreciation is a narrow one, it will generally find a violation of

---

24   Ibid, ¶67.

the Convention; where it considers that the margin of appreciation is wide, the respondent State will usually be "acquitted".

[11.34] They added the following points:

- While there is a lack of consensus in other countries in this matter, few of them have regulated on the express provision of religious symbols in government schools.[25]

- Giving regard to majority religion is not complying with the obligation of abstention from religious promotion required by the Convention.

- The state's obligations cover not only the curriculum, but the whole educational system, indeed all the 'functions' assumed by the State.[26]

- '…the individual is exposed without possibility of escape to the influence of a particular faith, to the acts through which it is manifested and to the symbols in which it is presented.'[27]

- The crucifix is predominantly a religious symbol and cannot be said to represent values independent of a particular belief.

[11.35] They concluded that strict denominational neutrality required by Article 2 of Protocol No. 1 and Article 9 ECHR applies not only to the content of teaching, but also extends to the general school environment, and as schooling is compulsory, religion should not be imposed on pupils.[28]

[11.36] Which decision was the right one? Opinions may differ, but it is interesting to note the intensive campaign by both governments and non-government organisations to influence the Grand Chamber's decision. There were 52 submissions by third parties: 10 governments, 4 non-government organisations and 33 European members of Parliament appeared and argued for retention of the crucifixes. Five non-government organisations argued against retention. One can surmise that the states were keen to maintain their relationship with religion. An argument presented strongly was based on the specific acceptance by the UN and European Council of the establishment of a state religion.

[11.37] It is suggested that the dissenting judgment is more in line with Rawls's model of justice as fairness and the principles underlying the belief provisions.

---

25   Ibid, dissenting opinion ¶1.
26   Ibid, dissenting opinion ¶3, citing *Folgerø and Others v. Norway* (2007) §84.
27   Ibid,, dissenting opinion ¶4
28   Ibid,, dissenting opinion ¶5

[11.38] The examples above illustrate the complexity of the issues that arise, based on conflicting values and ideals. The 'margin of appreciation', while potentially an avenue to justice and fairness, can throw into jeopardy, or at least obscure, the promise of equal belief rights.

Religious symbols at work

[11.39] In another matter that was dealt with in the case of *Eweida and Others v the United Kingdom* (2013) – a less conciliatory approach to the display religious symbols – was taken by the European Court on the wearing of religious symbols at work.

[11.40] In this case, two of the four applicants complained that they were restricted from wearing conspicuous crosses with their uniforms at work. Ms Eweida, a British Airways employee, and Ms Chaplin, a geriatric nurse, complained that this was a violation of their right to freedom of religion under the ECHR.

[11.41] The European Court recognised that religious freedom is primarily a private matter. It also ensures the freedom to manifest one's beliefs in private or public, any limitation of which must be prescribed by law, in pursuit of a legitimate aim and necessary in a democratic society.[29] The lack of explicit protection in the UK law in this area did not, in itself, mean that Ms Eweida's right to manifest her religion had been breached.

[11.42] Where someone claims that an employer has restricted their freedom of religion in the workplace, the court said that it should consider whether the restriction was proportionate to the harm caused.

[11.43] The Court considered that by prohibiting the applicant from wearing a visible cross, British Airways interfered unjustifiably with her right to manifest her religion. The Court said that a fair balance had not been struck between her desire to manifest her religious belief and her employer's wish to project a certain corporate image (no matter how legitimate that aim might be). The argument that the wearing of a crucifix would damage British Airways' image was also weakened by the fact that:

- they had previously authorised the wearing of religious clothing such as turbans and hijabs;

- after Ms Eweida's complaint, the company had amended the uniform code to allow for wearing visible religious symbolic jewellery

---

29   Ibid, ¶¶79–80.

[11.44] This, the Court held, indicated that the employer had not, in fact, seen the earlier prohibition as having crucial importance.

[11.45] On the other hand, the protection of health and safety on a hospital ward – the hospital's reason for asking Ms Chaplin to remove her cross – was one of much greater importance. The Court relied on the judgment of hospital managers, who, it said, were better placed to make decisions about clinical safety (it had no direct evidence to the contrary). The Court found that requiring the removal of the cross was disproportionate to the interference with her freedom to manifest her religion, as it was deemed necessary in a democratic society. Accordingly, there had been no violation of Article 9 as concerned Ms Chaplin.

[11.46] Two of the dissenting judges disagreed with the Court's conclusion that British Airways had acted disproportionately in relation to the first applicant. They pointed to the fact that Ms Eweida had for months concealed her cross without objecting, and the employer had acted on her complaint, offering her a temporary position in administration, where she could wear her cross openly. They held that the Court had not carried out a 'fair balance' of the competing interests, and concluded that Ms Eweida's rights had not been violated

[11.47] . The wearing of religious apparel and face covering in public places generally is considered at[5.32]ff.

Religious 'vilification' and freedom of speech

[11.48] Numerous resolutions calling on UN member States to take specific measures to 'combat defamation of religion', or oppose religious incitement to hostility or violence, through legislation and other measures have been passed by both the Human Rights Council (and the Human Rights Commission before it), as well as the General Assembly (see[2.32]]). Some governments and religious groups still insist on equating any questioning of religious beliefs with the criminal prohibition of incitement to religious hatred, thus giving a very wide interpretation to that offence, and repressing any comment unfavourable to, in particular, the Islamic religion.[30]

[11.49] Case law has demonstrated the difficulty in determining acceptable and unacceptable speech that offends. This is borne out, for example, by the extensive discussion (and individual reasoning of judges) in the UNHRC case of *Faurisson v France* (1993). In that case, an academic was convicted under laws that prohibited questioning, *inter alia,* the extermination of Jews in Nazi concentration camps. He publicly expressed doubt

---

30   Mchangama (2013).

about the Holocaust. While the UNHRC held that the author had a right to express an opinion in general, it concluded that two statements he made, indicating that the Holocaust was a 'myth' and a 'dishonest fabrication', served to strengthen anti-Semitic fervour.[31] The legislation prohibiting such statements was held to be compatible with the ICCPR, as necessary for respect of the rights and reputations of others. However, the UN General Assembly has recently issued a *General Comment* stating that laws penalising expression of opinions about historical facts are incompatible with obligations imposed by the ICCPR regarding freedom of expression.[32] Just what that means for drawing a distinction between offense and incitement to hatred and social disaffection by extremely repellent opinions such as Holocaust denial is open to question.

[11.50] The context surrounding particular speech was considered by the UNHRC in the case of *Ross v Canada* (see[10.13]). There the UNHRC considered not the author's beliefs as such, but the 'manifestation of those beliefs within a particular context'.

[11.51] The line to be drawn between speech that causes offence through ridicule and incitement to hatred and violence is debatable. Amir Butler, the executive director of the Australian Muslim Public Affairs Committee has argued, for example, that the Victorian legislation in Australia prohibiting 'religious vilification'[33] has 'served only to undermine the very religious freedoms' it was supposed to protect'.[34] He suggests that it is impossible to draft religious vilification prohibitions properly, because of their very nature, as religions are inherently sectarian:

> If we believe our religion is the only way to Heaven, then we must also affirm that all other paths lead to Hell…Yet this is exactly what this law serves to outlaw and curtail: the right of believers to passionately argue against or warn against the beliefs of another.[35]

[11.52] Steve Edwards points to claims that 'Muslims and Christians are using the legislation as a tactical weapon, engaging in mutual surveillance for the sole purpose of silencing one another'.[36]

---

31 *Faurisson v France* (1993), ¶9.6.

32 *General Comment 34* (2011), ¶ 49.

33 *Racial and Religious Tolerance Act* 2001 (Vic), s8. (1), 'A person must not, on the ground of the religious belief or activity of another person or class of persons, engage in conduct that incites hatred against, serious contempt for, or revulsion or severe ridicule of, that other person or class of persons'.

34 Butler (2004). See also Blake (2007).

35 Ibid. See also Edwards (2005). For an outline of Australian vilification laws, Whelan and Fougere (2002); Perkins (2005), 53; *Fletcher v Salvation Army Australia* (2005); *Islamic Council of Victoria v Catch the Fire Ministries Inc* (2004). Carolyn Evans (2007), presents concisely arguments both in favour of, and against, hate speech legislation, considering the benefits and pitfalls of each. See also Feenan (2006); Edge (2003); Clarke (2007), 94.

36 Edwards (2005), 33.

[11.53] The European Court has accepted applications relating to alleged religious vilification, and tended to allow suspension of material considered to offend the religious sensitivities of the public, applying the 'margin of appreciation' broadly.[37] In the case of *Otto Preminger-Institut v Austria* (1994) the applicant association announced a series of public showings of a film considered offensive to religion called *Council in Heaven*. The charge was 'disparaging religious doctrines' under section 188 of the Penal Code.

[11.54] The State Court of Appeal considered that artistic freedom was necessarily limited by the rights of others to freedom of religion and by the duty of the State to safeguard a society based on order and tolerance. It further held that indignation was 'justified' for the purposes of section 188 of the Penal Code only if the object of the offending speech was such as to offend the religious feelings of an average person with normal religious sensitivity.[38]

[11.55] The European Court, to which the case was then referred, agreed that prohibiting exhibition of the film was not a breach of Article 9, upholding, *inter alia*, what it declared as 'the legitimacy of measures repressing conduct incompatible with the respect for the religious feelings of believers as guaranteed in Article 9'.[39]

[11.56] The Court said:

> The Court cannot disregard the fact that the Roman Catholic religion is the religion of the overwhelming majority of Tyroleans. In seizing the film, the Austrian authorities acted to ensure religious peace in that region and to prevent that some people should feel the object of attacks on their religious beliefs in an unwarranted and offensive manner. It is in the first place for the national authorities, who are better placed than the international judge, to assess the need for such a measure in the light of the situation obtaining locally at a given time. In all the circumstances of the present case, the Court does not consider that the Austrian authorities can be regarded as having overstepped their margin of appreciation in this respect.[40]

[11.57] In the later case of *Wingrove v the United Kingdom* (1996) the Court continued this approach. *Wingrove* concerned a film allegedly offensive to religion. The Court upheld the refusal of the British Board of Film Classification to grant a licence for the distribution of the film. The Court said that the aim of the refusal

---

37   See, for a discussion of the case law Taylor (2005), 84ff.
38   *Otto Preminger-Institut v Austria* (1994), ¶13.
39   Ibid, ¶47.
40   Ibid, ¶56.

was to protect against the treatment of a religious subject in such a manner "as to be calculated (that is, bound, not intended) to outrage those who have an understanding of, sympathy towards and support for the Christian story and ethic," which is "fully consonant with the aim of the protections afforded by Article 9 (art. 9) to religious freedom."[41]

[11.58] In relation to religious belief, the Court held, this aim, imposes 'a duty to avoid as far as possible an expression that is, in regard to objects of veneration, gratuitously offensive to others and profanatory'.[42]

[11.59] Again, the Court favoured religious sensitivities in the case of *Murphy v Ireland* (2003). This case involved an advertisement on radio for a video 'on the evidence of the resurrection', which was suspended by the Government. Although the advertisement itself was not offensive, simply providing the date and time of showing of the purportedly factual video, justified its prohibition. The Court invoked the state's right to a margin of appreciation, deferring to what it referred to as the 'extreme sensitivity of the question of broadcasting of religious advertising in Ireland' and that 'religious advertising from a different church might be considered offensive and open to the interpretation of proselytism'.[43]

[11.60] It concluded that

a wider margin of appreciation is generally available to the Contracting States when regulating freedom of expression in relation to matters liable to offend intimate personal life stances within the sphere of morals or, especially, religion'.[44]

[11.61] However, the Court more recently has held that

a balance must be achieved which ensures the fair and proper treatment of people from minorities and avoids any abuse of a dominant position…Pluralism and democracy must also be based on dialogue and a spirit of compromise necessarily entailing various concessions on the part of individuals or groups of individuals which are justified in order to maintain and promote the ideals and values of a democratic society…It is precisely this constant search for a balance between the fundamental rights of each individual which constitutes the foundation of a "democratic society".[45]

---

41   *Wingrove v the United Kingdom* (1996), ¶48.
42   Ibid, ¶52.
43   *Murphy v Ireland* (2003), ¶73.
44   Ibid, ¶67. The Court dealt with the matter under Article 10 ECHR (freedom of speech).
45   *Leyla Şahin v Turkey* (2005), ¶108. See also *Young, James and Webster v the United Kingdom* (1981), ¶63; *Chassagnou and Others v France* (1999); *United Communist Party of Turkey and Others v Turkey* (1998), pp. 2122, ¶45; *Refah Partisi (the Welfare Party), and Others v Turkey* [GC] (2003), ¶99.

This approach was endorsed by the European Assembly in Resolution 1510 (2006), stating that 'freedom of expression should not be restricted to meet the sensitivities of any group in a democratic society'. In 2013 it repeated this view, including blasphemy.[46]

[11.62] Views as to how these seemingly contradictory approaches have been balanced will vary. Some may say there was a bias in the Court towards Christianity. Certainly, there will be those who disagree with particular findings, and conclude that even with the best of intentions, there is no way of guaranteeing a truly equal recognition of belief rights. Some firmer directions, however, could forge a more successful realization of belief freedoms by removing the special treatment formerly given to religion.

Education

[11.63] Choice is at the heart of belief, according to Rawls, and is implied in the belief provisions, but choice is an empty idea unless the individual has the capacity for choice, and the opportunity to be aware of beliefs from which to choose.

[11.64] People, as members of society, are imbued with a particular concept of the world and the meaning of life from early childhood, as determined by their parents, family and community, when they have little capacity or opportunity to evaluate and choose a belief for themselves. While these capacities and opportunities arrive with adulthood and many individuals change or revise their beliefs, upbringing has a very powerful influence which is difficult to shake off. It may not even occur to people to question, or they may be coerced, tricked or pressured into manifesting a belief that they do question.[47]

[11.65] Choice in adopting a belief thus becomes a particular issue in the education of children. This point is illustrated by the US Supreme Court judgement in *Wisconsin v Yoder* (1972). The respondents, members of the conservative Amish religion, refused to send their children to public or private school after they had graduated from the eighth grade, in contravention of the law, which mandated school attendance until the age of 16. Instead, children were kept in the community and restricted to learning the basic requirements for the simple Amish lifestyle. The Court:

---

46   See, e.g. European Assembly Resolution 1928 (2013), pars 5, 48.
47   E.g., 'Stereotypes are reinforced by persistent patriarchal attitudes and assumptions that women's place is in the home supported by men. Male superiority prevails, also in industrial societies, and can amount to an ideology': United Nations (2002), ¶92.

- accepted that the parents sincerely believed that attending high school was contrary to the Amish religion and way of life, and that compliance with the law would endanger the salvation of all concerned.

- upheld the Wisconsin State Supreme Court finding that compulsory mandatory secondary school attendance for the Amish was a violation of their First Amendment belief rights.

[11.66] Stating that the Amish way of life is one of deep religious conviction, 'intimately related to daily living' and that interfering with that would be interfering with their belief,[48] the Court went on to find that

> compulsory school attendance to age 16 for Amish children carries with it a very real threat of undermining the Amish community and religious practice as they exist today; they must either abandon belief and be assimilated into society at large, or be forced to migrate to some other and more tolerant region.[49]

[11.67] However, this case raises the question of choice. It is critical that the opinion of the students themselves was not considered by the court, only that of the parents. At grade eight they may well be old enough to decide if they wish to further their education. The Amish may be free to exercise their religious beliefs, but should they be free to prevent their children from such freedom? Douglas J. expressed an alternative perspective, dissenting in part from the majority and pointing out that the court had only considered the interests of the parents, not the children. He offered a different, and I agree, a better perspective from the majority of the court:

> It is the future of the student, not the future of the parents, that is imperilled by today's decision. If a parent keeps his child out of school beyond the grade school, then the child will be forever barred from entry into the new and amazing world of diversity that we have today... It is the student's judgment, not his parents', that is essential if we are to give full meaning to what we have said about the Bill of Rights and of the right of students to be masters of their own destiny. If he is harnessed to the Amish way of life by those in authority over him and if his education is truncated, his entire life may be stunted and deformed. The child, therefore, should be given an opportunity to be heard before the State gives the exemption which we honor today.[50]

---

48   *Wisconsin v Yoder* (1972), 216.

49   Ibid, 218.

50   Ibid, 245-6. Despite this, Article 14 of the Convention on the Rights of the Child, guarantees Freedom of belief, and gives parents the right to provide direction in exercising this right 'consistent with the evolving capacities of the child' *Convention on the Rights of the Child* (1990).

[11.68] The question of free will complicates the simple presumption that all individuals are free to choose their belief. While one should not dictate how people view the world, or set their personal values, as a matter of human rights in general, Rawls insists that in democratic society, appropriate compulsory education should be available to children to prepare them for participation in political life. This should provide them with the capacity and opportunity for choice, and the ability to realise their potential for autonomy. As a matter of belief rights, the belief provisions are further used to condone segregation for special education of children by religious groups, *requiring only that education in relation to belief be objective and impartial for those whose parents desire it to be exempt from religious instruction.*

Different tribunal approaches

[11.69] While the 'official' line seems to be well established – freedom to believe as one will, but only those acts that are directly expressive of a belief are protected, unless government can demonstrate necessity to restrict them – there is an apparent difference in emphasis between the UNHRC and the European Court. While the UNHRC in recent cases stresses the need for full justification of limitations placed on manifestation of belief, the European Court has shown a readiness to accept government assurances that limits are valid, based on the principle of 'margin of appreciation'. This is most clearly demonstrated in their differing rulings on mandatory removal of head covering for identity photos.

[11.70] The applicant was Shingara Mann Singh, a French national and a practising Sikh. The Sikh religion requires its male followers to wear a turban at all times. The applicant, had had his driver's licence renewed in the past after providing photographs which showed him wearing a turban. His request to replace his stolen licence was refused on the grounds that the identity photographs he had supplied showed him wearing a turban. Regulations had been changed to require requests for issuance of a new or duplicate licence to be accompanied by a photograph showing the person "bareheaded and facing forward". After exhausting all domestic avenues of appeal, Mr Singh took his case to the European Court,[51] arguing, *inter alia*, violation of his right to freedom to manifest his religious beliefs.

[11.71] The European Court acknowledged that the impugned regulations amounted to interference with exercise of the right to freedom of religion and conscience, but that the government was pursuing the legitimate aim of ensuring public safety. It dismissed the case, noting other cases where national security was held a valid reason for requiring removal of headwear for identity purposes, and said Article 9

---

51   *Mann Singh v. France* (2008).

- did not protect every act motivated or inspired by a religion or belief;

- did not always guarantee the right to behave in a manner governed by a religious belief; and

- did not confer on people the right, in practising their belief, to disregard limitations that are justified.

[11.72] The Court considered that the detailed arrangements for implementing identity checks fell within the respondent State's margin of appreciation, especially since the requirement for persons to remove their turbans for that purpose or for the initial issuance of the licence was an infrequent one. It therefore held that the impugned interference had been justified in principle and proportionate to the aim pursued.[52]

[11.73] Later, when Mr Singh applied for a passport and again was required to produce a photograph without his turban, he decided to take his case to the UNHRC, which found in his favour.[53] Firstly, it held that the French Government had not explained why adequate identification could not be made when the face was clearly visible, and why people who always appear in public with their heads covered would be better identified through bare-headed identity photographs.[54]

[11.74] Further, the Committee said that

even if the obligation to remove the turban for the identity photograph might be described as a one-time requirement, it would potentially interfere with the author's freedom of religion on a continuing basis because he would always appear without his religious head covering in the identity photograph and could thus be compelled to remove his turban during identity checks.[55]

[11.75] The Committee concluded that the disputed Decree was a disproportionate limitation on Mr Singh's freedom of religion.

[11.76] It seems that the European Court leaned toward emphasis on the 'equality' aspect of belief rights, emphasising its secular nature. The UNHRC, on the other hand, was concerned to

---

52   Press release issued by the Court Registrar, < http://www.hfhrpol.waw.pl/precedens/english-section/press-release-inadmissibility-decision-mann-sungh-v-france-27-11-2008.html >.

53   *Mann Singh v France* (2013).

54   Ibid [9.4].

55   Ibid [9.5].

ensure the 'freedom' side of the equation. Neither tribunal adequately examined the most pertinent issues. These, in my view were:

- the purpose of the identity photos (i.e. the circumstances under which a person's identity is to be established);

- factual aspects of identification when head cover does not cover the face. For example, given the ease of changing appearance, whether photographing the features of a person's head, such as presence or absence of hair, hair colour or hairline is essential for identification, or whether photographing the facial features only is adequate for identification if the head cover is later removed;

- the need to express the law in terms that apply to all, regardless of belief (i.e. it should apply to head cover, whether based on religion, culture, or choice); and

- whether the impugned government practice is in fact necessary in the public interest.

[11.77] Had these issues been more fully pursued, one would at least feel more satisfaction at the attempt to balance the interests of both Sikh followers and the public interest of state neutrality.

Conclusion

[11.78] There will always be difference of opinion and controversy regarding the right balance to strike between freedom and equality when in relation to belief rights. Despite the monitoring bodies' insistence that limitations are perforce restricted to those specified, and must be necessary to realise the objectives noted in the belief provisions, based on the public good and rights of others, a potentially overbroad discretion is allowed to states through 'proportionality', 'objective and rational justification', and a 'margin of appreciation'. While unavoidable, this, in addition to the religion-flavoured, indefinite and, at times, incongruous language of the belief provisions themselves, opens the door to skewing the balance in favour of particular political, religious or cultural biases and interests at best, and prejudice, unfairness and a drift towards theocracy at worst.

CHAPTER 12:
THE RESULT: MISSION UNACCOMPLISHED

Special treatment of belief as human rights

[12.1] From the very beginning, with the drafting of the UDHR, the idea of what became known as 'freedom of religion and belief' was compromised by a limited view of what was intended, tainted by interests in sectarian and cultural dominion. The drafters of the belief provisions did not consider the full impact of the institutionalisation of religion and belief, and the language of Article 18 further encouraged misconceptions and misuses. The demand for freedom of 'religion and belief' became more than a demand for fostering ideas and personal lifestyles, it was the catalyst for vast corporate-style, belief-based empires and militant battles for pre-eminence over people and property. As pointed out by Stephen Mutch, 'rights' language can be 'used as weapons by lobby groups to achieve their agendas', and, in relation to harmful activities by cults and apologists, often ensures that governments do nothing.[1]

[12.2] It has been argued that governments and religions have shown themselves eager to be associated with the idea of human rights, the widespread claim to follow them, based as it is on various religious and cultural backgrounds, 'signifies no more than rhetorical consensus'.[2] Most religions and other beliefs across the world, from East to West, proclaim adherence to human rights, but as Johan van der Vyver states, they do so 'on their own terms'.[3] Nations have insisted on maintaining their own laws on particular matters, or interpreting human rights according to Shari'ah or other religious dictates. This is demonstrated by the long list of reservations to the ICCPR by States Parties signing and ratifying it.[4]

[12.3] The state-belief relationships described in earlier Chapters means that societies are dominated by prevailing religious or other beliefs, and this affects the rights of women and children in particular. Government acquiescence, either formally or informally, plays a part in their continuance. In Afghanistan, for example, '[n]umerous reports demonstrate that authorities systematically fail to investigate and prosecute perpetrators of sexual violence…police and judicial officials are not aware or convinced that rape is a serious criminal offence'.[5] In some countries authorities may help to preserve and protect harmful traditional practices, for example, in covering up or

---

1   Mutch (2013).
2   van der Vyver (1996), xii.
3   Ibid.
4   Reservations are set out at <http://treaties.un.org/Pages/ViewDetails.aspx?src=TREATY&mtdsg_no=IV-4&chapter=4&lang=en>.
5   United Nations (2009), 24-5.

condoning crimes carried out in the name of 'honour'. They may fear retribution for interference with custom or culture.[6]

[12.4] As well as outright rejection of human rights as set out in the UDHR by some states, Jonathon Fox estimates that 85.1% (149) of the 175 states he examined either 'support some religions over others, place restrictions on some religions that are not placed on others, or both'.[7] When one considers that belief rights necessarily require freedom *from* belief (i.e. the unwanted influence of beliefs of others), practices such as prayer in Parliament, official mentions of God in national anthems (e.g. the UK, NZ), religion in state-funded education or a general bias towards one or more religions in official language and/or policy, the number, it is suggested, is closer to 100%. The promise of Article 18 is unrealised across the world.

[12.5] Fox concludes that '...no matter what one's perspective on the data, GIR [government involvement in religion] remains ubiquitous throughout the world'.[8] Even given acceptance of the need for state-belief separation, he continues, 'no matter how it is measured most states do not separate religion and state'.[9] Indeed, government involvement in religion has risen in 86 – almost half – of the states he reviews between 1990 and 2002.[10] He concludes that '[n]o matter how one views the larger picture, some aspect of religion remains a significant influence on at least some aspects of society and politics'.[11]

[12.6] At one end of the spectrum there are states that have, in effect, repudiated the human rights involved in belief rights: theocracies such as Iran and the Arab Emirates. Their constitutions provide that the state is subject to Islamic law. At the other end of the spectrum are states that provide for separation of government from religion. These states vary in the degree of actual separation that occurs, the two most prominently (but not completely) separationist being the US and France. Other nations fit into various positions along the spectrum. They all belong to the UN and all have signed the UDHR.

[12.7] Fox suggests that the following are reasons states privilege or suppress religion are:

- prevention of outside influence on indigenous culture (particularly in Orthodox Christian states of eastern Europe);

---

6 See, e.g., United Nations (2002), ¶197
7 Fox (2008), 353.
8 Ibid, 100.
9 Ibid, 359.
10 Ibid, 356.
11 Ibid, 364.

- exclusion of religions considered a threat to government or society (particularly in Western and Eastern Europe);

- maintenance of religion as national identity, or the basis of government (particularly in Muslim countries);

- maintenance of a symbiotic relationship between religion and state (particularly Middle Eastern states); or

- maintenance of belief practices resulting from historical inertia (to some extent in most states).[12]

[12.8] There is also the fact that governments seek to secure votes, and tend to be influenced by belief-based institutions seeking to increase their power and wealth through favourable treatment.

[12.9] What we find then, is that sectarian interests have largely overcome attempts at government impartiality towards belief. In many non-Western nations there is neither freedom to practise one or more beliefs, nor freedom from the unwanted influence of one or more beliefs. Individuals in Western democracies are still subject to a very prominent influence of one or more religions. Article 18 is represented in terms favourable to their cause.

Non-Western nations

[12.10] Non-Western nations have a record of more egregious human rights breaches sponsored or disregarded by government, including breaches against belief rights (which also can involve suppression of freedom of speech and assembly). There is plenty of evidence of this to be found in the press and the internet. The UN issues a daily bulletin that surveys human rights throughout the world,[13] and the US Commission on International Religious Freedom (USCIRF) publishes a yearly report of global human rights.[14] As mentioned in[2.23]ff., states members of the UN have rejected the terms of the UDHR in relation to belief rights.

[12.11] Fox documents increased government involvement in religion through limits and bans on minority beliefs over recent years. States identifying as Muslim have seen an increase in religious regulation of individuals, as well as discrimination based on religion since 1990. Some link religion with citizenship, e.g. Saudi Arabia, Iran, Kuwait and the UAE. Orthodox states also have heavy state involvement in religion.

---

12   Ibid, 354–5.
13   <https://www2.smartbrief.com/signupSystem/subscribe.action?pageSequence=1&briefName=un_wire>.
14   < http://www.uscirf.gov/>.

[12.12] States identifying themselves as Orthodox are considered to have separation of religion and state, but few of these states have extreme government involvement in religion. By contrast, nations identified as Muslim states can be found from one extreme to the other, but are more likely to have government involvement in religion. Despite adopting the notion of neutrality between state and religion, Western democracies all have some degree of state-belief accommodation.

[12.13] Like those with religious beliefs, those with non-religious beliefs suffer discrimination in relation to the right for such organisations to exist, to express their belief, to citizenship, public education and to employment. Sometimes apostasy or manifestation of unaccepted beliefs is punished with the death penalty.[15]

[12.14] Eastern religions, Van der Vyver points out, are increasingly questioning Western perceptions of human rights, and there is a 'struggle for supremacy' in the UN, particularly between the perceptions of human rights considered 'Western', and those based on Islamic shari'ah.[16]

[12.15] The attempt to incorporate all nations as member states results in a pragmatic approach by the UN that compromises genuine and equal belief rights. It is noted that Saudi Arabia, which has declared atheism a form of terrorism,[17] is a member of the UN Human Rights Council, among other hardline Islamic countries. As the UN approach to the belief provisions permits special treatment of religion, the Catholic Church has become an institutional feature at the UN. The Holy See, the Church's governing entity, an absolute theocracy with an unelected government, is given dubious recognition as a sovereign state,[18] by virtue of which it has direct access to the General Assembly and international UN conferences as a permanent observer.[19] It uses this

---

15   International Humanist and Ethical Union (2012), 9. For an updated report see International Humanist and Ethical Union (2013).

16   van der Vyver (1996), xiiiff.

17   See, e.g. <guardianlv.com/2014/04/saudo_arabia-labels-atheists-equivalent-with-terrorists/>. There is a wealth of information about discrimination on the basis of belief on the internet.

18   See, e.g., Robertson (2010); The Church itself recognises this dubious status: Catholics for Choice, (2013) cites the following statements by church hierarchy: 'The Holy See is not a state, but is accepted as being on the same footing as a state.' — Hyginus Eugene Cardinale, then Apostolic Nuncio, 1976, at p.2; 'The real and only realm of the Holy See is the realm of conscience.' — *Then-Archbishop and Holy See Permanent Observer to the United Nations Renato Martino at p. 13;* 'Of course the nature and aims of the spiritual mission of the Apostolic See and the church make their participation in the tasks and activities of the United Nations organization very different from that of the states, which are communities in the political and temporal sense.' – *Pope John Paul II, address to the General Assembly, 1979, at p. 11.*

19   Popes have been invited to address the General Assembly. The Holy See has an invitation to observe all open meetings of the intergovernmental subsidiary bodies of the General Assembly. It can intervene and participate in discussion and participate in private negotiations leading to the adoption of General Assembly decisions and resolutions and has the right to participate in the general debate of the General Assembly. The Catholic Church has used its unique power to influence resolutions and policies on human rights. These involve using its consideral influence on sexual and reproductive health issues: see, e.g. Catholics for Choice (2013), 17.

privileged status, granted to no other religion or belief organisation, to influence political agendas across all jurisdictions. It purports to act in the interests of international human rights, despite the fact that it has failed to ratify several key human rights treaties,[20] but insists on promoting its religiously-inspired views.[21] Other religious groups and NGOs also have influence, but this is not so formalised.

'Liberal Democracy' and accommodation of religion

[12.16] Focusing on the absence of freedom from belief (and religion in particular) highlights laws and policies that adversely influence the holding and practice of personal convictions. This approach is appropriate for liberal democracies. Those nations enjoy what is known as 'freedom of' belief, as people are not punished for their personal beliefs, or forbidden to practise them, within the parameters of democratic society. But currently this is a limited freedom, fashioned by social and political interests in the promotion of religious beliefs, as pointed out by Martínez-Torrón, and Navarro-Valls (see[6.36]]). People may find themselves facing the imposition of the doctrines of others, e.g. through enculturation or indoctrination in schools through religious influence and instruction, and through government policies and laws that enforce these doctrines or provide for the funding of religious organisations. This enables us to identify where the promise of the belief provisions is unrealised in liberal democracies, with its emphasis on liberty and consequent neglect of equality. Across the world, there are many ways in which citizens' autonomy is infringed by the undue influence of government entanglement with belief.

---

20   The Holy See has not signed the UDHR; or ratified the ICCPR; *International Covenant on Economic, Social and Cultural Rights,* the *Convention on the Elimination of All Forms of Discrimination against Women* (CEDAW), or the *Rome Statute of the International Criminal Court.* It has signed, but with critical reservations, the *Convention on the Rights of the Child* the *Convention against Torture and Other Cruel, Inhuman or Degrading Treatment or Punishment* 'insofar as it is compatible, in practice, with the peculiar nature of that State' and the *Convention relating to the Status of Refugees* (see Catholics for Choice, (2013), 3.

21   For example, a letter was sent on 24 June 2013 to the President of the Security Council from Archbishop Francis Chullikatt, Apostolic Nuncio, Permanent Observer Of The Holy See to The United Nations in relation to the Open Debate of the United Nations Security Council on "Women and peace and security: sexual violence in conflict". Archbishop Chullikatt stated that while the Holy See 'constantly strives to enhance development, freedom, and the dignity of all peoples and each person, from conception to natural death'

...we regret that the resolution just adopted goes beyond this noble call and instead seeks to promote a potentially destructive notion of health care, such as sexual and reproductive health, which too often is used as a justification for taking life rather than upholding it. Death of an innocent unborn child only visits further violence on a woman already in difficulty.

He continued 'International tribunals must adhere to the role of local national systems as the primary source for holding an individual accountable.' This rejection of an international approach to human rights favours nations that have signed concordats with the Holy See to adopt policies favourable to the Church.

Government alignment with religion

[12.17] The Queen of England is the UK Head of State, having that status 'by the grace of God' rather than as an elected head. She is the Supreme Governor of the Church of England (the established state church). Religious practices are part of government procedures, such as sessions of Parliament and local Council meetings. The Lord's Prayer, often used, invokes a desire for the coming of God's 'kingdom' and the doing of 'His' will, thus apparently declaring allegiance to a supernatural power instead of the nation. Other formal opening prayers indicate a similar sentiment. In some Western countries, the commencement of the legal year is marked with (Christian) religious ceremony and prayer attended by the legal profession, formally aligning the judiciary and legal profession with religious doctrine. Some national anthems (e.g. those of the UK and New Zealand) are prayers for God's protection of the monarch or the nation in general. In the US, with its official stance of 'separation of church and state', the pledge of allegiance invokes the (presumably) Christian God, and coins bear the invocation, 'In God we Trust'. US case law precedent is 'murky on prayer before government meetings', with contradictory decisions and confusion between allowing prayers if they are 'multifaith' and allowing any prayers at all.[22]

[12.18] In the UK, before every session in both the Lords and the Commons, members stand, turn to face the wall behind them, and pray. Attendance is voluntary, but the Speaker's Chaplain only ever reads out Christian prayers.[23] Prayers at other Parliamentary procedures there are said behind closed doors, and not as a formal part of sittings. This may be considered neutral in effect, but consider also that the House of Lords includes a significant number of unelected bishops. Despite the High Court recently finding that prayers cannot legally be part of formal business at council meetings, the Government decided to enact a 'general power of competence' to give local authorities power to include prayers as part of the formal business at council meetings. It issued a document, *Freedom To Pray: Advice To Parish Councils* to this effect.[24] The UK also has a Minister for Faith, who has considered calls for separation of church and state 'militant secularism', and has rejected claims that the Government doesn't 'do' God. He has stated that atheists should 'get over it' and 'recognise that the UK is a Christian country',[25] despite the declining proportion of Christians to those of other religions or no religion.[26]

---

22   Orlowski (2013).

23   Hickman (2010).

24   <https://www.gov.uk/government/uploads/system/uploads/attachment_data/file/5963/2092285.pdf>.

25   <http://www.huffingtonpost.co.uk/stephen-evans/eric-pickles-faith-minister_b_5657557.html>. See also <http://www.telegraph.co.uk/news/religion/10747980/Militant-atheists-should-get-over-it-and-accept-UK-is-Christian.html>.

26   Between 2001 and 2011 there has been a decrease [12%] in people who identify as Christian (from 71.7 per cent to 59.3 per cent) and an increase [<10%] in those reporting no religion (from 14.8 per cent to 25.1 per cent). There were increases in the other main religious group categories, with the number of Muslims increasing the most (from 3.0 per cent to 4.8 per cent): Office for National Statistics <http://www.ons.gov.uk/ons/index.html>.

[12.19] Even where there is no formally established state religion, e.g. in Australia and New Zealand, the Governments clearly favour Christianity economically, socially and politically.[27] The Queen is their Head of State as well. Their national flags bear the crosses of three Christian Saints, St George, St Andrew and St Patrick. Parliamentary sessions start with Christian prayers and the New Zealand National Anthem (*God Defend New Zealand*) is in effect a prayer. The former Australian Prime Minister, John Howard, and former Treasurer, Peter Costello, often invoked Australia's 'Judeo-Christian tradition' as determining our political values, and former Australian Prime Minister Kevin Rudd has argued for religious influence in politics.[28] In South Australia, a senior Catholic, Monsignor David Cappo, was appointed as an unelected member of the executive committees of the South Australian Government.[29]

[12.20] Nearly five million Australians (around 22.3%)[30] and 1.635 million New Zealanders[31] (around 41.9%) stated they do not belong to a religion in recent census findings. They are not officially recognised in these important formal state ceremonial representations that seem to ally the government with religion. The trend of diminishing religious affiliation is present throughout the Western world.

[12.21] This substantial proportion of the population is affected by the influence of Government entanglement with belief. The Australian High Court discounted the notion that there is a separation of 'church and state' in Australia, allowing state aid to religious schools for nominally non-religious purposes, despite the potential benefit for religious activities.[32] That case concerned Section 116 of the Australian Constitution, that prohibits the federal government from making law 'for the establishment of religion'. The applicants argued that legislation for funding of religious schools was a breach of this prohibition. The majority of the judges took a narrow approach to the meaning of 'establishing' a religion, stating that what is prohibited is the institution of a national church, involving, in one judge's words, the entrenchment of a particu-

---

27   E.g., Altman (2006), Chapter 3; Maddox (2005).

28   Rudd (2006), 22. See comment, Wallace (2008), 246.

29   *The Australian* 4-5 February 2006 noted that 'the appointment of a non-elected, non-government person to Cabinet – let alone a senior church figure – is unprecedented in Australia'.

30   *Herald-Sun* 29 December 2013 < www.heraldsun.com.au>; <http://en.wikipedia.org/wiki/Religion_in_Australia>.

31   <http://www.stats.govt.nz/Census/2013-census/profile-and-summary-reports/quickstats-culture-identity/religion. aspx> *New Zealand Catholic*, 10 December 2013.

32   Blackshield (2005), argues that according to the judgment, 'it would be constitutionally open to the Commonwealth "to patronise, protect and promote" a particular sect or religion' so long as this was not done pursuant to a perceived institutional obligation of patronage, protection or promotion', and that government aid to support the building of a cathedral would not infringe s.116: (at p. 98).

lar religion as 'a feature of and identified with' the government.[33] Funding of religious schools did not constitute establishment of religion. Three judges indicated that the Constitution does not create a separation of church and state in Australia.[34] While these statements were *obiter dicta*, (tangential to the ruling in the case), they appear to endorse state unity with religion (with a tendency towards theocracy), legitimising state privilege of religious individuals and organisations.

[12.22] Only one judge, (Murphy J.) approved the US approach of interpreting prohibition of establishment as involving separation of church and state.[35] The US Constitution also prohibits the government from establishing a religion. This has been given a different meaning by the US Supreme Court as meaning a strict 'separation of church and state', influenced by Thomas Jefferson's opinion that the prohibition creates a 'wall of separation' between the church and state.[36] This approach has recently been modified, evolving into what judges call 'benevolent neutrality', which I argue is accommodation by another name (see[13.8]]). Indeed, Derek Davis argues that:

> Given the time-honored right of religious bodies to be active participants in the American political process, it is not surprising that the US Supreme Court has not seriously challenged this basic right.[37]

Exemptions from laws of general application

[12.23] Exemptions from legislative provisions are provided for religious organisations – such as health and safety, anti-discrimination or other generally applicable requirements. Examples are the exemption for Sikh adherents from the requirement to wear hard hats on worksites and when riding motorcycles, or for Jewish and Islamic followers from otherwise generally applicable regulation of the slaughter of animals.[38]

---

33   In *Attorney-General (Vic.), Ex Rel. Black v The Commonwealth* (1981), Barwick CJ held that 'establishing any religion' 'involves the entrenchment of a religion as a feature of and identified with the body politic, in this instance, the Commonwealth' (p. 582). Of the other judges Gibbs J considered that establishing a religion means 'conferring on a particular religion or religious body the position of a state (or national), religion or church' (p. 604), and Stephen J. said "establishing" means the constituting of a religion as an officially recognized State religion (p. 605).

34   Ibid: Barwick (by implication) at 579, Wilson at 652, Stephen at 609, 652.

35   Ibid, p.622-3.

36   This phrase was used by Thomas Jefferson in his reply to correspondence from the Danbury Baptist Association in1802, reproduced in Boston (2003). See, e.g., *Everson v Board of Education* (1947), which established the requirements for separation of religions and state. The case of *Lemon v Kurtzman* (1971) established a three-part test for legislation to ensure state-belief separation: the law must have a secular purpose, neither advance nor inhibit religion, and not foster excessive governmental entanglement with religion.

37   Davis (2001), 9.

38   Knights (2007), 191, *Employment Act* (U.K.), 1989. Knights outlines other exemptions in the U.K., ibid, Chapter 7.

[12.24] In Australia, people are exempted from compulsory voting[39] and provision of union access to the workplace because of conscientious objection on religious grounds.[40]

[12.25] In the US, Marci Hamilton points to examples of religious influence on the legislature.[41] These include exemption from prosecution for medical neglect of children where this is based on religious conviction by the Nixon administration and the requirement by the Clinton administration of a state interest to be 'compelling' before it can burden the manifestation of religion.[42] She also notes the increased promotion of 'faith-based initiatives' (involving government approval and funding of religiously inspired and administered social services) under the Bush administration. This increases the access of churches to recruits. Hamilton cites the 'publicly-groomed perception of incapacity or powerlessness' of, and widespread discrimination against, faith-based groups, which is supported by the notion that only faith-based groups are capable of providing welfare.[43] Sean Faircloth points to the currently unprecedented number of 'theocrat' members of Congress (those who expressly endorse religious bias in law).[44]

[12.26] Clergy are often privileged from having to disclose criminal activity of penitents to the authorities.[45] In Australia, clergy generally are not required, under mandatory reporting legislation, to report crime such as child or spousal abuse.[46]

Government funding and grants

[12.27] The focus on granting freedom to act on belief has resulted in the belief provisions being interpreted to countenance the conferring of privileges on belief organisations. As a result of favourable treatment by government, religious institutions throughout the world are very

---

39   See the Australian Electoral Commission website at <http://www.aec.gov.au/Elections/australian_electoral_system/ electoral_procedures/Electoral_Offences.html>. Conscientious objection to voting on religious grounds is recognised: see, e.g. Report 42 (1984), – Community Law Reform Program: Sixth Report - Conscientious Objection To Jury Service: '3. Conscientious Objection in Legislation' at <http://www.lawlink.nsw.gov.au/lrc.nsf/pages/R42CHP3>.

40   Bachelard (2008), 176ff.

41   Hamilton (2004-5), 1163ff; Hamilton (2005), Part 1. In *God vs. the Gavel* (2005), Hamilton notes that legislation in the U.S. provides exemption from reporting child abuse, even out of the confessional (p.9, 12ff.); for causing death through neglect for religious reasons (p.34ff); discrimination legislation by religious bodies (173ff). See also Challans (2007): <http://www.usafa.af.mil/jscope/ISME2007/Papers/Challans_Rawls_v._Habermas.doc>, 9; Harris (2004), 45.

42   Hamilton (2004), 1153. She quotes Justice Stevens as stating that this law was 'a legal weapon that no atheist or agnostic can obtain': *City of Boerne v Flores, Archbishop of San Antonio* 521 U.S. 507,537. See also generally, Hamilton (2005), Part 1.

43   Hamilton (2004), 1168.

44   Faircloth (2012).

45   Canon law of the Catholic and Anglican churches provide for clergy-penitent confidentiality, while common law in the U.K. and Australia is unclear. In Australia, Victoria, the NT, the Commonwealth, New South Wales and Tasmania include priest-penitent confidentiality privilege in their Evidence Acts and in the U.K. it is subject to common law principles: Mabey, (2006), <https://elaw.murdoch.edu.au/archives/issues/2006/2/elaw_Renae%20Mabey%20Priest%20Penitant%20Privilege.pdf>. In the United States legislation also varies from state to state (See, e.g., Sippel (1994). In all jurisdictions it is uncertain.

46   Wallace (2001) 555.

wealthy – to the tune of billions of dollars in many countries.[47] This amounts to what Max Wallace, considering the financing of religious institutions in Australia, calls 'soft theocracy': 'a state where church and government purposes coincide to garnishee taxpayers' money and resources, structurally through tax exemptions and functionally through grants and privileges'.[48]

[12.28] Governments such as Greece, Denmark, Finland and Italy fund the maintenance of church buildings and provide subsidies for religious personnel and activities. Despite French constitutional secularism and a 1905 law banning subsidisation of religion,[49] it was estimated in 2006 that the French state subsided private (mainly Catholic) schools to the tune of €8.2 billion. In addition, individual municipalities gave €530 million, and regions and local authorities up to €499 million.[50]

[12.29] This is not seen as breaching the belief provisions, so long as individuals are not specifically prevented from having or practising a particular belief.

[12.30] Providing millions of dollars of taxpayers' money in government grants to religious organisations, such as the provision of funding and facilities for the recurrent international World Youth Day gatherings held by the Catholic Church in different countries, is not considered a breach of Article 18 ICCPR despite the resulting discrimination.[51] It is reported, for example, that the Australian Commonwealth Government contributed $55 million for the Catholic Church's week-long 'World Youth Day' Rally ('WYD') in 2008,[52] as well as formally associating itself with the activity.[53] The NSW Government chipped in an extra $100 million. It is also

---

47   Wallace (2007) discusses church wealth, especially in relation to the Catholic Church and Australia.

48   Wallace (2010), 72.

49   *Loi du Décembre 1905 Concernant la Séparation des Églises et de L'État (Law of December 1905 Concerning the Separation of Church and State).*

50   National Secular Society, UK, 'French Secularists Fight To End Massive Catholic Subsidies' <http://www.secularism. org.uk/74110.html?CPID=a9792377ce69b66e4aa9fc7643727e56>. The Department of Alsace Moselle, part of Germany in 1905, is exempt the 1905 law, as are the French Overseas Territories, allowing for a further funding of €72 million. More than 2,000 priests are paid out of public funds to teach religion in state-owned schools. See also Dominique Goussot, Libre pensée (France) *Le livre noir des atteintes à la laïcité : états généraux de défense de la laïcité, Paris, 9 décembre 2006, Bourse du travail* Paris, Fédération nationale de la libre pensée, 2006.

51   Article 26 ICCPR (prohibition of discrimination on the ground of, *inter alia*, religion). Discrimination occurs when it is either favourable or non-favourable.

52   The Commonwealth committed $35 million towards security and visa costs, with an additional 'pledge of $20 million to help relocate racehorses from Randwick': Morris (2007).

53   Prime Minister Kevin Rudd was personally involved in Government support given to the Catholic Church World Youth Day by the Federal Government. He appointed an Ambassador to the Vatican to 'enable Australia and the Holy See to be able to work together on the great challenges we face in the world': Linda Morris, et al (2008, News 3, <http://www.smh.com. au/news/world-youth-day/fischer-to-be-our-man-in-vatican/2008/07/21/1216492357011.html>). Rudd also appointed a Christian minister as his personal adviser on moral and ethical policy: Andrew West, 'Rudd Spiritual Adviser Sees a Leadership Role', *Sydney Morning Herald* 26 February 2008, 2.

reported that the South Australian Government paid $70,000 for a memorial service in Adelaide for Pope John Paul II.[54]

[12.31] Prime Ministers have publicly associated themselves with religious activities of many denominations by formally addressing religious conferences and gatherings, and offering financial assistance for these and other activities.[55] The Australian Government has devoted up to $700 million for programs providing religious chaplains in public schools. Chaplains are provided mainly by Christian organisations. Despite two rulings by the Australian High Court that this funding program is constitutionally invalid, the Government has indicated that it supports the programs and is considering other means for ensuring that they continue.[56] As indicated below [12.61]]ff), some governments either fund or mandate religious instructions in schools.

Church taxes

[12.32] By omission, the ICCPR, and by specification, the ECHR,[57] do not provide any person or association with an *inherent* entitlement to exemption from general taxes that include allocation of funds to belief organisations or activities, however, there is no prohibition from *state-endowed* entitlement to such a privilege. The UNHRC stated that, while Article 18 ICCPR protects the right to hold and manifest belief, 'the refusal to pay taxes on grounds of conscientious objection clearly falls outside the scope of the protection of this Article'.[58]

[12.33] The European Commission has likewise held that taxation for the purposes of general government spending, in which no person directs their contribution to any specific cause, but which is appropriated for religious purposes, is permitted by the ECHR.[59]

[12.34] Religious or other belief organisations may impose taxes on their adherents, and these may be administered and enforced by the state, for example in Denmark, Finland, Germany (about 80% of church income) and Iceland, and this has been allowed by the European Commission.[60] This involves disclosing one's belief to the government, and/or notifying the government

---

54   Kate Reynolds, Democrats Member of the Australian Parliament 'revealed documents showing the church simply sent a one-sentence invoice to the government for $70,000 after it requested funding to hold a memorial service in Adelaide for Pope John Paul II':see, e.g. Catholic News 3 February 2006 <http://cathnews.acu.edu.au/602/22.php>.

55   See, e.g., John Warhurst 'The Religious Beliefs of Australia's Prime Ministers' <http://www.eurekastreet.com.au/article.aspx?aeid=24159>.

56   <http://www.news.com.au/national/high-court-rules-against-federal-government-funding-of-school-chaplains/story-fncynjr2-1226959661271>

57   ECHR First Protocol, Article 1; *C v United Kingdom* (1983), 142, 148. *Iglesia Bautista "El Salvador" v. Spain*, at 261.

58   *J P v Canada Communication* (1991), ¶4.2. See also *J.v.K. and C.M.G. v.K-S. v The Netherlands*, (1992); *K. V. and C. V. v Germany*, (1994), p. 365.

59   *C v United Kingdom* (1990), ¶47ff.

60   *Gottesmann v Switzerland*, (1984).

if one leaves a religious organisation, a requirement otherwise considered unacceptable under Article 9 ECHR. The Commission held that for the purposes of Article 9, governments have a wide discretion in how they determine on what condition a person may be validly considered to leave a particular denomination for the purposes of taxation on behalf of a state church.[61] While it recognised that the required reporting formalities attached to adopting or leaving a religious belief may deter people, the European Court held that a state church system must provide adequate safeguards so that no one may feel forced to enter, or be prohibited from leaving, a state church.[62]

[12.35] The case of *Darby v Sweden* (discussed above[9.47]) drew the distinction between taxes imposed by a church for direct religious purposes, and those imposed for the provision of state-related activities carried out by the church, such as maintenance of records of births, deaths and marriages, or management of cemeteries. Taxes for religious purposes are the prerogative of the church, and can only be imposed on members, and taxes for stat-related purposes are applicable to members and non-members alike.[63]

[12.36] The European Court has established that maintenance of birth and death registers or responsibility for burial sites by a religious body are '[t]asks of a non-religious nature which are performed in the interest of society as a whole' and the state can decide who will carry them out and how they should be financed. It also has a wide margin of appreciation in these decisions.[64] Thus, a 'dissenter's tax' levied on non-members of the Swedish Church, less than that imposed on Church members and reflecting the proportion church activities comprising such 'civil' tasks, was not a violation of Article 9 ECHR.[65]

Church exemption from tax

[12.37] Exemption of religious organisations from taxes such as income tax, property tax and council rates, can amount to a very considerable financial benefit to an organisation, particularly where it participates in commercial or other activity not directly related to the charitable purposes. They also result in considerable lost revenue by the state. Countries such as the UK, Australia and New Zealand allow blanket exemption from taxation from all major forms of church income. The 'advancement of religion' is considered in itself a charitable purpose, auto-

---

61   *E & G. R. v Austria*, (1984); Taylor (2005), 40.
62   *Darby v Sweden* (1990), ¶45.
63   *Darby v Sweden* (1990), ¶51. The Commission estimated that 30% of the Lutheran Church's tax could be held to be applicable to non-religious activities.
64   *Lundberg v Sweden* (2001), 7. See discussion by Evans and Thomas (2006), 713.
65   *Lundberg v Sweden* (2001).

matically making religious organisations charities, whether or not they carry out any genuine charitable activity.[66]

[12.38] It has been estimated that the total cost of concessions to registered religious organisations in Australia exceeds $31 billion, money that would have otherwise gone into consolidated revenue.[67] To what extent this figure includes non-religious activity is unknown. The exemption of religious institutions from the same financial reporting requirements that apply to other charitable organisations makes accuracy difficult. It also means they are not accountable for the extent and use of their wealth.

[12.39] Generous tax exemptions for religious organisations are also available in the US. W. Cole Durham, for example, points out that religions benefit more than secular non-profit organisations in relation to tax exemptions. He states that while non-religious groups must 'file extensive information establishing their charitable character' to obtain tax-exempt status, religious groups do not have to do so.[68] As a consequence of 'added protection for religious groups against various types of governmental regulation and red tape, it is not surprising that a large percentage of groups elect to organize their affairs as some type of religious corporation'.[69] The annual loss to US consolidated revenue through religious tax exemptions has been recently estimated at $71 billion.[70]

[12.40] The European Commission has allowed singular tax exemption for the Catholic Church based on a Concordat with the Holy See providing for reciprocal obligations (exemption in return for the Church placing historical, artistic and documentary material at its disposal).[71]

Faith-based welfare and financial benefits

[12.41] Governments have outsourced and funded many of their welfare responsibilities to Church-based agencies that offer religious services as part of their activities, and use their work as a 'religious mission'.[72] These welfare agencies are also often granted exemption from anti-discrimination legislation in hiring staff and conditions of work.

---

66 The Australian Government, for example, exempts all religions based on belief in the supernatural from income tax: section 23(e), *Income Tax Assessment Act 1936*. The High Court has held that religion involves belief in the supernatural: *Church of the New Faith v. Commissioner of Pay-roll Tax* (Vic), (1983), 154 CLR 120. See also Australian Government Tax Office (2006).

67 Perkins et al (2009).

68 Durham (2004), 321, 341 n 110. This is also the case in Australia.

69 Ibid, 341.

70 Cragun et al (2012).

71 *Iglesia Bautista "El Salvador" and Ortega Moratilla v Spain* (1992).

72 See, e.g. Monsma and Soper (2009), 121.

[12.42] The 'commercialisation' of charitable activities by religious or other groups has led to an industry with an increasingly high management sector, with well-subsidised personnel and property, and a corresponding increase in political and social influence. This gives them a commercial edge over non-religious enterprises. It has been reported, for example, that in Australia: 'The five big churches had revenue of more than $21.7 billion in 1994'.[73] The Sydney Catholic Archdiocese has a net worth of $1.24 billion.[74]

[12.43] It is impossible to accurately estimate church wealth from its disparate sources (including donations, bequests, government funding, foregone taxes, property, artworks, buildings and income).[75] Governments demand varying degrees of financial accountability on the part of religious bodies, exempting them either partially or fully from reporting, so the extent of their wealth and how it is spent is not readily available. Some money purportedly acquired for specified charitable activities may be sent overseas e.g. to the Vatican for dispersal through secretive channels, or even to religious extremists fighting sectarian wars.[76]

Negotiating privilege

[12.44] Governments have adopted an approach to providing religious freedom by direct negotiation with various groups concerned, to determine with them what would provide a satisfactory outcome. Negotiation between government and interest groups has been used in many other circumstances, from ensuring equal opportunity and welfare for different sectors in society to paving the way for industrial and property development.[77] It has also been advocated for use in relation to different religious groups, in the sense that governments and parties involved come to an agreement based on mutual interests.[78] In relation to remedying some aspects of lifestyle inequality, it may well be a legitimate process. Rather than ensuring state disassociation from religious or other belief, this has resulted in a *de facto* entanglement of state and belief, and the potential marginalisation of those excluded from these benefits.

    a)   *Religious mediation and judicial procedures*

---

73   Ferguson (2005), 45. The income from non-religious activity (including commercial properties and private enterprises such as hospitals and nursing homes), would admittedly constitute a substantial proportion of this income and thus of public revenue foregone in taxes.

74   Testimony by Cardinal George Pell to the Royal Commission on Institutional Child Abuse. He said that the funds are "ultimately controlled by – owned by, if you like – the archbishop of the day": *Sydney Morning Herald*, March 25, 2014 < http://www.smh.com.au/national/sydneys-catholic-archdiocese-has-assets-over-1-billion-royal-commission-told-20140325-35fu8.html>.

75   A search of the internet gives a feel for the vast global wealth of religious organsations.

76   For example see Wallace (2007) 105ff re the Vatican and wealth. Examples of charities accused of ties to terrorism by the US in 2007 can be found at http://en.wikipedia.org/wiki/List_of_charities_accused_of_ties_to_terrorism.).

77   On negotiating privilege, see McClain (2004); Richmond, et al (1999).

78   For examples of negotiation of religious privilege in Spain see Bloß (2003), 39ff.

[12.45] One form of 'negotiated equality' that has been rejected by the European Court is the acceptance of diverse legal systems within the one jurisdiction. This has taken the form of religious 'courts' or tribunals whose judgements are considered legally enforceable by the state.

[12.46] A distinction should be drawn between mediation bodies and arbitration tribunals. The function of mediation bodies is to bring disputing parties (such as those with family or business disputes) to foster an agreed outcome by the parties. Compliance with the agreed outcome is voluntary, as they are advisory, and not legally enforceable. Arbitration tribunals, on the other hand arose to provide quicker, less expensive procedures for settling commercial disputes, and are enforceable at law (subject to compliance with legal principles).

[12.47] Mediation and arbitration bodies based on religious law have been established in most Western nations. Britain is a good example of their operation, along with what Catholic and Jewish Beth Din 'courts' have been doing for years. Muslim shari'ah Arbitration Tribunals are classified as arbitration tribunals under the UK *Arbitration Act* 1996, which makes their rulings binding in law, provided that both parties in the dispute agree to this. The Arbitration Act provides that arbitrators may make their decisions according to the rules agreed by the parties, 'subject only to such safeguards as are necessary in the public interest'[79] and long as it is not done in 'bad faith.'[80]

[12.48] However, especially when mediation councils or arbitration tribunals are used for disputes over personal issues such as family law or personal behaviour, and based on religious belief, the voluntary nature of all parties to participate and agree with recommendations is questionable, due to social and religious pressure.[81] The 'basis for determining "bad faith" is blurry'[82] A judgment considered fair according to religious law could offend the principles of the British legal system.

[12.49] The line between mediation and arbitration is easily confused. There are many 'Shari'ah Councils' in Britain that represent themselves as tribunals, requiring applicants to sign an agreement to abide by their decisions, but these Councils are supposed to be mediation bodies,[83] In

---

79   Arbitration Act, 1996, c. 23, § 1(a), (b) (U.K.)

80   *Halpern v. Halpern*, [2007] EWCA Civ 291, [2008] Q.B. 195, 214 (C.A.).

81   See, e.g. Fortuyn (2013)

82   Reiss (2009), 741. Reiss, Maria 'The materialization of legal pluralism in britain: why Shari'a council decisions should be non-binding' (2009) *Arizona Journal of International & Comparative Law Vol. 26, No. 3, 739*. Ee, e.g. Cranmer (2012), and (2013); Fraser, (2014); Boyd (2004).

83   Civitas (2009).

2008 the House of Lords held that shari'ah law is discriminatory, especially against women, and incompatible with human rights[84] Maria Reiss argues that

> [u]nless the British legislature amends the Arbitration Act to prevent its use in matters involving religious law, Britain will be inadvertently sanctioning a parallel legal system which no longer embodies the values of British law regarding equal judicial treatment of men and women.[85]

[12.50] The Government of Ontario recently considered the institution of shari'ah courts. Responding to critics[86] the Premier, Dalton McGuinty announced in September 2005 that there should be one law for all in Ontario and Canada. This prompted him to reject not only introducing shari'ah tribunals, but also all religious tribunals acting under the Arbitration Act.[87]

[12.51] The European Court considered the entanglement of church and state by government endorsement of religious courts in the case of *Refah Partisi v Turkey* (2003). In that case, the Court upheld the dissolution of a political party advocating the establishment of legally recognised religious courts for relevant religious adherents as necessary in a democratic society to protect the rights and freedoms of others. The Refah Partisi adopted a platform aimed at setting up a plurality of legal systems, applying shari'ah to the internal or external relations of the Muslim community, and expressing the possibility of recourse to force as a political strategy.[88]

[12.52] The Court went on to hold that a plurality of legal systems was inimical to the values of the ECHR. There is no guarantee of individual rights and freedoms by the government as legal plurality endorses the requirement of individuals to obey laws of their religious group rather than those that apply to the general population.[89] Such a move would 'do away with the State's role as guarantor of individual rights and freedoms and the impartial organiser of the practice of the various beliefs and religions in a democratic society'. Individuals would be obliged to obey the 'static' rules imposed by religion rather than the democratic laws of the state. It would also 'infringe the principle of non-discrimination undeniably between individuals as regards their

---

84   *EM (Lebanon) (FC) (Appellant) (FC) v Secretary of State for the Home Department* [2008] UKHL 64 http://www.publications.parliament.uk/pa/ld200708/ldjudgmt/jd081022/leban-1.htm.

85   Reiss (2009), 741.

86   A detailed consideration of the issues surrounding the adoption of Shari'ah Courts/Tribunals in Canada and an outline of submissions from interested parties, are contained in Boyd (2004). See also Dominic McGoldrick (2009), who discusses issues surrounding the adoption of Shari'ah law and points out that both formal and informal sharia'ah courts and tribunals have been operating in the UK quoting an estimate that there are as many as 85 such bodies (p.35).

87   Thomas (2005).

88   *Refah Partisi v Turkey* (2003) esp ¶81ff, 116ff.

89   Ibid, ¶119.

enjoyment of public freedom' and govern 'individuals in all fields of public and private law according to their religion'.[90]

[12.53] The European Court said in the *Refah Partisi* case of shari'ah, that 'principles such as pluralism in the political sphere or the constant evolution of public freedoms have no place in it'. It concluded that the introduction of shari'ah cannot be reconciled with 'the fundamental principles of democracy, as conceived in the Convention taken as a whole', as shari'ah also offends rights relating to criminal law and the status of women, and interferes in all aspects of public and private life.[91] The *Refah* case thus holds that laws incompatible with human rights are not protected by the ECHR, which 'precludes any legal system where divine mandate means that some or all laws are considered beyond challenge'.[92]

[12.54] In sum, the *Refah* case 'demonstrates that establishment of a religion must at least not have a profound effect on the political and legal system of a country'.[93] However, the boundary line is characteristically imprecise.

b) *Concordats*

[12.55] Another method of negotiated privilege for particular religious beliefs is the use of Concordats. These are treaties (sometimes secret and rushed) between a country and the Holy See. The excellent website, *Concordat Watch*,[94] describes the many concordats in effect and translations of them. It also has general background Articles, related documents and expert commentary. Among other matters, concordats provide privileges to the Catholic Church such as funding of

---

90   Ibid.
91   Ibid, ¶ 123. The question of just what constitutes shari'ah law is not always clear. Sharia'ah refers to 'not a single set of laws, but the several overlapping legal systems', however 'all forms of shari'ah use the Qur'an and the Sunnah, the narrated traditions of the prophet as their basis' which Ha-Redeye calls the 'immutable Basic Code': Ha-Redeye (2009), 4–5. Abdullahi An-Na'im states that

> It would be heretical for a Muslim who believes that Shariah is the final and ultimate formulation of the law of God to maintain that any aspect of that law is open to revision and reformulation by mere mortal and fallible human beings. To do so would allow human beings to correct what God has decreed: An-Na'im (1987), 10.

> Although he believes some social and political aspects of shari'ah can and should be adapted to modern society, An-Na'im argues that 'Belief in the Qu'aran as the final and literal word of God and faith in the Prophet Mohammed as the final prophet remain the essential prerequisites of being a Muslim' (ibid, 17). All Muslims seem to be agreed that there is some fundamental, immutable core of Shari'ah law, but not precisely what it is.

92   Evans and Thomas (2006), 712. As noted above Shari'ah is subject to different interpretations. See, e.g., Ha-Redeye (2009), who, however, has to concede there that there is an unchanging, immutable portion of Shari'ah, the Q'ran and the Sunna. This is separate from 'ever-evolving interpretive law (*fiqh*)' (at 4), that is dependent on judicial rulings ('discretionary public policy practices'), to 'address social ills' (at 7). These are not determined by the people, but by the (male), scholars and imams. The very fact that Shari'ah is based on religion and not the will of the people means it is not democratic.
93   Evans and Thomas, ibid, 713.
94   <http://www.concordatwatch.eu>.

church buildings and both commercial and religious activities, as well as tax exemption, immunity from state criminal law and exemption from reporting child abuse to civil authorities. They promote Catholic Church involvement in policy and legislation relating to such matters as family planning and abortion. This adds to its political influence across the globe. Concordats can thus greatly inhibit the experience, perceived or real, of freedom from the influence of particular beliefs.

[12.56] As concordats are treaties between recognised sovereign states, national laws are subject to their provisions and can only be changed or abrogated by mutual agreement between the government and the Holy See. This can result in the continuance of concordats made with dictators who are long gone (e.g. concordats with Mussolini and Hitler). By their entrenched institutional concession to religion, concordats thus 'represent a fundamental threat to both democracy and human rights'. [95]

[12.57] The basis of Italy's recognition of the Vatican as a sovereign state is a concordat with Mussolini. [96] Despite a constitutional guarantee of state neutrality from religion, Italian law is subject to a directive made by the fascist Minister Rocco in 1926 regarding state promotion of the Catholic religion. The directive was later endorsed by the Lateran Pacts which included a Church-State Concordat between Italy (under Mussolini) and the Papacy in 1929. The Lateran Pacts established the Holy See as a sovereign state in return for its recognition of the Kingdom of Italy and exclusion from participating in Italian politics. It also involved a concordat, which provided privileges to the Church in Italy. The Catholic religion was declared the 'only religion of the State', and Catholic religious symbols were compulsory in schoolrooms and government premises.

[12.58] The socialist Prime Minister Craxi renewed the Concordat in 1984, removing many of the Catholic Church's privileges. [97] The Catholic religion was no longer to be the sole religion of the Italian State. The state was to support other religious groups, Christian and non-Christian, with special tax exemptions as well. However, some special privileges for the Catholic religion remain in the Agreement, [98] which can be altered without Constitutional amendment. As recently as 19 November 2005, the Pope and the Italian Prime Minister agreed that the Italian Govern-

---

95   Ibid, *What's the harm in Concordats?* Concordats (treaties), with the Holy See exist between, *inter alia,* Austria, France (Alsace Lorraine), Germany, Italy, Latvia, Lithuania, Luxembourg (the 1801 concordat with France), Malta, Poland, Portugal, Slovenia and Spain.

96   The validity of the Vatican's claim to sovereignty is questioned as valid under internatonal law: see Robertson (2010), Chapter 5.

97   *Agreement Between the Italian Republic and the Holy See* <http://original.religlaw.org/template.php?id=578>.

98   Article 8 of the 1929 Conciliation Treaty still prohibits public insults against the Pope's speeches, acts, or writings with a penalty of up to 5 years in prison.

ment and the Catholic Church would continue to 'collaborate within the framework of the Lateran Treaty',[99] thus compromising the constitution and separation of Church and State.

[12.59] The powerful influence of the Catholic Church in Italy can be seen by the fact that there was a nationwide protest after Adel Smith won a court order for the removal of crosses at the school his children attended in 2003, resulting in the order being reversed.[100] In 2007 the Italian Court in Camerino sentenced Judge Luigi Tosti to seven months in gaol and one year of exclusion from public buildings, as well as suspension from functions and remuneration. He had refused to sit in a courtroom in which a crucifix was displayed. This conviction was despite the Italian Constitutional *de facto* separation of church and state.[101]

[12.60] However, the Court of Cassation (Supreme Court) in Rome acquitted Judge Tosti of all charges. By contrast, the ECtHR bowed to the influence of the Church in *Lautsi and Others v Italy* (2011) (discussed above[11.31]]) when the Grand Chamber of the European Court ruled that compulsory display of crucifixes in government schools was not a breach of Article 9 ECHR.

c) *Religion and Schools*

[12.61] Neither the ICCPR[102] nor the ECHR[103] prohibit state funding of belief-based schools, with their advancement of religion through propagation of religious or other belief. Governments pay clergy to teach religious instruction in public schools in Austria, Italy, Poland and Spain. While there is no obligation to provide for religious instruction,[104] many European states require religious education or instruction to be given in public schools, usually with a distinct bias towards Christianity. The UNHRC has stated that

> if a State party chooses to provide public funding to religious schools, it should make this funding available without discrimination. This means that providing funding for the schools

---

99   International Humanist and Ethical Union (2006).

100   <http://www.secularism.org.uk/judge-tosti-wins-secularism-batt.html>

101   <   http://www.secularism.org.uk/judge-tosti-wins-secularism-batt.html>;   <http://www.iheu.org/judge-tosti-cleared>.

102   ICCPR article 18(4). ICCPR *General Comment 22*, ¶6 states that article 18.4 ICCPR 'permits public school instruction in subjects such as the general history of religions and ethics if it is given in a neutral and objective way'. It also states that children should be granted non-discriminatory exemptions or alternatives from religious instruction that 'accommodate the wishes of parents and guardians' including those who do not believe in any religion. *Leirvåg v Norway* (2004), ¶14.2; *Hartikainen v Finland* (1981), ¶10.4.

103   Protocol No. 1 to the *European Convention for the Protection of Human Rights and Fundamental Freedoms* (1952). See, for a similar approach to the UNHRC, the ECHR case of *Folgerø and Others v Norway* (2007).

104   Carolyn Evans (2001), 88ff. This was specifically held by the European Commission in *X & Y v United Kingdom* (1982), 31; *X. v United Kingdom,* 14 Eur. Comm'n H.R. Dec. & Rep. 179, 180 (1978).

of one religious group and not for another must be based on reasonable and objective criteria.[105]

[12.62] As will be argued in Chapter 13, equal funding of all groups that claim to be 'religious' is not practicable, not to mention the Committee's failure to include non-religious beliefs. General education about religion, as opposed to religious instruction, is recognised under the belief provisions. The UNHRC and European Court require such teaching to be 'objective, critical and pluralistic'.[106] It may well be considered an important part of government school curricula. Religious instruction may be delivered in non-denominational schools, however, but only with parental consent.[107] Unfortunately,

> while the tests, such as 'general and objective' teaching, seem appropriate in the abstract, in application the Commission and Court have been reluctant to explore the way in which such teaching may put pressure on students to take religiously specific instruction and to reveal their religion to the State and school authorities.[108]

[12.63] The result of such pressure is seen in the cases of *Folgerø and Others v Norway,* (2002)[109] and *Leirvåg v Norway* (2004),[110] both of which chronicled the stigmatisation of children, and problems within the family caused by the withdrawal of children from religious instruction in school. In another case, a Polish student claimed that she faced employment and social discrimination because her school record showed that she had refused to participate in a Catholic education class.[111] Cathy Byrne has found examples of students traumatised by the influence of religious instruction or the presence of religious chaplains in schools in Australia.[112]

[12.64] Religious instruction, in the form of indoctrination, as distinguished from the provision of a general understanding of different religious beliefs and their function in society, is prevalent

---

105   *Waldman v Canada* (1999), ¶10.6.
106   See, e.g., *Hartikainen v Finland* (1981), ¶10.4; *Leirvåg v Norway* (2004), 203; *Folgerø and Others v Norway* (2007), ¶84(h).
107   *Angeleni v Sweden* (1986), ¶4.1; *The Norwegian State Church Knudsen v Norway* (1985).
108   Carolyn Evans (2001), 96.
109   ¶65-68.
110   An expert in minority psychology concluded that both children and parents (and in all likelihood the school), experienced conflicts of loyalty, pressure to conform and acquiesce to the norm, and for some of the children bullying and a feeling of helplessness (at ¶2.5). There was also conflict of loyalties between school and home (at ¶3.3); a daughter was teased because she did not believe in God, and when excused from religious instruction, 'she was placed in the kitchen where she was told to draw, sometimes alone, and sometimes under supervision. When her parents became aware that banishment to the kitchen was used as a punishment for pupils who behaved badly in class, they stopped exempting her from lessons', ¶4.2
111   *CJ JJ & EJ v Poland* (1996); see also Carolyn Evans (2001), 95-96.
112   Byrne (2014).

in government-funded schools throughout the world.[113] The state has relatively wide discretion when it comes to what religions may be taught in schools, with the potential to shore up the dominant religion.[114]

(a) Religious vilification and apostasy

[12.65] While they may be considered measures for providing for belief rights, laws prohibiting blasphemy, apostasy or 'defamation' of religion can privilege religious belief, as noted above [11.48]([11.48]ff).

[12.66] A PEW survey of 198 world countries and territories shows that as of 2011, almost half (47%) have laws or policies penalising blasphemy, apostasy or 'defamation of religion'.[115] The following chart, compiled from that survey, indicates the number of countries by region.

Table 8: Countries with Blasphemy, Apostasy and Defamation of Religion Laws (2011)

Countries Surveyed	Middle East and Northern Africa	Asia-Pacific Region	Sub-Saharan Region	Americas (incl. Brazil & Canada)	Europe
198	20 Countries	50 Countries	48 Countries	35 Countries	45 Countries
Blasphemy (Total 32)	13 (65%)	9 (18%)	2 (4%)		
Apostasy (Total 20)	11 (55%)	5 (10%)	4 (8%)		
Defamation of Religion (Total 87)	15 (75%)	17 (34%)	13 (27%)	6 (17%	36 (80%)

Conclusion

[12.67] The above examples of state-belief entanglement show a failure to implement obligations under international law to secure equal belief rights for all citizens. This is not just because of the lack of clarity in the belief provisions, but a lack of will on the part of governments. A state that is truly impartial to belief does not promote religious or any other belief: it assures 'freedom

---

113   For a global overview, see <http://en.wikipedia.org/wiki/Religious_education_in_primary_and_secondary_education>

114   See, e.g Malcolm Evans (1997), 342-62; Carolyn Evans (2001), 95ff.

115   PEW Research: *Laws Penalizing Blasphemy, Apostasy and Defamation of Religion are Widespread* <http://www.pewforum.org/2012/11/21/laws-penalizing-blasphemy-apostasy-and-defamation-of-religion-are-widespread/>. Anti-blasphemy and apostasy laws are most common in the Middle East and North Africa, while laws forbidding defamation of religion or hate speech against members of religious groups were far more common worldwide. In Europe most laws were against hate speech directed at specific persons or groups, while in the Middle East and North Africa they were mostly against 'defamation' of religion itself.

from belief' as a necessary corollary to 'freedom *of* belief'. The same can be said, of course, for non-religious belief.

[12.68] When state impartiality towards one or more beliefs is lacking, one life stance (most often a religious one) will predominate in the public sphere to the detriment of other worldviews.[116] Not only will this favour the circumstances of those belonging to privileged denominations, the influence of the dominant religion can result in persecution or denial of important services, such as marriage, medical services (e.g. reproductive services) and education. As indicated, it also influences the use of public money, with the loss of substantial amounts of revenue to the furthering of sectarian interests (not counting genuine charitable services) at a cost to more general social interests.

[12.69] States should not be concerned with judging the competing truth claims of religions or belief systems. But they do have the moral, and indeed legal duty (as signatories of the ICCPR and/or ECHR), to foster common values such as those expressed in international human rights. This will sometimes necessitate government intervention in the practices of particular beliefs – not advancing or restricting any belief as such, but promoting the commonly accepted values of human rights. These values may coincide with particular religious doctrines, but it is because they are *politically accepted* values, not religious or other life stance ones, that they are implemented by the state.

[12.70] State establishment or advancement of a particular religion is recognised internationally as consistent with belief rights, with their prohibition of suppression or coercion in relation to the liberties of others. As noted, this acceptance of state-belief entanglement is made clear in the *travaux préparatoires*,[117] *General Comment No. 22*,[118] and decisions by human rights tribunals as described above. Nevertheless, while *General Comment No. 22* makes it clear that not only is discrimination against those not belonging to the state-sponsored religion to be avoided, it also cautions against 'giving economic privileges to them'.[119] As can be seen, this principle is more honoured in the breaking than the observance.

[12.71] Formally, belief rights are described as involving state neutrality in relation to religion or other belief. However, as foreshadowed in previous Chapters, the term 'neutrality' is subject to various interpretations. The next Chapter considers these interpretations, seeking the best one for maximising equal belief rights for all.

---

116   Gogineni and Gule (2008), 705ff.
117   Bossuyt (1987), 360. See UN Doc. A/2929, 48 (¶108)
118   ICCPR General Comment 22, ¶9.
119   Ibid.

CHAPTER 13
THE ANSWER: ACCOMMODATION OR SEPARATION?

[13.1] Interpretations of the principle of state neutrality in relation to belief rights have ranged between

- ***accommodationism:*** acceptance of state-belief entanglement of religious doctrines in government policy-making and/or funding of religious institutions so long as no-one is specifically prohibited from, or punished for, manifesting their belief; and

- ***state-belief separation:*** insistence on strict state impartiality in relation to belief doctrines in legislation and policy.

It has been argued in previous Chapters that the belief provisions and their interpretation by the tribunals tolerate some degree of accommodation of belief, albeit unclearly determined. Consequently, the term 'neutrality' has been used to describe most government positions along the scale, with acceptance of 'neutrality' as either 'benign' (accommodation of majority beliefs) or purportedly equal treatment for all religions. The term 'neutrality' is too vague. We should draw a simple distinction in non-theocratic regimes between degrees of state-belief accommodation and state-belief separation.

Why 'no' to state-belief accommodation

[13.2] Criticism here of the differential treatment of beliefs through state accommodation is not based solely on the fact that it violates the essential liberal-democratic principle of equal citizenship. There are other fundamental issues involved that are dealt with in this Chapter.

Proselytising

[13.3] Accommodation of belief involves the state in advancing the cause of particular religion(s) or other belief. It is the role of religion, for example, to evangelise and bear witness. *The case of Kokkinakis v Greece* (1993) noted that 'Christian witness', which corresponds to 'true evangelism', was described 'in a report drawn up in 1956 under the auspices of the World Council of Churches as 'an essential mission and a responsibility of every Christian and every Church'.[1] Belief-based associations that perform state responsibilities may well implement the supplementary agenda of

---

1   *Kokkinakis v Greece* (1993) ¶48.

proselytising: that is their job.[2] The distinction between religious and non-religious activity of these associations could be difficult to draw, as many religions consider they have a mandate to proselytise, recruit and influence government, even when carrying out secular functions.[3] This distinction becomes irrelevant in countries that have adopted English precedent which provides that the 'advancement of religion' *per se* is to be considered a benefit to society, and therefore eligible for classification of 'charity'.

[13.4] Those individuals and bodies qualifying as a 'religion' thus receive the added benefits for which charities are eligible, without being required to do good works, or to account for their expenditure of public moneys.[4] They can benefit from tax exemptions and other advantages in commercial activities and investments. The arbitrary nature of determining a religion has been discussed at [8.31]ff.

Accommodation tolerates inequality

[13.5] Writers who argue for an accommodationist approach to state–belief neutrality[5] prioritise freedom for (some) individuals at the expense of equality of that freedom for all. They favour a policy that *purports* to treat all religions equally (non-religious organisations are not generally considered) while in fact not doing so. Their focus is on liberty to manifest belief at the expense of responsibility to ensure *equality* of that liberty. This approach is based on the false view that the state can (and should) equally privilege everyone in their beliefs.

[13.6] Rather than providing equal participation in belief rights, however, government accommodation of any personal worldview leads to inequality. This right applies to everyone, so each person has an obligation not to impinge on the freedom of others. As beliefs and interests can be diverse and incompatible, unfettered freedom for all to manifest their belief is impossible if one is to maximise *equality* as well as freedom.

---

2   In their study of funding of religious welfare groups in Australia, Monsma and Soper point to the officially endorsed 'religious mission' of such groups. In Australia, for example this has been openly acknowledged by religious groups in the education and welfare sectors as the underlying function of their educational or welfare activities: Monsma and Soper (2009), 121.

3   See, e.g., ibid.

4   Wallace (2007), esp. Part 2, gives a comprehensive study of the effects of the financial privileging of religion in Australia. See also above [12.27]ff.

5   See, e.g., Monsma (2002), esp Ch 13; Monsma and Soper (2009). As noted above, there is an extensive discussion of the separation and neutrality approach the judgments in *Mitchell v Helms* (2000). William Marshall states the reasons against restricting the role of religion in political decision-making are, firstly, restriction is artificial if not impossible; secondly it 'undercuts society's ability to make informed moral and political judgments'; and thirdly it inappropriately forces religious and religious values to be 'privatized' or 'marginalized': Marshall (1993), 843.

[13.7] Consequently, state support of all personal beliefs cannot be equal, as the needs, resources and interests of different belief groups are diverse and often incompatible. As Rawls indicates, accommodationism is unfair.[6] It is inevitably discriminatory, with state discretion in identifying what a belief is in the first place, and judgment is required as to what is equal in very unequal and diverse circumstances. It often results in the diversion of public money and resources to sectarian interests, when political and social influence is weighted in their favour. It causes marginalisation, disadvantage to 'other' beliefs and their interests, and the inability for equal manifestation by everyone of their individual beliefs. This is considered more fully below.

[13.8] Church-state partnership through indirect means was endorsed in the US case of *Mitchell v Helms* (2000), which ruled that Government aid (in this case to religious schools) does not amount to advancing religion, providing, said the Court, the aid is offered for education generally, and not for specifically religious purposes.[7] The Australian High Court has also taken this approach.[8] A term to cover this sort of approach, 'benevolent neutrality' was coined earlier, somewhat confusingly, by the US Supreme Court in *Walz v Tax Commission of the City of New York* (1970). There, Chief Justice Burger, delivering the opinion of the Court, endorsed a 'benevolent neutrality which will permit religious exercise to exist without sponsorship and without interference'.[9] Consequently, 'benevolent neutrality' is not so rigid a form of neutrality as to prevent any deviation from drawing an 'absolutely straight line' between church and state.[10]

[13.9] 'Benevolent neutrality' has also been called 'informed neutrality' by Professor Paul Rishworth.[11] He describes informed neutrality as making 'exceptions for religious rituals that are judged not sufficiently harmful that they must be banned whatever their motivation' on the pretext of equal consideration for all. The term is thus used to legitimise state accommodation of religion or belief deemed to fulfil the requisite requirements.

[13.10] This terminology is confusing in its attempt to deal with complex reality. It is suggested, however, that true neutrality means in fact just that: it is neither 'benevolent' (favouring) nor 'malevolent' (disfavouring), not only in intention, but also in effect. The concepts such as 'neutrality' and 'benevolent neutrality' have been used to condone some degree of entanglement of state and belief, while purporting to maintain disengagement of the state from favouring particular belief systems. It allows government aid that is nominally earmarked for a secular purpose,

---

6   Rawls (2005d), 458ff, esp. 460.
7   Davis (2002), 81.
8   *Attorney-General (Vic.), Ex Rel. Black v. The Commonwealth* (1981): see above [12.21][12.21].
9   *Walz v Tax Commission of the City of New York* 397 US (1970), p. 664.
10   Ibid, 669.
11   Religion and Schools Forum, 14 September 2007 www.hrc.co.nz/hrc.../14-Sep-2007_11-21-43_Forum_Summary. doc.

whether or not it is actually used for that purpose. The US Supreme Court case in *Mitchell v Helms* (2000) noted the difficulty of dealing with 'divertibility' of aid from secular to religious purposes acknowledging that 'any aid, with or without content, is "divertible" in the sense that it allows schools to "divert" resources'.[12] Only the purported secular *aim* of the aid is important (such as money for materials, remedial education services, interpreters for the deaf, etc.) even if these resources free up other resources for indoctrination.[13]

[13.11] It is not difficult for the government to fund a particular belief group for secular services in a way that is theoretically 'neutral', by drafting terms that on the face of them are neutral,[14] such as providing funds for 'education' to religious schools, or for provision of welfare services to a religious institution. In such cases the provision of public funds leaves the institution's resources available for religious activities that would otherwise be required for non-religious activities, allowing for religious incursion into otherwise secular services.

[13.12] Given the increasing involvement of religious and other private organisations in erstwhile government activities such as welfare, education, and other administrative activities, the line between government and these organisations has become blurred in effect, if not in intention. The arguments presented in favour of separation shows how it addresses this unfairness and imprecision of accommodationism.

Accommodation and culture

[13.13] Many who reject strict separation of state from religious organisations, maintain that separation denies any place in the public arena for the history or identity of particular societies. For example, Rex Ahdar and Ian Leigh suggest that a degree of church-state entanglement and discrimination in favour of a particular religion is acceptable: 'the point is surely not to treat all religions equally... but to treat all religions with due concern and respect'.[15] They propose that religions historically entrenched and perceived as socially useful should be given preference over others, invoking 'classical' justifications (e.g. God, as the ultimate source of authority; religious underpinnings providing legitimacy for secular institutions; and governmental responsibility for spiritual welfare).

---

12 *Mitchell v Helms* (2000), 820ff. Interestingly, *divertisement* in French, applies to misappropriation of funds.
13 See, e.g., *Mueller v Allen* (1983), (tax credits for parents to send their children to religious school); *Witters v Washington* 474 U.S. 481 (1986), (financial support for blind student at bible college); *Zobrest v Catalina Foothills School District* 509 U.S. 1 (1993), (interpreter for hearing impaired student at religious school); *Agostini v Felton* 521 U.S. 203 (1997), (remedial services to children at religious school), *Mitchell v Helms* (2000), (financial aid for materials for religious schools).
14 Souter J, in *Mitchell v Helms* (2000), 51n1.
15 Ahdar and Leigh (2004), 671ff. They conflate social services with belief.

[13.14] This misconstrues the intention of the human rights provisions, which do recognise society's entitlement to the preservation of culture and values that sustain social cohesion. However, the separation part of the equation relates to the exercise of coercive power by the state, which must accord with the political conception of justice. Culture and belief are not to be coerced, but protected within the parameters of political liberalism.

[13.15] Given that his view that liberal democracy involves separation of church and state,[16] and is based on an overlapping consensus, I conclude that Rawls rejects accommodationism and, by implication, advocates political secularism, providing for state-belief separation.

Accommodationism tends towards theocracy

[13.16] In many cases, preferment of cultural or belief-based activities in practice intentionally promotes the advancement of a religion or belief. Indeed, evangelism is fundamental to religious belief.[17] Throughout the world,

> [i]n the East, more so than in the West, human rights perceptions are…conditioned by uncompromising tenets of religious belief'. This has 'permeated the entire spectrum of particular rights, including the very notion of religious freedom *per se.*'[18]

[13.17] Recognition or preference of some religions over others by the state through 'benevolent neutrality' has led to disadvantage for non-favoured faith-based beliefs (particularly those of minority groups) and non-religious individuals and associations.[19] Proponents of favouring religion argue that it is necessary to allow such organisations to maintain their religious identity. This approach to state-belief neutrality would also allow such activities as prayer and religious instruction in schools, the display on government property of religious symbols, and use of government premises for any religious activity on a theoretically non-discriminatory basis.

[13.18] Government sponsorship of religious organisations providing non-religious, charitable activities such as education, health care and welfare creates a tendency towards theocracy. In effect, the government adopts religious values in the guise of providing community services.

[13.19] The 'neutralist' view maintains that equal amounts of aid to religious and non-religious schools will have exclusively secular and equal effects, both on external perception and incentives

---

16   Rawls (2005d), 476.
17   *Kokkinakis v Greece* (1993), ¶48: 'Christian witness…corresponds to true evangelism, which a report drawn up in 1956 under the auspices of the World Council of Churches describes as an essential mission and a responsibility of every Christian and every Church'.
18   van der Vyver (1996), xii.
19   E.g., Fox (2008), discusses different levels of support and privilege granted religion in former Soviet Bloc countries as they are considered 'part of the traditional heritage', at 150ff.

to attend different schools. In fact, such aid may be used indirectly (if not directly) for religious purposes. As noted in Chapter 12, no matter what the supposedly secular purpose of the law granting it, aid may be diverted to religious schools to directly support religious teaching in addition to secular education, or, by providing resources for non-religious teaching, can leave teachers or resources free for religious activities:[20]

> in practical terms, neutral disbursements of public aid to religious institutions cannot remain purely neutral. Some criteria must exist by which government agencies determine their beneficiaries…by forcing the public to fund … institutions that may or may not adhere to beliefs and practices consistent with those of the larger society, an inherently contentious situation is created'.[21]

[13.20] The 'benevolent neutrality' principle thus fosters the development of publicly funded, religiously-based programs such as public libraries, recreational facilities, welfare programs and day care centres. While such services are beneficial when untainted by religious objectives, providers may be influenced, for example, in the library materials they offer or services they provide by religious or other belief. Brownstein argues that funding of religious groups for such services fosters

> a particular kind of politicizing of religion that results when the proprietary interests of faith communities become susceptible to political deliberation and manipulation and there is increasing fragmentation of both political and public life along religious lines.[22]

[13.21] In this way, government funding of non-religious activities by belief-based groups can result in undue influence on the part of those organisations.[23] Evans and Thomas point to the 'underpinning of the central role' of particular belief values and organisations through money and prestige bestowed by government privilege. Official endorsement may become a reason for the attraction of a particular belief to the detriment of others.[24]

[13.22] That attractiveness, one could argue, is enhanced by benefits to be received, the ease of 'going with the flow' and difficulty in opposing it, as well as general social approval seen to be attached to accepting the *status quo*.

---

20   So held in *Mitchell v Helms* (2000), (edited and reproduced in Monsma (2002), 81). Money can be diverted to religious means, as to require otherwise would be 'unworkable' (see summary of Court's decision in the first paragraph of Justice O'Connor's decision, reproduced in Monsma, ibid, 21). See also Meyerson (2008), 55-57.
21   Davis (2002), 90.
22   Brownstein (2002), 161.
23   See, e.g., Tushnet (2000); Lupu (1991), esp. 582ff.; Smith (2005a); Marshall (1993).
24   Evans and Thomas (2006), 713.

[13.23] Evans and Thomas point to the fact that where church tax is compulsory and enforced through the government (such as in Germany) citizens are required to register their religious affiliation, and to apply to the government if they relinquish their religion in order to gain remission from the tax. This, they note, is 'an intrusion into privacy that the [European] Court views with surprising equanimity'.[25]

[13.24] Further, they maintain that '[t]he danger of establishment to religious minorities should not be overlooked'[26] and point to 'cases where an established church intruded too far into the lives of non-believers and the Court struck down the law in question'.[27] Such a program may discriminate against other belief groups who provide different but socially advantageous activities, or who do not apply for funding. (A particular group may not countenance the idea of government funding, or is too small to qualify for it).[28]

Neutrality under accommodationism is not feasible

[13.25] Different types and areas of exemptions from the law on religious grounds raise different issues (for example, exemptions from military service, monogamy, Sunday closing, etc.). But specifics aside, they all highlight the same fundamental problem: they promote institutionalised discrimination between individuals and between religious and non-religious institutions. They provide enormous wealth and power on the basis of personal, often invalid and unsubstantiated assumptions.

[13.26] Wojciech Sadurski explains that neutrality in relation to belief rights means the maintenance of 'normality'. 'Normality' is described as a base-line set of circumstances determined by an impartial government as a normal state of affairs 'by reference to which all departures from the baseline may be judged as non-neutral'.[29]

[13.27] In normal circumstances people are not prevented by the state from attending church or otherwise practicing their beliefs. The state may deprive a person of the exercise of his or her beliefs through, e.g. limits to freedom in the military or prisons, and thus may be expected to compensate for that loss of (normal) freedom.[30] However, children are not deprived of the

---

25   Ibid, 714.

26   Ibid, 707 n 41. Arcot Krishnaswami, in his UN-sponsored study of religious discrimination warned that the mere existence of an established church 'usually connoted severe discrimination – and sometimes even outright persecution – directed against dissenters' although this is not always the case: Krishnaswami (1960), 46-7.

27   E.g., the requirement for MPs to swear an oath of allegiance: *Buscarini and Others v San Marino* (1999). Greek laws that made it especially difficult for minority religions to gain government permission to establish places of worship were held to be in breach of the ECHR. See *Manoussakis and Others v Greece* (1996).

28   Brownstein (2002), 160.

29   Sadurski (1990), 433.

30   Ibid, 451.

opportunity for having or practising religious belief by going to school, as they do not suffer a loss of normal freedom. Thus the state should not be expected to compensate them by provision of religious instruction and observance in schools.[31] It is, however, suggested that 'compensation' here does not *necessitate* state-funded facilities or services, but rather liberty to access religious services where they can be independently funded and made available.[32]

[13.28] In a liberal society, those involved in government are not deprived of the normal means of accessing religious activity. Therefore, prayers and religious practices are not a legitimate part of government activities. It also follows that the promulgation of religion-based policies are not a 'normal' state function in liberal society, and thus cannot be legitimised as being 'neutral'.

[13.29] Accommodationists say they are neutral in their accommodation, but they are not, and cannot be.

[13.30] As noted above, the principles of liberty and equality are claimed to be mutually incompatible when the liberty to manifest belief is burdened by state intervention in religious activities in the name of equality.[33] On the contrary, Sadurski maintains that both the free exercise and non-establishment principles should not be seen as two separate injunctions. They are 'unified within a common scheme of state neutrality' towards belief.[34] This is evocative of Rawls's view that the apparent contradictions of liberty and equality can be reconciled (see abov[4.27]7]).

Why 'yes' to State-belief Separation?

[13.31] Following are the reasons why state-belief separation – by ensuring both freedom *to,* and freedom *from* adopting and manifesting a belief – has the potential to minimise the unfairness of accommodationism and its inevitable inequality.

State-belief separation = protection rather than privilege

[13.32] Eisgruber and Sager argue that it is religion's vulnerability to discrimination that warrants its protection.[35] *Protection* rather than privilege is at the basis of freedom of religion. On this reasoning, any belief vulnerable to discrimination warrants protection. It is not a question of privileging religion, they argue,

---

31   Ibid, 454.
32   This is based on the understanding that no belief-based services are funded by the state.
33   E.g., wearing religious regalia, religiously-approved food preparation, consuming otherwise illegal drugs, etc.
34   Sadurski (1990), 433.
35   Eisgruber and Sager (2005), 1245-1315.

[w]hat properly motivates constitutional solicitude for religious practices is their distinct vulnerability to discrimination, not their distinct value; and what is called for, in turn, is protection against discrimination, not privilege against legitimate governmental concerns.[36]

[13.33] If a democratic society is indeed based on liberty and equality, one would expect an interpretation of the belief provisions to lead to a 'levelling out of the playing field' to allow all personal life stances equal protection, whether they involve 'religion' or not.[37]

[13.34] Both adjudication and a consideration of the literature points to the preservation of belief rights through determining the context and purpose of the provisions in which they appear. This involves giving effect to the principles they are stated to embody, rather than debate over nuances of language. It indicates a broad, inclusive approach to all fundamental freedoms, including freedom of thought, opinion, belief, speech[38] and association,[39] that underlie the rights to dignity, autonomy and personal integrity.[40] This approach proposes a dispassionate outlook on both religious and other personal life stances, questioning the views of writers such as Peñalver[41] who favour religious belief over others.

[13.35] In this way, both religious and other personal life stances are placed in perspective, enmeshed in a plethora of rights that reach across the whole spectrum of human activity, leading to acceptance of people regardless of their opinions and beliefs. Most importantly by forsaking the special mention of religion, states will then:

- uphold the principles of democracy;

---

36 Ibid, 1248.
37 van der Vyver (2004), 117.
38 For example, van der Vyver (2004), at p. 108, points to *Kokkinakis v Greece* (1993), ¶55), and *Larissis and Others v Greece* (1998), (at ¶51), as cases demonstrating the 'complementary interaction' between the right to freedom of religion or belief and the right to freedom of speech.
39 At ibid, 110 van der Vyver points to *Sidiropoulos and Others v Greece (*1998), and the *United Communist Party of Turkey and Others v Turkey* (1998), as highlighting the 'entanglement of freedom of religion or belief with freedom of assembly and association'.
40 Nickel (2005), 946. These rights are listed as: Freedom of belief; thought and inquiry; communication and expression (UDHR Art. 19, ICCPR Art. 19, ECHR Art. 10); association (UDHR Art. 20, ICCPR Art. 21, ECHR Art. 11); peaceful assembly (UDHR Art. 20, ICCPR Art. 22, ECHR Art. 11); political participation (UDHR Art. 21, ICCPR Art. 25), and movement (UDHR Art. 13; ICCPR Art. 12); economic liberties (UDHR Art. 17; ICCPR Art. 26 (equality before the law)); privacy and autonomy in the areas of home, family, sexuality and reproduction (ICCPR Art. 17, ECHR Art. 8), and the right to freedom to follow an ethic, plan of life lifestyle or traditional way of living (UDHR Art. 18; ICCPR Art. 18; ECHR Art. 9), at p. 941.
41 Peñalver (2006), 2249 ff. argues that legal interference with the practice of religion is uniquely problematic: 'problematic in a way that is unlike the harm inflicted by interfering with other sorts of expressive conduct'. See also Horwitz (1997), 127; Garry (2005). Also favouring the view that religious belief is 'special' are Fish (1997); McConnell (2000); Greene (1994). Those specifically rejecting such a view include Smith (2005b); Eisgruber and Sager (1994a); Nickel (2005); Sadurski, esp. (1990); Tushnet (2000).

- recognise the depth and comprehension of non-religious life stances, such as humanism, rationalism[42] and other non-theistic philosophies, and that these have elaborate structures that are just as important to some as religion is to others;[43]

- require public policy justification through public reason, eliminating bias and discrimination in favour of or against belief-based organisations and practices.[44] State deference to religion or any other belief for its own sake would then be weighed against the principles of democracy and found wanting;

- focus on the effect of actions resulting from manifesting a particular belief, rather than on the nature of the belief itself, i.e. whether these actions are inimical to the proper functioning of the state or the rights of others;[45]

- avoid the fallacy of equating personal moral principles (their social benefit in the eyes of those concerned) with society-wide, political objectives.[46] The depth of conviction for the individual believer as the sole test of whether he or she should be entitled to special exemption from the law is an unacceptable basis for determining the right to manifest belief;[47] and

- eliminate resentment and social disharmony that results from marginalisation (and thus denial of protection) of non-adherents of recognised mainstream religions, thus securing both religious and non-religious beliefs.[48]

---

42   For a brief explanation of the beliefs of humanism and rationalism see, e.g., Hobson and Jenkins (2005). Gogineni and Gule (2004), 699.

43   See Nickel (2005), 957; Gunn (2003), 200ff.

44   It has been pointed out that biased or unreasonable restrictions on registration of religion are:

> ...a violation of religious freedom since the right to organize religious services, study and teach religion, publicize one's own beliefs and other activities have a direct impact on the human right to freedom of religion: 2005 Human Rights Organizations' Report on Ukraine, cited in *Svyato-Mykhaylivska Parafiya v Ukraine* (2007), ¶91.

45   The broad and therefore often vague interpretation given to 'worship, observance, practice or teaching' is discussed above [10.10]ff. See discussion in Malcolm Evans (1997), 215ff (UN), and 304ff (European Bodies), who argues that their approach is in fact strict and exclusive of beliefs that are unconventional. As noted, the case of *Arrowsmith v the United Kingdom* (1978), held that not all belief-inspired action is protected.

46   See Nickel (2005), 954.

47   Carolyn Evans (2001), 32; Nickel (2005), 952.

48   As Nickel states:

> Religious liberty is more secure when non-religious people see it, not as a special concession to the orthodox, but rather as simply an application of liberties and rights that all enjoy. If nonbelievers dislike religion and have no desire to protect it as such, reflection will nevertheless reveal to them that undermining religious liberties would come at the cost of undermining their own liberties of thought, expression, association, assembly, and so on. (Nickel (2005), 951. See also Rawls (2003), 6ff.)

[13.36] No-one would have a privileged access to the common resources of society simply because of 'their [sectarian] conceptions of the good': [49]

> The believer, the religion shopper, the founder of a new religion, the syncretistic new age seeker, the theologian, the doubter, and the atheist all find shelter in the broad basic beliefs [of civil society]'.[50]

State-belief separation = no state interference in personal convictions

[13.37] It has been argued[51] that religious or other practices are 'sheltered' from unfair state interference by its impartiality towards belief. Government funding or favouring of belief-sponsored activity is often subject to specific conditions as to where and how these activities may be carried out. This control can compromise the tenets of the religious body, through pressure to amend practices and beliefs to qualify for government support. It can cause division within the religious community, divert church resources to fulfil government requirements, and even force changed religious tenets or practices. [52]

[13.38] State-belief separation thus avoids state interference in *personal and/or religious moral principles*, as opposed to *society-wide, political moral principles*. Personal convictions are private, and not the state's business. They are not the plaything of politics. Unfair financial and political influence on particular belief organisations should be avoided.[53]

Other benefits of state-belief separation

[13.39] Separation from belief interests mean that government resources (taxpayer dollars) would not be applied to activities that promote particular religious (or other) beliefs to which many do not subscribe. This would save millions, if not billions, of dollars that are lost to state revenue through tax exemptions for religious organisations 'advancing religion'.[54] Direct funding of religious activities also amounts to millions of dollars (see above [12.27]). Government also avoids funding the conflicting moral interests of different belief systems.

---

49   *PL* 330.

50   Nickel (2005), 951.

51   Evans and Thomas (2006), 713. See also e.g., Tushnet (2000); Lupu (1991), esp. 582ff.; (2005a); Marshall (1993).

52   Tushnet (2000), 250.

53   For example, in Australia, for the purposes of tax exemption 'religion' is limited to a 'religious institution'. A religious organisation is one that has a belief in a supernatural being, thing or principle and the acceptance of associated canons of conduct: Australain Tax Office webpage <http://www.ato.gov.au/nonprofit/content.aspx?doc=/content/34269. htm&page=10>). These characteristics are necessary but not enough, the Government tax website tells us, 'for an organisation to be an institution. Its activities, size, permanence and recognition will be relevant.'

54   See, e.g., Australian Government Tax Office (2006).

[13.40] Prayers in Parliament or local council meetings would be eliminated – surely an official sign of government commitment to religious doctrine: not the 'normal' practice of democratic government.

[13.41] Finally, state-belief separation avoids unjust marginalisation of non-members of favoured associations, and consequent denial of protection or privilege. With separation, only activity that is contrary to the welfare of others is restricted.[55] Separation is overall socially *inclusive,* not *exclusive*.

Conclusion

[13.42] The argument, then, is that separation of the institutions of government and state involvement of religious or non-religious belief is a cornerstone of public reason, on which Rawls's idea of liberal democracy is based, and on which the form of government that best expresses the globally adopted UDHR. Legislation and policy become subject to justification that is acceptable to members of a pluralist society, regardless of belief. Promoting separation of religion and state increases the possibility that no belief system or organisation is perceived by the state to be privileged.

[13.43] It is recognised that, politically, a strict state-belief separation may be, in practical terms, difficult to achieve, but it is the only logical approach to a 'pure' model of belief rights, and in practice worth pursuing in order to maximise equal freedom for all. Toleration of state-belief entanglement is a potential threat to the free and equal exercise of one's beliefs. State-belief entanglement promotes uncertainty and unfair inequality, as well as potential undue political religious influence. This entanglement, I argue, is inconsistent with liberal democracy.

[13.44] Rawls says it simply: state-belief separation protects 'religion from the state, state from religion, and citizens from their churches'.[56]

[13.45] The problems with interpretations and implementation of Article 18 have been canvassed in the foregoing Chapters. Chapter 14 considers a way of overcoming these problems, and facilitating realisation of its promise.

---

55   That is, limitations that are prescribed by law and are necessary to protect public safety, order, health, or morals or the fundamental rights and freedoms of others: Article 18.3 ICCPR .
56   *PL* 476.

CHAPTER 14:
REALISING THE PROMISE

Introduction

[14.1] The preceding Chapters demonstrate that the implementation of the principles underlying the belief provisions would be facilitated by the adoption of a perspective that no longer accommodates special treatment by the state of any particular personal worldview. This approach recognises the need for meticulous state impartiality towards belief and separation from religious or any other institutionalised ideology. The aim is to *protect*, not privilege, all beliefs.

[14.2] Although the state-belief relationship is volatile in some nations, it is clear that most, if not all, governments do not, whether intentionally or otherwise, adequately recognise the principles underlying belief rights. That is, to protect absolutely the holding and adoption of all beliefs as defined above, while also protecting the right to be free from interference and undue influence of the beliefs of others.

How do we achieve true belief rights?

[14.3] Rawls has offered a roadmap for belief rights. In establishing state-belief separation, he points to the difference between

- what he nominates as the *human rights* of illiberal but decent societies – essential, but falling short on both liberty and equality, and

- what he nominates as the *basic liberties* of liberal democracies, which seek to maximise both.

[14.4] The question then becomes, how do we work towards maximising equal belief rights for every citizen? Answers can be deduced from the facts described in earlier Chapters. These indicate that there are multiple factors that need to be addressed.

[14.5] If we are to enjoy full and equal opportunity to have and exercise our beliefs, the above analysis suggests that governments must, in a sincere and honest way, seek to implement the principles of human rights and democracy as promoted by the UN, rather than defining human rights in their own terms. It is proposed that this requires:

a) a liberal democratic regime, with political values that maximise equal opportunity for self-realisation, through the legal institution of a Bill of Rights (preferably attached to the Constitution); and

b) a change in perspective on belief – and religion in particular – that would require a shift in thinking of somewhat seismic proportions, at least in most states.

[14.6] It is proposed that the state must recognise the place of 'public political culture', and that illiberal decent societies should be acknowledged where they provide for nominated human rights. However, as Rawls recognised, it is critical to the full and equal enjoyment of human rights that the 'public political culture' becomes one based on an overlapping consensus of political (as distinct from personal) values that can be agreed to by all. The fact that all nations have officially adopted the UDHR as a form of consensus indicates that these values have been identified (at least at the formal international level) as most likely to provide maximum human self-realisation and potential.

[14.7] A more liberal public political culture cannot be achieved with force, or inordinate pressure on societies who do not recognise such values. Evidence seems to show that such an approach fuels militant opposition to such measures. To expect all nations to spontaneously and wholeheartedly adopt the UDHR would have been, and still would be, overly optimistic. This is the lesson we have learned from the past seventy years of struggle for compliance by human rights bodies. Maximising belief rights requires measures outlined below.

1. Change of perspective

[14.8] Those supporting the accommodation of religious practices by the state must no longer hide behind the claim of a special status (be it superior or otherwise) for religion or any other belief, to further their own agenda. They must recognise that 'freedom of belief' necessarily involves freedom *from* belief. Whether religious or not, personal life-stances do not attract privilege: they attract protection where unduly threatened. This includes states refraining from making laws that discriminate purely on the grounds of religious or other belief.

[14.9] Not only must the state respect and protect religion and other beliefs, then, belief systems must respect the state. Freedom to act must be tempered by the obligation to allow others the same freedom: ensuring equal *worth* of the freedom to manifest belief for everyone. Belief rights, like other benefits of true democracy, do not come without a cost, which all must be prepared to pay. The time for pretence is over – the state is either separationist, or it privileges one or more beliefs through accommodation or theocratic policies.

[14.10] This change in perspective may seem a hopeless ideal, particularly in those nations wracked with religious conflict and hostility. While the UN has achieved a revolutionary milestone in its work towards belief rights and other human rights, many states and/or individuals persistently resist human rights, including the equal exercise of belief for all. Despite outbursts of sectarian militancy, awareness of the need for political secularism is being more clearly articulated, and is slowly growing in the developed and developing world. It has taken centuries for nations to give at least lip service to the need for universal human rights, and the work of realising them has a long way to go.

2. Removal of political inequality

[14.11] It seems clear that societies with top-down rule such as dictatorships and tyranny are anathema to human rights. It is also difficult to fully exercise such rights, especially belief rights, in societies with a sovereign (no matter how benign), who is hereditary, often appointed 'by the grace of God' not man, with their associated elite class and institutionalised entitlement and privilege based on birth and regal preferment and prerogative. Most monarchies are linked to an established state church, or require the monarch to belong to a nominated religion. Such a society is in principle inconsistent to the social and political equality required by human rights. Strengthening of the rule of law, with recognition of one law for all, as well as removal of social inequalities that prevent full enjoyment of human rights, is necessary for ensuring belief rights. It is noted that those nations most resolute in supporting state–belief separation are Republics. Political equality negates class and privilege.

3. Removal of special consideration of religion

[14.12] Lack of direction is caused by the fact that belief provisions are ambiguous, the rulings of the belief tribunals recognise accommodation of religion and that they are at times confusing and contradictory. The specific association of the provisions with religion narrows and distorts the intention of the provisions, distracting from the basic principle of autonomy of thought and action, circumscribed by the principle of equality. This brings ambiguity and uncertainty into the search for the true worth of belief rights, and this ambiguity is often used as a tool to justify the sectarian interests that are promoted in the name of human rights. Those who wish to instigate genuine attempts for belief rights are distracted and obstructed by the need to traverse the minefield of literal and legal niceties created by the imprecision of the belief provisions and their propensity for bias.

[14.13] Unfortunately, despite its good intentions, and in the light of hindsight, it can be seen that the UN got it somewhat wrong when settling on the wording of Article 18. Religion, and the desirability of its accommodation by the state was very much in the minds of the drafters, and became the focus of the provisions. This was a fundamental flaw, and central to achieving belief rights is the removal of the focus on 'religion' in conceptions of the right, and recasting language to clearly establish that the freedom covers all beliefs. While the human rights tribunals are quite clear that belief rights are to be 'construed broadly' to include personal life stances other than religion itself, the language of the belief provisions, in the attempt to be clear, has in fact had the opposite effect of muddying the waters.

[14.14] Removal of religious connotations caused by the words 'religion', 'conscience' and 'belief' would underscore the broad coverage of the belief provisions. Ideally, It is concluded that the interrelationship between action based on life stances, that include cultural values, and other modes of thinking (such as ideas and opinions) and consequent speech, assembly and association is recognised. Looking beyond religion is not just a philosophical nicety: it is essential for adequately protecting the principles of liberty and equality.

4. Due recognition of political secularism

[14.15] To fulfil the promise of belief rights, the UN must infuse determinacy, consistency and clarity into the understanding of just what freedom to manifest belief entails. Attempts to unravel the nuances of language detract from the underlying principles of autonomy (the liberty to act as you will) and the qualifying requirement of equality (the limitation of action where necessary for the public good and the same liberty for others). The employment of these principles has often fallen victim to political, economic and social pressures that prevent their effective realisation.

[14.16] While accepting the principle that a person must be free to hold and exercise their personal belief, it is essential to acknowledge more fully the necessary restrictions this imposes on the individual to ensure everyone else has that same freedom. This is consistent with the basic principles that underlie democracy, and established in the international human rights treaties that contain within themselves *limits* as well as liberties. This is best recognised by a constitutional expression of freedom both *of* one's own belief and *from* the beliefs of others. Where a state is avowedly secular, the European Court has argued that it is not just a matter of asking whether someone's (religious) practice is hampered, but rather, whether the principle of secularism is being eroded. This, it is argued, is closer to the spirit of the belief provisions as we should understand them.

5. Requirement of state–belief separation

[14.17] Further contributing to the undue influence of religion and (in some countries) other beliefs is the fact that the international human rights treaties do not require state-belief separation, while this, it has been argued, is the most effective way to ensure that individuals are unimpeded in having and expressing their beliefs. Areas of positive entanglement of state and belief are countenanced by the belief provisions under the ICCPR'[1] and the ECHR.[2] The Euro-

---

1   See discussion in Taylor (2005), 153ff.
2   Evans and Thomas (2006).

pean Court has more effectively recognised the importance of secularism, but has not insisted on a policy of rigorous state-belief separation. The human rights organisations have consequently condoned much state-belief collaboration through consideration of cultural context (such as the margin of appreciation) which, while potentially beneficial, can lead to bias and prejudice on the part of tribunal members. Discretion on the part of the tribunals should be subject to tighter and more specifically enunciated principles, so that sectarian and cultural biases and beliefs are not given undue weight in judgments and rulings. The balance is often a fine one, and views as to the best approach may differ, but the focus must be on maximising the 'worth' of the equal belief rights for everyone.

6. Consideration of Rawls's model of 'political liberalism'

[14.18] The above analysis suggests a different understanding and approach is needed to facilitate freedom to have and manifest belief in line with the principles of liberal democracy outlined in the UDHR and favoured by Rawls. His model of political liberalism, while it is a theoretical ideal, offers a flexible and realistic analytical tool for considering different societies and their varying approaches to the exercise of rights and liberties. The model is flexible to the extent that human rights principles are recognised, according to which national culture may be adapted for governance. It is realistic in that it works to maximise basic liberties compatible with modern democratic society. It places due emphasis on the fact that political equality creates a citizenship based as much on restriction as on freedom – on the understanding that belief, and the values underlying belief, are private, and not a matter for state governance. Citizenship, instead, is based on principles generated by public reason and adopted by overlapping consensus.

[14.19] Whilst the realisation of those principles is far from being achieved, the evidence that they are accepted as feasible is there in the nations' affirmation of their commitment to these rights. Indeed, it is argued a[1.15]4], no better model of liberal society has yet been propounded, and to a large extent Rawls's principles are already recognised. The purpose of the belief tribunals, and indeed the UN itself, involves the promotion of public reason based on them.

[14.20] We can thus judge the extent to which the interpretation and implementation of the belief provisions meet the requirements of a just and fair society, through the concept of public reason. Public reason is based on the purported overlapping consensus on the nature and values of government, and this consensus is expressed in the civil and political rights set out in the UDHR and similar declarations and Conventions. Nations have proclaimed their commitment to this 'overlapping consensus' through membership of the UN, but overwhelmingly neglect its implementation. They may well have signed the UDHR for political purposes other than guaranteeing the rights it promotes. Not taking their undertakings seriously, however, is a betrayal of those who rely on governments to honour their commitments. Nations enjoy the privileges of belonging to the UN while avoiding the obligations of membership.

Article 18 as stated is problematic

[14.21] Statements setting out the terms on which a society is to be governed, that are meant to have the force of law or direct behaviour should be adequately precise, to ensure clarity and certainty. Article 18 is best considered a statement of general principle only, with governments establishing the liberties and limitations it involves in more defined terms. This leads me to conclude that:

a) *Article 18 as expressed is an unsatisfactory directive for ensuring belief rights for all.* There are inherent contradictions in the very notion of freedom of thought, religion and conscience.[3] Religion and cultural practices often prevent true freedom of thought and conscience. Tolerance of different (and often contradictory) beliefs based on religion and culture signifies a contradiction in terms: tolerance of intolerance, as claims to be the sole holder of the truth generates intolerance. Article 18 raises issues that are unnecessary and divert from the purpose of what is at the heart of human rights: autonomy, personal integrity and rights to freedom of expression, assembly and association. It also provides an excuse for the privileging of religion by government and individuals, and the potential oppression of minority religious or non-religious beliefs. It also provides an excuse for ignoring the harm that religious practices can do the name of religious freedom.

b) *We do need belief rights, but in other terms.* The language of Article 18 appears to give special protection to religious belief and its manifestation. It is suggested that freedom to adopt and practise a system of personal ethical doctrines should be recognised, but freedom of expression, association and assembly are already contained in the relevant international documents. This is not to deride discussion and promotion of the idea of freedom to adopt and practise religious and alternative comprehensive doctrines, but to argue for recognition that they are part of the general right to freedom of self-realisation that underlies the institution of universal human rights.

[14.22] While Article 18 is the time-honoured expression of belief rights, nations could well adopt more effective language in constitutional or other legislation. It is suggested, then, that governments legislate to recognise belief rights, as meaning the adoption of, and action pursuant to, belief, as defined above.

---

3   Perkins, (2012), 162

How would we re-write belief rights?

Constitution or ordinary legislation?

[14.23] Differences of opinion between having a Bill of Rights attached to a constitution or as a stand-alone piece of legislation were discussed a[2.71]1]ff. As state-belief separation is a fundamental part of the institution of government, the entrenchment of such a provision in the Constitution could well be seen as appropriate.

[14.24] It has been argued in Chapter 13 that state neutrality should eschew any form of government entanglement with belief systems. Describing neutrality as 'benevolent neutrality', involving some degree of accommodation of belief, is to misrepresent the idea of neutrality, as 'benevolent neutrality' is an oxymoron. Provision for rigorous state–belief separation is required to provide for true equality in the enjoyment of belief rights, as state–belief entanglement necessarily involves discrimination: between religious beliefs, within religious beliefs and between religious and non-religious beliefs. Religious agencies should be subject to requirements of transparency and public accountability just like any other association. For tax purposes, charitable works that receive government financial assistance should be considered separately from activities fostering the advancement of religion. The government should neither fund nor support the advancement of belief as a form of 'charity'.

Non-establishment of belief?

[14.25] Australia and the US have provision in their constitutions prohibiting the government making laws in relationship to the establishment of a religion. This has been seen by many as the answer to prevention of state entanglement with religion, by requiring a separation of 'Church and State', and the US Supreme Court has held accordingly. However, we have seen that this does not work. In the US, the Court has watered down the idea of separation of state and belief to mean 'benign neutrality' (see abov[13.8]ff). In addition, the Court has upheld exemption from laws of general application on the grounds of religious belief.[4] In Australia, the High Court held that 'establishment' is to be defined narrowly to mean the declaration by government of a national state-instituted religion, allowing for widespread accommodation of religion. Some of the judges indicated their view that there is no separation of church and state in Australia (see abov[12.21]1] and footnote). Moreover, both constitutions refer only to 'religion'. Prohibiting 'establishment', then, is not enough to ensure true and equal belief rights, as can be seen from the subsequent prevalence of religious belief in government activities and policies in those countries.

---

4   Burwell, *Secretary of Health and Human Services, et al. v Hobby Lobby Stores, Inc., et al*, (2014)

[14.26] Providing for state-belief separation by ordinary statute also poses problems with its vulnerability to repeal. Because it is so necessary in democratic society to ensure individual autonomy in the way we think, adopt central values for living, and manifest these in the way we live, the freedom to do so, according to the public political conception of justice, should be expressed clearly as principles underlying the constitution of, and rules for, government.

Example: Fiji Constitution

[14.27] It is instructive that the tiny republic of Fiji, in instituting a new democratic regime, has been able to do for belief rights what other democracies have failed to do over centuries. Recently, a new Fiji Constitution was promulgated, which includes a bill of rights, incorporating, at Article 22, the 'right to freedom of religion, conscience and belief', with limitations similar to those in Article 18.

[14.28] In a country divided racially and religiously, some strongly influential religious groups wanted Fiji to be declared a Christian nation. Chairman of the Commission to draw up a draft Constitution, Professor Yash Ghai, stated: 'we cannot be endorsing human rights if we strive to make Fiji a Christian State because the two issues contradict each other'.[5] His Committee recommended provision, additional to Article 22 and later adopted, for a declaration that Fiji is a secular state, and detailed provisions for separation of religion and state. The Commission's (leaked) Report on the Draft Constitution stated that

> [T]he separation of state from religion and culture does not mean that the state is opposed to religion and culture. On the contrary, this separation is in the interests of religion and culture, freeing them from the regulation by the state. Culture is always evolving and it is only in this way that it will remain relevant to the people and enable them to cope with changing social and economic circumstances. In order words, culture and religion will be responsibilities predominantly of civil society...[6]

[14.29] The Draft Constitution was revised, but draft provisions on separation of state from religion and culture were retained in the final version of the Constitution which was adopted in 2014. Not only is Fiji declared a secular state, but with 'religious freedom' a founding principle, there is specific provision that 'religion is personal', and religion and the state are pronounced to be separate. The Constitution then sets out a comprehensive statement on just what separation

---

5   Draft Constitution: The Explanatory Report p (2012), 52, at . <http://www.fijileaks.com/uploads/1/3/7/5/13759434/thursday_the_explanatory_report_two-4.pdf.>.
6   Ibid.

means in practice.[7] Taking these provisions as a model, and replacing the inclusive concept of 'belief' for 'religion' it is proposed that, for Article 18 to be fully effective, belief rights could well be expressed in a Constitution along the following lines:

1. Freedom to adopt and practice a belief (defined to include all personal worldviews) is declared a founding principle of the state;

2. The state is declared secular;

3. Belief is declared to be private;

4. A person shall not be compelled to

    a) act against his or her conscience,

    b) take an oath contrary to his or her belief,

    c) receive religious instruction contrary to his or her belief, (or that of parents if a child) or

    d) participate in religious observance against his or her beliefs (or that of parents if a child);

5. The above provisions are subject to limitations similar to those in Article 18.

6. State-belief separation is specifically prescribed. This means that all persons holding a public office,

    a) must regard all beliefs as having equal significance,

    b) must not mandate the holding or practice of any belief,

    c) must not benefit by any means any particular belief or any institution in advancing any particular belief.

7. No Person shall assert any belief as a legal reason to disregard the Constitution or any other law.

---

7   Section 4 of the Fiji Constitution, entitle 'Secular State' provides:

     4.   (1) Religious liberty, as recognised in the Bill of Rights, is a founding principle of the State.

          (2) Religious belief is personal.

          (3) Religion and the State are separate, which means—

             (a), the State and all persons holding a public office must treat all religions equally;

             (b), the State and all persons holding a public office must not dictate any religious belief;

             (c), the State and all persons holding a public office must not prefer or advance, by any means, any particular religion, religious denomination, religious belief, or religious practice over another, or over any non-religious belief; and

             (d), no person shall assert any religious belief as a legal reason to disregard this Constitution or any other law.

[14.30] Provision in these terms not only prohibits government financial or other support of belief, it also negates the confusing idea of 'equal treatment' of all beliefs, and establishes that fully secular, charitable work is not included in the prohibition of favourable treatment. It also provides that no Parliament or government department, council, school or public function is to pressure anyone to participate in belief-based worship, practices, observance or instruction. It affirms that religion or other belief is not above the law. In other words, it ensures not only 'freedom of belief', but also 'freedom from belief'.

[14.31] The provisions lead to the proposal that 'freedom of belief' is not just a matter of government recognising the integrity of beliefs (religious or otherwise), but equally one of beliefs recognising the requirements of reciprocity according to public reason. If not, society tends towards theocracy or dictatorship. Independent scrutiny of government policy for state-belief neutrality, certifying its accordance with underlying principles of human rights, would facilitate avoidance of conflict with the conscientious requirements of particular groups when this is not necessary in the public interest. Perhaps Australia and New Zealand could learn from their near neighbour.

The worth of belief rights

[14.32] If we look at Rawls's requirements for a just societ[3.11]1] where the worth of belief rights is maximised for all, we can see that the above provisions promote these requirements. There is a measure of agreement over conceptions of justice, based on universally adopted human rights – in this case the rights to have and practise one's belief, speech and assembly – to be equally enjoyed through the rule of law. Society is organised both at the governmental and individual level to promote the legitimate expectations of liberal democracy including freedom of and from belief through government impartiality. There will be a general understanding and acceptance of the need for social cooperation to maximise freedom and equality in relation to belief. Finally, legislative and judicial processes will be geared to apply fairly the means to correct and prevent infractions that jeopardise the promise of belief rights.

[14.33] The fact that these provisions have been recently set out in one nation's Constitution, and provisions along similar lines have been adopted in others, indicate that the perception of belief rights may be changing in some areas of the globe, and with the growing influence of the internet and consequent awareness of the benefits of liberal democracy, belief rights may one day no longer be an unfulfilled promise.

BIBLIOGRAPHY

Ahdar, Rex and Leigh, Ian (2004) 'Is Establishment Consistent with Religious Freedom?' 49 *McGill Law Journal*, 635.

Ahdar, Rex (ed) (2000) *Law and Religion*, Aldershot, Ashgate.

Alston Phillip and James Crawford (eds), (2000) *The Future of UN Human Rights Treaty Monitoring*, Cambridge, Cambridge University Press,

Alston Philip (ed), (1992) *The United Nations and Human Rights: a Critical Appraisal*, Oxford, Clarendon Press.

Altman, Dennis (2006) *51st State?* Melbourne, Scribe, Chapter 3.

An-Na'im, Abdullahi (1987) 'Religious Minorities under Islamic Law and the Limits of Cultural Relativism' 9 *Human Rights Quarterly,* 1.

An-Na'im, Abdullahi Ahmed (2005) 'The Interdependence of Religion, Secularism and Human Rights' 11(1) *Common Knowledge*, 56.

Arneson, Richard (2006) 'Justice After Rawls' in John Dryzek, et al (2006) 45.

Artz, Donna (1990) 'The Application of Human Rights Law in Islamic States' *Human Rights Quarterly* 12, 202-230.

Australian Government Tax Office (2006) *Getting started - Income tax guide for non-profit organizations* <http://www.ato.gov.au/print.asp?doc=/content/34263.htm>.

Australian Human Rights and Equal Opportunity Commission, (2008) '*Combating the Defamation of Religions: Report to the United Nations High Commissioner for Human Rights*' <http://www.humanrights.gov.au/partnerships/religiousdefamation/>.

Australian Human Rights Commission (2011) *Freedom of Religion and Belief in 21st Century Australia* http://www.humanrights.gov.au/frb/Report_2011.pdf.

Ayaan Hirsi Ali (2006) *The Caged Virgin*, New York, Free Press.

Aymonier, Jean Francios (2000) Material held by the author.

Bachelard, Michael (2008) *Behind the Exclusive Brethren,* Melbourne, Scribe.

Bacik, Ivana (2009) 'Is Ireland Really a Republic?' *Philip Monahan Lecture, UCC* <http://www.ucc.ie/en/government/Bacik-Lecture.doc>.

Baggini, Julian (2006) 'The Rise, Fall and Rise again of Secularism' December 2005-February *Public Policy Research,* 204.

Bancquart, Marie-Claire (1999) (ed), *Anatole France: Oeuvres*, Vol. 2 Gallimard, 1987) 329.

Barbier, Maurice (2005) 'Towards a Definition of French Secularism' *Revue des Revues de l'adpf, sélection de Septembre 2005* <http://www.diplomatie.gouv.fr/en/IMG/pdf/0205-Barbier-GB-2.pdf>.

Barro, Robert J. and McCleary, Rachel M. (2005) 'Which Countries Have State Religions?' *The Quarterly Journal of Economics*, November 2005, 1331.

Barry, Brian (2001) *Culture and Equality: An Egalitarian Critique of Multiculturalism* Oxford, Polity.

Batabyal, Amitrajeet (2000) Book Review: 'John Rawls The Law of Peoples' 13 *Journal of Agricultural and Environmental Ethics*, 269.

Baubérot, Jean (2004) 'The Place of Religion in Public Life: The Lay Approach' in Lindholm, et al (2004). 441.

Bedau, H. (1975) 'Inequality, How much and Why?' 6 *Journal of Social Philosophy,* 25.

Bielefeldt, Heiner (2011) *Report of the Special Rapporteur on Freedom of Religion or Belief,* Agenda Item 3, UN Human Rights Council 19th Session A/HRC/19/60.

Bielefeldt, Heiner (2012) 'Freedom of Religion and Belief A Human Right under Pressure' *Oxford Journal of Law and Religion,* 1.

Benito, E. Odio (1989) 'Study of the Current Dimensions of the Problems of Intolerance and of Discrimination on grounds of Religion or Belief' *Human Rights Study Series No 2,* UN Sales NO E.89. XIV.3.

Bentham, Jeremy (1843) extracts of his *Anarchical Fallacies*, reproduced in Waldron (1987) 46. (The only complete form is in the Bowring edition of *The Works of Jeremy Bentham* (Edinburgh, William Tait, 1843).

Berg, Thomas (1998) *The State and Religion in a Nutshell*, Minnesota, St Paul University Press.

Berg-Sørensen Anders, (2007) 'Politicizing Secularism' *Journal of International Affairs* Fall/Winter, 253.

Bhargava, Rajeev (2006) 'Political Secularism' in Dryzek et al, (2006) 636.

Blackburn, Simon (2001) *Ethics: A very Short Introduction,* Oxford, Oxford University Press.

Blackshield, Tony (2005) 'Religion and Australian Constitutional Law' in Radan et al, (2005).

Blake, Garth (2007) 'Promoting Religious Tolerance in a Multifaith Society: Religious Vilification Legislation in Australia and the U.K.' 81 *The Australian Law Journal* 386.

Bloß, Lasia (2003) 'European Law of Religion – organizational and institutional analysis of national systems and their implications for the future European Integration Process' Jean Monnet Working Paper 13/0 NYU School of Law New York, NY 10012 USA, <http://www.jeanmonnetprogram.org/archive/papers/03/031301.pdf>.

Bocock, Robert and Thompson, Kenneth (1991) *Religion and Ideology* , Manchester, Manchester University Press.

Bonett, Warren ed., (2010) *The Australian Book of Atheism,* Carlton North Australia, Scribe.

Bossuyt, M J, (1987) *Guide to the Traveaux Préparatoires of the International Covenant on Civil and Political Rights* The Hague, Martinus Nijhoff.

Boston, Robert, (2003) *Why the Religious Right is Wrong about Separation of Church and State*, Amherst, N.Y., Prometheus Books.

Bowman, Harold (1996) 'Religious Rights in Russia at a Time of Tumultuous Transition: A Historical Theory' in van der Vyver et al (1996) 285.

Boyd, Marion (2004) *'Dispute Resolution in Family Law: Protecting Choice, Promoting Inclusion'* Report to the Ontarian Attorney-General <http://www.attorneygeneral.jus.gov.on.ca/english/about/pubs/boyd/fullreport.pdf>.

Brownstein, Alan (2002) 'The Souter Dissent: Correct but Inadequate' in Monsma (2002) 151.

Butler, Amir (2004) 'Why I've Changed My Mind on Vilification Laws', *The Age* (Melbourne), 4 June.

Byrne, Cathy *Religion in Secular Education: What, in Heaven's Name, are we Teaching our Children?* Brill Academic Publishers (2014).

Callinicos, Alex *Equality* (2000) Cambridge, Polity Press.

Cane, Peter, Evans, Carolyn and Robinson, Zoë (eds), (2011) *Law and Religion in Theoretical and Historical Context*, Cambridge, Cambridge University Press.

Cannold, Leslie (2011) 'Australia's fading separation between church and state.' *ABC Religion and Ethics* 13 May 2011, <http://www.abc.net.au/religion/articles/2011/05/13/3216153.htm>.

Carozza, Paul (2008) 'Human Dignity and Judicial Interpretation of Human Rights: A Reply' *The European Journal of International Law* Vol. 19 no. 5, 931.

Carter, April and Stokes, Geoffrey (1998) *Liberal Democracy and its Critics* Cambridge, Polity Press.

Catholics for Choice, (2013) *The Catholic Church at the United Nations: Church or State?*, Washington, DC, <http://www.catholicsforchoice.org/topics/politics/documents/CFC_See_Change_2013.pdf>.

Challans, Timothy (2007) 'Rawls versus Habermas on Religion, Politics, and War' *School of Advanced Military Studies International Symposium on Military Ethics*, <http://www.usafa.af.mil/jscope/ISME2007/Papers/Challans_Rawls_v_Habermas.doc>.

Charbonneau, Louis (2010) 'UN Committee Moves to Keep out Gay-Lesbian NGO', <http://www.reuters.com/article/idUSTRE6526BQ20100603>.

Charlesworth, Hilary (2005) 'The Challenges of Human Rights Law for Religious Traditions' in Janis et al (2005).

Churchill, Bob (2013) 'Believe or Die: 4 Member States of the Human Rights Council Where Apostasy Means Death' *Huffington Post* 17/12/2013, <http://www.huffingtonpost.com/bob-churchill/believe-or-die-4-member-states_b_4462310.html>.

Civitas (2009) 'Shari'a Law or One Law for All', <http://www.civitas.org.uk/pdf/Shari'aLawOrOneLawForAll.pdf>.

Clarke, Ben, (2007) 'Freedom of Speech and Criticism of Religion: What are the Limits?' 14(2) *Murdoch University elaw Journal* 94.

Concise Oxford Dictionary (1982) Oxford, Clarendon Press.

Concordat Watch (webpage) 'List of concordats 1801-2004' <http//www.concordatwatch.eu>.

Constitution Commission of Fiji (2012) *Draft Constitution: The Explanatory Report,* <http://www.fijileaks.com/uploads/1/3/7/5/13759434/thursday_the_explanatory_report_two-4.pdf.>.

Cooke, Bill (2006) *Dictionary of Atheism, Skepticism, and Humanism* New York, Prometheus Books.

Coorey, Phillip (2008) 'Australia Rejects Call for Islamic Courts' *Sydney Morning Herald* Feb 9-10, <http://www.smh.com.au/news/national/australia-rejects-call-for-islamic-courts/2008/02/08/1202234167178.html>.

Cragun R.T., Yeager, S. and Vega D. (2012) Research Report: 'How Secular Humanists (and Everyone Else) Subsidize Religion in the United States' *Free Inquiry*, vol 32 issue 4, <http://www.centerforinquiry.net/newsroom/u.s._loses_over_71_billion_in_religious_tax_exemptions/>.

Cranmer, Frank (2012) *Sharia law, the Arbitration Act 1996 and the Arbitration and Mediation Services, (Equality) Bill* <http://www.lawandreligionuk.com/2012/10/24/sharia-law-the-arbitration-act-1996-and-the-arbitration-and-mediation-services-equality-bill/>.

Cranmer Frank (2013) *Religious tribunals in the United Kingdom and the United States,* <http://www.lawandreligionuk.com/2013/04/13/religious-tribunals-in-the-united-kingdom-and-the-united-states/>.

Dacey, Austin (2008) *The Secular Conscience* New York, Prometheus Books.

Davie, Grace (2007) *The Sociology of Religion* London, Sage Publications.

Davies, Margaret (1994) *Asking the Law Question* Sydney, Law Book Company Limited.

Davis, Derek (2001) 'Separation, Integration and Accommodation: Religion and State in America in a Nutshell' 43 *Journal of Church and State* 5.

Davis, Derek (2002) 'The Thomas Plurality Opinion: The Subtle Dangers of Neutrality Theory Unleashed' in Monsma (2002).

Dawkins, Richard (2006) *The God Delusion,* London, Bantam Press.

De Schutter, Olivier (2010) *International Human Rights Law*, Cambridge, Cambridge University Press.

de Sousa e Brito, José (2004) 'Conscientious Objection' in Lindholm et al (2004).

Douzinas, Costas (2000) *The End of Human Rights: Critical Legal Thought at the Turn of the Century*, Oxford, Hart Publishing.

Dryzek, John, Honig, Bonnie and Phillips, Anne (eds) (2006) *The Oxford Handbook of Political Theory*, Oxford, Oxford University Press.

Durham, W. Cole (1996) 'Perspectives on Religious Liberty' in van der Vyver et al (1996).

Durham, W. Cole (2004) 'Facilitating Freedom of Religion or Belief Through Religious Association Laws' in Lindholm et al (2004) 321.

Dworkin, Ronald, (1978) *Taking Rights Seriously* London, Duckworth.

Edge, Peter (2003) 'Extending Hate Crime to Religion' 8 *Journal of Civil Liberties* 7.

Edge, Peter (2006) *Religion and Law* Aldershot, Ashgate Publishing Limited.

Edwards, Steve (2005) 'Do We Really Need Religious Vilification Laws?' 21(1) *Policy* 30.

Eisgruber, Christopher and Sager, Lawrence (1994a) 'The Vulnerability of Conscience: The Constitutional Basis for Protecting Religious Conduct' 61 *University of Chicago Law Review* 1245.

Eisgruber, Christopher and Sager, Lawrence (1994b) 'Why the Religious Freedom Restoration Act is Unconstitutional' 69(3) *New York University Law Review* 437.

Eisgruber, Christopher and Sager, Lawrence (1996) 'Unthinking Religious Freedom' 74 *Texas Law Review* 577.

European Commission of Human Rights (1956) 'Preparatory Work on Article 9 of the European Convention on Human Rights: Information Document' <Document No. DH (56) 14>.

Evans, Carolyn (2001) *Freedom of Religion under the European Convention on Human Rights* Oxford, OUP.

Evans, Carolyn and Thomas, Christopher (2006) 'Church-State Relations in the European Court of Human Rights' *Brigham Young University Law Review* 699.

Evans, Carolyn (2007) 'Religious Freedom and Religious Hatred in Democratic Societies' *Human Rights 2006: The Year in Review,* University of Melbourne Legal Studies Research Paper No. 236; Marius Smith, ed., pp. 155-168, Monash University, <http://ssrn.com/abstract=993654>.

Evans, Malcolm (1997) *Religious Liberty and International Law in Europe* Cambridge, Cambridge University Press.

Evans, Malcolm (2000) 'The United Nations and Freedom of Religion: The Work of the Human Rights Committee' in Ahdar (2000) 35.

Evans, Malcolm (2004) 'Historical Analysis of Freedom of Religion or Belief as a Technique for Resolving Religious Conflict' in Lindholm et al (2004) 2.

Evans, Malcolm (2008) 'Freedom of Religion and the European Convention on Human Rights Approaches, Trends and Tensions' in Cane et al (2004) 291.

Faircloth, Sean (2012) *Attack of the Theocrats!* Pitchstone Publishing, Virginia.

Feenan, Dermot (2006) 'Religious Vilification Laws: Quelling Fires of Hatred?' *Alternative Law Journal* 31.

Feldman Stephen (ed), (2000) *Law and Religion: A Critical Anthology*, New York, New York University Press.

Ferguson, Adele (2005) 'Charity Inc.' *Business Review Weekly* (Sydney), 24-30 March, 45.

Ferguson, Adele (2006) 'God's Business', June 29-July 5 *Business Review Weekly* 43.

Ferrara, Alessandro (2009) 'The Separation of Religion and Politics in a post-secular society' 35 *Philosophy and Social Criticism* 77.

Fish, Stanley (1997) 'Mission Impossible: Settling the Just Bounds Between Church and State' 97(8) *Columbia Law Review* 2255.

Fortuyn, Pim (2013) 'One Law for All: On the Moral Bankruptcy of Shari'a Courts' <https://peshawarnights.wordpress.com/2013/05/28/one-law-for-all-on-the-moral-bankruptcy-of-sharia-courts/>.

Foster, Sir John (1971) 'Enquiry into the Practices and Effects of Scientology' London, Her Majesty's Stationery Office.

Fox, Jonathon (2008) *A World Survey of Religion and the State* Cambridge, Cambridge University Press.

France, Anatole (1987) 'Le Lys Rouge' in Marie-Claire Bancquart (ed) *Anatole France: Oeuvres, Vol. 2*, Gallimard, 329.

Franck, Thomas (1992) 'The Emerging Right to Democratic Governance' 86(1) *American Journal of International Law* 46.

Fraser, Muriel (2008) 'Secularism' *Concordat Watch* <http://www.concordatwatch.eu> 8.

Fraser, Muriel (2014) *Religious courts in England* on Website *Concordat Watch* <http://www.concordatwatch.eu>.

Freeman, G. C. (1983) 'The Misconceived Search for the Constitutional Definition of "Religion"' 71 *Georgetown Law Journal* 1519.

Freeman, H. A. (1958) 'A remonstrance for Conscience' 106 *Pa. L. Rev.* 806.

Freeman, M D A (2001) *Lloyd's Introduction to Jurisprudence* London, Sweet & Maxwell 7th ed.

Freeman, Samuel (1994) 'Political Liberalism and the Possibility of a Just Democratic Constitution' 69 *Chicago-Kent Law Review* 619.

Freeman, Samuel (2003) *The Cambridge Companion to Rawls* Cambridge, Cambridge University Press.

Freeman, Samuel (2004) 'Public Reason and Political Justifications' 72 *Fordham Law Review* 2021

Freeman, Samuel (2007a) *Rawls* London and New York, Routledge.

Freeman, Samuel (2007b) *Justice and the Social Contract* Oxford, Oxford University Press.

Galleoti, Anna (2002) 'Globallity, State and Society' (Paper presented at the Globalism Project Conference, Mexico City, Feb. 19-22, <http://polanyi.concordia.ca/conf/pdf/Yeatman.pdf>).

Galleotti, Anna (2006) 'Identity, Difference, Toleration' in Dryzek, (2006) 564.

Galligan, Brian (1989) 'No Bill of Rights for Australia', Paper originally presented at the third Senate Seminar on Parliamentary Law and Practice at Parliament House on 8 May 1989 <http://www.aph.gov.au/library/intguide/law/civlaw.htm#bill >.

Gardiner, Tim (2006) 'The RFRA Needs to be Repealed Now' *Humanist Network News* <www.//NetworkNews.org>.

Garry, Patrick (2005) 'Religious Freedom Deserves More Than Neutrality: The Constitutional Argument for Nonpreferential Favouritism of Religion' 57(1) *Florida Law Review* 1.

Gearty, Conor (2000) 'Democracy and Human Rights in the European Court of Human Rights: A Critical Appraisal' 51(3) *Northern Ireland Legal Quarterly* 381.

Gearty, Conor (2001) 'Reflections on Human Rights and Civil Liberties in Light of the United Kingdom's Human Rights Act 1998' 35(1) *University of Richmond Law Review* 1.

Gearty, Conor (2004) *Principles of Human Rights Adjudication* Oxford, OUP.

Gearty, Conor (2006) *Can Human Rights Survive?* Cambridge, Cambridge University Press.

Geering, Lloyd (2007) *In Praise of the Secular* Wellington, St Andrew's Trust for the Study of Religion and Society.

Gibbs, Harry (1992) 'Does Australia Need a Bill of Rights?' *Inaugural Conference of The Samuel Griffith Society* <http://www.samuelgriffith.org.au/papers/html/volume6/v6chap7.htm>.

Gogineni, Rajaji Ramanadha Babu and Gule, Lars (2004) 'Humanism and Freedom from Religion' in Lindholm et al (2004).

Good, B. J. (2001) 'Belief, Anthropology of' *International Encyclopedia of the Social and Behavioural Sciences* 1137 <http://www.sciencedirect.com>. Pages noted are those of downloaded printout.

Goodenough, W. H. (1990) 'Evolution of the human capacity for beliefs', 92 *American Anthropologist* 597.

Green Phillip (ed), (1999) *Democracy,* New York, Humanity Books 192. (excerpted from *Engendering Democracy*, London, Polity Press 1991 pp. 156-68).

Greene, Abner (1994) 'Is Religion Special? A Rejoinder to Scott Idleman', *University of Illinois Law Journal* 535.

Greschner, Donna (2001) 'Does Law Advance the Cause of Equality?' 27 *Queen's Law Journal* 299.

Griffin, Leslie (1977) 'Good Catholics should be Rawlsian Liberals' 35 *Southern California Interdisciplinary Law Journal* 297.

Griffin, Leslie (2010) 'Fighting the New Wars of Religion: The Need for a Tolerant First Amendment', 62(1) *Maine Law Review* 23.

Grinberg , Maxim (2006) 'Defamation of Religions v Freedom of Expression: Finding the Balance in a Democratic Society', 18 *Sri Lanka Journal of International Law.*

Gross, Tom (2013) 'The UN Promotes a Slave-Owning Nation' *Huffington Post* 25/2/2013. <http://www.huffingtonpost.com/tom-gross/mauritania-un-human-rights-council_b_2758719.html >.

Guichon, Audrey (2007) 'Some Arguments on the Universality of Human Rights in Islam' in Rehman et al (2007) 167.

Gunn, T Jeremy, (1996) 'Adjudicating Rights of Conscience under the European Convention on Human Rights' in van der Vyer (1996) 305.

Gunn, T Jeremy (2003) 'The Complexity of Religion and the Definition of "Religion" in International Law' 16 *Harvard Human Rights Journal,* 189.

Gutmann Amy (ed), (1994) *Multiculturalism: Examining the Politics of Recognition*, Princeton, Princeton University Press,

Hamilton, Marci A (1998) 'The Constitutional Rhetoric of Religion', 20 *University of Arkansas Little Rock Law Journal,* 619.

Hamilton, Marci A (2004) 'What does "Religion" mean in the Public Square? Review Essay: *Democracy and Tradition* by Jeffrey Stout, Princeton University Press 2004' 89 *Minnesota Law Review,* 1153.

Hamilton, Marci A (2005) *God vs. the Gavel* Cambridge, Cambridge University Press.

Hamilton, Marci (2007) 'The Dangers of Accommodation of Religion based on Religious Status, as Opposed to Religiously Motivated Practice, and the Duty of Religious Individuals to Obey the Law' *Findlaw Writ* <http://writ.news.findlaw.com/hamilton/20070405.html>.

Hammond, Phillip and Mazur, Eric (1995) 'Church, State, and the Dilemma of Conscience', 37 *Journal of Church and State* 555.

Ha-Redeye, Omar (2009) 'The Role of Islamic Shari'ah in Protecting Women's Rights' <http://ssrn.com/abstract+1526868>.

Harris, D. J., O'Boyle, M. and Warbrick, C. (1995) *Law of the European Convention on Human Rights,* London, Butterworths.

Harris, Sam (2004) *The End of Faith* London, Free Press.

Henkin Louis (ed), (1981) *The International Bill of Rights: The Covenant on Civil and Political Rights*, New York, *Columbia* University Press.

Heywood, Andrew (2003) (3rd ed) *Political Ideologies* New York, Palgrave Macmillan.

Hickman, Leo (2010) 'The Government's Secret Prayers' *The Guardian,* <http://www.guardian.co.uk/commentisfree/belief/2010/jan/12/mps-prayers-parliament>.

Hobson, Alfred and Jenkins, Neill (2005) *Modern Humanism: Living without Religion,* Washington, North East Humanists.

Horwitz, Paul (1997) 'Scientology in Court: A Comparative Analysis and Some Thoughts on Selected Issues in Law and Religion' 47 *De Paul Law Review* 85.

Hudson, Deal (2008) *Onward, Christian Soldiers: The Growing Political Power of Catholics and Evangelicals in the United States* New York, Threshold Editions.

Humphrey, John (1975) 'The Revolution in the International Law of Human Rights' 4 *Human Rights,* 205.

Hurd, Elizabeth (2008) *The Politics of Secularism in International Relations* Princeton, Princeton University Press.

Huscroft Grant and Paul Rishworth (eds), (1995) *Rights and Freedoms,* Wellington NZ, Brookers.

International Humanist and Ethical Union (2004) *Discussion of Religious Questions Now Banned at UN Human Rights Council* transcript of debate available at <http://www.iheu.org/node/3193> (Video of UN Human Rights Council debate available at <http://www.shariahfinancewatch.org/blog/2008/07/04/videos-of-the-un-human-rights-council-silencing-free-speech/>).

International Humanist and Ethical Union (2006) 'Call for the Acquittal of Judge Tosti' (2006) <http://www.iheu.org>.

International Humanist and Ethical Union (2008) 'Universality of Human Rights under attack at the UN' <http://www.iheu.org/node/2874>.

International Humanist and Ethical Union (2012) *Freedom of Thought 2012 A Global Report on the Legal Status, and Discrimination Against Humanists, Atheists and the Nonreligious* <http://freethoughtreport.com/download-the-report/>.

International Humanist and Ethical Union (2013) *A Global Report on the Legal Status, and Discrimination Against Humanists, Atheists and the Nonreligious* <http://freethoughtreport.com/download-the-report/>.

Jahangir, Asma *Report of the Special Rapporteur on Freedom of Religion or Belief* A/UNHRC/10/8/Add.1, 16 February 2009.

Janis, Mark, Kay, Richard and Bradley, Anthony (eds) (2000) *European Human Rights Law* (2nd ed.) Oxford, OUP.

Janis, Mark and Evans, Carolyn (2005) *Religion and International Law* Leiden/Boston, Marinus Nijhoff Publishers.

Jordan, David (2002) 'The Dark Ages of Islam, Ijtihad, Apostasy and Human Rights in Contemporary Islamic Jurisprudence' 9(55) *Washington and Lee Race and Ethnic Anc. Law Journal* 55.

Kant, Immanuel, (1795) 'Perpetual Peace: A Philosophical Sketch' in Reiss, H., *Kant: Political Writings* (1995) Cambridge Cambridge University Press 93.

Kennedy, Paul (2006) *The Parliament of Man: The United Nations and the Quest for World Government,* Penguin.

King, Ursula (2004) 'Hinduism and Women: Uses and Abuses of Religious Freedom' in Lindholm (2004) 523.

Kitching, Kevin (ed) (2005) *International Discrimination Law: A Handbook for Practitioners*, London, Inter-rights.

Knights, Samantha (2007) *Freedom of Religion, Minorities and the Law*, Oxford, Oxford University Press.

Krishnaswami, Arcot (1960) 'Study of Discrimination in the Matter of Religious Rights and Practices', UN Doc. E/CN.4/Sub.2/200/Rev.1, UN Pub. No. 60.XIV.2.

Kukathas, Chandran (1997) 'Cultural Toleration' in Shapiro et al (1997) 69.

Kukathas, Chandran (2006) 'Moral Universalism and Cultural Difference' in Dryzek (2006) 581.

Kurtz, Paul (2007) *What is Secular Humanism?* Amhurst, NY, Prometheus Books.

Kuru, Ahmet (2007) 'Passive and Assertive Secularism: Historical Conditions, Ideological Struggles, and State Policies toward Religion' 59 *World Politics* 568.

Kymlicka, Will (1995a) (ed) *The Rights of Minority Cultures*, Oxford, OUP.

Kymlicka, Will (1995b) *Multicultural Citizenship: A Liberal Theory of Minority Rights*, Oxford, Oxford University Press.

Kymlicka, Will (2001) *Politics in the Vernacular*, Oxford, Oxford University Press.

Langlois, Anthony (2001) *The Politics of Justice and Human Rights*, Cambridge, Cambridge University Press.

Lauterpacht, Herscht (1945) *An International Bill of Rights of Man,* London, Columbia University Press.

Lawson, Stephanie (1995-96) 'Occidentalising Democracy' Nov.1995 - Feb 1996 *Pacific Research.*

Laycock, Douglas (1990) 'The Remnants of Free Exercise' *Supreme Court Review* 1.

Lazarus, Liora et al (2009) 'The Relationship between Rights and Responsibilities' *(U.K.) Ministry of Justice Research Series 18/09* <www.justice.gov.uk/publications/research.htm>.

Lerner, Natan (1996) 'Religious Human Rights Under the United Nations' in van der Vyver (1996).

Letsas, George (2010) 'Strasbourg's Interpretive Ethic: Lessons for the International Lawyer' *The European Journal of International Law* 21(3)509.

Lewis James R ed (2009) *Scientology,* Oxford OUP 365.

Lewis, Tom, 'What Not to Wear: Religious Rights, The European Court, and the Margin of Appreciation' *International and Comparative Law Quarterly* vol 56, April 2007, 395.

L'Heureux-Dube, Claire (1999) 'Conversations on Equality' 26 *Manitoba Law Journal* 273.

Lichter, Ida (2014) 'United Nations No Defender of Muslim Women's Rights' *Huffington Post* 1/8/2014 <http://www.huffingtonpost.com/ida-lichter-md/united-nations-no-defende_b_4515337.html>.

Lichter, Ida (2009) *Muslim Women Reformers: Inspiring Voices Against Oppression,* New York, Prometheus Books.

Lindholm, Tore, Durham, W and Tahzib-Le, Bahia (eds) (2004) *Facilitating Freedom of Religion or Belief: A Deskbook*, Leiden, Martinus Nijhoff.

Lindholm, Tore (2004) 'Philosophical and Religious Justifications of Freedom of Religion or Belief' in Lindholm et al (2004).

Lindholm, Tore (2005) 'The Strasbourg Court Dealing with Turkey and the Human Rights to Freedom of Religion and Belief: A Critical Assessment in the Light of Recent Case Law (*Leyla Şahin v Turkey*, 29 June 2004)' <tore-lindholm@nchr.uio.no>.

Little, David (1996) 'Studying "Religious Human Rights": Methodological Foundations' in van der Vyver (1996).

Lupu, Ira (1991) 'Reconstructing the Establishment Clause: The Case Against Discretionary Accommodation of Religion' 140 *University of Pennsylvania Law Review* 555.

Lupu, Ira and Tuttle, Robert (2003) *The State of the Law 2003: Developments in the Law Concerning Government Partnerships with Religious Organisations* (The Roundtable on Religion and Social Welfare Policy <http://www.rockinst.org/pdf/faith-based_social_services/2003-12-the_state_of_the_law_2003_developments_in_the_law_concerning_government_partnerships_with_religious_organizations.pdf>.

Mabey, Renae (2006) 'The Priest-Penitent Privilege in Australia and its Consequences', <https://elaw.murdoch.edu.au/archives/issues/2006/2/elaw_Renae%20Mabey%20Priest%20Penitant%20Privilege.pdf>.

Macklem, Timothy (2000) 'Faith as a Secular Value' 45 *McGill Law Journal* 1.

Maddox, Marion (2010) 'God under Gillard', *Quest,* Macquarie University Research Journal, Issue 3, 16.

Maddox, Marion (2005) *God under Howard,* Sydney, Allen & Unwin.

Marr, David (2009) 'Politics and religion: crossed paths' *Sydney Morning Herald* December 26.

Marshall, William (1993) 'The Inequality of Anti-Establishment' 63 *Brigham Young University Law Review* 71.

Marshall, William (1993) 'The Other Side of Religion' 44 *Hastings Law Journal* 843.

Marshall, William (2000) 'What is the Matter with Equality? An Assessment of the Equal Treatment of Religion and Nonreligion in First Amendment Jurisprudence' 75 *Indiana Law Journal* 193.

Martin, Rex and Nickel, James (1980) 'Recent Work on the Concept of Rights' 17(3) *American Philosophical Quarterly* 165.

Martin, Rex and Reidy, David (eds), (2006) *Rawls's law of Peoples: A Realistic Utopia?*, Oxford, Blackwell Publishing.

Martínez-Torrón, Javier and Navarro-Valls, Rafael (2004) 'The Protection of Religious Freedom in the System of the Council of Europe' in Lindholm et al (2004).

Mason, Anthony (1987) 'Future Directions in Australian Law' 13 *Monash University Law Review* 149.

Matisson, Jean-Marie (2003) *'Audition du Comité Laïcité République Devant la Commission Stasi: Commission de Reflexion sur L'application Du Principe De Laïcite Dans La Republique'* (2003). Intervention De Jean-Marie Matisson, Président du Comité Laïcité République Mardi 18 Novembre 2003. <http://www.communautarisme.net/commissionstasi/Audition-de-M-Jean-Marie-Matisson,-President-du-Comite-Laique-et-Republicain-et-M-Patrick-Kessel-huit-clos-_a41.html>.

McCallum, Gerald (1967) 'Negative and Positive Freedom' 76(3) *The Philosophical Review* 312.

McCarthy, Anna-Lena (1998) *The International Law of Human Rights and States of Exception* The Hague, Kluwer Law International.

McClain, Linda (2004) 'Negotiating Gender and (Free and Equal) Citizenship: The Place of Associations' *Fordham Law Review*, Vol. 72, p. 1569, Social Science Research Network Electronic Paper Collection <http://ssrn.com/abstract=588425>.

McConnell, Michael (1990a) 'Free Exercise Revisionism and the *Smith* Decision' 57 *Chicago Law Review* 1109.

McConnell, Michael (1990b) 'The Origins and Historical Understanding of Free Exercise of Religion' 103 *Harvard Law Review* 1409.

McConnell, Michael (1992) 'Religious Freedom at the Crossroads' 59 *University of Chicago Law Review* 115.

McConnell, Michael (2000) 'The Problem of Singling out Religion' 50 *DePaul Law Review* 1.

McGoldrick, Dominic (2009) 'Accommodating Muslims in Europe: From Adopting Sharia Law to Religiously Based Opt Outs from Generally Applicable Laws' *Human Rights Law Review* November 12, 1.

Mchangama, Jacob (2013) A Questionable Victory for Free Speech *National Review Online* March 4, <http://www.nationalreview.com/articles/342072/questionable-victory-free-speech-jacob-mchangama>.

McKinnon, Catriona (2007) 'Democracy, Equality and Toleration' 11 *Journal of Ethics* 125.

McLean, Ian and McMillan (2003) Alistair, *The Concise Oxford Dictionary of Politics* Oxford, Oxford University Press.

McLean, Ian, (2003) 'Democracy' in McLean et al (2003).

Merrills, J.G. (1988) *The Development of International Law by the European Court of Human Rights* Manchester, Manchester University Press.

Meyerson, Denise (2006) *Essential Jurisprudence* Sydney Routledge-Cavendish.

Meyerson, Denise (2008) 'Why Religion Belongs in the Private Sphere, Not the Public Square' in Cane et al (2008) 44.

Mill, John Stuart (1996) *On Liberty* Hertfordshire, Wordsworth Classic Edition.

Minnerath, Roland (2004) 'The Right to Autonomy in Religious Affairs' in Lindholm et al (2004) 291.

Moeckli, Daniel Sangeeta Shah, Sandesh Sivakumaran and David Harris, eds., (2010) *International Human Rights Law* Oxford, Oxford University Press.

Monsma , Stephen (2000) 'Substantive Neutrality as a Basis for Free Exercise - No Establishment Common Ground' 42 *Journal of Church and State* 13.

Monsma, Stephen (ed) (2002) *Church-State Relations in Crisis: Debating Neutrality*, Lanham, Rowman & Littlefield Publishers, Inc.

Monsma, Stephen and Soper, Christopher (2009) *The Challenge of Pluralism,* Plymouth, Rowman & Littlefield Publishers Inc. (2nd ed).

Morgan, Jenny (2004) 'Equality and discrimination: Understanding context' 15 *PLR* 314.

Morris, Linda (2007) 'Taxpayers' $95m bill for World Youth Day' *The Sydney Morning Herald,* 16/11/07) <http://www.smh.com.au/news/national/taxpayers-95m-bill-for-world-youth-day/2007/11/15/1194766868787.html?page=fullpage>.

Morris, Linda, Dart, Jonathon and Davies, Mark (2008) 'Fischer to be Our Man in Vatican' *Sydney Morning Herald* (Sydney), 22/7/2008, News 3, <http://www.smh.com.au/news/world-youth-day/fischer-to-be-our-man-in-vatican/2008/07/21/1216492357011.html>.

Mortensen, Reid (1995) 'The secular Commonwealth: Constitutional government, law and religion' University of Queensland, T.C. Beirne Department of Law, 478 <http://espace.library.uq.edu.au/eserv/UQ:184004/the10180.pdf>.

Mutch, Stephen (2013) 'Religious Cults, Human Rights and Public Policy: The Secular Perspective' Unpublished Paper, base on an oral presentation at the ICSA Annual Conference, 'Manipulation, Abuse and Maltreatment in Groups' Trieste, Italy, 4-6 July 2013.

National Human Rights Consultation Committee (2009) *National Human Rights Consultation Report* Canberra <http://www.humanrightsconsultation.gov.au/www/nhrcc/nhrcc.nsf/Page/Report_NationalHumanRightsConsultationReportDownloads>.

Nickel, James and Reidy, David (2010) 'Chapter 2: "Philosophy"' in Moeckli et al (2010). Also at <https://docs.google.com/fileview?id=0B_VH8cWdlkJSYjZiOTE4YTMtODQ3Yi00NjViLTllOWUt-Mjg1MWU4NmY3Y2Ew&hl=en&pli=1>.

Nickel, James (1993) 'How Human Rights Generate Duties to Protect and Provide' 15 *Human Rights Quarterly* 77.

Nickel, James (1993-4) 'Rethinking Rawls's Theory of Liberty and Rights' 69 *Chicago-Kent Law Review*, 763.

Nickel, James (2003) 'Rawls's Theory of Human Rights in Light of Contemporary Human Rights Law and Practice'. <http://homepages.law.asu.edu/~jnickel/rawlsessay.pdf>.

Nickel, James W (2005) 'Who Needs Freedom of Religion?' 76 *University of Colorado Law Review* 941.

Nickel, James (2006a) 'Are Human Rights Mainly Implemented by Intervention?' in Martin et al (2006) 263.

Nickel, James, (2006b) 'Human Rights' *Stanford Encyclopedia of Philosophy* <http://plato.stanford.edu/entries/rights-human/> accessed 11/01/07.

Nickel, James (2008) 'Rethinking Indivisibility: Towards A Theory of Supporting Relations between Human Rights' 30 *Human Rights Quarterly*, 984.

Nicklin, Lenore (1998) 'God's Property' *The Bulletin* 14 April, 20.

Nowak, Manfred (1993) *UN Covenant on Civil and Political Rights: CCPR Commentary* Kehl am Rhine, N.P. Engel.

Nowak, Manfred and Vospernik, Tanja (2004) 'Permissible Restrictions on Freedom of Religion or Belief' in Lindholm (2004).

Nussbaum, Martha (2000) *Women and Human Development* Cambridge, Cambridge University Press.

O'Brien, Joanne and Palmer, Martin (2007) *The Atlas of Religion* London, Earthscan.

Office of the High Commissioner of Human Rights (1997) 'Cairo Declaration of Human Rights' *A Compilation of International Instruments: Volume II: Regional Instruments* Geneva, United Nations,) 477.

Omar Ha-Redeye (2009) 'The Role of Islamic Shari'ah in Protecting Women's Rights' <http://ssrn.com/abstract+1526868>.

Opsahl, Turkel (1992) 'The Human Rights Committee' in Alston (1992) 421.

Orlowski, Aaron (2013) 'Case law precedent murky on prayer before government meetings' *Rapid City Journal* 24/2/2013 <http://rapidcityjournal.com/news/case-law-precedent-murky-on-prayer-before-government-meetings/article_a72d2866-d6f5-591d-8d21-d6be0f14ad1d.html>.

Palayret, Gallianne (2004) 'Compatibility/Incompatibility of Shia Islam with Human Rights Standards' <www.hrni.org>.

Pannikar, K.M. (1982) 'Is the Notion of Human Rights a Western Concept?' in Steiner et al (2000).

Partsch, K J (1981) 'Freedom of Conscience and Expression, and Political Freedoms' in Henkin (1981).

Patterson Dennis (ed), (1999) *A Companion to Philosophy of Law and Legal Theory* Malden, Mass., Blackwell Publishers.

Paul, Gregory (2005) 'Cross-National Correlations of Quantifiable Societal Health with Popular Religiosity and Secularism in the Prosperous Democracies' 7 *Journal of Religion and Society*, 1 <http://moses.creighton.edu/JRS/pdf/2005-11.pdf>.

Peñalver, Eduardo (2006) 'Treating Religion as Speech: Justice Steven's Religion Clause Jurisprudence' 74 *Fordham Law Review* 2241.

Pena-Ruiz, Henri (2005) *Histoire de la Laïcité: Genèse d'un idéal*, Paris, Gallimand.

Perez-Estervez (1998) 'Intercultural Dialogue and Human Rights: A Latinamerican Reading of Rawls *The Law of Peoples*': Paper presented at the Twentieth World Congress of Philosophy, Boston Mass., August 10-15).

Perkins, John, (2012) *Islam, Arrogance and Delusion: A Reply to people like Waleed Aly*, Vivid Publishing.

Perkins John and Gomez, Frank (2009) 'Taxes and Subsidies: the Cost of "Advancing Religion"' *Australian Humanist No. 93 Autumn* 6-8, < http://home.alphalink.com.au/~jperkins/TaxesAndSubsidies. htm>.

Perkins, John (2005) 'Religion and Vilification' *Dissent* Autumn/Winter, 53.

Pew Research Center (2014) *Religious Hostilities Reach Six-Year High* <http://www.pewforum. org/2014/01/14/religious-hostilities-reach-six-year-high/>

Phillips, Anne (1999a) 'Engendering Democracy' in Green (1999) (excerpted from *Engendering Democracy* London, Polity Press 1991 pp. 156-68).

Phillips, Anne (1999b) *Which equalities matter?* Malden, Mass, Polity Press.

Plowden, Philip and Kerrigan, Kevin (2002) *Advocacy and Human Rights: Using the Convention in Courts and Tribunals* London, Cavendish.

Podoprigora, Roman (2004) 'Freedom of Religion and Belief and Discretionary State Approval of Religious Activity' in Lindholm, (2004) 425.

Post, Robert (2006) 'Democracy and Equality' 603 *The Annals of the American Academy of Political and Social Science* 24.

Preston, Noel (2001) *Understanding Ethics* 2nd edition, Sydney, Federation Press.

Prusak, Bernard (1998) 'Politics, Religion and the Public Good: an Interview with Philosopher John Rawls' *Commonweal* Sept 25, 1998. <http://findarticles.com/p/articles/mi_mi1252/is_n16_v125/ ai_21197512/print>.

Puls, Joshua (1998) 'The Wall of Separation: Section 116, the First Amendment and Constitutional Religious Guarantees' 26(1) *Federal Law Review* 139.

Radan, Peter, Meyerson, Denise and Croucher, Rosalind (eds) (2005) *Law and Religion: God, the State and the Common Law*, London, Routledge,

Radan, Peter (2005) 'International Law and Religion: Article 18 of the International Covenant on Civil and Political Rights' in Radan et al (2005) 9.

Ramcharan, B. G. (1981) 'Equality and Nondiscrimination' in Henkin ((1981) 246.

Ranan, David (2006) *Double Cross: The Code of the Catholic Church*, London, Theo Press.

Rath, Jan et al (1999) 'The Politics of Recognizing Religious Diversity in Europe' *Netherlands Journal of Social Sciences* 53.

Rawls, John (1999) *The Law of Peoples* Harvard, Harvard University Press.

Rawls, John (2003) *Justice as Fairness: a Restatement*, Cambridge, Belknap Press.

Rawls, John (2005a) *A Theory of Justice* (Cambridge MA, Harvard University Press (revised edition).

Rawls, John (2005b) *Political Liberalism*, New York, Columbia University Press (expanded edition).

Rawls, John (2005c) 'Reply to Habermas', reprinted in Rawls (2005b) 372: (originally published in *Journal of Philosophy* 92, March 1995, 132-180).

Rawls, John (2005d) 'The Idea of Public Reason Revisited' reprinted in Rawls, (2005b), 435-490: (originally published in *University of Chicago Law Review* 64, Summer 1997, 765-807).

Raz, Joseph (1998) 'Disagreement in Politics' 43 *American Journal of Jurisprudence* 25.

Raz, J (1986) *The Morality of Freedom* Oxford, OUP.

Rehman, Javaid and Breau, Susan (eds), (2007) *Religion, Human Rights and International Law: A Critical Examination of Islamic State Practices* Leiden, Martinus Nijhoff, 167.

Renucci, Jean-François (2005) *Article 9 of the European Convention on Human Rights* Strasbourg, Council of Europe.

Richmond, Penni, Hughes, Kate and Schucher, Karen (1999) 'The Role of Unions in Furthering Women's Equality' paper prepared for the LEAF National Forum on Equality Rights, *Transforming Women's Future: Equality Rights in the New Century* 4-7 November, Vancouver, B.C.

Rishworth, Paul (1995) 'Coming Conflicts over Freedom of Religion' in Huscroft (1995) 255.

Roberts, Keith (1984) *Religion in Sociological Perspective* Belmont, Wadsworth Publishing Company (2nd edition).

Robertson, G (2010) *The Case of the Pope* Penguin.

Rothstein, Mikael (2009) '"His name was Xenu. He used renegades…" Aspects of Scientology's founding myth' in Lewis (2009) 365.

Rudd, Kevin (2006) 'Faith in Politics' *The Monthly*, October, 22.

Sadurski, Wojciech (1990) 'Neutrality of law towards religion' 12 *Sydney Law Review* 450.

Sadurski, Wojciech (1990b) *Moral Pluralism and Legal Neutrality* Dordrecht, Kluwer Academic Publishers.

Sadurski, Wojciech (2005) 'Rawls and the Limits of Liberalism: Reflections on the "Law of Peoples"' 1 *Ius et Lex* 197.

Sadurski, Wojciech (2008a) *Equality and Legitimacy*, Oxford, OUP.

Sadurski, Wojciech (2008b) 'Legitimacy, Political Equality, and Majority Rule' 21(1) *Ratio Juris* 39.

Sadurski, Wojciech (2008c) '"Reasonableness" and Value Pluralism in Law and Politics' European University Institute Working Paper LAW 2008/13' <http://www.eui.eu/>.

Sadurski, Wojciech (2009) 'Rights and Moral Reasoning: An Unstated Assumption - A Comment on Jeremy Waldron's "Judges as Moral Reasoners"' 7(1) *I.CON* 24.

Sager, Lawrence (2002) 'Constitutional Justice' 6(11) *New York University Journal of Legislation and Public Policy* 11.

Sager, Lawrence (2008) 'The Moral Economy of Religious Freedom' in Cane et al (2008) 16.

Sajó, András (2008) 'Preliminaries to a Concept of Constitutional Secularism' 6(3-4) *International Journal of Constitutional Law* 605.

Sandel, Michael (2009) *Justice: What's the Right Thing to Do?* London, Penguin.

Schwarzschild, Maimon (2000) 'Constitutional law and equality' in Patterson (2000) 156.

Scott, Joan (2008) 'Secularism: Forced to be Free' 90 *Australian Humanist* 4.

Sen, Amartya (2004) 'Elements of a Theory of Human Rights' 32(4) *Philosophy and Public Affairs* 315.

Sen, Amartya (2006) 'Human Rights and the Limits of Law' 27 *Cardozo Law Review* 2913.

Sen, Amartya (2009) *The Idea of Justice*, London, Penguin.

Shapiro Ian and Kymlicka Will (eds) (2000) *Ethnicity and Group Rights* New York, New York University Press.

Sheen, Juliet (2004) 'Burdens on the Right of Women to Assert their Freedom of Religion or Belief' in Lindholm (2004) 513.

Sher (1997) George, *Beyond Neutrality: Perfectionism and Politics* Cambridge, Cambridge University Press.

Siaroff, Alan (2005) *Comparing Political Regimes* Peterborough, Ontario, Broadview Press.

Singer, Peter (1993) *Practical Ethics* Cambridge, Cambridge University Press.

Sippel, Julie (1994) 'Comment: Priest-Penitent Privilege Statutes: Dual Protection in the Confessional' 43 *Catholic University Law Review* 1127.

Smith, Steven (1990) 'The Restoration of Tolerance' 78 *California Law Review* 305.

Smith, Steven (2005a) 'The Tenuous Case for Conscience' 10 *Roger Williams University Law Review* 325.

Smith, Steven (2005b) 'What Does Religion Have to Do with Freedom of Conscience?' 76(4) *University of Colorado Law Review* 911.

Spano, Robert (2014) 'The European Court of Human Rights: Anti-democratic or Guardian of Fundamental Values?, *speech given Chatham House London, 13 October 2014,* <http://ukhumanrightsblog.com/2014/11/19/the-european-court-of-human-rights-anti-democratic-or-guardian-of-fundamental-values-judge-robert-spano/#more-24811>.

Steiner, Henry and Alston, Phillip (eds) (2000) *International Human Rights in Context* Oxford (2nd ed., OUP).

Steiner, Henry (1988) 'Political Participation as a Human Right' 1 *Harvard Yearbook of International Law* 77.

Steiner, Henry (2000a) 'Do Human Rights require a Particular Form of Democracy?' in Steiner et al, (2000) 1315.

Steiner, Henry (2000b) 'Individual Claims in a World of Massive Violations: What Role for the Human Rights Committee?' in Alston et al (2000) 15.

Sterba, James (1999) 'Reconciling Public Reason and Religious Values' 25(1) *Social Theory and Practice* 1.

Stuart, Alison (2010) 'Freedom of Religion and Gender Equality: Inclusive or Exclusive?' 10(3) *Human Rights Law Review* 429.

Schwarzschild, Maimon (2000) 'Constitutional law and equality' in Patterson (2000) 156.

Schwartzman, Micah (2004) The Completeness of Public Reason *Politics, Philosophy & Economics* [2004] vol. 3, 19.

Tahzib, Bahiyyih (1996) *Freedom of Religion and Belief: Ensuring Effective International Legal Protection* Martinus Nijhoff.

Taylor, Charles (1994) 'The Politics of Recognition' in Gutmann (1994) 25.

Taylor, Paul (2001) 'The Basis for Departure of European standard under article 9 of the European Convention on Human Rights from Equivalent Universal Standards' 5 *Web Journal of Current Legal Issues* <http://webjcli.ncl.ac.uk/2001/issue5/taylor5.html>.

Taylor, Paul (2005) *Freedom of Religion: UN and European Human Rights Law and Practice* (Cambridge, Cambridge University Press).

Thomas, Douglas, (2005) 'Great news for Canada' <http://www.americanhumanist.org/hnn/archives/?id=208&article=8>.

Tooker, E (1992) 'Identity systems of Highland Burma: "belief," Akha Zan, and a critique of interiorized notions of ethno-religious identity' 27 *Man* 299.

Troper, Michel (2000) 'French Secularism, or *Laïcité*' 21 *Cardozo Law Review* 1267.

Tushnet, Mark (2000) 'Questioning the value of Accommodating Religion' in Feldman (2000) 245.

UN Human Rights Committee (1991) 'Report of the Human Rights Committee Concluding Observations, Sudan' (UN Doc. CCPR/A/46/4).

United Nations (1984) *UN Sub-Commission on Prevention of Discrimination and Protection of Minorities, Siracusa Principles on the Limitation and Derogation of Provisions in the International Covenant on Civil and Political Rights,* Annex, E/CN.4/1984/4.

United Nations (2002) Committee on Freedom of Religion or Belief and NGO Committee on the Status of Women 'Study on freedom of religion or belief and the status of women in the light of religion and traditions' <http://www.wunrn.com/un_study/english.pdf>.

United Nations (2004) 'Guidelines on International Protection: Religion-Based Refugee Claims under Article 1A(2) of the 1951 Convention and/or the 1967 Protocol relating to the Status of Refugees (High Commission for Refugees) HCR/GIP/04/06'16 (3) *International Journal of Refugee Law* 500.

United Nations (2009) *Silence is Violence: End the Abuse of Women in Afghanistan* (Assistance Mission in Afghanistan) Geneva, United Nations High Commissioner for Human Rights <http://unama. unmissions.org/Portals/UNAMA/vaw-english.pdf>.

van Boven, Theo (2004) 'The United Nations Commission on Human Rights and Freedom of Religion or Belief' in Lindholm (2004) 173.

van der Vyver Johan and Witte John (eds), (1996) *Religious Human Rights in Global Perspective: Legal Perspective* The Hague, Martinus Nijhoff.

van der Vyver, Johan (2004) 'The Relationship of Freedom of Religion or Belief Norms to other Human Rights' in Lindholm (2004) 86.

van Dijk, P. van Hoof, F., Van Rijn A. and Zwaak, L., (2006) *Theory and Practice of the European Convention on Human Rights*, 4th edition, Antwerrp, Intersentia.

van Krieken, Robert et al (2000) *Sociology: Themes and Perspectives* Sydney Pearson Education, Australia.

van Mierlo, J.G.A. (1996) 'Public Entrepreneurship as Innovative Management Strategy in The Public Sector: A Public Choice Approach' (Paper Originally Presented at the 65th Annual Conference of the Southern Economic Association, November 18-20, 1995) < http://arno.unimaas.nl/show. cgi?fid=585>.

Van Wyk, Marius (2001) *Equal Opportunity and Liberal Equality* (Doctoral Thesis, Rand Afrikaans University, <http://152.106.6.200:8080/dspace/browse-title?top=10210%2F2978>.

Vanaik, Achin (1992) 'Reflections on communalism and nationalism in India' 196 *New Left Review* 43.

Vink, Maartin (2007) 'Dutch Multiculturalism : beyond the Pillarisation Myth' 5(3) *Political Studies Review* 337.

Wacks, Raymond (1999) *Jurisprudence* (London, Blackstone Press.

Waldron, Jeremy (1984) *Theories of Rights* Oxford, Oxford University Press,.

Waldron, Jeremy (ed) (1987) *Nonsense upon Stilts: Bentham, Burke and Marx on the Rights of Man* London, Methuen.

Waldron, Jeremy (1991) 'The Substance of Equality' 99 *Michigan Law Review* 1350.

Waldron, Jeremy (1993) 'Religious Contributions in Public Deliberation' 30 *San Diego Law Review* 817.

Waldron, Jeremy (1995) 'Minority Cultures and the Cosmopolitan Alternative' in Kymlicka (1995a) 93.

Waldron, Jeremy (1999) 'How to Argue for a Universal Claim' 30 *Columbia Human Rights Law Review* 305.

Waldron, Jeremy (2009) 'Judges as Reasoners' 7(1) *I.CON* 2.

Wallace, Margaret (1985) 'The Legal Approach to Discrimination and Harassment' 57(1-2) *The Australian Quarterly* 57.

Wallace, Max (2007) *The Purple Economy: Supernatural Charities, Tax and the State* Melbourne, Australian National Secular Association.

Wallace, Max (2010) *Realising Secularism: Australia and New Zealand* Australia and New Zealand Secular Association.

Wallace Max and Nola, Robert (2013) 'Asset rich churches should pay fair tax' *New Zealand Herald*, 8 August 2013 , <http://www.nzherald.co.nz/nz/news/article.cfm?c_id=1&objectid=10909537>

Wallace, Meg (2001) *Health Care and the Law* (Sydney, Lawbook Co. 3rd ed.

Wallace, Meg (2008) 'Parliament is not a Church: Rudd Rawls and the Secular State' 15(2) *Murdoch University elaw Journal* 246.

Wallace, Meg (2007) 'Liberty to Believe: What Has Religion Got to do With It?' 86 (Winter) *Australian Humanist* 9.

Weller, Paul (2006) "Human Rights', 'Religion' and the 'Secular': Variant Configurations of Religion(s), State(s) and Society(s)' 1 *Religion and Human Rights* 17.

Whelan, Jenni and Fougere, Christine (2002) 'Proscription of Hate Speech in Australia' (Paper presented at the XVIth Congress of the International Academy of Comparative Law, Brisbane, 14th - 20th July).

Wilkins, Burleigh (2007) 'Rawls on Human Rights: A Review Essay' *The Journal of Ethics* <feedraider.com/item/245698/Springerlink-Journal>.

Wilkins, John (2010) 'The Role of Secularism in Protecting Religion' in Bonett, (2010).

Wilson, Richard (1997) *Human Rights, Culture & Context*, London, Pluto Press.

Wolff, Jonathon (1998) 'John Rawls: Liberal Democracy Restated' in Carter et al 119.

Yeatman, Anna (2000) 'Who is the Subject of Human Rights?' 43(9) *American Behavioural Scientist* 1498.

Young, Kathryn (2009) 'The Rise of Shar'ia' *The Brief* http://www.hklaw.com/files/Uploads/Documents/In%20the%20Headlines/TheRiseofShariah080909.pdf.

Yourow, Howard (1996) *The Margin of Appreciation Doctrine in the Dynamics of European Human Rights Jurisprudence,* The Hague, Kluwer Law International.

Zimmermann, Augusto (2008/09) 'Eight reasons why Australia should not have a federal charter of rights' (79) *National Observer* 34, <www.nationalobserver.net>.

INDEX

A

Accommodation of religion 9, 113, 207, 227, 239, 243
Alignment with religion 9, 208
Apostasy 48, 53, 54, 88, 206, 223

B

Basic liberties 6, 24, 48, 69, 70, 71, 73, 74, 76, 87, 91, 92, 93, 94, 95, 113, 237, 241
Belief Declaration 8, 12, 23, 46, 48, 50, 61, 119, 125, 130, 131, 159, 160, 171, 172
Belief Provisions 12, 22
Belief rights 6, 12, 22, 23, 28, 48, 61, 74, 88, 238
Belief tribunals 23
BIBLIOGRAPHY 11, 247
Burdens of Judgment 23

C

Cairo Declaration 23, 33, 52, 53, 113, 260
Civil liberties 5, 33, 34, 35, 46
Communalism 7, 100
Comprehensive doctrine 25, 30, 75, 91, 93, 94
Concordats 114, 219, 220
Conscientious objection 8, 155
Cultural Relativism 247

D

Defamation of Religion 12, 54, 223
Democracy 9, 16, 34, 133, 134, 207, 249, 253, 254, 256, 258, 261, 263, 266, 267

E

ECHR 5, 6, 8, 15, 16, 17, 18, 19, 20, 23, 28, 36, 41, 46, 48, 54, 55, 59, 60, 61, 62, 83, 84, 104, 105, 106, 107, 109, 121, 122, 123, 124, 125, 126, 132, 133, 134, 135, 136, 137, 138, 139, 140, 141, 144, 149, 150, 155, 157, 158, 160, 161, 162, 165, 167, 168, 171, 173, 175, 177, 178, 179, 185, 186, 188, 189, 190, 192, 193, 197, 213, 214, 218, 219, 221, 224, 231, 233, 241, 267
Education 9, 16, 19, 117, 139, 140, 144, 198, 210, 249, 265, 267
Equality 7, 33, 83, 84, 86, 248, 249, 250, 253, 256, 257, 258, 259, 261, 262, 264, 265
Essential human rights 6, 69, 71, 87, 91, 95
European Commission 8, 23, 24, 59, 63, 104, 121, 122, 128, 132, 133, 134, 139, 140, 155, 161, 162, 163, 166, 167, 168, 173, 177, 213, 215, 221, 251
European Court 3, 23, 24, 41, 55, 59, 61, 62, 83, 104, 105, 107, 108, 110, 111, 122, 123, 128, 132, 133, 134, 135, 137, 138, 139, 140, 149, 150, 151, 157, 163, 164, 166, 168, 173, 175, 176, 177, 178, 185, 186, 187, 190, 193, 196, 200, 201, 214, 217, 218, 219, 221, 222, 240, 241, 251, 253, 257, 258, 263
European tribunals 9, 23, 124, 133, 139, 161, 173, 176, 181, 185
Exemption from tax 10, 214

F

Faith-based welfare 10, 215

Fiji 11, 26, 114, 244, 245, 250

Forum internum 8, 155, 156, 157, 158, 159, 160, 162, 164, 165, 169, 170, 181

Freedom of speech 9, 36, 41, 44, 61, 64, 94, 121, 126, 133, 135, 136, 139, 141, 149, 150, 174, 175, 186, 194, 197, 205, 233

G

General Comment 22 8, 13, 57, 118, 119, 130, 131, 141, 159, 160, 172, 174, 176, 186, 221, 224, 268

H

Human Rights 3, 5, 6, 8, 12, 13, 14, 23, 24, 25, 27, 28, 33, 39, 40, 47, 48, 51, 52, 53, 54, 55, 56, 58, 59, 62, 63, 65, 70, 94, 95, 104, 121, 128, 130, 140, 144, 160, 161, 163, 177, 184, 194, 206, 221, 234, 247, 248, 249, 250, 251, 253, 254, 255, 256, 257, 258, 259, 260, 261, 262, 263, 264, 265, 266, 268, 270

Human rights tribunals 24

I

ICCPR 5, 6, 8, 13, 16, 18, 20, 23, 24, 26, 35, 36, 46, 48, 49, 50, 51, 52, 53, 54, 55, 56, 57, 58, 60, 61, 62, 69, 70, 81, 83, 104, 116, 118, 119, 120, 121, 125, 126, 127, 128, 129, 130, 131, 135, 136, 141, 144, 149, 150, 157, 159, 160, 161, 167, 171, 172, 174, 175, 176, 178, 184, 186, 195, 203, 207, 212, 213, 221, 224, 233, 236, 241, 268

J

Judicial procedures 216

Justice 6, 24, 25, 71, 72, 73, 74, 76, 89, 90, 93, 94, 144, 155, 164, 211, 227, 230, 247, 252, 256, 260, 262, 263

Justice and reason 6, 76

Justice as fairness 6, 24, 73, 76, 89, 93, 94

L

Liberal democracy 30, 31, 35, 39, 66, 69, 70, 73, 74, 75, 76, 77, 89, 92, 93, 94, 95, 110, 144, 229, 236, 241, 246

M

Manifestation of belief 8, 9, 28, 37, 50, 61, 63, 104, 105, 108, 138, 155, 158, 159, 160, 162, 163, 164, 166, 170, 171, 172, 173, 174, 176, 178, 179, 183, 184, 186, 191, 200

Margin of appreciation 9, 107, 108, 124, 133, 149, 150, 151, 178, 185, 186, 187, 188, 189, 190, 191, 192, 193, 196, 197, 200, 201, 202, 214, 241

Mediation 216, 217, 250

Military 8, 57, 91, 108, 155, 160, 161, 163, 164, 173, 177, 178, 184, 231

N

Negotiating privilege 10, 216

Neutralist paradigm 44

Neutrality 31, 45, 94, 98, 102, 108, 109, 110, 119, 120, 122, 124, 144, 190, 191, 192, 202, 206, 210, 220, 224, 225, 226, 227, 229, 230, 231, 232, 243, 246

O

Obligations 5, 26, 37, 38, 46, 47, 62, 103, 132, 141, 158, 162, 167, 184, 192, 195, 215, 223, 242
Organisation of the Islamic Conference 24, 48, 52
Overlapping consensus 30, 72, 73, 75, 77, 91, 95, 113, 176, 229, 238, 241

P

Perfectionist paradigm 94
Personal worldview 23, 27, 30, 31, 40, 42, 93, 127, 226, 237
Pillarisation 7, 99, 100, 265
Political conception of justice 6, 24, 30, 72, 74, 75, 76, 77, 78, 89, 91, 93, 103, 111, 171, 229, 244
Political Virtues 24
Primary Goods 24
Private sphere 7, 8, 86, 157, 165, 169
Procedural justice 6, 75, 78, 79, 81, 82, 89, 93, 107, 110, 171
Proselytising 106, 175, 226
Public political culture 24, 75, 91, 93, 95, 101, 238
Public reason 24, 76, 79, 89, 91, 93, 95, 104, 144, 176, 234, 236, 241, 246

R

Rawls 1, 5, 6, 7, 10, 12, 23, 24, 25, 29, 30, 31, 34, 38, 39, 46, 67, 69, 70, 71, 72, 73, 74, 75, 76, 77, 78, 79, 80, 81, 82, 84, 85, 86, 87, 88, 89, 90, 91, 92, 93, 94, 95, 96, 97, 101, 102, 103, 104, 107, 110, 111, 113, 118, 125, 127, 133, 134, 150, 159, 169, 171, 180, 183, 187, 192, 198, 200, 211, 227, 229, 232, 234, 236, 237, 238, 241, 246, 247, 248, 249, 252, 257, 259, 261, 262, 266
Reason 6, 7, 23, 24, 25, 27, 29, 31, 34, 38, 41, 44, 50, 59, 76, 77, 79, 87, 89, 91, 92, 93, 94, 95, 96, 99, 104, 119, 124, 137, 144, 162, 163, 176, 180, 194, 200, 230, 234, 236, 241, 245, 246
Reasonable 'comprehensive doctrine' 25
Reasonable person 25
Reciprocity 25, 34
Reflective Equilibrium 25
revolution 36
Revolution 5, 33

S

Schools 3, 106, 140, 150, 172, 192, 207, 209, 210, 212, 213, 221, 222, 223, 227, 228, 229, 230, 232
Secularism 7, 10, 31, 96, 97, 98, 99, 100, 101, 102, 103, 104, 105, 106, 107, 108, 109, 110, 111, 113, 114, 122, 123, 124, 127, 147, 180, 208, 212, 221, 229, 238, 240, 241
State-belief accommodation 10, 206, 225
State-belief separation 10, 31, 92, 102, 115, 118, 122, 204, 210, 225, 229, 232, 235, 236, 237, 239, 240, 241, 243, 244
Symbols 9, 107, 110, 115, 152, 172, 176, 189, 190, 191, 192, 193, 220, 229

T

Taxes 214, 261
Tribunals 217, 218, 261

U

UDHR 3, 12, 25, 27, 29, 35, 36, 46, 47, 48, 49, 50, 51, 52, 53, 55, 61, 62, 66, 69, 76, 77, 81, 95, 113, 119, 125, 127, 131, 136, 140, 141, 143, 171, 172, 203, 204, 205, 207, 233, 236, 238, 241
United Nations Human Rights Committee 6, 8, 23, 24, 25, 56, 94, 104, 128
United Nations Human Rights Council 6, 51, 53

V

Vilification 9, 194, 195, 196, 223

W

Weller 7, 97, 99, 100, 266
Worth of liberty 6, 80, 90

www.ingramcontent.com/pod-product-compliance
Lightning Source LLC
Chambersburg PA
CBHW080527090426
42733CB00015B/2509